The Musical Topic

Musical Meaning and Interpretation
Robert S. Hatten, editor

RAYMOND MONELLE

The Musical Topic

Hunt, Military and Pastoral

INDIANA UNIVERSITY PRESS
Bloomington and Indianapolis

This book is a publication of

Indiana University Press
601 North Morton Street
Bloomington, IN 47404-3797 USA

http://iupress.indiana.edu

Telephone orders 800-842-6796
Fax orders 812-855-7931
Orders by e-mail iuporder@indiana.edu

© 2006 by Raymond Monelle

The paper used in this publication meets the minimum requirements of American National Standard for Information Sciences—Permanence of Paper for Printed Library Materials, ANSI Z39.48-1984.

Manufactured in the United States of America

Library of Congress Cataloging-in-Publication Data

Monelle, Raymond, date
   The musical topic : hunt, military and pastoral / Raymond Monelle.
      p. cm. — (Musical meaning and interpretation)
   Includes bibliographical references and index.
   ISBN 0-253-34766-1 (cloth : alk. paper)
 1. Music—History and criticism. 2. Hunting music—History and criticism. 3. Military music—History and criticism. 4. Pastoral music (Secular)—History and criticism. I. Title. II. Series.
   ML160.M686 2006
   781.5′9—dc22

                                                                                2006002650

1 2 3 4 5   11 10 09 08 07 06

To

Joseph Kerman

with

respect and admiration

Contents

Plates

1. French hussar of the Napoleonic period (painting by François Fleming). Peter Newark's Military Pictures.
2. Antoine Watteau, *The Shepherds* (ca. 1719). Schloss Charlottenburg, Berlin.
3. Bartolomeo Pinelli, *Shepherd Musicians Before a Shrine* (1807), detail. Florence, Uffizi.
4. Player of the double *aulós*. Red-figure painting on a drinking bowl, ca. 480 B.C. Staatliche Antikensammlungen, Munich.
5. Titian, *The Three Ages of Man*, detail. National Gallery of Scotland, Edinburgh.
6. The angel's visitation to the shepherds. From the Book of Hours of Jeanne d'Evreux (fourteenth century). Metropolitan Museum of Art, New York.
7. Pieter Bruegel the elder, *Dance of the Peasants* (ca. 1568). Kunsthistorisches Museum, Vienna.

Plates follow page 114.

Preface

Musical topics are more than mere labels. Since the full elucidation of a topic, both as signifier and signified, must depend on investigations of social history, literature, popular culture, and ideology as well as music, each topic must lead to a lengthy cultural study. This is the kind of exercise that is three times embarked on here. It becomes clear that musical topics map whole tracts of human reality; that even a single topic involves an almost inexhaustible quest, far beyond anything possible in these few pages. Topic theory, in fact, may signal the moment when musicology ceases to be wholly, or even primarily, about music.

This kind of undertaking—"interdisciplinary studies", or nowadays "comparativism"—carries two dangers. You can do it for amusement, leading your reader out of her specialty into wider fields and making wild connections. Or you can frustrate her, by failing to give a proper account of music, literature, painting, social history, philosophy, or anything else. The present book errs in both respects. Academic minds, somebody said, are either arrows or storage rooms. Most of us spend our early years trying to become arrows, but if you were born a storage room you had better find some way, finally, to be yourself. As a lifelong storage room and an erstwhile modern historian, I have found myself continually drawn out of positivistic musical analysis into reflections on semantics and general culture.

This book has much to say about general culture. Here is a kind of musicology that may sometimes even lose sight of music altogether. If this is so, let us say that hunting is often good fun even when you lose the scent, that military maneuvers may achieve useful results even when not in pursuit of the enemy, and that there may be other sheep which are not of this fold. The most perfectly focused work of musicology ever written was Ludwig Köchel's *Chronologisch-thematisches Verzeichnis sämtlicher Tonwerke Mozarts,* but few of us have ever read it for pleasure. There is more pleasure in going down the road of Paul Ricoeur's "split or cleft reference" where doors may unexpectedly open on insights scarcely sought.

It is pointed out in the text that this is not a comprehensive study of musical topics, though that was how it started out. Such a study would occupy twenty volumes and a lifetime's work. There are whole categories of topics that are not mentioned: topical dance measures, icons (such as the noble horse and the *pianto*), stylistic references (the French overture), and passing fashions (the Turkish topic). These have been excellently covered by other writers, and I have said something about a couple of them in my last book, *The Sense of Music.* The three great topical genres, hunting, soldiering, and shepherding, are chosen here because they represent major cultural themes. In any case, comprehensive lists of topics are probably of little use and are not the way to do topic theory. As Agawu has said, the inventory of topics expands constantly as we work. Topical analysis works best when we proceed ad hoc, allowing musical texts to suggest new topics as they arise.

Much of this book has been heard at conferences, in lectures worldwide, and indeed published in various places. I am grateful to have had the reactions, sometimes even sympathetic, of audiences and readers, and of my eminent academic friends. As well as this, distinguished musicologists and other outstanding scholars have helped with invaluable advice. I was even helped by huntsmen and soldiers: my thanks to them. Undoubtedly, I should have consulted a shepherd or two. It would be odious to select for thanks any particular names, and a full list would occupy an extensive space. I thank them for their help and inexplicable sympathy.

I wish, however, to mention two outstanding figures whose work has inspired me, not only in the present work but for many years. The first of these is Leonard Ratner of Stanford University. My past criticisms of Ratner's work have led some people to think of me as his attacker or opponent. I wish to lay this idea to rest. Without Ratner there would have been no topic theory in its modern form. Ratner has been one of the most intuitive and inspired writers on music of the last half-century. I only regret that, living on the other side of the world from Stanford, I never had the opportunity to be his student.

The other warrior-hero of my musicological story has been Joseph Kerman, whose writings have excited and inspired me since I was a student. He has never sold out to fashionable positivisms but has always found music meaningful, and has somehow communicated the greatness and truthfulness of music, without solemnity. I never knew Tovey or Riemann, but I am profoundly happy to know Kerman. This book is respectfully dedicated to him, with his kind permission.

A tribute of gratitude also to Mhairead, who encouraged me always and took my ideas seriously, even the maddest ones.

It is usual to say that "any faults to be found in this book are, of course, my own." I feel uneasy about this, for there has hardly been a book on music so profoundly dependent on the research of others, in many, many different fields. Could a few faults have crept in that were not my own? I hope so. Then maybe mine will not seem so bad.

Permission is gratefully acknowledged to reproduce the following items:
Figure 4.1, used by permission of the Trustees of the National Library of Scotland; figures 4.4a, 4.4b, 5.1, 13.2, and 13.3, used by permission of the British Library; figure 4.4c, used by permission of the Staatliche Kunstsammlungen, Dresden; figures 4.5 and 9.4, © Edinburgh University Collection of Historical Musical Instruments; figure 4.6, used by permission of Lüder H. Niemeyer, Ridinger Gallery Niemeyer; figures 6.11 and 7.4, © used by kind permission of Schott Musik International GmbH & Co. KG, Mainz, Germany; figures 6.20 and 14.4, used by permission of BMG Ricordi, S.p.A—Casa Ricordi; figure 7.7, © Copyright 1898 by Josef Aibl Musikverlag. © Copyright assigned 1932 to C. F. Peters. Reproduced by permission of Peters Edition Ltd., London; figures 7.11 and 7.12, reproduced by kind permission of Faber Music Ltd. © Copyright 1922 by Ralph Vaughan Williams. Exclusively licensed to J. Curwen & Sons Ltd. for the World (excluding

Note on Titles of Musical Works

In this book, titles in italics are authorized by the composer (for example, *Pastoral Symphony*), while titles in quotation marks are attributed by others (for example, "Military" Symphony). The distinction is significant, in that the authority of the composer may be considered to guarantee the topical content of the piece, while added names simply confirm that topics are often recognized in scores without evocative titles. This applies only to main titles, however: arias and single movements of symphonies appear in quotation marks.

Part One.   *Topic Theory*

1 Topic and Expression

(a) A musical morning

Just before the reprise of the first movement of Haydn's Symphony no. 6, entitled *Le Matin*, the orchestra suddenly stops, leaving a solo horn in D to play the first figure of the main theme, a simple triadic motive like a hunting call, which had earlier been played by the flute. After a couple of measures, flute and strings take over and the theme is heard in its original form.

The movement began with a slow introduction that represented a sunrise. Presumably, the subsequent allegro theme, first proclaimed by the flute and later briefly echoed by the horn, has something to do with the program of the symphony; that is, it is meant to suggest the "morning". Though written in 3/4 time rather than the hunting 6/8, it sounds like many of the calls of the great brass *trompe de chasse*, an instrument that broadly resembled the crooked *Inventionshorn* in Haydn's orchestra and probably sounded similar. Haydn elsewhere used his orchestral horn to suggest the hunting horn (notably, in the oratorio *Die Jahreszeiten*), and here it is reminding us that the courtly hunt of the period took place during the morning, a fact we can ascertain from social history. French hunting horns were usually in D, so the key of the symphony is well chosen. As for the original presentation of the theme on a flute, this is a very typical witticism. Haydn seems to ask: do you recognize the character of this tune, in spite of its wrong timbre? If you do not, I will later reveal all by playing it on the horn. This witty effect was famously copied by Beethoven in his Third Symphony, though for him the horn was associated with the heroic rather than the matutinal.

To appreciate the meaning of this gesture, not to mention its elusive wit, you have to know that it suggests the idea of the hunt, and that hunts were morning affairs. The tiny figure that starts the allegro is a kind of musical term or word; it has a conventional meaning, understood by all hearers. It does not "express emotion", except insofar as all linguistic syntagmas carry some kind of emotion. It is a simple statement about the time of day, and the activities and sensations associated with that time, as well as the sort of people who enjoyed them. It carries a "literal" meaning, together with a cluster of associative meanings.

Leonard Ratner has taught us that we need to know such associations if we are to understand classical music. He calls them "topics" and speaks of "a thesaurus of characteristic figures" that were "subjects for musical discourse" (Ratner 1980, 9). He divides them into three categories: dance measures, styles, and examples of word painting. His short article on the movements and associations of dances—the minuet, passepied, bourrée, contredanse, and so on—has been much amplified by Wye Jamison Allanbrook (in *Rhythmic Gesture in Mozart*, 1983). Allanbrook explains that dances were associated with social class, and that the bourgeois contredanse was the popular dance of the late eighteenth century. Minuets were still danced but were considered aristocratic and old-fashioned. Thus, social commentary could be written in terms of dance measures, a point that she illustrates with much perspicuity from Mozart's operas.

Topics that are styles, Ratner's second category, include "military and hunt music", the French overture, the singing and brilliant styles, Turkish music, *Sturm und Drang*, *Empfindsamkeit*, and others. These, too, carry traditional associations; for instance, the French overture has the "serious, elevated tone" of "punctilious ceremony" (20). We may surmise that the military style carries suggestions of soldiering and thus, perhaps, of heroism and gallantry. The hunt style, as we have seen, can suggest the morning.

Finally, Ratner notices that eighteenth-century composers liked pictorialism and word painting. He refers to Haydn's "Drum Roll" Symphony, no. 103 in E flat, which may illustrate the Battle of Vienna of 1683. Clearly, this kind of musical work puts together some of the preexistent associative topics, like drum rolls and fanfares.

(b) Kinds of topics

As well as Allanbrook, other scholars such as Kofi Agawu, Elaine Sisman, and Robert Hatten have taken up Ratner's idea of topics (Agawu 1991; Sisman 1993; Hatten 1994). It seems clear that an understanding of topics is necessary in interpreting classical music. Indeed, such an understanding may be important for a much wider range of music, including Romantic and modern repertoires. Agawu admits that "topics abound in the music of Romantic composers" (137), but he finds a dislocation of topics from their conventional meanings in the nineteenth century. Yet some topics are to be found throughout our culture, from the sixteenth century through the twenty-first; I have elsewhere described (in *The Sense of Music*, 2000, 66–73; henceforth *Sense*) the topic of the *pianto*, the falling minor second that signifies weeping, which begins its life in Italian madrigals and can still be found today in a piece like Kurtág's *Stele*, not to mention popular music and *Gebrauchsmusik*.

Perhaps we must revise Ratner's three-fold classification of topics, in semiotic terms. Reservations about the historical universality of topics, such as those of Agawu, may arise from the tendency to generalize unduly about topics. For these figures are of many types. The *pianto*, which has just been mentioned, is a useful paradigm. In an early madrigal it may set a text like "pianto" or "lagrime". Dido sings this topic when she laments her fate at the beginning of Purcell's opera, though the words "weeping" or "tears" do not appear. The orchestra plays it when Donna Anna enters in *Don Giovanni*, stricken after the death of her father. Alberich in *Das Rheingold* cries "Wehe! ach Wehe" to this topic. Famously, it recurs in the "Adagietto" from Mahler's Fifth Symphony, qualifying this movement to become the theme-tune of Visconti's elegiac movie *Death in Venice*.

At first sight, it has a unitary, simple signifier, the falling minor second, with an equally simple iconic signified that is not limited historically; the sound imitated is that of someone weeping, and people have wept, alas, in all ages. Yet behind both signifier and signified we find a cluster of associations. The signifier branches into subtopics like the *passus duriusculus* and the operatic lament, and in the eighteenth century yields the topic of *Empfindsamkeit*, making of it a major feature of our cultural history (*Sense*, 66–77). Similarly, the signified extends from mere weeping to the general idea of grief, and even to other dysphoric feelings such as disappointment, anger, and fear.

The topic of the noble horse is somewhat similar in pattern. It is described in *Sense*, 45–65. The signifier is a more or less rapid compound duple or triple rhythm, typified by the 6/8 of Schumann's *Wilde Reiter*, from *Album for the Young;* the 9/8 of Wagner's Valkyries; the 12/8, in effect, of Schubert's *Erlkönig*. The representation depends on mimicking the hooves of a horse at the gallop; there is a semiotic reason for the gallop of the musical horse, based on a cultural connection between the medieval warhorse and its fast pace. However, this signifier is much simpler than that of the *pianto;* the "noble horse" rhythm is its only feature. There is, so to speak, no equestrian *passus duriusculus*. The signified, which is again iconic, is initially the familiar animal, but embraces all the associations of the literary horse, noble, active, virile, adventurous. The signified of this topic is the *cheval écrit*, the horse in culture and literature. It differs from the *pianto* in one other important respect: it becomes current suddenly in the 1790s, though there are a few earlier appearances.

The signifier seems the controlling feature of these topics, but there are others in which all the emphasis is on the side of the signified. The *Dance of Death*, described by Reinhold Hammerstein (1980) and Robert Samuels (1995, 119–131), is a medieval literary and visual image with musical associations, which was revived in a new musical guise in the nineteenth century; its signifiers are variable and somewhat ad hoc, but this topic nevertheless becomes an important motif.

On the other hand, certain topics have a simple signifier but a less focused signified. These are no more than stylistic traits. Agawu lists the *alla zoppa* (limping) rhythm, a recurrent syncopated effect, which may be simply an aspect of Italian style (and thus indexical of a particular cultural world, though not necessarily of any detail within it). The "singing" style, described by Koch (1802, column 1390), is an essential aspect of classical construction as well as a particular instrumental manner, because singing style alternates with "flowing" or "brilliant" styles to form the temporal amalgam of the classical movement, which is extended in time by the interposition of passages of progressive temporality or *Gänge*, which tend to contrast stylistically with lyric evocations (see *Sense*, 100–110).

At the other extreme, there are great topical worlds that constitute musical and cultural genres. Here, the signifiers may be multifarious, and the signifieds complex and elusive. The pastoral genre is an example: flute and oboe timbre, the meter of the siciliana, and bagpipe drones may all act as signifiers, and the signified encompasses courtly shepherdesses, sunlit tranquility, peaceful landscapes, amorous play, and the lyric spirit, not to mention Christmas and the Christian heaven. Of course, the pastoral topic has its origin in literature, including that of the ancients. The military genre, too, is connected with literature, reflecting the classical image of the hero; and like the pastoral, it has several signifiers, notably the military march and the trumpet fanfare. The hunt topic is similar, though less extended into literature; the signification of this topic echoes, not great poetry and drama but famous hunting manuals like the *Livre de Chasse* of Gaston Phoebus (1387). The signifier is more unified than that of the military topic, though still somewhat complex. A common feature of the great genres is the noncontemporaneity of signifier and signified; while signifiers were generally contemporary with the music in which they appeared, signifieds were usually mythical and nostalgic. These three complex topical genres, pastoral, military, and hunting, form the main study of this book.

Topics that are dance measures, analyzed by Allanbrook, have simple signifiers and signifieds: the rhythm of the sarabande initially means "sarabande", though of course the associations of the sarabande are of primary importance. High decorum, stately dignity, and noble feelings are embodied. Dance topics differ from the great genres in that musicians are more aware of the contemporaneity, or otherwise, of signifier and signified, because they know perfectly well when a cited dance is contemporary, and when it is no longer seen in the dance hall. Signification is social; an "old-fashioned" dance signifies some aspect of society that is thought to be passing or for which one may feel nostalgia, but contemporary dances figure largely in the topical repertoire. Neither Ratner nor Allanbrook thinks to extend the inventory of dance topics backward into the sixteenth century, where the dance pairs of pavan-galliard and passamezzo-saltarello form the structure of instrumental and vocal pieces, or forward into the twentieth, where the waltz, though still a contemporary dance, is made in *Der Rosenkavalier* to evoke an old-world nostalgia, though with a trace of anachronism; Strauss's waltzes are similar to those of his nineteenth-century namesakes, but *Der Rosenkavalier* is set in the previous century. It seems that the world of dance topics is, after all, quite extensive and complex.

Each of these topics can be observed over a wide span of our musical history. But some topics are limited to shorter periods, and are no more than fashions. The Turkish topic, found in Mozart's *Die Entführung aus dem Serail,* in the Sonata in A, K. 331, and in Beethoven's *Ruins of Athens* and Ninth Symphony, is an aspect of fashionable orientalism in a Vienna released from the threat of invasion after the repulsion of the Turkish army in 1683. The centenary of this event in 1783, and subsequently the Austro-Russian war against the Ottomans in 1788–90, made Turkish orientalism current in Mozart's Vienna (see especially Head 2000). There is another aspect to this, however; with the sultan a diplomatic ally, janissary bands were exported to European courts and their instrumentation influenced the development of military music (though Head, basing his judgments on Ralf Martin Jäger's article in *Die Musik in Geschichte und Gegenwart,* doubts that Europeans had an accurate knowledge of Turkish military bands, as Farmer and Signell thought; Farmer 1912, Signell 1967). Matthew Head makes a convincing argument for the articulation of the Turkish topic as an aspect of racial and cultural estrangement, an identification of the cultural Other in a West that was dominating and colonizing the Orient. He links the general idea of exoticism with the aspect of the carnivalesque, and ultimately the intrusion of open forms into classical symmetry; thus he is able to continue his narrative into the nineteenth century as a more general aspect of Western psychology. However, the specifically Turkish was no more than a passing fashion. Its most important function was to bring about a vital development of the military genre, in which bands were enlarged and became capable of playing for marching. This is chronicled below.

Topics, then, can resemble linguistic terms; they can be simple signs, joining a unitary signifier to a defined signification, though both signifier and signified usually have more complex associations. They can be mere stylistic traits, with only generalized significations. And they can be like literary genres; with a group of signifiers, they can embrace a complex world of fantasy and myth.

(c) A dictionary of topics?

Among Agawu's important achievements is his demonstration that the idea of the topic was discussed by contemporaries, though they used different language (Daube speaks of "figures"; Burney of "ideas"; Castil-Blaze of "effects"; see Agawu 1991, 28, 29), and by modern writers not actually topic theorists, like Pestelli, Kerman, and Rosen (Agawu 1991, 31, 32). It is probably futile to seek a specific account of every topic in the writings of eighteenth-century theorists, but the general theory is strongly supported. Castil-Blaze, for example, having discussed the "tragic and brilliant effects" produced by trumpets, trombones, and kettledrums, comments that such effects "are to music what figures are to oratorical discourse" (quoted by Agawu 1991, 28), a remarkable parallel to the literary topic theory of Ernst Robert Curtius, discussed below.

It is, perhaps, ill-advised to strive for a comprehensive dictionary of topics. Agawu provides a useful checklist of twenty-seven (1991, 30), but nevertheless believes that the lexical method is not the best way of approaching topics, because new topics continually emerge from analysis. The odor of topicality permeates our music, extending into every aspect. Haydn's horns always suggest the hunting field, even when they are merely filling out the harmony. The triadic shape of the military trumpet fanfare lends a sense of strength and pride even to a lyric tune like *The Star-Spangled Banner;* the grave dignity of the sarabande is sensed even when played without accompaniment, in the lonely purity of a fugue subject like that in B flat minor from the second book of the *Wohltemperirte Clavier.* The dysphoric sentiment of the *pianto* colors the discordant oxhorn blasts in *Götterdämmerung,* and even conjures terror in John Williams's music for the movie *Jaws.*

Ultimately, the assemblage of topics illuminates the "world vision of a civilization" (Eco 1979, 79), for "semiotics is mainly concerned with signs as social forces" (65). It would be rash to seek the genome of such a global aggregate.

(d) The historical perspective

Both Ratner and Agawu feel that musical topics appear chiefly, or at least work best, in classical music, the music of the late eighteenth century. These authors write almost exclusively about music of the classical period. Agawu does not deny that Romantic composers make use of topics, but he notices "a dislocation of the signifer from the signified" in the nineteenth century: "It appears . . . that while the *morphology* of various topics is retained by Romantic composers, their conventional association is displaced. Thus, one way of describing the Classic-Romantic relationship is in terms of a morphological continuity and a referential discontinuity" (137). *Simpliciter:* you can still hear topics in Romantic music, but they do not mean the same thing. As will be seen later, Agawu is certainly right in finding changes in the physiognomy of topics in Romantic music. This is splendidly illustrated by Ariane Jessulat, who shows that the musical *question,* a mere recitative formula in baroque music, turns into a symbol of instability, transition, and fateful change in the Romantic period (notably in the *Schicksalskundemotiv* from the *Ring;* Jessulat 2000, 194–203). Agawu finds also that "the sign assumes symbolic status" in the Romantic period. Whereas in classical music the signified was "self-evident" (thus, the topic of the hunt always meant just itself, rather than any individualistic program of hunts, real or psychological), in the later repertoire the meaning is apt to be colored, modified, altered by some particular concern of the composer. Thus the signification of Wagner's leitmotivs or of the manifest musical signs of Mahler is complicated, unique, many-layered.

This is an important consideration. But it is not a good reason to ignore the topics of Romantic music; and indeed, when Ratner came to write his more recent book on the Romantic period (1992), he often spoke of topics. The opening of Schubert's String Quartet in A minor, D. 804, with its droning cello and viola, is "frankly lyric, gentle, vibrant, in the manner of a musette" (105). The beginning of Tchaikovsky's Fantasy Overture *Romeo and Juliet* is a "solemn march" with a flavor of "archaic ecclesiastic modality, to indicate the presence of Friar Lawrence" (70). Ratner also discerns in Romantic music the *stile legato* and the *stile gravis;* the first of these, with its steadily melting suspensions, and the second, with its *alla breve* meter, are combined in Chopin's Prelude in E Minor, Op. 28 no. 4 (39).

In any case, the "self-evident" quality of classical topics may be only apparent. There are, in addition, topics that appear *only* in the later period, and therefore have escaped Ratner's and Agawu's nets, and there are topics, like the *pianto*, which overarch our entire history, from the sixteenth to the twenty-first centuries. In any case, the division of classical from Romantic, as Agawu admits, is ultimately false. Topics in Brahms are not much different from the same topics in Haydn; even the ironic inflexion of topics—the military topic, for instance—though this seems a bit postmodern, is possible for Mozart (in "Non più andrai"), for Boieldieu (in "Quel plaisir d'être soldat" from *La Dame Blanche*), and for Mahler (in *Rewelge*).

(e) The relationship to analysis

Many have found it troubling that topical hermeneutics does not lead immediately to *analysis.* Syntactic analysis of music has become such an ingrained habit that a critical method more paradigmatic than syntagmatic may appear useless.

Agawu is very concerned with the role of topics in the unfolding of music. Some topics are more appropriate to transitions and development sections, because they are inherently unstable (the *Sturm und Drang* topic, for instance). Topics may be combined to give character and life to a particular movement; the menuet of Haydn's String Quartet, Op. 20 no. 4, combines the dance topic with the *alla zingarese* style. Topics may be used to articulate the hierarchic regions of the form, as when the "second subject" may present itself in "singing style". The meaning of topics is primarily contextual, dynamic, and processual; for this reason we should refrain "from assigning fixed signification to topics".

In fact, Agawu is more interested in the contribution of topics to the dynamic structure of the work than in the question of signification. He gives his topics simple labels, but their more profound significance—their history in literature and culture, their reflections in contemporary social life—is not his main concern.

He develops his conviction that musical meaning lies at the heart of structure, first by introducing the concepts of beginning, middle, and end, derived from ideas of rhetoric; later by linking topical identification with Schenkerian analysis. His emphasis, therefore, is at a different pole from the present work; perhaps it could be said that Agawu's book is complementary to this enterprise.

William Caplin continues Agawu's discussion, attempting to list topics according to their preferred formal functions (Caplin 2002). Thus, the Mannheim rocket appears commonly at the beginning; the military fanfare may also come at the beginning, but its function is more general. The hunting call is often a cadential topic. Other topics—the *passus duriusculus*, *Sturm und Drang*, the learned style—are inherently unstable and tend to come in the middle. It may even be possible to trace a kind of formal irony when a topic appears in an uncharacteristic position (for example, the topic of "horn motion" begins Beethoven's Sonata in E flat, Op. 81a, although this topic is more typically cadential).

Caplin concludes very sensibly that the "anxiety" of certain scholars to link topic theory with formal analysis may simply be mistaken.

> But if we find in the end that topical analysis has little, or even no, syntactical basis, there is no reason for regret. Many modes [of] musical organization, such as timbre and dynamics, are clearly nonsyntactic, yet they are no less significant organizers of musical forces. Even if the relation of *topoi* to form is ultimately a fragile one, this in no way invalidates the potential that topics may have for their primary function as bearers of conventionalized musical meaning. (Caplin 2002)

Is topic theory relevant to analysis? It may be that such questions are redundant, as Caplin suggests. However, in another sense, topics may control the extension of a musical composition, since forms are also topics. When Mahler begins the recapitulation of the first movement of the Fourth Symphony in an unexpected way, he invokes the topic of the sonata-allegro (in order to challenge it; see Samuels 1995, 140–143, and *Sense*, 181–183).

All musical signification is social and cultural, and no signification is "purely musical" or "purely linguistic" because topics are paradigms, signifying in relation to culture, not in relation to syntagmatics. Along with everything else, musical topics are signs of our connections with our sisters and brothers in literary criticism, art history, cultural theory, and social history; many of these connections are complex and elusive. The primary concern of the topic theorist is to give an account of each topic in global terms, showing how it reflects culture and society, not to focus on music alone. There are, then, many riddles to be solved in the elucidation of topic theory. Where all seemed self-evident, an abyss of unsolved questions opens up.

2   The Literary Source of Topic Theory

(a) The literary topic

The idea of the topic or *topos* had its birth in literary studies. Though using the term "motif" rather than topic, M. H. Abrams calls it "an element—a type of incident, device, or formula—which recurs frequently in literature . . . an older term for such recurrent poetic concepts or formulas is the *topos* (Greek for 'a commonplace')" (Abrams 1971, 101). The tradition of these recurring motifs did not arise by accident. Aristotle compiled a book of *Topica*, "a collection of general arguments which a rhetorician might consult for help in treating a particular theme" (Allanbrook 1983, 329; see Aristotle 1958). Students of rhetoric, from the Middle Ages to the eighteenth century, were taught such habitual references and turns of phrase (the "figures [of] oratorical discourse," in the passage of Castil-Blaze quoted above), which were then worked into the language when a high style was sought. Topics appear in poetry, also. They are a sign of the sophisticated and educated speaker.

But their relevance to the world of the audience may be oblique to the point of grotesqueness. Rhetorical topics are always considered to refer to a literary world, not to the contemporary social world. This literary world may be very distant from the present; indeed, it may never have existed at all. Topics seem perfectly natural to the hearer or reader, but in referring to the exotic, the antique, the fantastic, they may be, on the face of it, absurd.

Our understanding of literary topics has been much broadened by the seminal book *European Literature and the Latin Middle Ages*, by Ernst Robert Curtius. Often in medieval and Renaissance literature, references appear which seem quite out of place. For example, in the *Nibelungenlied* of about 1200, Siegfried, hunting in the forests of Burgundy, kills an "enormous lion" (Curtius 1990 [1948], 126). Lions are not part of the fauna of Burgundy, and a modern commentator comments, "His delight in Siegfried's exploits leads the poet to tell tall stories." But no such reservation is needed. Lions abound in the *poetry* of medieval Europe. "Alcuin [an eighth-century English writer] hopes that a traveler will not be attacked by lions and tigers on his road," Curtius informs us. "English shepherds are warned to beware of lions [in Bede's *Life of St Cuthbert*]. . . . The French epic swarms with lions" (184).

The lions come, not from the northern forest, but from Ovid's *fulvi leones* in the *Heroides*. Literary historians recognize many such conventional references. Olive trees, for example, "were extraordinarily abundant in the medieval North," though of course olives did not *grow* in the north; and such out-of-place phenomena persist as late as Shakespeare's Forest of Arden in *As You Like It*, where there are olive trees, lions, and palms (the Forest of Arden is near Birmingham, England).

These references come, not from observation or from some topographic description, but from "the rhetorical school exercises of late Antiquity". Latin authors of the Middle Ages learned their craft by studying the rhetoric and poetry of the ancient Roman world. This was full of topoi, which had their origin in Ovid, Virgil, Petronius, Tiberianus, and other classical authors. Topoi continued to be created and added to the stock throughout the period of Latin literature, which lasted, of course, into the seventeenth century. Some of these are of the most general kind; the figure of the hero, for example, begins with Achilles and Aeneas and reappears in Siegfried, Roland, and Bayard.

Because these literary topoi adopted significations from elsewhere and from other times, they did not refer to any aspect of the real social world of their time, but rather to an imaginative world. Curtius gives a very striking example. Ekkehard IV, an eighth-century monk of the abbey of St. Gall in Switzerland, wrote a set of graces on food, which were long thought to provide a typical monastery menu for the period, the successive graces specifying the courses of the meal. A modern commentator describes the resultant banquet:

> First they filled their bellies with various kinds of bread, with salt, after which came at least one course of fish, fowl, meat, or game (all without sauces, vegetable, or other side dishes), after which came milk and then cheese. Then a dish containing the most pungent spices and sauces, together with honey, flat cakes, and eggs, after which vinegar was happily drunk . . . presumably as an apéritif for the following courses, which consisted of at least one dish each of legumes, native fruit, southern fruit, and fresh edible roots. Thirst was quenched first with divers wines, next with beer, and finally with water. (Quoted by Curtius 1990 [1948], 183)

This meal seems preposterous. It has now been shown, however, that the dishes to which Ekkehard provides the graces are drawn from the *Etymologiae* of Isidore of Seville (ca. 560–636). He gives himself away by quoting a grace for figs ("southern fruit"), which do not grow in Switzerland. The monk, selecting dishes for his pious attentions, does not think of invoking the food he consumes every day in his own abbey; like any other writer of his time, he looks to literary tradition.

It could be said that topics in Latin literature were signs not of natural objects or events, but of style. The author who frames her description according to a conventional topic is showing herself to compose within a particular genre; she is engaging with the reader's competence and sympathy by giving assurance of their mutual knowledge. It is easy to trace this conventionality in later poetry and writing, though Curtius, our best authority on the subject, stops at the Renaissance (because he is especially interested in literature in Latin rather than the vernacular). An example is given below (the *locus amoenus*) of a Latin topos which transferred to English literature and has persisted into modern times; and the survival of traditional genres is illustrated later at some length, in the discussion in part 4 of the pastoral, which is still alive in the late eighteenth century, in the poetry of Salomon Gessner (d. 1788) and André Chénier (d. 1794).

Two conclusions are to be drawn from this survey of the literary topic. First, in

the case of topics, the signifier and signified are not necessarily contemporary or local to each other. The lions mentioned by Sedulus Scottus, a poet of ninth-century
Liège, can be traced to Ovid. Similarly, the intrepid huntsmen evoked by Haydn's
quotation of the "sourcillade," a horn call first notated in 1742, probably inhabit
the hunting books of Gaston Phoebus and Alfonso XI of Castile (both fourteenth
century).

Second, the topical signified may be wholly imaginary, a reflection of cultural
fantasies. The pastoral topos, when it appears in recent centuries, is clearly not contemporary with its signification; Fontenelle, Pope, Gessner are not thinking of the
contemporary countryside. But if, on the other hand, they are thinking of the
countryside as known by Homer, Theocritus, and Virgil, then this scene is no less
imaginary. There was never an idyllic countryside like that described in the pastoral
tradition. Those fortunate, musical, refined shepherds and shepherdesses are pure
inventions. Compared to the poets, musicians are at one remove further from the
classical shepherd, because they are obliged to evoke him with modern means;
Corelli and Handel invoke the pastoral tradition with the droning bass of the bagpipe, which could not have been played by the shepherds of Virgil. Theorists of the
literary and musical topic, therefore, must take care not to assume that signifier and
signified are necessarily contemporaneous, or even that the signified was ever part
of the social and material world.

(b) The *locus amoenus*

Since the model for German theorists was literary criticism, let us illustrate
the operation of a literary topic in ancient and modern times. There was a literary
topos that governed writing from the first century into modern times, passing easily
from Latin into the European vernaculars. The pleasance or *locus amoenus* became
the "principal motif of all nature description" (Curtius 1990 [1948], 195) from the
time of the Empire (27 B.C.–476 A.D.) onward: "It is . . . a beautiful, shaded natural
site. Its minimum ingredients comprise a tree (or several trees), a meadow, and a
spring or brook. Birdsong and flowers may be added. The most elaborate examples
also add a breeze" (Curtius 1990 [1948], 195). Such scenes are to be found in classical poets like Theocritus and Virgil, but merely as pastoral backgrounds. In its
own right, the *locus amoenus* first appears in Petronius (first century).

> Mobilis aestivas platanus diffuderat umbras
> Et bacis redemita Daphne tremulaeque cupressus
> Et circum tonsae trepidanti vertice pinus. . . .

A moving plane cast summer shadows, so too the laurel crowned with berries, and the
tremulous cypresses, and, all around, the shorn pines with their swaying tops. Among
them, in wandering streams, played a foamy brook, fretting the pebbles with complain-
ing waters. . . . Witness the wood-haunting nightingale and the town-haunting swal-
low both, who, flitting over the grass and tender violets, beautified the place with their
singing. (Quoted by Curtius 1990 [1948], 195)

A later, more elaborate passage is quoted by Curtius from Tiberianus (fourth century). It is quoted here only in part, in the metrical translation of J. W. and A. M. Duff.

> Amnis ibat inter herbas valle fusus frigida,
> Luce ridens calculorum, flore pictus herbido.
> Caerulas superne laurus et virecta myrtea
> Leniter motabat aura blandiente sibilo . . .

> Through the fields there went a river;
> Down the airy glen it wound,
> Smiling mid its radiant pebbles,
> Decked with flowery plants around.
> Dark-hued laurels waved above it
> Close by myrtle greeneries,
> Gently swaying to the whispers
> And caresses of the breeze.
> Underneath grew velvet greensward
> With a wealth of bloom for dower,
> And the ground, agleam with lilies,
> Coloured 'neath the saffron-flower,
> While the grove was full of fragrance
> And of breath from violets . . .
> Dewsprent trees rose firmly upright
> With the lush grass at their feet:
> Here, as yonder, streamlets murmured
> Tumbling from each well-spring fleet . . .
> Through those shades each bird, more tuneful
> Than belief could entertain,
> Warbled loud her chant of spring-tide,
> Warbled low her sweet refrain.
> Here the prattling river's murmur
> To the leaves made harmony,
> As the zephyr's airy music
> Stirred them into melody.
> (Quoted by Curtius 1990 [1948], 196–197)

Rhetorical lawgivers were aware of the necessary components of this topic. Libanius (314–ca. 393) specifies six "charms of landscape," "springs and plantations and gardens and soft breezes and flowers and bird-voices."

Medieval poets, aware of these rules, naturally reproduce the topic of the *locus amoenus*. Writers on style discuss it as a necessary ingredient of stylish description; books on poetics, "which began to appear in increasing numbers from 1170", describe it in painstaking detail. Finally, Peter Riga (d. 1209) wrote *De Ornatu Mundi* (On earth's ornaments), a whole poem devoted to the *locus amoenus*, adding further delights to the classical list: spices, balsam, honey, wine, cedars, and bees. It was associated with Virgil's description of the Elysian Fields, which was adapted by Christian poets for Paradise; but Christians had to add the theme of fruit trees in order to make room for the forbidden fruit (Curtius 1990 [1948], 200n).

It is scarcely surprising that the *locus amoenus* enters English verse in precisely these terms. It appears as the description of Eden in Milton's *Paradise Lost*, in a passage which, if both are read in full, closely resembles that of Tiberianus quoted above.

> Thus was this place,
> A happy rural seat of various view;
> Groves whose rich trees wept odorous gums and balm, . . .
> Betwixt them lawns, or level downs, and flocks
> Grazing the tender herb, were interpos'd . . .
> . . . meanwhile murmuring waters fall
> That to the fringes bank with myrtle crown'd,
> Her crystal mirror holds, unite their streams.
> The birds their choir apply; airs, vernal airs,
> Breathing the smell of field and grove, attune
> The trembling leaves . . .
> (Book IV, ll. 246–266)

But the topic persists in many different contexts. Because of its conventional character, Shelley presents it as a dream in his poem *The Question:*

> I dreamed that, as I wandered by the way,
> Bare winter suddenly was changed to spring;
> And gentle odours led my steps astray,
> Mixed with a sound of waters murmuring
> Along a shelving bank of turf, which lay
> Under a copse . . .

Even Wordsworth, in spite of his impatience with "science and art", is equally in thrall to the ancient topic in *Lines Written in Early Spring.*

> I heard a thousand blended notes
> While in a grove I sat reclined. . . .
>
> Through primrose tufts, in that sweet bower,
> The periwinkle trail'd its wreaths;
> And 'tis my faith that every flower
> Enjoys the air it breathes.
>
> The birds around me hopp'd and play'd . . .
> The budding twigs spread out their fan
> To catch the breezy air . . .

The *locus amoenus* appears in opera, too. Giovanni Schmidt, librettist of Rossini's opera *Armida* (1817), imagines at the start of act 3 a charming landscape; but as in Shelley's case, this landscape is a dream, an illusion created by the sorceress of the opera's title. The composer responds with various musical topics: pastoral horns, woodwind birdsong. "An enchanted garden, a complete picture of the simplicity of Nature. Trees and plants, loaded with fruit. Hedges and bushes blooming with all kinds of flowers: running water courses, still pools and varieties of birds on them; more brightly colored birds flitting from tree to tree; on one side, some moss-covered grottoes; the scene is ringed by pleasant hillsides next to shady valleys." Musicians sometimes complete the topical allusion, if it is not already complete in the text. When the fourth door of Bluebeard's castle is opened in Bartók's opera, a beautiful grove is seen, "suffused with a bluish-green light". Béla Balázs's text mentions "branches heavy with blossom . . . lovely flowers" and a "sweet, fragrant garden, hidden under rocks and boulders"; the composer provides the missing topic of birdsong in the woodwind of the orchestra, though this is not mentioned in the libretto. Thus, the topic of the *locus amoenus* finds its way at last into music.

(c) German and Anglo-Saxon traditions

There has been a separate German tradition of musical topic theory, ignored by the American writers. Since Germany was the scene of the development of *literary* topic theory, the musicologists have been preoccupied with topics which resemble those of literature or have a strongly linguistic pattern. The most important of these is Hermann Jung's study of the pastoral (1980), a magnificent enterprise that traces the literary tradition as well as defining the musical signifier in all its variety from the beginnings up to 1750. Karl H. Wörner (1972) has written of the musical representation of death and eternity, Reinhold Hammerstein (1980) has examined the medieval theme of the Dance of Death in literature, visual art, and music, Peter Rummenhöller (1992) has investigated the idea of the *Liedhaft*— the echo of traditional song—in Brahms, and Ariane Jessulat (2001) has described the *Frage,* the musical question.

A comparison of Hammerstein's study with Robert Samuels's examination of the same theme will illustrate the difference between the German and Anglo-Saxon schools. Hammerstein considers a large number of written texts, from the fifteenth to the eighteenth centuries, and a similar repertoire of wall paintings and printed illustrations, to sketch the essential features of the medieval and Renaissance Dance of Death. He begins promisingly, by showing that Claudius's poem *Der Tod und das Mädchen,* set to music by Schubert, relates closely to a medieval poem on the same theme. But he does not pursue the topic of the Dance of Death in modern times; his book is a painstaking summary of the theme as understood in its heyday.

He shows, for example, that early writers characterize the Dance of Death as a *mattachins* or *branle,* dances performed by dancers holding hands in a chain linked into a ring. The true *branle* progressed to the right, but in the Dance of Death—in which the chain was led by a skeletal figure of Death, playing a musical instrument—the progression was usually *widdershins,* to the left. The earliest texts in Latin refer to the devilish instruments as either *fistula,* interpreted by artists as flute and fife, shawm, cornett, bagpipe, and bladder pipe, or *tympanum,* represented as a drum of some kind; the two instruments together make up the fife and drum combination of the medieval entertainer. Both the music and the dance are described as strange and unfamiliar, grotesque, so that the devilish visitors have to teach it to those who are being snatched away.

A turning point came with Holbein's woodcuts, published in Basel in 1526, in which each living figure, instead of joining hands in a chain, is separately dragged away by a figure of Death; there are no musicians as such, but some of the skeletal figures play instruments, psaltery, xylophone, and drum. It is not clear that all characters are dancing. The image of an individual figure dragged away by a figure of Death—a king, knight, churchman, merchant, or young woman—lies behind the poem of Claudius, of course. In subsequent illustrations of this type, a greater variety of musical instruments is shown, and indeed there is a slight suggestion of matching the instruments to the persons called; emperor, king, or knight may be called by Death playing a trumpet or horn, while a young person, male or female, is called by a stringed instrument, such as a lute or a vielle. Correspondingly, the character called by Death is sometimes herself a musician, holding or casting away her instrument.

These pictures inaugurate a certain freedom with the musical instruments chosen for this cultural theme. One very interesting image comes from a printed text of 1621, which is accompanied by etchings that reproduce a fresco of 1568, long since destroyed. In this portrayal the musician has thrown away an instrument—a recorder—but is also holding in one hand a pommer. Both would count as "Pfeife" or *fistulae*. Death calls the musician away by playing a *viola da braccia* with six strings. In a later watercolor copy of this same image, dating from 1773, the instrument is a violin, with four strings (illustrations 253 and 254 in Hammerstein's book). There is a similar wall painting, from Bleibach in the Black Forest, dating from 1723, in which Death's instrument is a violin, his victim's a shawm. Here Death's words are recorded:

Mit deiner schallmeyen thue jetzt schweigen,
Ein hopper tantz dir ich will geigen.
Ja unser spill wär gar nit gantz,
Wan du nit wärest bey unserem tantz.

Your shawm must now be silent—I will fiddle a sprightlier dance for you. Our music would not be complete, if you join not in the dance.

Hammerstein thinks the social standing of the instruments is compared, commenting that stringed instruments had become more prominent during the sixteenth century. "Death's violin," he says, "is thus the instrument of greater value and higher standing, compared to the primitive shawm of the musician" (Hammerstein 1980, 108). This seems wrong; probably the status of the fiddle as a *dance* instrument is being stressed, against the more solemn associations of the wind instruments. The antic posture of Death, and his invitation to the dance, would support this view. Thus, the later idea of the devilish violin, found in Saint-Saëns, Mahler, and Stravinsky, is foreshadowed, though Hammerstein does not say this.

This writer refers chiefly to material from Germany, Austria, Switzerland, and France, and his study ends in the early eighteenth century, when traditional representations of the Dance of Death cease. He is a chronicler, not a critical theorist. He shows little interest in references to the Dance of Death in the Romantic period, either literary or musical; by this time, the theme was popularized and misunderstood. As for its reflection in music not specifically connected to the theme, like Mahler's symphonies, Hammerstein would see no reason to consider such things.

Robert Samuels, in his book on Mahler's Sixth Symphony (1995), comes from exactly the opposite angle. He summarizes very briefly the medieval topic, referring to several authorities, including Hammerstein. He is chiefly interested in the individual summons of Death (rather than the round dance), because it leads to a nineteenth-century image that is erotic and prurient, in other words, kitsch. The grim figure of Death lures away a young woman, partly naked, who is portrayed as a bride, her bridal veil turning into a shroud. In a parallel development of the ancient theme, the sexual risk and scandal of the waltz, a new dance, led some writers to compare it to the Dance of Death. In particular the masked ball seemed a wild and threatening affair; it makes Samuels think of Bakhtin's idea of the carnivalesque. Indeed, the cartoonist Charles Rowlandson published in 1814–16 a set of engravings called *The English Dance of Death*, in which one tableau is entitled "The Waltz" and another "The Masquerade." Both show the skeletal figure of Death in a scene of dancing.

Both Goethe and Baudelaire wrote poems about the Dance of Death, and of course there were musical interpretations, notably Saint-Saëns's *Danse Macabre*. But these are not the focus of Samuels's interest. He stresses that this theme had become a cliché and an aspect of kitsch. Consequently, serious artists could not refer to it directly. It is chiefly important as an intertextual feature of Romantic art, part of the necessary context of certain texts, though never named. Here Samuels refers to Michael Riffaterre's idea of "presuppositions", which are "the implicit and requisite preceding conditions of an explicit statement" (Samuels 1995, 128). "These figures," Riffaterre explains, "refer to sign complexes that they substitute for and repress, as it were, pushing them back into intertextual latency." In Mahler's scherzos the figure of the Dance of Death is intertextually necessary to understanding, but is never specified in the text. It "remains outside the text, in the sense that it is not the subject of direct reference; but it animates the treatment of generic materials and its presence is signalled by the presence of clichés within the music" (129). Since the scandalous waltz had become associated with the Dance of Death, the near-banality of the waltz tunes in the scherzo of the Fifth Symphony represent a dangerous hankering after kitsch and cliché, and along with this comes the more threatening shadow of an eroticized Dance of Death, "the dreadful Other". In this section, Samuels relies not on historical chronicles but on a work of literary hermeneutics, Sarah Webster Goodwin's *Kitsch and Culture* (1988).

If Samuels, the self-avowed semiologist, may be criticized for his imperfect understanding of the medieval theme, then Hammerstein, the positivistic documentary historian, may be seen as too unwilling to trace the later implications of this theme, including its importance as a merely implicit or intertextual feature. In this respect, both writers reflect their scholarly heritage, one Anglo-Saxon, the other

German. A marriage of these traditions would obviously benefit the study of musical topoi.

(d) The complexity of topics

It is not possible to identify musical topics with mere labels. The complexity of literary topics shows this. Musical topics must behave similarly, and in any case are themselves often aspects of literary and cultural topics, inheritors of long histories. In order to understand a topic, we need to relate a long narrative of fantasy and imagination, as well as to understand social and technological history. This was demonstrated in *The Sense of Music:* the signification of the horse, or the *pianto*, in nineteenth-century culture extended far back into earlier times and was deeply ramified by its associations with other texts, other media, other worlds. Both signifier and signified must be investigated if we are to reach some grasp, at least provisional, of the meanings and evocations of each musical topic.

3   Signifier and Signified in Music

(a) The chimera of referentialism

It is often commented that topic theory embodies a *referential* view of music. The idea of "referential", "extramusical", or "extrageneric" meaning is apt to arouse resistance in some quarters; music cannot, it is believed, "refer" to anything, because its reference can only be known from a verbal text or title. This may turn out to be a false problem, because "referentiality" is not really a semiotic idea at all.

It is explained in a famous work of literary theory, *The Meaning of Meaning* by C. K. Ogden and I. A. Richards (1923), and is developed further in Richards's *Principles of Literary Criticism* (1925). Ogden and Richards were grappling with Aristotelean theories of meaning in their 1923 book, and they felt that the term "object", as descriptive of the contents of thought, was misleading.

> The word "thing" is unsuitable for the analysis here undertaken, because in popular usage it is restricted to material substances—a fact which has led philosophers to favour the terms "entity", "ens" or "object" as the general name for whatever is. It has seemed desirable, therefore, to introduce a technical term to stand for whatever we may be thinking of or referring to. "Object", though this is its original use, has had an unfortunate history. The word "referent", therefore, has been adopted. (Ogden and Richards 1923, 13n)

Next, the authors make it clear that "referential" meaning is the kind of meaning attributed to the "reflective, intellectual use of language," as opposed to the affective/volitional use. They are confirmed Darwinists, understanding communication and symbolism in behaviorist and psychological terms; hence they consider the "scientific" or cognitive view of meaning to be paramount. They point out that the common view of meaning—that a word means some "thing" in ordinary life—is elliptical, overlooking an important stage in the process of signifying. The word is, first of all, a "symbol," and its immediate "meaning" is a "thought" or reference, a mental phenomenon. This kind of meaning is causal and verifiable; a word may, at this level, be "wrongly" understood. The thought or reference then evokes a "referent"; this kind of meaning is "adequate" as it cannot be verified in universal terms. The word "dog" (Ogden and Richards's illustration) means the idea of a dog, which is a thought. The thought may then guide our attention to a real dog that we see in the street. Finally, we assume that "dog" means the dog in the street, overlooking the essential stage of reference, at which the word means an idea, and the idea relates to the real object in the outside world. "Between the symbol and the referent there is no relation other than the indirect one, which consists in its being used by someone to stand for a referent. Symbol and Referent, that is to say, are not connected directly . . . but only indirectly" (14).

Ogden and Richards criticize Saussure for "neglecting entirely the things for which signs stand", which cut him off "from any contact with scientific methods of verification" (8). To speak simply, Saussure saw the relation of the "symbol" (in Ogden and Richards's terminology) to the "reference", but had no use for the "referent".

In philosophical terms, Ogden and Richards were *realists*, Saussure a *nominalist*. On some level, the English writers believed in a real world that words "mean", a world that could be examined objectively and studied by science. Saussure, however (especially as he was revised by Benveniste, 1971 [1939], 45), saw that every property of the real world was attributed to it by language. Of course there is a real world, but nothing can be said of it; therefore, you cannot speak of a "real dog", but only of the meaning of "dog", which is to say a semantic dog. Signs refer to other signs, not to real objects. Nominalist views were repugnant to the positivistic climate of thought of the 1920s.

The field of meaning, to the realist, is external to that of expression. Thus, thought and language need a "world" of extension within which the meaning can be located, and to which the expression can refer; a thought that has no counterpart in the real world is just a dream or chimera. Language is operating "referentially", then, when it invokes a part of the external world as meaning. Referential meaning is logical, denotative, and objective—not emotional or volitional, as Ogden and Richards insist. To parody the idea of the "extramusical", referential meaning is "extralinguistic" and "extraliterary", because it postulates a world outside of the expressive system. This is a *metaphysical* issue; Eco speaks of the "metaphysics of the referent" (1979 [1976], 70).

Most semiotic writers cannot accept this view; indeed, they speak of the "extensional fallacy". The view that language—and other semiotic systems—refer to an extended or external world must fall when we consider imaginary meanings and lies. The idea of referentiality implies that the meaning of a sign "has something to do with its corresponding object" (Eco 1979 [1976], 62). But let us consider the term "horse". If its meaning depends on extension, then this term is meaningful while the term "unicorn" is meaningless. Similarly, sentences may seem to have their meaning in relation to states of affairs in the world. "All horses have wings", then, cannot have meaning. But it is clear that "all horses have wings" and "all horses have four legs" are sentences of exactly the same standing from the semiotic point of view, just as the status of "unicorn" is exactly equivalent to that of "horse". The status of a sentence or term as a semiotic entity is not guaranteed by its relation to a real state of affairs, but by its interpretability within a code. We understand a given expression because we can attribute to it "the content or the contents that one or several codes usually and conventionally assign to it".

According to this view, if we consider musical topics to form a code, then they need not refer to a "world" of extension, and their meaning is not "referential". On the contrary, they must refer to semantic values, defined and implied by the signs themselves. There may, in fact, be a musical "horse", as I have shown elsewhere. This has its own nature, defined by the musical sign, not by "experience". Indeed, there can be musical horses whether there are horses in the world or not. "A sign is everything which can be taken as significantly substituting for something else. This something else does not necessarily have to exist or to actually be somewhere at the moment in which a sign stands in for it" (Eco 1979 [1976], 7). The meaning of the musical sign is not to be sought in the world at all. It is to be sought within the system: the semantic web of a language, or other signifying system including music, lies back-to-back with the phonological and syntactic pattern, like a sheet of paper printed on both sides, so that "one cannot cut the front without cutting the back at the same time" (Saussure 1974 [1959], 113).

Musical meaning cannot be referential. But even linguistic meaning is only referential when, in ordinary life, we use context and pragmatics to negotiate meaningful communication. The world is not a material realm but a "semiosphere", an interconnected universe of signs. Ultimately, all signs, including musical signs, operate across the nexus of signifier and signified, expression and content.

(b) Correlation

Robert Hatten, agreeing that musical meaning cannot be called "referential", offers the term *correlation* for the relation of expression and content in music (it comes from Eco 1979 [1976], 49). This kind of nexus works on many levels; clearly, the relation of topical signifier and signified is one of correlation, but Hatten finds the process at work in simple oppositions like minor/major, which correlates with the cultural opposition tragic/nontragic (Hatten 1994, 11–12). He is especially interested in oppositions of this kind, since, as a hermeneutist, he wishes to use correlative relations as a key to the interpretation of works; in this interpretation he makes adroit use of the theory of markedness, which is dependent on binary oppositions.

Correlation is defined as an association that has become "a conventional part of the style" (269). Thus, in Peircean terms, it is symbolic, based on rule or convention (note the difference from the common use of "symbol"). As Peirce admits, it may reflect an original motivation which has been lost (as when the falling minor second indicates "grief" without need to think of its iconic origin). The ability to discern correlations is constitutive of *competence* in the style. Indeed, the very first stage of musical understanding is "identification of the structural types that exist in the style and their correlation with expressive types" (32). The finding of correlations ("decoding") is distinguished from interpretation, though the two "need not be completely separable stages" (33).

Undoubtedly, the finding of topics in music is such a process of decoding. A pattern of oppositions may, in fact, be inherent in the universe of topics; "importantly for reconstructing correlations . . . topics invoke a well-established oppositional network of meanings" (81). Thus, the Turkish march in Beethoven's Ninth Symphony seems out of place until one realizes that it confronts the heroic "Ode to Joy" on the axis low style/high style, and that the simple nobility of common people is meant (82). In the *Hammerklavier* the topics *aria* and *hymn* are opposed, the first "foregrounded and personal", the other "more distanced and objective" (17). The pastoral topic may work as an oppositional pole to the tragic, especially in Beethoven's Piano Sonata in A, Op 101. In this connection, Hatten agrees that certain topics may represent whole genres, though his sense is slightly different from that of the present work: he finds in the pastoral, for example, a formative theme that may determine the whole spirit of a work and even, in part, its structure (83). Furthermore, as a hermeneutist he is able to show that topics may be juxtaposed and may condition each other; there may be "pastoral tragedy", "learned rustics", and so forth. These are luxuries that are, perhaps, special to music.

Above all, the notion of correlation dispels the problems connected with terms like "reference" or "denotation", without suggesting that musical meaning is somehow personal or subjective or that the business of music is only to stimulate emotion. Hatten describes correlation as yielding "literal" meaning (165). "Correlations in music are characterized by their immediacy—involving merely an act of recognition. . . . [They] are encoded in a given musical style and transparently recognized by a listener." The nexus of expression and content is direct, not dependent on a listening mind. This seems a most admirable way of conceiving musical meaning.

(c) Cultural units

Musical meanings are to be found in a conventional world, the world of semantics, related by correlation to the world of expression. But what is the relation between this semantic world and the *external world*? What, for example, connects the cultural horse to a real horse? The external world is known through experience, in which the encounter with horses is a natural event. But a horse in literature or music is a constellation of conventional attributes; in literature, for example, horses may be anthropomorphic (they may be devoted, loving, loyal, fearless). Even the *linguistic* horse (as opposed to the literary horse) has some conventional aspects, since language, too, relates to a semantic universe; it is dependent not only on experience, but also on definition. A horse must stand at least 14.2 hands high (56.8 inches or 144 centimeters); smaller animals are called *ponies*. A horse is, generically, an animal of a certain kind, but the term can also be opposed to "mare", in which case "horse" is a male horse (in more specific terms, a stallion). These conventional qualifications may be different in other languages; German has to say "kleines Pferd" for a pony, though the English word is also used in Germany. Thus the semantics of language is primarily conventional. Language—much less literature or music—cannot bring real horses into being by a process of hypostasis.

Still, most people would consider horses to be manifested in experience, independently of definition and attribute. Yet the conventional aspect of the literary horse is found by Eco throughout the world of signs—even in the linguistic horse. All horses are cultural; there is no "real" horse. "Every attempt to establish what the referent of a sign is forces us to define the referent in terms of an abstract entity which moreover is only a cultural convention," writes Eco (66). "What, then, is the meaning of a term? From a semiotic point of view it can only be a *cultural unit*" (67). Eco quotes David Schneider's definition of a cultural unit: "A unit . . . is simply anything that is culturally defined and distinguished as an entity. It may be a person, place, thing, feeling, state of affairs, sense of foreboding, fantasy, hallucination, hope or idea. In American culture such units as uncle, town, blue (depressed), a mess, a hunch, the idea of progress, hope and art are cultural units" (Schneider 1968, 2, quoted by Eco 1979 [1976], 67). Cultural units, then, have their being within a culture, rather than within language. They may, conceivably, bridge gaps between languages; a French-speaking Louisianan presumably understands the units of American culture as well as someone from Virginia or Maryland, though she may express them in French. Even in polyglot Europe, languages— especially related languages like French and Italian—often seem to signify exactly similar lexical contents, though there are usually differences of detail between significations in different languages. No one would doubt that a perceptual unity embraces *horse*, *Pferd*, and *cavallo*.

Cultural units are clearly signifieds, but in order to understand Eco's explanation of the process of translation across semiotic modes, we need to turn again to the semiotics of C. S. Peirce. In place of Saussure's signifier and signified, Peirce speaks of the *representamen* and the *object*, which are joined by a third sign, the *interpretant*. For example, a road sign may have as its object a "dangerous bend". In order for this representamen to be joined to this object, there must be a thought in the mind of an observer who interprets the sign; or alternatively, somebody, seeing the sign, may slow down and beware the danger. Either of these, the thought or the behavior, may constitute an interpretant. But apparently the sign does not "mean" the thought or the behavior.

Consider, now, the expression of a cultural unit in terms of two semiotic modes; for instance, in language and in a drawing. "I can make the drawing of a dog correspond to the word /dog/," remarks Eco (1979 [1976], 70). If we transfer a cultural unit from one mode to another, each mode furnishes an interpretant for the sign in the other mode. A word within the linguistic lexicon, a conventional theme in literature, a musical topic, or a representation by a painter may form a constellation of signifiers around the same cultural signified. Thus, the linguistic interpretation of a musical topic is an *interpretant*, not the *object* of the musical figure. A label— *Empfindsamkeit*, the *pianto*, the sarabande—is such a linguistic interpretation.

There will, however, be something strikingly different about the information given by music, painting, and literature, compared to the lexicon of language. This difference must be examined. The rhythm of the piano accompaniment to Schubert's song *Erlkönig*, and of the leitmotiv of Wagner's Valkyries, means "horse". Similarly, the painting of the racehorse Baronet, by George Stubbs, which was the first work of art to popularize the attitude of the *galop volant*, a conventional portrayal of the gallop which lasted for almost a century, means "horse" at some level. But clearly, the musical and visual terms convey a great deal of cultural information which is not contained in the semantic field of "horse". Apparently, this extra information lies in that area which is usually called "imaginative". A musical horse carries a much greater burden of imaginative signification than the simple linguistic term. The musical horse is noble, masculine, adventurous, warlike, and speedy. It corresponds ill to any animal that may be enclosed in a lexical definition. It has a nature and a history that cannot be matched in the lexicon or in simple communication, though it can be matched to a great degree in literature, especially that of the Middle Ages and Renaissance.

The musical horse, then, may be interpreted by the linguistic horse, because both horses correlate to a semantic horse, which is a cultural unit. But the musical horse provides more information than the linguistic horse because it adds the imaginative dimension. The horse in music is always associated with nobility; for this reason the musical topic is called the "noble horse". For certain, the *literary* horse adds the same sort of increment. We are justified in asking why the musical and literary horses place us so much nearer to the cultural horse; why, that is to say, music and literature are more imaginative than ordinary language.

The answer: music, like literature, is not merely language, but *text*. Literary texts, unlike music, are fashioned out of language, of course. But in the text, language is made to work, to do a task. "Faire de la langue un travail," writes Julia Kristeva, to make language do a job is to put the literary text in opposition to language, because language is considered to be "a carrier of meaning", while the text *transforms meaning* (Kristeva 1969, 9). Texts began in magic, myth, and poetry, where language also was germinated. Though made of language, the text questions and changes language, detaching it "from its thoughtless automatism, its everyday routine" (10). It "sinks into the surface of language a vertical where are sought the models of that signification which representative and communicative language does not recite, even though it is marked by them" (11).

This signification forms culture, and culture defines society. Literary texts, therefore, are social processes as well as imaginative utterances. In the best sense, they are revolutionary, for it is within texts that signification is made and culture is changed. "Within the substance of language and within social history, the text places itself in the reality that generates it: it forms part of the vast process of material and historical movement" (11). "In other words, since the text is not just language as codified by grammar, it does not content itself with *representing*—with *signifying* reality. At the moment of signifying . . . it participates in the shifting, in the transformation of reality which it grasps at the very moment of its non-closure" (11).

Music is not made of language, but is text through and through. The failure to distinguish language from text has presumably led to the many unfruitful views of "music as language". And because music is not made of language, even the "terms" of music, if we may describe topics thus, are no inert pointers. In this respect, music and literature are different. When the literary author speaks of a horse, she engages with a processual signified, the developing theme of the literary horse; but she must use a linguistic term that is also to be found in ordinary communication, which may be defined in a dictionary, and which is easy to think of in referential and extended terms. When a musical text evokes a horse, as in Schubert's *Erlkönig*, there is never a question of referentiality or extension, but always of the acceptance and formulation of a cultural unit. Language can seem to represent a "real" horse, but music is bound to invoke a textual horse, a *cheval écrit*. Of course, literary texts can no more speak of "real" horses than can music. This is why we call texts "fiction"; they are *materia ficta*, something made or fashioned, and something that fashions.

Musical topics mean by virtue of their correlation to cultural units. This meaning is not "referential". Cultural units combine to form a culture, as words combine to form a language. Culture defines society, and society operates within history. In order to describe musical topics, there must be a full account of cultural mythology, of literary genre and symbolism, and of social history.

(d) Sign and ground

It has been shown that the linguistic term "horse" may be the interpretant of the piano figure in triplets accompanying Schubert's song *Erlkönig*. In this case, the musical topic and the linguistic expression betoken a cultural unit which may be considered the signification of the terms. This cultural unit is complex; it is a wide-branching sememe, intensionally composed of other sememes and ultimately of semes, irreducible and abstract semantic atoms. The linguistic expression, as has been shown, is a comparatively poor representative of the cultural unit; in the case of "horse", it is probably biological in large part, though there will be cultural components (like "taller than 144 centimeters"). The cultural unit itself, lying behind these various expressions, has many contextual semes which allow it to signify beyond the merely scientific or material. One of these may be "gallop", since the most rapid pace of the horse signifies as part of the nature of the unit. Of course, horses move at other paces, but these are not parts of the sememe that constitutes the unit; "gallop" is contextually significant because it links with the horse's cultural associations of nobility, power, and adventure. Thus, two semiotic modes (music and painting) have abstracted "gallop" in order to signify "horse" during the nineteenth century (see *Sense*, 45–63).

What, then, is the logical status of "gallop" in a pattern of signification in which the signifier is a particular musical rhythm, and the signified a world of social and literary associations connected with horses? Let us turn again to the semiotics of Peirce. The musical rhythm may be called the *representamen*, the horse (at least, the horse as cultural unit) the *object*. They are joined, whenever the sign is manifested, by an *interpretant*, vouchsafing their connectedness; this may be a thought in somebody's mind, an interpretation in another semiotic mode, or other things.

However, the nexus of representamen and object does not obtain in *any* respect, but with regard to a particular aspect. "The sign stands for something, its *Object*. It stands for that object not in all respects, but in reference to a sort of idea, which I sometimes call the *ground* of the representamen" (Peirce, quoted by Greenlee 1973, 51). A weathercock signifies the wind by reference to its direction, for example, so in this case the direction is the ground of the sign function (Greenlee 1973, 64). The musical horse always gallops, because its pace is the essential bearer of its cultural significance. The gallop is the ground of the sign called "noble horse" or *cheval écrit*. It is thus necessary that the cultural unit forming the object of the sign present in Schubert's piano accompaniment in *Erlkönig* contain the component "gallop". It will be noticed that the linguistic expression is simpler than the musical term, and linguistic horses can trot or amble, sleep or graze. It is not, however, merely a *musical* convention, since the gallop serves as the ground of signs in literature and painting, which are to be found in contemporary pictures and in much older literature (in particular, the *chansons de geste*). The gallop is the ground of the cultural horse as sign.

Typically, a musical *topos* signifies a cultural unit by virtue of some intensional component of that unit, which furnishes a ground for the sign function. The relation of the sign to the ground may conform with certain modes of relation, which Peirce calls *icon, index,* and *symbol*. The icon relates to the ground by resemblance. "A figurative painting is an icon, or the imitation of a nightingale or cuckoo by an orchestral instrument" (Monelle 1992b, 197; hereafter *LSM*). The index "is a sign which refers to the Object that it denotes by virtue of being really affected by that Object. . . . [It is] in dynamical (including spatial) connection both with the individual object, on the one hand, and with the senses or memory of the person for whom it serves as a sign, on the other hand" (Peirce 1940, 102, 107). A weathercock and a footprint are indices. The symbol (already mentioned above, in connection with Hatten's definition of musical content) signifies by virtue of a conventional rule that has to be learned; words in language are symbols, or road signs (though many of these are also icons). In the case of the musical horse, the relation of sign to ground is iconic, because the musical figure *resembles* the sound of the gallop. It must be insisted that Schubert's piano rhythm does not signify a horse (in the sense of a real animal), nor is the linguistic expression "horse" the *object* of the term, but an *interpretant*.

This pattern of sign, interpretant, cultural unit, contextual semes, and ground is a little harder to discern in the case of a topic like that heard in the leitmotiv of the "sword" in Wagner's *Ring*. This resembles not any sound that a sword may make, or that may be associated with a sword, but an item from another musical repertoire, namely the military trumpet call. It may initially seem that, like the gallop, Wagner's figure may be related to a trumpet call by *resemblance*. But if that is the case, there must be a contextual component within the unit "trumpet call" which forms the ground of the resemblance. Indeed, it might be possible to invoke such contextual features; it is triadic (an essential feature of the old cavalry trumpet repertoire), it is brazen and stirring, and it is played, nowadays, on a B-flat orchestral valve trumpet, which in timbre somewhat resembles the long natural trumpet of the cavalry. However, the operatic motive and the military signal are expressed in the same semiotic mode, namely music. Thus, the motive cannot resemble the signal, except in the way that a painting of another painting (*Olympia* in the background of Manet's portrait of Zola, for example) is related by resemblance—yet it is, apparently, merely a repainting of the original painting. Viewed in one way, Wagner's motive is related to a military signal in the same way that the military signal is related to another such signal; they clearly resemble each other, yet they are not signs of each other. But this would make the motive, like each signal, merely a token of a type, which is not a sign relation at all; indeed, in a few cases the topical reference is a literal quotation, like Mahler's quotation of the military signal *Abblasen* in the Third Symphony (*Sense,* 184). This is a case of a duplicate, which cannot be taken as a sign: "a duplicate is not a sign by virtue of merely being a duplicate" (Esposito 1999). Clearly, the musical topic is a sign, just as much in this case as in the case of the musical horse.

In fact, Wagner's topic is a *sign of a class* (not merely a member of the class). This relates it to one of Peirce's descriptions of indices: "They refer to individuals, single units, single collections of units, or single continua" (Greenlee 1973, 86). Such indices are connected to their objects by "blind compulsion" or "associational compulsion", and not by resemblance. The motive is an index of a collection of units, namely the repertoire of military trumpet signals.

For this reason I have previously classified topics as iconic and indexical, according to their representation either of natural sounds or of musical events. The methodologies in studying these two kinds of topic are somewhat different, for the iconic topic is musical only in its signifier; the signified is natural, social, cultural, and historical. Neither the object of the "noble horse" topic, nor the ground (which is the sound of the gallop) is musical; only the signifier—a kind of rhythm in 6/8 time—is musical. A study of the signified, then, will be cultural and social, but not musical. There is a world of associative signification beyond the initial object (what I have elsewhere called the "indexicality of the content"; see *Sense,* 17); an account is needed of the cultural unit that embraces the object and all its associations, viewed through social history, literature, and perhaps the other arts.

In the case of the indexical topic, there is much musical work to do on the side of the initial signified also, since this, like the signifier, is musical. The topic of the military trumpet call signifies by invoking the trumpet calls that were being played in contemporary armies, many of which we can observe. This repertoire and phenomenon must be described, including their organological aspects. And, as with the iconic topic, there is a world of associative signification beyond the musical repertoire, of course, embedded in literature and social history. These associations are related to moral character: heroic, adventurous, virile, dangerous (but not necessarily to "emotion", that perennial distraction in the study of musical signification).

Perhaps the chief difference in studying indexical and iconic topics is in the importance of the ground. In the case of the indexical topic, we must examine the musical original to see how closely it is reproduced; how far the original timbre is copied, how far the rhythms, melodic motives, or tempi relate to the repertoire echoed. But the iconic topic has no musical original; its musical content is an imitation of nature, though it is also conventional (horses do not gallop exactly in 6/8 time, though we believe they do). It would, perhaps, be of passing interest to examine the relation between the signifier of the "noble horse" topic and recordings of horses at the gallop, or to attempt to transcribe the sound of forest murmurs in musical terms, in order to compare this with the topic of "forest murmurs" (found in *Siegfried* and in Vivaldi's motet "Vos aurae per montes", RV 634, for example). But the result would likely be rather inconclusive, because the nexus of topical signifier and real sound is largely conventional. The chart shows examples of topics in the various categories (fig. 3.1).

	Signifier	Example
	dance measures	the Sarabande
Indexical topic	concert music	the French overture
	functional music	the hunting fanfare
	imitation of natural sound	the noble horse
Iconic topic	imitation of human sound	the pianto
	reference to literary theme	the Dance of Death

Figure 3.1.

(e) Interpretation and culture

There are certain difficulties in applying Peirce's theory of the sign to musical topics. Douglas Greenlee criticizes Peirce for certain of his underlying assumptions that are never properly argued: first, the assumption that all signs are "representations". If "anything should be a Sign, it must 'represent,' as we say, something else," writes Peirce (quoted by Greenlee 1973, 51). Greenlee finds this idea troubling. Clearly, some signs (names, for instance) do represent their objects, and an account of their objects is necessary in elucidating these signs. Other signs (connectives like "and"; abstract classes like numbers) seem meaningful, and appear to "stand for" something, but without obviously being representations, and in these cases a description of the object can be problematic. But in fact Peirce uses words like "refers to", "represents", and "stands for" interchangeably; he would not, perhaps, insist on a specific meaning for "represents".

A corollary to this objection is the complaint that some signs do not manifestly have "objects". If every sign stands for an object, then in some cases it is extremely difficult to see what it is. "I suggested that objects as diverse as words and piano sonatas are signs. Now the everyday use of language is prepared to admit words and linguistic expressions into the range of signs but would be strained to admit most piano sonatas. And does not one of the reasons lie in the fact that words often 'stand for' things, whereas most piano sonatas do not?" (Greenlee, 54). In such problematic cases, the mark of a sign is not its standing for something else, but its being interpreted: "Interpretation is the essential condition" (55). Here the logician Greenlee proposes a kind of hermeneutic semiotics, a little strange in the context of Peirceanism but very relevant to the interpretation of music. The desire to name an object for every sign may lead to false trails. Signs may be meaningful, without having any clear unitary meaning. This has been mentioned above, in relation to the *alla zoppa* rhythm.

The musical topic locates music in history and in culture. Its study is a corrective to the "abstract" analysis of music, which tends to deculturalize this most social of arts. At every point in the study of topics there is a need to seek historical reality. Both signifier and signified have their roots in the social, cultural, and technological world. In the case of indexical topics, the signifier—the sign, embodied in a musical event—will naturally tend to be contemporary. The hunt topic in the eighteenth century could only be signified by the music of the brass *trompe de chasse*, though its object was in many ways not contemporary. The innocent world of the shepherd was best evoked with bagpipes and flutes, although the classical shepherd, whose world lay behind modern pastoralism, had played the reed *aulós* and the syrinx.

The signifier of an indexical topic, then, was normally a component of the social world of its day. The signified, too, had its roots in the contemporary world, but in a more complex way. It is a little surprising to find that the heroic, manly, noble hunt evoked by music, portrayed in operas and described in hunting books, was not very much practiced in the lands of its chief currency, the Austro-German territories of eighteenth-century Europe. Hunting was cowardly and ignoble, and the fanciful mythology of the noble hunt was cultivated partly to redeem this. The musical topic was significative of an older, more sporting hunt, but it was also significative of the falseness of contemporary heroism; indeed, the brass hunting horn was itself a feature of baroque redundancy, since it was adopted largely for its festive sound, rather than its practical superiority to the older oxhorns and *cornets de chasse*.

Social and cultural history must be investigated for the central meaning of the topic. Since topics normally have roots in distant times, this means returning to the literature of much earlier eras; in some cases to antiquity itself, though of course nothing of antique music was known. This study will lead us to construct a mythology; the imaginative world of topical signification is alive within consciousness, but not to be found *tout simple* in the world of everyday reality.

Yet the world of contemporary reality must itself be understood, for it is reflected in cultural units along with the imaginative world of the time. When Schubert portrayed the horse of the father and son in the *Erlkönig*, horses were almost uniquely the only means of land transport in Europe, and were an important component of armies and warfare. Nevertheless, the musical horse was not the same as the horse of everyday life. This opposition evidently structures the musical horse of Schubert's time, because ordinary horses were everywhere. Today, horses are almost nowhere; they are clearly not central enough to society to generate an opposition to musical horses. Paradoxically, the horse has passed away, apart from metaphoric horses and a few horses ridden for sport and recreation, while the musical horse lives on strongly. In the everyday modern world, the hearer of *Erlkönig* seldom sees a real horse in her everyday life. The opposition between cultural horses and ordinary horses is no longer alive. In spite of this, we perfectly understand the musical term, and we understand, for example, why Schubert's horse has to gallop, although Goethe's poem does not mention the pace of the horse.

(f) A performance of Brahms

A final logical excursus. It is Thursday evening. I attend a concert at the Queens Hall, Edinburgh. One of the items is Brahms's Horn Trio. In the finale, the horn player sounds something that resembles a call of the great brass hunting horn; this gives the music a heroic, virile, outdoor, adventurous character. Topical semiosis is at work.

The topical signified is clear: it is the heroic character lent to the music by the hunt-like instrumental melody. But what is the signifier? (No apology is made for using the Saussurean terms *signified* and *signifier,* instead of the Peircean *object* and *representamen.*) Apparently, the performance of the horn player, Brahms's score, my listening sensitivity as interpretant of the sign, these are signifiers. But this sign, the one which gave special meaning to Brahms's finale, is the same sign that I might have heard in other works by Haydn, Strauss, or Delibes. Same signified, and presumably also same signifier. The details of the work, of the performance, of the hall and the evening are not relevant to a theory of the sign. I must progress a little further than a mere glance at the social and practical circumstances, this Thursday evening.

In the above two paragraphs, I think only of the manifestation of the sign, a Peircean *second* (a *dicent*). I need to consider the sign itself, which, since it is only a possible semiosis, is a *first* (a *rheme*). (Incidentally: viewed thus, my *theory* of the sign is an *argument*—a *third.*) The initial signifying effect of the player's performance is to guide my sensitivity to the eighteenth-century hunting horn and its repertoire of field calls (I do not need to know this, of course, and certainly not to think about it). This, on a provisional level, is the signification of the performance, but not of the sign. The hunting horn and its repertoire now function semiotically, signifying a myth of the heroic hunt, the splendor of the hunt as eighteenth-century huntsmen thought of it, and as they would like us to think of it. On this level—which is the level of the *second first*—the signifier embraces the hunting instrument developed in the late seventeenth century, and the collections of horn calls published during the next two centuries, perhaps including calls that were not written and have been forgotten.

This is the context in which the remainder of this book is written. Circumstantial interpretants—social and psychological considerations about manifested performances, or discussions of the "emotional" effects of the music—are a different matter, and are rather foreign to the world of semiotics. Semiotics is a logical study. The logic of signification demands that we examine the sign, not its manifestations, though these are also signs. Many manifestations will be surveyed in what follows here (in the sense of musical scores, not performances), but only in order to give a comprehensive account of signifier and signified; of representamen and object, if you will.

(g) A red herring

Within the music of our civilization, as in our literature, we may find heroes, riders, journeys, pomp and ceremony, weeping and dancing, the woodland, the church, the salon. The tradition of abstract analysis, focusing on development, distribution, comparison, has obscured this obvious fact, but most writers on music in the more popular traditions have continued to acknowledge it. Although the images of literature are shared by visual art, architectural ornament, furniture, and porcelain decoration, it is often denied that they have any place in music. Music, it is proclaimed, must always escape the constraints of meaning; it is a "concept-free discourse" (Adorno), "grammar without semantics" (Lévi-Strauss; both quotations from memory).

I have written elsewhere that "there has never been a gesture that was 'purely musical'" (*LSM* 326). The present book rests firmly on the assumption that music is a semiotic. Music is interesting because it is meaningful, and its meaning is as apparent as that of literature, painting, architectural decoration, or anything else. "Music is a species of thought; and thus, the idea that music is sign and depends on significative processes, or semiosis, is obviously true" (Martinez 1998, 2).

Unfortunately, many authorities have located musical meaning in the area of *emotion*, presumably because significations in music do not often converge on a single term, and one often passes easily from understanding to emotional response. Also, the emotional interpretation of music is individual and subjective, congenial to the Romantics, for whom "the source of the work of art was the soul of the artist" (Allanbrook 1983, 3). Allanbrook quotes Liszt's famous pronouncement that music "embodies feeling" without compelling it "to contend and combine with thought".

This attempt to wall music up in the emotive area, detached from the area of understanding, has received support because the terms of music are so transparent that we overlook them. One is commonly not aware of the musical terms which are intermediaries to one's feelings of triumph, agitation, grandeur, sadness, or calm, and one is then led to accept emotional responses as the signification of the music. The opening of the *Ring* gives an immediate feeling of immense cosmic depth, of vast spaces, mysterious powers hanging darkly over the world; one forgets that the horns playing this passage speak to us of the woodland and of the hunt. The theme of the sword Notung sounds dynamic, proud, resolute. We do not need to reflect on its origin as a military trumpet signal. The second subjects of Dvořák's Cello Concerto and Tchaikovsky's Sixth Symphony are sad and sweet, poetic and touching. Most persons will not notice that, as pentatonic tunes, they are part of the engagement with the nation and the people, utterances of the mysterious *Volksseele* with its involvement in soil, roots, and the homeliness of the tribe. All these meanings are inherent significations, not dependent on the listener; they are *lexical*, or in common language they are "literal" meanings. In this respect semiotics is distinguished from hermeneutics. The semiologist does not seek an "interpretation" of music. She seeks merely an elucidation of music's meaning, if you will, a "neutral" account of the music.

Part Two.　　　　　*Huntsmen*

4 Signifier:
The Hunting Horn

(a) The *trompe de chasse*

The topic of the hunt, with its associations, is perhaps the classic case of a separation of signifier and signified in the world of musical topics. The signifier was a musical style rooted in the calls of the great brass hunting horn, which was a relatively new instrument in the eighteenth century. At the same time, the heroic parforce hunt of the Middle Ages was in decline. Nevertheless, the ethos and mythology of the hunt continued in the *Jagdlieder,* the festivals of St. Hubert, the noble hunting orders, and in the many treatises on hunting. As we shall see, much hunting was ignoble, squalid, and cruel during this period. This was little reflected in writings about hunting, or in hunting music. The cultural hunt—the *chasse écrite*—remained heroic and glorious, and its association with the forest bore rich fruit in the Romantic period.

We should, therefore, enlarge on Leonard Ratner's account. "Military and hunt music was familiar throughout the eighteenth century . . . ," he says; "the hunt was a favorite diversion of the nobility; horn signals echoed and re-echoed throughout the countryside" (Ratner 1980, 18). Presumably this observation is merely an inference from the ubiquity of the hunt topic in music. Ratner offers no description of contemporary hunting, and apparently does not know of the hunting manuals which give copious details of this. We may observe intuitively that hunting music evoked the nobility, the outdoors, the forest, adventure, and action. But the brilliance, the heroism, the manliness of the musical hunt may not necessarily be inherent in the hunt of the day—that is, of the eighteenth century.

Let us survey, however, the *signifier* of this topic, based on the calls of the brass hunting horn. Its predecessor, the medieval hunting horn, was a natural oxhorn called *cor de chasse* or *Hifthorn* (because it hung at the owner's hip). A very luxurious version, the *oliphant,* was made from ivory. These crude instruments sounded a single note, and their calls were therefore merely rhythmic (though one writer has considered that they could achieve three harmonics; see Halfpenny 1953–54). Some of the calls are recorded in hunting manuals like those of Gaston de Foix, called Phoebus (about 1387) and Hardouin de Fontaines-Guérin (1394; see Taut 1927, 74–106). Some modern writers have thought that hunting calls varied from region to region, quoting Hardouin's precept: "De tant pais tantes guises", so many lands, so many styles (Taut 1927, 113). Yet there is a distinct pattern of relations between the various manuals of the period. For example, the calls transcribed by Jacques du Fouilloux in his book *La Vénerie*, which appeared about 1561 (du Foui-

Figure 4.1.

lloux 1606 [1561]), are copied verbatim by Sigismund Feyerabend in his *New Jag und Weydwerckbuch* of 1582, though du Fouilloux was writing in the Limousin, Feyerabend in Frankfurt (Taut 1927, 124). Even more surprising, one of du Fouilloux's calls, the *curée*, the call played after the kill when the hounds are given parts of the dead prey as a reward, is quoted by Purcell in *Dido and Aeneas*, as described below (Ringer 1953, 149–150). Evidently these calls were widely known and remained current, even 128 years after the book's appearance.

Du Fouilloux was accustomed to hearing calls played on the *cornet de chasse*, a brass or copper instrument, semicircular in shape with a loop in the center (fig. 4.1 shows one of his fine illustrations); although his cited hunting calls are all on a single pitch, this instrument may have been capable of the fourth harmonic, making it possible to play notes a fourth apart. As early as the mid-fourteenth century, such calls appear in the ritornello of the *caccia* "Tosto che l'Alba" by Gherardello da Firenze (d. 1362 or 1363; Ringer 1953, 148). The horn call, sung to the words "suo corno sonava", is shown in figure 4.2. This type of call continues to be found in *caccie* of the fourteenth century, and horns of the cornet shape are seen in woodcuts of the mid-fifteenth century (Baines 1976, 148). Baines calculates that such

suo   cor - no   so - na - va,

Figure 4.2.

horns in F (written)

longo

Figure 4.3.

calls would require a tube of at least 75 cm in length, awkward to carry on horse-back but reducible to an overall length of about 30 cm with the addition of a central loop. But true melodic calls, so familiar after the invention of the brass *trompe*, depend on the higher harmonics: the fifth harmonic (the major third) seems to be the essential ingredient.

Rather astonishingly, calls of this kind are echoed in a work of the nineteenth century, Franck's *Le Chasseur Maudit*. The unaccompanied extract shown in figure 4.3 could be played on three cornets in A, D, and G. Perhaps this is merely a coincidence. Franck can scarcely have known of the early horn calls in fourths; the symphonic poem dates from 1882, before the repertoire of fourteenth-century *caccie* had been studied. Even more surprising, there are simple horn calls spanning a fourth in the *Jeu du Rapt* section of Stravinsky's *Rite of Spring*.

The technique of bending brass tubes, known to the Romans, had been lost in the Middle Ages, but was rediscovered during the fourteenth century. In those early times, the distinction between horn and trumpet was not established. Today, to speak very generally, trumpets are considered to be predominantly cylindrical, and to be played with a cup-shaped mouthpiece; horns are conical, with a funnel-like mouthpiece. The brilliance of the trumpet, and the comparatively mellow tone of the horn, are caused by these technical differences. Alongside the *cornets de chasse*, early huntsmen seem to have played small, tightly wound, snail-like instruments, some of which were trumpets, some horns. This type of instrument was called *cor à plusieurs tours* by Mersenne (1636); in this case "cor" did not necessarily imply a horn. Mersenne's illustrations of the *cornet de chasse* and the *cor à plusieurs tours* are shown in figure 4.4a,b; oddly, he shows the instruments without bells.

The earliest surviving instruments are in Dresden's Staatliche Kunstsammlungen; they are tiny horns, conical and with funnel mouthpieces, pitched high in the trumpet range (fig. 4.4c shows a horn of 1575–80, made by Valentin Springer). On the other hand, Praetorius (1619) illustrates an instrument "wound like a snake" called a *Jäger Trommet* (huntsman's trumpet), which appears to be cylindrical and has a trumpet-type mouthpiece. Some instrument of this kind—a horn or a trum-

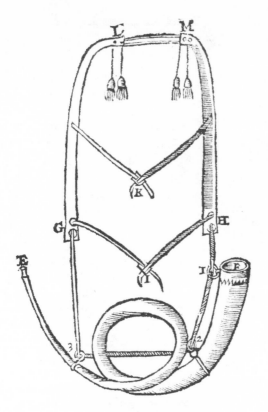

Figure 4.4a.

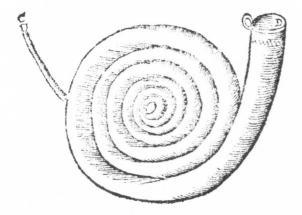

Figure 4.4b.

Figure 4.4c.

pet—may be suggested in a few compositions of the sixteenth century apparently showing hunting calls with the fifth and sixth harmonic, some of which are mentioned below.

The spiral-wound trumpet survived into the seventeenth and eighteenth centuries; a 1727 portrait of J. G. Reiche, Bach's principal trumpeter, clearly shows a coiled trumpet (Baines 1976, plate 7/4). According to one interpretation, it became the *tromba da caccia* of Telemann (Baines 1976, 143–144). This name would indicate that it was still thought of as a hunting instrument, though in the field it had been superseded by the *trompe de chasse* (a horn) at this late date; it owed its association with the hunt to its shape, not to its sound or its technical construction, for it was clearly a trumpet. Even Altenberg much later spoke of Praetorius's *Jäger Trommet* as a horn (1795, 6).

The medieval hunting horn was primarily a signaling instrument. During the course of hunting, personnel and hounds could become dispersed over a wide area, and it was often necessary to communicate certain messages. The first sight of the quarry, the loss of the scent, the plunging of the quarry into water, the release of "relays" (*relais,* small teams of huntsmen and hounds posted along the probable route of the hunt), the stag at bay, the stag killed, and many other important steps in the process of hunting needed to be broadcast to the various members of the hunting party. The sound of the horn was also found to stimulate the hounds.

At some time during the seventeenth century, the conical tube of the *cor à plusieurs tours* and the hoop-like central loop of the *cornet de chasse* were combined to produce a large circular instrument, single-wound, which was capable of a full range of harmonics. A portrayal of this instrument in its early stages is to be found in tapestries at Fontainebleau, dated about 1655 (Fitzpatrick 1970, 4). Curt Sachs admits that its origins are hard to discern (Sachs 1940, 384). The earliest surviving example is German, made in Nuremberg in 1667, though this is pitched much higher than the later hunting horns (in F, an octave above later horns in F; see Baines 1976, 152). German makers remained prominent, although the instrument was eventually inseparable from its association with the French court. For example, the Dresden builder Johann M. Koch made a horn in eight-foot C in 1689, thus again an octave higher than later hunting horns in C (Csiba and Csiba 1994, 46).

It would be helpful to know whether this started as a concert instrument and was adopted by the hunt soon afterward, or whether the reverse was the case. Fitzpatrick lists horn fanfares in works of Cavalli (*Le Nozze di Teti e di Peleo*, 1639) and Lully (*Les Plaisirs de l'Isle Enchantée*, 1664), at a time when such fanfares were probably not yet established in the hunting field (Fitzpatrick 1970, 5–6).

The decisive adoption of the brass *trompe de chasse* as a hunting instrument is associated with the reign of Louis XIV (1643–1715). It is instructive to find that some huntsmen of the time disliked the new horn, finding it a distraction from the good order of the hunt and a cause of the decline of effective hunting. A certain "Mr. De Selincourt" (a pen name of Jacques Espée, according to Dunoyer 1863, Part 1, 229n4), writing in 1683, was particularly hostile.

> We must demonstrate how to sound the horn without confusing the hounds, and to convey to them what is desired of them, according to the occasions that arise in hunting. . . . [Sometimes the beast is lost through confusion] . . . the hounds being deafened by the various ways in which the horn is sounded nowadays, against all good order and reason. . . .
>
> Indeed, it may be said that the inventors of the horns used at present are responsible for breaking up the good order that used to be observed in the staghunt, and that they are more interested in the horns than in the huntsmen, and thus have introduced a licence to play the horn more in the style of the masters of the Pont-Neuf than to observe the old rules, so right and appropriate to the dignity of the staghunt. (Selincourt 1683, 12, 19)

Reservations about the brass hunting horn continued into the next century. Practical huntsmen sometimes showed impatience with this glorious instrument, which made a wonderful sound but was possessed of an effect more aesthetic than practical. An important German commentator, H. W. Döbel, deplores the disuse of the older horns, oxhorns and *cornets de chasse*, in favor of the new brass horns which were less effective in encouraging the hounds. In his day, the old horns were still carried by huntsmen, but they were not used; indeed, the modern people were unable to play them. "Nowadays the baldrick and oxhorn are carried more for show than for use. Many a man wears a baldrick with an oxhorn hanging from it, who cannot blow it, nor ever could, all his days" (Döbel 1783 [1754], Part 3, 114). Formerly, horns were not merely for show or aesthetic effect. "Let us consider the time of our forefathers, who used the oxhorn not just for decoration or show, but also with the hounds—hunting-hounds, staghounds and boarhounds—to stimulate them, and also to give signals. In those days they either knew nothing of the great brass horns, or simply did not use them". (Döbel 1783 [1754], Part 3, 114). Apart from being better signal instruments, the "Hifthörner" were better for encouraging the hounds. "Also, it is certain that the oxhorn stimulated the hounds better than the brass horns. This may be observed, when I blow the oxhorn with hunting hounds, wolfhounds and the like, even with the little badger-hounds, if they are taking a while to start baying loudly, even when they are in the kennels or indoors. Therefore, since the hounds bark loudly when they hear the oxhorn, it must be in their nature that it raises their spirits" (Döbel 1783 [1754], vol. 2, 107; vol. 3, 114).

The baroque hunting horn was poised between musical expression and practical utility. Less effective than the oxhorn as a signaling tool, it was more evocative of the splendor and exhilaration of the hunt. Thus, the signifier of the hunt topic was already halfway to being its own signified. It was implicated in the imaginative re-creation of the hunt as a cultural unit. It may well have originated as a theatrical instrument. Such was baroque culture; the world was a stage.

Returning to the mid-seventeenth century: the horn in C, mentioned above, was comparatively high in pitch ("C alto"). The new *trompe*, which in its final form would dominate the eighteenth-century hunt, was much longer. An exemplar in the Paris Conservatoire Museum is 4.54 m in overall tube length (14.9 feet) and thus sounds in D, a seventh below the little C horn (Bourgue 1982, 27). With its single coil, it is 73 cm in diameter, unwieldy for a mounted huntsman. The Paris horn-maker Lebrun wound this instrument into two and a half coils, reducing its diameter to 55 cm ("after 1729", Bourgue says; but this is too late, as there is a fine example of the new, smaller horn, with a diameter of 54.5 cm, in the Collection of Historic Musical Instruments of the University of Edinburgh, dated 1721, shown in fig. 4.5). This instrument became the standard French *trompe de chasse* in the eighteenth century. Lebrun called it the *Cor Dauphine*, in honor of the birth of Louis XV's first son, though it goes also by other names.

The mouthpiece and bell of this horn are almost parallel, and it was played bell down, gripped by the player's right hand, leaving the other hand free to control the horse (fig. 4.6, the etching "Parforce Jäger mit der Meute" by Johann Elias Ridinger). Some horns had the interior of the bells blacked, to protect following horses from reflected sunlight. This horn was capable of all harmonics up to the sixteenth, and could thus play diatonic melodies in its highest register. It remained the French hunting horn of the eighteenth century. The final modification took place in the 1830s, when the coils were increased to three and a half, reducing the diameter further to 45 cm. This was called the *demi-trompe* or *trompe d'Orléans* (after the Duke of Orléans, for whom the new horn was made) or *trompe Périnet*, after François Périnet, apprentice to the original maker. It is the modern French hunting horn. The angle between mouthpiece and bell has been opened out in this instrument, making it easier to play bell up over the shoulder.

Nevertheless, the charming story of Count von Sporck is often retold. This Bohemian nobleman visited the court of Louis XIV in 1680–82. He heard the new *trompe de chasse* and was so pleased with the sound that he had two of his servants

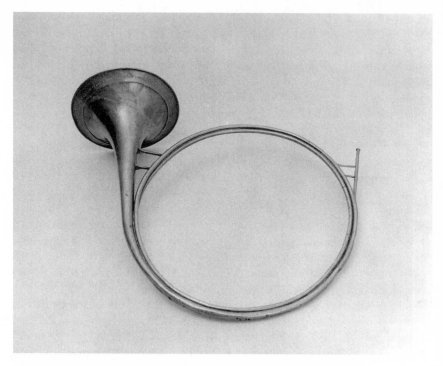

Figure 4.5.

taught to play, and took some horns back home with him. For this reason, Bohemia became the home of a school of horn players, a tradition which continued into the age of the orchestral horn (Fitzpatrick 1970, 11–16, based on Gerber, *Lexikon*, 1792, ii, 146).

German hunting horns are extant in a number of different keys, but it is clear from the concert repertoire that E flat was thought of, by the end of the eighteenth century, as the essential German hunting key. This contrasted with the use of D in France; Haydn strikingly uses both keys in his hunting scene in *Die Jahreszeiten*. There are some irregularities in this connection—Rossini, writing a hunting chorus in *Guillaume Tell*, with a Parisian audience in mind, chooses to write in E flat—but on the whole this distinction of keys applies to French and German hunting music throughout the succeeding centuries.

(b) The hunting repertoire

It would seem to be a simple matter to describe the hunting calls of the eighteenth and nineteenth centuries, to show how they are literally quoted by concert composers, and to demonstrate how the style was copied when the topic of the hunt was manifested. Indeed, there are plenty of sources for the French diatonic hunting melody. But the case is much more difficult than this. First, there were

Par force Jäger mit der meute.   Chasseur par force avec la meute.

Figure 4.6.

apparently two distinct periods of hunting melodies: the early period, in which tunes were chiefly in the third register of the instrument, and were thus mainly triadic like military trumpet calls, and the later period in which calls moved up into the fourth register and became largely diatonic. Most of the published calls are of the second type. (Figure 4.7 shows the harmonics available on an open brass tube; the fundamental is usually weak, but the second register, with two harmonics

Figure 4.7.

available, is good on most instruments, while the third, triadic register is the home of most music for natural brass, though the out-of-tune seventh harmonic is not generally usable; the fourth or clarino register has eight notes and is the site of many eighteenth-century notated hunting calls, as well as the virtuosic trumpet music of the period, but several notes are not in tune—for example, harmonic 13 is about halfway between A and A flat in equal temperament. Furthermore, no brass instrument produces harmonics that are exactly in tune with the mathematical series; strictly, we should speak of "natural notes" rather than "harmonics".)

There is some reason to suppose that the earlier, simpler calls, triadiclike trumpet calls, continued to be used, especially in Germany. The hunting style, as a musical topic, is associated to a great degree with the third-register calls of the early style, yet there are very few extant collections of these. Indeed, publishers of hunting collections sometimes speak contemptuously of the earlier calls; "I shall not reproduce here the *vieille mort*," writes Le Verrier (1778, 443), "which is an ancient fanfare that most people nowadays scorn to play."

To understand the nature of hunting calls before the style began to change, we may consult three sources, two French, one German. André Danican Philidor l'aîné (ca. 1647–1730), as part of his duties as musician and composer in the French royal chapel, established a library of music at Versailles, and one of the documents it contained was a set of horn calls (ms. 178, library of Versailles). This dates from about 1705 and is apparently the earliest recorded set of melodic horn calls. It is shown in its entirety in figure 4.8, with notation partly modernized (the original is written an octave lower in the alto clef). Notice that the eleventh harmonic is freely used (written as F; its pitch would be almost exactly halfway between F and F sharp). Some of the calls have names which became standard, though not for these melodies which are archaic in style. "Pour le chien" suggests the later "ton pour chiens", played to encourage the hounds; "pour la voye" prefigures the later "vue", played when the quarry is first sighted; "la retraite" became a standard name. The last call, "la sourcillade", was named for M. de Sourcy, hunting-master for Louis XIV, according to Marolles, who also tells us that it was played in place of the "vue" (Marolles 1979, 48). One hesitates to doubt the word of Gaston de Marolles, the great old master of French hunting, but *sourcil* means "eyebrow" and eyebrows were certainly raised when the stag, at first followed blind, appeared at last to view. Oddly, the name reappears in a later collection (Serré de Rieux 1734), but for a different tune.

Various archaic features appear. Many of the calls are in 3/4 time instead of the

Figure 4.8.

La Retraite

La Sourcillade

Figure 4.8. *Continued*

6/8 which later became universal. The first two calls are entirely triadic and hardly stray at all into the fourth register. There are many repeated notes, recalling the even older calls played on the oxhorn and *cornet de chasse*. The final "sourcillade", however, is almost entirely modern in style, chiefly situated in the fourth register, firmly in 6/8 time and composed of two strains, each repeated, in the manner of a little binary number (there is, in fact, a third strain which is different in style).

Contemporary with the Philidor collection is the cantata *La Chasse du Cerf* by Jean-Baptiste Morin, performed at Fontainebleau on 25 August 1708. With a hunting horn in the orchestra, this work prefigures hunting calls from the later "Dampierre" canon, as well as containing calls not found elsewhere, some of which may have been composed by Morin. Indeed, one of them (merely called "fanfare") is identical with the "sourcillade" later recorded by Serré de Rieux (but not with the "sourcillade" of Philidor); it may be seen in figure 4.9a. There is a chorus headed "l'halali"—the voices repeat the word "halali" over and over—which bears no relation to the famous "halali" tune, attributed to Dampierre, which appears in every collection later in the century and survives into modern times. Most of the calls in Morin's cantata seem more modern than the Philidor calls; they exploit the fourth register and are largely in 6/8 time, though 4.9b (the "halali") is in 3. The final call (4.9c), again entitled "fanfare", would later be named "la Dampierre". As well as these horn calls, the chorus sings many real hunting cries, "Ah, tayaut, tayaut . . . Y perce çavant . . . Ah, ça va la haut".

Almost contemporary with the Philidor collection and the Morin cantata is a small collection of hunting calls published in Germany. This appears in H. F. von

(a)

(b)

(c)

Figure 4.9.

Wann die Hunde losgekuppelt werden.

(?)

Figure 4.10.

Wann die Hunde anfangen zu jagen.

Wann sie die Fährd wieder gefunden.

Wann der Hirsch erleget worden.

Figure 4.10. *Continued*

Figure 4.10. *Continued*

Flemming	Meaning	French title
Wann die Hund losgekuppelt werden	uncoupling of pack	*La queste*
Wann die Hunde anfangen zu jagen	hounds on scent	*Quand les chiens vont bien*
Wann sie die Fährd verlohren	hounds have lost scent	*Hourvari*
Wann sie die Fährd wieder gefunden	hounds have recovered scent	*Le relancé*
Wann die Hunde gar gut jagen	encourage hounds	*Ton pour les chiens*
Wann der Hirsch erleget worden	the kill	*Halali*
Wann die Jagd zu Ende und vollbracht ist	hunt over, party returning home	*La retraite*

Figure 4.11.

Flemming's comprehensive hunting manual *Der vollkommene teutsche Jäger* (Flemming 1724, 1:311–312). Four of the seven calls are shown in figure 4.10. Their titles reveal that they fulfill similar functions to several of the common French calls, as shown in the table in figure 4.11.

What is particularly striking about this comparison is that these German calls were played "sonderlich bey der par Force Jagd" (especially for the parforce hunt; Flemming 1724, 310) rather than for the *chasse aux toiles* (see below). Few of them would have any function in the *chasse aux toiles*. This suggests that parforce hunting was practiced in Germany at this period. Yet Flemming's text elsewhere contradicts this. Perhaps the names of the calls were merely emblematic in Germany.

The style of these calls is even more archaic than that of the Philidor collection, except for one feature: they are almost throughout in 6/8 time. Apart from this, they are predominantly in the third register, even descending into the second (the incursions into the fourth register all amount to reprises of the same little tune, as though it were a special trick of the player). Thus, these calls are mainly triadic, like military trumpet calls. They would, of course, have sounded much lower than the military trumpet, since the trumpet in D was exactly half the length of the horn in D. There are many passages of repeated notes, recalling the ancient calls of the oxhorn and *cornet de chasse*.

(The pitch of brass instruments needs to be clarified. By a lucky chance, a tube of about 8 feet in length has a fundamental on the C below the bass stave and sounds middle C as fourth harmonic. A cavalry trumpet in C would be such an instrument; the player, reading figure 4.7, would sound the notes written, without transposition. A tube of about 16 feet in length has its fundamental an octave lower than this, and sounds middle C as eighth harmonic; however, the player reads exactly as a player of the trumpet, reading middle C as the fourth harmonic. Such an instrument is the horn in C; written middle C sounds *bass* C and the instrument transposes an octave downward. A tube of about 4 feet in length has its fundamental on bass C; middle C [sounding] would thus be the second harmonic, and the important octave above middle C would lack its third. Such an instrument, more or less, is the modern orchestral trumpet in B flat, which, disregarding its valves, is about 4½ feet in length. However, the player reads *as though the instrument were double the length* and there is no transposition, apart from the obvious transposition of a tone downward in the case of the orchestral trumpet, which is able to supply the missing third—and many other notes—by means of valves. Broadly speaking, horns transpose *downward* because they have lengths of 16 feet or less. The orchestral horn in F, regardless of its valves, is about 12 feet in length, and the *trompe de chasse* in D has a length of about 14 feet. Most trumpets transpose *upward;* the cavalry trumpet in D is about 7 feet in length, thus higher than the 8-foot norm. The modern valve trumpet is clearly exceptional.)

As will be argued later in this chapter, there is some reason to think that simple calls, like those of Flemming, remained common in Germany throughout the period of aristocratic hunting. Most eighteenth-century collections of hunting calls record the later, more sophisticated style of call, perhaps because such difficult calls needed the support of written records. But in any case, these collections are mainly French. The earlier and simpler calls were more informal, easier to play, better suited to musicians who were also huntsmen, grooms, and horse-minders. Josef Pöschl, the leading modern authority, even considers that hunting calls were composed, as well as played, by "stable-boys and huntsmen" rather than composers who were "outsiders" (Pöschl 1997, 204).

But soon, new sets of calls were composed. Since the new horns were especially suitable for merely exuberant or celebratory calls, many melodies were written with no signaling purpose at all, named for their composer or for a noble person to whom they were dedicated. Central to the new repertoire was the Marquis Marc Antoine de Dampierre (1676–1756), a French nobleman who served as *Lieutenant des Chasses* to the Duke of Maine from 1709 and to Louis XV from 1727 (Fitzpatrick 1970, 6). Marolles's account of Dampierre's importance is of some interest, not least because he gives no sources for his information.

> In 1723, the Marquis of Dampierre, having chosen the horn in D, an octave below the trumpets, began his series of fanfares; he preserved them in a personal collection,

numbered and without title; this collection seems to have passed, at his death, into the hands of M. Bouron, royal secretary. This was his way of presenting them as a souvenir to Mme Bouron, formerly Mlle de Beaufort, for whom he had a fancy—which was returned—and who was a very good musician; she seems to have cooperated in the composition of these fanfares.

M. de Dampierre had fortunately given a copy of all his fanfares to one of his pupils, who published the collection *in extenso* in 1778, twenty-two years after the death of their composer. The collection had been virtually finished in 1734; but the "Fontenoy," by the Marquise de Pompadour, and the first "Champcenetz," were added afterward. (Marolles 1979, 48)

It is hard to know how much of this information, retold by one of France's greatest experts, is hard fact. Apparently, the first publication of Dampierre-type hunting calls appeared in an appendix to a curious work called *Les Dons des Enfans de Latone*, published in 1734. This consists of two long poems, one on music and the other on hunting, brought together by the conceit that Apollo and Diana both had Latona as mother, and music and hunting were therefore brother and sister. The hunting calls are headed "Tons de Chasse et Fanfares, a une et deux trompes composées par Mr. de Dampierre gentilhomme des plaisirs du Roy pour faire connoitre aux Veneurs le Cerf que l'on cours, ses divers Mouvemens, les differentes operations de la Chasse, et le lieu ou l'Occasion où les dites fanfares ont eté faites"— hunting calls and fanfares for one and two horns composed by M. de Dampierre, gentleman of the king's pleasures to inform huntsmen what beast is pursued, its various movements, the different operations of the hunt, and the positions or occasions where the said fanfares are sounded (Serré de Rieux 1734, end). The distinction is made in this title between what would now be called "fanfares de circonstance", calls which declare important stages in the hunt, and "fanfares d'animaux", which give information on the animal pursued: whether it be a *cerf à dix cors*, a fully grown stag with at least ten tines to the antlers, a *daguet* or immature stag, a *daim* or fallow deer, a *chevreuil* or roe-deer, or other creatures. The most important calls in this collection are shown in appendix 1.

These calls are not, in fact, all by Dampierre. The compiler attributes some of them to other composers, to King Louis XV himself, to the Marquis de Tressan, to Jean-Joseph Mouret, and to Jean-Baptiste Morin, while some (including the important "la sourcillade", wrongly ascribed by Ringer to André-Danican Philidor the elder) are anonymous. It may be the case that Dampierre's reputation as a composer of hunting calls, and his prestige as royal hunting-master, caused many calls to be attributed to him. As Marolles comments, a beautiful presentation volume of his calls was published after his death, the music pages separated by sumptuous engravings of hunting scenes, and by this time it is clear that many calls, formerly attributed to others, had now been imported into the "Dampierre" canon (Dampierre 1776). This collection has another important feature: each call is quoted first as a monody, then again as a note-against-note duet for two horns. It is evident that horn calls were often played as *bicinia*, in two parts (and even in three parts), and this feat is still accomplished today by mounted French huntsmen.

(a) Latone

(b) Gaffet

(c) Zuckerová

Figure 4.12.

Yet hunting fanfares were not learned from books of music, but practically, in the field, "for the simple reason that the huntsman or the horn-player does not always read music" (Didier de Martimprey, in Chambry 1994, 9). We are told this also by the leading German contemporary, Heinrich Wilhelm Döbel, who justifies his failure to publish the hunting calls by saying, "solches ist aber in der Praxi besser zu begreiffen, als hier zu setzen, oder zu beschreiben"—it is better to learn such things in practice, rather than to set them forth or describe them here (Döbel 1783 [1754], 2:107). It is easy to believe Dampierre's editor of 1776 when he speaks of "the lack of accuracy and precision with which most trompe-players execute Monsieur de Dampierre's fanfares on this instrument". This situation is easily inferred from the slight variations in the calls, as they are recorded by different authorities. The commonest call, which is quoted several times in concert music, was the "halali" (accent on the second syllable so that it almost rhymes with "Bali"), attributed to Dampierre. It was played when the stag was at bay (when, through exhaustion, it had ceased running and turned to face the hounds), though in some sources its two parts are separately designated "halali sur pied" (stag still on its feet, about to be killed with a hunting knife) and "halali par terre" (the stag dead; see Bourgue 1982, 35). Versions of this call from the *Enfans de Latone*, and from two other sources, are shown in figure 4.12. (Fig. 4.12b is from Gaffet 1742, 4; 4.12c from Zuckerová 1983, 19—Zuckerová attributes it to Ondrej Anton, 1754–ca. 1817, a trumpeter at the castle of Český Krumlov. This particular call is dated 1794.) The first phrase only is shown; apparently, players liked to echo the last few notes. Notice also that Gaffet shifts the barlines so that the tune begins without anacrusis.

Essentially, then, we are dealing with an oral repertoire. The attribution of calls to individual writers may be treated with some reservations, since the written calls are usually transcriptions of music heard in the field. Nor can we assume that the calls were played exactly as written or as they would be played by a modern concert musician reading the scores. The art of the hunting horn is still alive in France, with over 160 groups of players (*corps de chasseurs*) hunting with 6,000 hounds from October to March over a total area of 900,000 hectares, about 3,500 square miles (Pöschl 1997, 181). These players affect an extraordinary style of perform-ance, described in detail by Bourgue. All notes are played *en pleine trompe*, "brassy, hard, making the whole instrument vibrate". Groups of eighth notes are played in a dotted rhythm, the *ton de vénerie*. Longer notes are *roulé*, played with a series of soft tonguings which give the effect of a broad vibrato. Important notes are ap-proached with a rapid ascending glissando, the *hourvari*, which "could be com-pared to the howl of a dog". Some long notes are *tayauté*, lengthened with an echo tone (Bourgue 1982, 29–30). This style of playing is widely affected by modern players; its effect, broad and vulgar, is a great shock to musicological ears. It has been recorded a number of times. Bourgue is sure that eighteenth-century hunts-men played in this way, and indeed he attributes the *ton de vénerie* to Dampierre. He adds that the *ton de vénerie* is affected only by French and Belgian huntsmen (speaking, of course, of the modern hunt). There is some evidence to suggest that this style was adopted by eighteenth-century players. In a preface to his *Sinfonia di Caccia*, Leopold Mozart advises: "At first the G horns must be played very harshly, as is customary in hunting, and as loudly as possible." As I suggest later, this in-struction is perhaps meant to be satirical.

Indeed, we may have some reservations about the *ton de vénerie* in the eight-eenth century. Some writers advised playing with good taste and with a soft, well-modulated tone. "It remains for me to say," writes Le Verrier de la Conterie, "that the horn is not really pleasant unless one draws from it a mellow, natural and light sound; not everyone is gifted in this way." You can only correct bad performance "if you can learn to play in tune, lightly and with taste" (Le Verrier 1778, 431).

It is of some importance that the subsequent eighteenth-century collections of hunting calls were printed in France rather than in Germany, for the most elaborate hunting manuals were German. Yet the big German treatises normally do not in-clude pages of music. Clearly, this is because the standard hunting calls were fea-tures of the parforce hunt, which was little practiced in Germany, as will be ex-plained later. The printing of sets of hunting calls continued in France in the nineteenth century. France may, indeed, be considered the home of the hunting horn, even though the orchestral horn owed much of its development to German virtuosos and makers.

The German hunting horn had a different history, however. Its decline, caused by the universal practice of the *chasse aux toiles*, was reversed by the influence of Hans Heinrich, Count of Hochberg, who was elevated in 1854 by the King of Prus-sia to the rank of Prince of Pless (Fürst Pless). He became director of the Prussian court hunt in 1878. Not content with reintroducing the horn, he became himself a fine player and published a book of fanfares, interspersed with hunting tales (Pöschl 1997, 45). His favored horn, however, was a small instrument with three valves, in B flat, of length 131 cm and thus sounding with the orchestral trumpet. This horn, now called the *Fürst-Pless Horn*, was itself virtually a trumpet, since it was predominantly cylindrical and was fitted with a cup mouthpiece (see Fensterer 1984, 8). It continues to be used by modern German huntsmen as their principal signaling instrument, alongside parforce horns in B flat alto and E flat (Pöschl 1997, 46), and even a horn that combines the two pitches, with a single valve permitting movement from one to the other.

(c) The parforce hunt

There were two main types of staghunt in Europe. The first was the hunt *par force de chiens,* or simply *parforce.* A single animal was pursued by mounted huntsmen and a pack of hounds across open country or at large within a spacious deer park (the largest of these, that of Fontainebleau, extended to 16,856 hectares, about 65 square miles: see Fehr 1954, 13). It was finally dispatched with a knife. It was, at first, never shot, as firearms were considered unsporting. Firearms gradually established themselves during the seventeenth century, however; Louis XIV wished everyone to notice that he was a particularly good shot, and furthermore the manufacture of the *petit plomb*—the small musket ball—was a royal monopoly (Jullien 1868, 231–232).

The other kind of hunting—the *chasse aux toiles*—will be described later. In any case, horn signals are particularly applicable to the parforce hunt. During the eighteenth century this became largely a French speciality; it is still much practiced in France and the rest of Europe, and was until recently the style of the British fox-hunt.

In the classic period, the actual hunting was largely accomplished by paid staff, in the French royal hunt the Grand Véneur with his Lieutenants de la Vénerie, Gentilshommes, Pages, Maréchal des Logis, and so on (Gaffet 1742, 28). The night before a hunt, the king or the nobleman in charge gives orders for the following day. Before first light, individual huntsmen set off with specialized hounds (*limiers*) on leads, to move stealthily through the forest in order to locate stags suitable for hunting, which at this stage are hidden within the coverts. When a hunt-worthy stag is located (though not seen, of course), the huntsmen approach the king with an approved formal sentence, informing him that he "believes" a stag has been found. The hunt is then assembled with the blowing of the "Appel" (or *Anbruch*). As soon as all are prepared to begin, the hounds, which are normally tethered in couples, are released, with the blowing of the "quête". Taking up the scent, the hounds begin to run. To encourage them, huntsmen sound the "tons pour chiens", which are usually rather simple calls as they have, perhaps, to be played on a horse in motion (most of this account is based on Goury 1769, 40–49, while the identification of the horn calls comes from Le Verrier 1778, 433–444).

At this stage, only the hounds have contact with the quarry. But eventually the animal is sighted by a huntsman, who then informs his fellows by blowing the "vue". At some point, the stag will try to shake off the hounds by trying a ruse; it may turn back along its own track for a short way and then fly off at right angles, so that the unwary hounds will follow the scent until it appears to come to an abrupt end. Or perhaps the beast may mingle with a group of other stags, hoping that another animal may run off with the hounds in pursuit (this is called a *change*). The new quarry would have an unfair advantage, being less tired than the hounds. When the huntsmen realize that this has occurred, they blow the "hour-vari", which indicates that the stag has tried to deceive the hunt. Another call, the "retour", was reserved specifically for the first of these deceptions, the double-back and sideslip.

A favorite trick of the stags was to plunge into a lake or river, where the pack would lose the scent. But experienced huntsmen were wise to this also, and at this point they would blow the "bat l'eau". It was a dangerous moment; hounds were often drowned when they followed the quarry into the water, and huntsmen, taking to boats, might find themselves stuck fast amidst reeds and boggy land. Goury even recommends that water-borne stags should be shot to avoid these dangers.

However, the animal eventually leaves the element not natural to it, which requires the blowing of the "sortie de l'eau". If these kind attentions cause the stag to leave the woodland and break out into open country, the "debuché" is sounded.

The quarry becomes increasingly tired. Being a heroic beast (the hunting manuals remind us of this) it conceals this from the hunt; although a tired stag runs with its head lowered, the moment it understands that it can be seen by the hunt it raises its head and runs proudly. But even heroism cannot overcome nature, and eventually the exhausted animal turns on its pursuers and makes a stand. As the yelping hounds surround it, the huntsmen blow the "halali" (or the "halali à pied"). The stag is then dispatched with a knife, and the "halali par terre" is blown. Many collections make no distinction between the two halves of the "halali" call, which, musically, are obviously parts of the same melody, and a late source gives the whole call as "halali sur pied", following it with a quite different call as "halali sur terre" (Bretonnière 1860, 26).

Traditionally, the hounds were given certain parts of the dead stag as a reward; the animal having been skinned, these parts were spread out on the *nappe* or skin (Goury 1769, 48). This meal was called the "curée", and it was accompanied by its own horn calls. Finally, the hounds were again tethered in pairs, and the whole company set off home to the sound of the "retraite" (these are by no means all the hunting calls listed by the various authorities. In addition, the names vary somewhat from one authority to another; see fig. 4.13, which lists the names used in four sources).

(d) The "Dampierre" style

The style of the Dampierre hunting calls, whether composed by Dampierre or by others, is sharply defined. All are in 6/8 time, and all are limited to the area between the sixth and the twelfth harmonics (between low and high G, as written, spanning the third and fourth registers). Some tunes omit the sixth harmonic (the "halali" is an example) and thus lie in the interval between eighth and twelfth harmonics (between C and G at the top of the stave). There are no incursions into the area above; the thirteenth harmonic (high A) is never found, perhaps because it is so flat. The seventh harmonic, likewise, is never employed, though the eleventh harmonic, equally "out of tune", is used freely. The fourth and fifth harmonic (low C and E) are reserved for the second-horn parts in *bicinia*.

Latone (1734)	Gaffet (1742)	Le Verrier (1778)	Dampierre (1776)
Ton pour la quete*	La queste	Quete	
Ton pour chien	Ton pour les chiens	Des tons pour chiens	
	Premiere vue	Vue	
Pour la requete	Le requete		
	L'ourvari	Hourvari	
Pour le debuche	Le debuche	Debuche	Le Debuche
	Le relance	Relance	
	Le raproche	Rapproche	
Pour l'eau	Quand le cerf est a l'eau	Le bat l'eau	L'eau
	Le cerf sort de l'eau	Sortie de l'eau	
	Le hallaly	Halali	L'Halali
Pour l'appel	L'apel	Appel simple	
	La retraite manquee	Retraite manquee	
La Retraite	Retraite prise		La retraite prise

*Eighteenth-century sources often omit accents in French. Thus the accents (acute, grave, circumflex) are missing from many of these terms.

Figure 4.13.

Unlike the earlier style of hunting tune, the Dampierre tunes are resolutely me-lodic. They do not sound like signals. In fact, they sometimes echo French folk-songs, many of which are in 6/8 time ("Malbrouk s'en va-t-en Guerre" and "La Carmagnole" will be known to English-speaking readers). The first phrase of the call "La Royalle" is identical to the famous folk tune "Il était un' bergère". Most calls are either implicitly or expressly in binary form, the two sections repeated, with a cadence at the end of each section; some are in rounded-binary, with the first phrase repeated at the end of the second section. Some are in *rondeau* form, with two contrasting *couplets*, the main section recurring each time (ABACA); in the Dampierre "L'eau" the passage marked "deuxième couplet" is also marked "Quand le cerf a passé l'eau", when the stag has left the water. In these formal respects they resemble some folksongs, but more obviously the contemporary dance number, notably the dances found in harpsichord suites (the harpsichord piece *Fanfare* by Kirnberger is mentioned elsewhere; see *Sense*, 33–34). The brief "vol ce l'est" in the Dampierre collection (1776) manages to accomplish a rounded-binary unit in nine measures.

Huntsmen liked echo effects. The echoes that were clearly popular in the "halali" are matched in other calls; they were probably an *ad lib* device, for in Dampierre 1776 "la petite royalle" is given in two forms, the first for a solo horn, the second for two instruments. In the second version echoes are introduced, marked "doux". There are other subtleties: "la Chantilly" includes a cross-rhythm, the stressed note occurring twice on the weak second beat.

In short, the Dampierre-style fanfares are sophisticated musical numbers. Performed in the sonorous harmony of two or three horns, they must have become a joyous musical accompaniment to the chase, rather than just a signaling system. It is hard to employ this style as a musical topic, since such charming melodies, already part of the art-music world, melt into the texture of concert music. In spite of this, such melodies do appear in music of all centuries from the eighteenth onward. But manifestations of the hunt topic, as it appears in instrumental music, are usually much simpler, more wedded to the third-register triadic shapes of the older fanfares.

It is striking—and, as we shall see, significant for the history of hunting music— that most of the sources of hunting calls are French. The French sources agree generally on the names and occasions of the main calls; four sources, the "Latone" collection, Gaffet de la Briffardière, Le Verrier de la Conterie, and the late edition of Dampierre, are compared in figure 4.13. German hunting manuals usually do not give the music. Even Döbel's monumental *Jäger-Practica* gives no hunting calls. Sometimes they talk about the calls, but do not transcribe them; the Bohemian hunting-master J. W. von Pärson laboriously lists the moments in the hunt when calls are blown (sounding as though he is simply copying from some French manual) but does not give the calls (Pärson 1734, 75–76). The only significant eighteenth-century German source is H. F. von Flemming, whose rather primitive hunting calls have been mentioned. These calls are mainly in the second and third register and are thus triadic rather than diatonic.

References in concert music to the field hunting call do not always evoke the Dampierre style. The little triadic tag which precedes the recapitulation in Haydn's *Le Matin* slightly suggests the simple calls of Philidor, but bears no comparison to the great heroic melodies of Gaffet and the 1776 "Dampierre" collection. Probably, then, eighteenth-century huntsmen had their own way of playing the horn. Most, perhaps, could not master the Dampierre calls, with their brilliant exploitation of the clarino register. Yet the Dampierre calls undoubtedly were played sometimes, since when written down they were obviously transcribed aurally rather than copied from a written source. And finally, concert composers were perfectly able to quote real Dampierre calls, especially the "halali". Both the simple triadic tunes, and the great clarino melodies, form components of the hunt signifier.

(e) Compositions for hunting horns

From the earliest days of the brass horn, huntsmen have enjoyed playing musical numbers composed for the instrument. Augustus the Strong, Elector of Saxony and King of Poland (1670–1733), kept an octet of hunting horns as part of his musical establishment. Modern German collections of *Jagdhorn* music usually add a few concert numbers for horn ensemble, called *Vortragstücke*, after the hunting calls. These are impeccably in hunting style, mostly in 6/8 time, arranged for three or four horns in homophony, often in "horn motion".

The most elaborate items in this repertoire are the *Jägermessen*, arrangements of the ordinary of the mass for voices and horns, used to celebrate hunting saints' days, particularly St Hubert's day on 3 November. The composers have normally been hunting specialists, like J. C. Pez (*Missa venatoria*, 1706) and J. Ries (*Missa Sancti Huberti*, 1756). The tradition continued into the next century, yielding the *St. Hubertus-Messe* of Anton Wunderer. These examples are provided by Pöschl, who gives many more illustrations from the twentieth century (Pöschl 1996, 1314). A standard modern collection, the *Handbuch der Jagdmusik* edited by Reinhold Stief, includes a complete *Hubertusmesse* (as part 4) and many short pieces with names like "Kaiserfanfare" and "Marsch der Jäger", arranged in four parts. This music is strictly for specialists, except in revealing that hunting-horn players have always engaged in recreational and concert playing as well as sounding field calls.

5 Signified: Hunts Noble and Ignoble

(a) The *chasse aux toiles*

In determining the theoretical nature of the topical signified, the social reality of the eighteenth-century hunt must first be investigated. It is easy to assume that musical topics signified aspects of contemporary society, and that a historical account of this must illuminate our understanding of the musical feature itself. Since this is often not the case, we must begin by surveying the contemporary hunt, especially the hunting style chiefly characteristic of the German lands, including Austria, where much of the definitive concert music of the period was composed. There ought to be no anomaly in the picture of a manly, adventurous, highly organized pursuit, associated with a style of music-making that was noisy, exuberant, and magnificent. But this was not how it was.

Many manifestations of the topic come from the concert repertoire of Germany, Austria, and central Europe. In these areas, the parforce hunt was very little practiced. Even in France, other styles of hunting existed alongside the exciting and dangerous parforce. From an early date—probably in the fifteenth century, perhaps earlier—parforce hunting had co-existed with another type of hunt, the *chasse aux toiles*. A large enclosure of canvas screens, some three meters high, called an *accourre* or *Laufft*, was erected somewhere in the park, into which the game was herded by professional huntsmen. The aristocrats who funded the activity were then able to slaughter the game at their leisure; in Germany this usually meant that the animals were shot.

Apparently, this type of nonsporting hunt had its origin in a medieval style called *chasse aux haies;* in earlier times, the deer park was furnished with a permanent arrangement of hedges which served the same purpose as the later canvas *Rolltücher* (Dunoyer 1863, 349–355). Both styles of hunting were practiced in France and Germany. For example, Louis XIII and Louis XIV favored the *chasse aux toiles*. The latter often attended such a hunt after dinner, riding in his coach in the company of ladies and visiting notables. His successor, Louis XV, however, who was obsessed with hunting, returned to the parforce hunt. Louis XVI enjoyed what were by then called *hourailleries*, or *chasses aux toiles* using firearms, after the German model. But the use of "toiles" in hunting was suppressed in 1787, and after the Revolution (in 1792) the redundant canvas was used to make tents for the army (Dunoyer 1863, 362).

It was generally recognized that the *chasse aux toiles* was a German stock-in-trade; indeed, it was often called *chasse allemande* or *deutsche Jagd* (Dunoyer 1863,

389*n*M). As early as the mid-sixteenth century, when the hunting horn still sounded only a single note, the German hunt was of this type (Taut 1927, 126). It is suggested that the dense forests of Germany made parforce hunting difficult, while French woodland was more penetrable (Fehr 1954, 12). Unsurprisingly, the technical terms of the parforce hunt were French, and often remained in French when they were quoted by the German writers, while the "German hunt" had its own German terminology.

There are a number of lengthy descriptions of this kind of hunt, both German and French (Flemming 1724, 1:271–278; Döbel 1783 [1754], 2:3–86; Gaffet 1742, 141–147; Goechhausen 1751 [1710], 249–256; Dunoyer 1863, 3:363–391), of which Flemming's and Döbel's are the most elaborate. Most typically, the *Laufft* was in the shape of a figure-eight, the narrow center being spanned by a rope from which hung sheets of canvas (*Lappen*), forming a weak barrier through which animals could be driven. Within one side of this enclosure a pavilion or *Schirm* was erected. Game was herded into the other side, the nobility took up their position with guns within the Schirm, and when all was ready the staff drove the animals through the division (terrified, they were unable to find their way back out), and the noble "huntsmen" fired at them as they ran past. Outside the enclosure, spectators watched the excitement, including ladies and musicians; and when all was accomplished, there was music. After the playing of required horn calls and the shouting of the accepted cries, celebratory music was played by trumpets and drums (Goechhausen 1751 [1710], 256).

Figure 5.1 shows one of Döbel's illustrations; only the right half of the Laufft is shown. The Schirm is shrouded in gunsmoke, and the numerous beasts are being reduced to a graveyard of bodies (in the center), some of which have already been moved into a cart (bottom left). Here and there, stags are being harassed by dogs. A horn player can just be discerned (bottom right, facing away), refreshing himself before contributing his music.

Döbel calls this kind of hunt *eingerichtete Jagd* ("well-equipped hunt") or *Bestätigungs-Jagen* ("confirmed hunt", presumably because the outcome was never in doubt); he admits that it is often called simply *deutsche-* or *Zeug-Jagen*. A modern writer connects it with the introduction of firearms, once strictly excluded. "When firearms, previously considered unhuntsmanly, began to appear as hunting weapons towards the end of the sixteenth century, the so-called 'equipped' (*eingerichtete*) or 'prepared' (*eingestellte*) hunt developed in Germany out of the parforce hunt" (Eckardt 1976, 52). The aristocratic "huntsmen", in fact, did no hunting at all.

There was even a certain nationalistic rivalry between the Germans and the French, with regard to the types of hunt. "The French behave," wrote Flemming, "as though this idea was invented by them alone of all nations in the world, namely, to defeat a stag, a bold and noble animal, in the open field with heroic spirit, and not, like other nations, to make use of underhand methods, screens, nets, boxes, special breeding, and the like; whereby these parforce huntsmen, because of such rumors, live in open hostility to the German huntsmen, and an antipathy grows up between them" (Flemming 1724, 1:294).

Figure 5.1.

The "German hunt" may seem disgracefully unsporting to modern sensitivities, but in this respect it was much exceeded by other types. These are listed by Döbel, and are described in a cruelly objective way by Eckardt. First, the *Wasserjagd*. "In the 'water hunt' the game is chased by the pack through runs, prepared beforehand and fenced off with hedges, into lakes, ponds or rivers. They are then shot from boats or artificial islands, or the hunting party merely watches as the hounds tear the game apart as they swim. Animals that reach the bank alive are laid low without trouble" (Eckardt 1976, 54, based on Flemming). This sort of hunt could be taken to grotesque extremes. Dunoyer describes paintings hanging in the castle of Rastadt, near Baden.

> The eighteenth-century pictures preserved in the castle of Rastadt . . . initiate us into refinements whose strangeness passes all belief. The animals, driven toward ponds decorated with sumptuous constructions, are forced to leap into the water, passing through windows and arcades or through fireworks; others, crowded into enclosures are bombarded with hand grenades by soldiers or shot by huntsmen while they are trying to get away along raised galleries or hanging bridges.
>
> Some wild boar, caught as they run, are rigged out with wings and hitched to carts, while live cats are fired from mortars to celebrate this extravagant butchery, worthy of the Roman Decadence. (Dunoyer 1863, 390–391)

Next comes the *Sprengjagd*. The animals were driven to the summit of a high cliff, or to the top of an artificially erected platform, from which they were forced to jump. Sometimes they fell into water, whereupon a *Wasserjagd* was started; sometimes they fell on hard ground. If they were not instantly killed, they were finished off by the huntsmen (Eckardt 1976, 54 [based on F. X. Smoler, *Historische Blicke auf das Forst- und Jagdwesen, seine Gesetzgebung und Ausbildung von der Urzeit bis zu Ende des 18. Jhdts*, Prague, 1847]).

It is hard to understand how the *Kampjagd* could be described as a hunt at all. This "Lustbarkeit" took place in the courtyard of the *Jagdschloss*, watched from the windows. Selected animals were set to tear each other to pieces. Bears were placed with dogs, stags with wolves, and even exotic animals were imported—lions and tigers—and were allowed to dismember horses, cows, and calves.

Without trying to excuse or justify this barbarous theater, it is worth saying that the German hunt was thought of less as a sport than as a courtly festivity and a means of showing off wealth. Hunts took place on occasions of celebration: birthdays, name-days, homecomings, visits of foreign nobility. The birthday celebrations of Duke Karl Eugen of Württemberg in 1763 lasted three weeks; their culmination was a lavish hunt in which 5,000 animals were driven into an artificial lake and slaughtered (Eckardt 1976, 55).

Apart from celebration and entertainment, these kinds of hunts obviously had little use for horn signals. Indeed, the various hunting calls were named after the stages in the parforce hunt rather than the "German hunt", and their names were French. The best descriptions of the parforce hunt were written by Frenchmen, just as the most elaborate accounts of the *eingerichtete Jagd* are by the Germans, Flemming and Döbel. One German commentator finds uses for a few of the parforce fanfares; "special calls are blown for the beginning and end of the hunt [*An- und Abblasen des Jagens*], also there are special calls to indicate the animal that is being hunted. . . . This is the custom with the screens [*Tüchern*]" (Pärson 1734, 75). Perhaps this writer was thinking of the calls of the *Flügelhorn,* a much simpler instrument used by the paid staff, which is described in the next part of this work. Clearly the elaborate code of parforce horn calls had little application to the *niedrige Jagd* [low hunt, Pärson's term], and eventually the horn began to disappear from the ordinary hunting field in Germany; after 1848 it was heard only in *Prunkjagden,* the sort of lavish celebrations already described. By the end of the nineteenth century it was considered a French specialty and was ostracized for political reasons, being replaced by the *Fürst-Pless Horn* (see above). After the Second World War, however, there has been a renaissance of the parforce hunt, with its brass horns and horn signals, in Germany (Pöschl 1997, 189).

(b) Aristocrats and professionals

Were the hunting horns played by noble amateurs, or were the horn players, like most of the practical huntsmen, professional specialists? Goury and other writers tell us that the horns were played by *piqueurs* ("stingers," the same word as Spanish *picador*). These were undoubtedly professionals; Gaffet, having described the horn playing of these employees, remarks, "On ne peut donc trop payer les bons Piqueurs, puisque tout le succès et l'agrément d'une chasse roulent sur eux" [you can't pay good *piqueurs* too highly, for the whole success and delight of a hunt depends on them; Gaffet 1742, 103–104]. Fitzpatrick explains how the staff who played horns in the hunting field became recruits for the horn departments of court orchestras (Fitzpatrick 1970, 18n2). Unfortunately, Fitzpatrick also expresses the view that aristocrats played the horn, citing Flemming and Döbel. But the passages he quotes refer to the *Jägermeister* and *Ober-Jägermeister,* who were certainly paid employees. It is clear from Fitzpatrick's own illustrations—like those reproduced facing his page 18, taken from paintings at Fontainebleau—that horns are played by men in livery. On the reverse of this illustration (facing page 19) he shows a plate from J. E. Ridinger's *Der Fürsten Jagd-Lust* (Augsburg, 1729) in which an aristocrat, distinguished by his wearing a sword, is neither carrying nor playing a horn, while liveried horn players surround him. Thus, aristocratic horn players like the Marquis de Dampierre must be considered exceptional.

In fact, the role of aristocratic patrons in the hunt itself was variable. In France, they often remained at the center of things; a true enthusiast like Louis XV rode with the hunt and took a major part in its actions and decisions. But German noblemen were advised to leave the dirty business of hunting to paid staff; it was enough for them to ride along with the hunt as observers.

> However, the nobleman can make up his own mind about this, and go along with the hunt himself. For this work, the direction of the hunt and the managing of the hounds, belongs to the appointed huntsmen, piqueurs and auxiliary hands. . . .
> But if the nobleman and lord rides along with the hunt, he should take care; it is

not necessary for him to follow the huntsmen through thick and thin, but only to remain with the hunt so that he can hear the pleasing and well-sounding noise of the hounds, huntsmen and hunting horns. (Döbel 1783 [1754], Part 2, 87)

Truth to tell, the German nobleman disliked the inconvenience and dangers of the parforce hunt; it was "dangerous" and led to many "unfortunate accidents" (Flemming, quoted in Wendt 1908, 2:298). Flemming was in favor of "comfort" and "convenience"; ways had been found "whereby high society can hunt the game in greater safety". The real hunting was "a job for the hunting staff and the pack of hounds". The aristocratic "huntsmen" simply tagged along and, Eckardt thinks, were allowed to kill the animals when they were at last brought to bay (Eckardt 1976, 53).

There was a further, and probably stronger, reason for the eighteenth-century German aristocracy to hunt. Hunting rights were confined to the landed nobility. In an area that contained free cities like Leipzig, ruled by bourgeois *Rathäuser*, and in a time when wealth was being redistributed in favor of trade and the towns, it seemed vital to the aristocracy to preserve their exclusive right to hunt. This was what distinguished them, what confirmed their continuity with the landed aristocracy of the past. Ferocious penalties were put in place against hunting by unauthorized persons. It seemed unthinkable that a "noble stag" could be hunted by a peasant or a townsman. Hunting was necessary for the self-identification of the nobility; "The hunt played a major role for most men of position, especially for those who led a patriarchal, withdrawn and old-fashioned aristocratic life, just as it had for their forefathers, princes and counts of the Empire" (Eckardt 1976, 50). In medieval society, hunting rights were confined to royalty, though they could be conferred on favored subjects. In the eighteenth century, especially in the German-speaking lands, they remained the identifying feature of the landed nobility, which was increasingly threatened by the power of the towns.

This was not merely a matter of self-interest and self-protection. Noblemen traditionally felt themselves the keepers and protectors of their dominions, and hunting showed their care for the land. Hunting country had to be properly maintained: Döbel makes this clear. Hunting was inseparable from the conservation of the countryside, as it was in England during the controversy of 2002–04 over the outlawing of the foxhunt. "Also, it is a matter of standing for a prince and a great lord . . . not only lavishly to maintain the hunt, but also to possess a suitable district, territory or forest, not only for hunting, but also to see that it is properly hedged, and is known to be for hunting" (Döbel 1783 [1754], Part 2, 87).

(c) The noble hunt

Eighteenth-century hunting presents a squalid picture, especially in Germany. Why, then, did composers continually evoke the hunt by writing hunting pieces as program music, and by their understanding of certain melodic figures, and the timbre of the horn, as a significant topic? Clearly, the signification of the hunt topic had to do with a myth of hunting that transcended contemporary practice; people thought about the hunt in a way that was scarcely reflected when they went out to hunt.

The noble ideals of hunting were often mentioned by writers of the eighteenth century, especially the French. The stag was a noble animal; the hunt was a scene of courage, joy, and oneness with nature; hunting accustomed a man to hardship and sacrifice; it was a training for war and a kind of substitute for military actions. Considering the decadence of the contemporary hunt, this high-mindedness may seem curious.

> Mankind and the hunt were created together. The Creator, in making man, subjected him to many evils, yet also wished him to be happy; it was the concern of the great Architect to balance pain and pleasure, and of all pleasures the most honest, the most noble and innocent, was that of the hunt with running hounds, in which we contemplate the wonders of nature. . . .
>
> The practice of the hunt is so noble that it is authorized by the example of the greatest kings on earth; in all periods, it occupied the leisure of heroes, who chose to make it a successor to their labors. The management of horses and arms are talents common to huntsmen and soldiers; the habits of movement and fatigue, so necessary to support and further courage, are learnt in the hunting field and transferred to warfare; it is the pleasant school of a necessary art. (Le Verrier 1778, 1–3)

Even German writers attributed great dignity to the hunt. Von Lohenstein, in his long poem *Arminio*, which tells the story of the first-century hero Hermann (Arminius), reproduces all the standard eulogies of hunting.

> Wie vielerley Ergötzlichkeit
> Die Menschen je erfunden haben
> Kürzt keine besser nicht die Zeit,
> Und keine kan mehr Leid vergraben,
> Als wenn man Menschen nicht den meisten Abbruch thut,
> Und seinen Stahl senckt ein in wilder Thiere Blut . . .
> [Die Jagd] ist zwar kurtzweil, doch ein Krieg;
> Nur dass er nicht auf Menschen wütet. . . .
> Die Jagd macht hertzhafft und geschickt,
> Zum Krieg und hurtigen Geschäfften;
> Klug, dass uns niemand leicht berückt,
> Stärckt Glieder, mehrt die Lebens-Kräfften.
> Sie räumet geiler Lust nicht Zeit und Wachsthum ein,
> Wer nun die Tugend liebt, der muss ein Jäger seyn.
> (Quoted by Flemming 1724, 11–12)

> Of any amusement invented by man, none passes the time better, and none banishes care more effectively, than when, without harming humans, one sinks one's steel into the blood of a wild beast. . . . [The hunt] is a pastime, yet also a kind of war, except that it is not waged against humans. . . . It makes us hearty and skillful in war and in speedy actions; clever, so that no one imposes on us; strengthens our limbs, in-

creases our vital powers. It gives no time for lascivious desires to develop: whoever loves virtue, must be a huntsman.

For contemporary sensitivities, the hunt was no mere diversion or display, nor a prudent and selfish manifestation of aristocratic land-rights. It expressed the nobility of man, his kinship with nature, his courage and idealism, and it prepared him for warfare. Here it should be remarked that warfare, also, was decadent in the eighteenth century; but like the hunt, it was still spoken of as heroic and noble (see below, part 3). Both activities were presented in two forms, one manifested, the other cultural.

Fitzpatrick, writing of the German and Bohemian lands, confirms that high ideals operated, even in the country of the *chasse aux toiles*. "The hunt stood for all that was desirable in worldly virtue, representing a new embodiment of the older *ritterlich-höfisch* . . . ideals which were at the centre of aristocratic thought. . . . These ideals and aspirations . . . lay at the very heart of the *adelisches Landleben*" (Fitzpatrick 1970, 20). This modern author associates the ideals of the hunt with von Lohenstein's notion of *Tugend*, "a fundamental concept of seventeenth-century Austrian aristocratic thought . . . [which was a] complex mixture of bravery, industry, honesty, and chivalry" (20n1).

Much later, and in the comparatively marginal land of England where foxhunting (rather than staghunting) was the standard pursuit, the same themes are repeated.

> An early benefit conferred by the pursuit of wild animals was the courage, address, and skill in combat, which it produced. For the capture of such as were formidable by their size and ferocity, man learned to devise weapons suited to place him on an equality with them; and having so done, his courage would be increased by his additional prospect of success, and his endeavours would be multiplied to insure it. . . . The connection between sporting and martial enterprise was therefore early and intimate, and so it has continued. . . .
>
> It was from the war which man necessarily, and in his own defense, made on animals, that he learned the art of offence (Blaine 1852, 154).

Clearly the perceived cultural realities of the hunt differed radically from the manifestation. Since musicians were obviously expressing the cultural realities, we must pursue these realities to their source. Hunting manuals had been written since the fourteenth century; the earlier treatises, concerning themselves exclusively with the parforce hunt, expressed the moral aspects at great length.

"All my life I have taken special delight in three things: arms, love and hunting" (Gaston 1994 [1387], 13R). Thus wrote Gaston, Count of Foix, called Gaston Phoebus, in the *Livre de Chasse* of 1387, one of the most famous hunting books of all time, which was admired, copied, and translated by many other writers. "Now, I shall show you how huntsmen have more joyful lives in this world than other folk. For when the huntsman gets up in the morning, he sees the sweet and fine morning air, the clear and healthy weather, and the song of the birds, singing sweetly, melodiously and lovingly, each in its own language. . . . And when the sun rises he sees the sweet dew on the branches and the grasses, gleaming in the good sunlight, and bringing pleasure and joy to the heart of the huntsman. . . . Thus it is said that huntsmen go to paradise when they die, and live in this world more joyously than any other people. Thus I assure you that huntsmen live longer than any others" (Gaston 1994 [1387], 15R).

These glowing praises of the hunting life are universal in medieval writings. There were many medieval treatises; some are listed here.

William Twiti, *The Art of Hunting*, about 1328; Alfonso XI, King of Castile, *Libro de la Montería*, fourteenth century; Anon., *Les livres du Roy Modus et de la Royne Ratio*, fourteenth century; Hardouin de Fontaines-Guerin, *Trésor de Vénerie*, 1394; Charles IX, King of France, *La Chasse Royale*, about 1570; Jacques du Fouilloux, *La Vénérie*, 1561; George Turbervile, *The Noble Art of Venerie or Hunting*, 1575 or 1576.

We shall adopt John Cummins, a modern writer, as our guide through this corpus. "Medieval literature on the theme is permeated by a sense of dedicated enjoyment, the fulfilment of an enduring compulsion to retain a link with nature" (Cummins 1988, 2). First of all, the idleness which so easily leads to sin is occupied by the delightful diversion of hunting. But there is another, more magical benefit. Wild animals have certain qualities which men need to acquire; this he may achieve by "studying, hunting, and defeating them". Thus the hearing of the boar, the sight of the lynx, the taste of the stag, the touch of the spider, may be sought by man. All writers describe the hunt as a preparation for war, in a sense a kind of substitute warfare, the "preparation and mirror of warfare" and "praeludium belli" (Eckardt 1976, 50).

As Gaston Phoebus suggests, hunting was connected to courtly love. There was an erotic side to hunting. The quarry, after capture, might be presented to a lady, the hunting field might become a setting for lovemaking, and the courtly love tradition often portrayed love as a hunt (Cummins 1988, 7–8). Andreas Capellanus described love as a "kind of hunting" (Rooney 1993, 46). Hunting was *exotopic*; it took a man into distant and unfamiliar environments, detached him from his friends and home, subjected him to danger and the unpredictable (Cummins 1988, 74).

The pursued hart took on magical qualities in these narratives; he was often white, as in Malory, and might have sacred associations. In the story of the conversion of St. Eustace (also called St. Hubert), a hart appeared with an image of the crucified Christ between his antlers, a scene often portrayed by artists.

The medieval hunt was aristocratic, warlike, manly, adventurous. It was dangerous and unpredictable. The hart, a noble animal, conferred nobility on its pursuers. The hunt was at once erotic and idealistic. An aspect of high culture, it was intimately linked to the poetry of courtly love and to the life of refinement and breeding.

Anne Rooney, in her book on Middle English literature, shows that the literary hunt could be split up into a number of hunting "motifs", subtopics which permeated English and foreign texts. These include the *Devil as Hunter*; the tenacious ruses of the Devil in trying to ensnare the believer are presented as the techniques of a cunning huntsman. Also the *Wild Hunt*, which is similar to the witches' ride, classified elsewhere as an aspect of the dysphoric horse (*Sense*, 62–63); the huntsman is a baneful spirit, Odin, Diana, or Herne the Hunter, who sets off in pursuit of the faithful. Rooney even comments that the hunt was directly connected to adventure; it was sometimes "the means of beginning an adventure. The hunt is either interrupted or leads the hunter into isolation, and some adventure follows" (Rooney 1993, 58).

There are a few extra associations of the hunt, which are not specifically mentioned by medieval writers, but may be inferred from musical references in the eighteenth century. In this case, it could be said that the topic refers to contemporary life, though without doubt these references would have rung equally true in the Middle Ages.

First, the hunt took place, most typically, in the morning. As previously explained, the command for the next day's hunt was issued the previous evening; the *limiers* needed to go out before first light to find suitable quarries. The author of the *Enfans de Latone* makes this clear:

> Avant que le Soleil des monts dore la cime
> Menez-le [the *limier*] au bois, chargé du trait qui le reprime. . . . (Serré 1734, 207)

> Before the sun gilds the mountaintops, send the limier to the woods, with the task assigned to him. . . .

It will be recalled that the librettist of Bach's "Hunting Cantata" (*Was mir behagt*, no. 208) spoke of a hunt which began at dawn.

> Was mir behagt, ist nur die muntre Jagd!
> Eh noch Aurora pranget
> Eh sie sich an den Himmel wagt
> Hat diese Pfeil
> Schon angenehme Beut erlanget!

> The only thing to please me is the merry hunt! As soon as the dawn shows its beauty, as soon as it touches the sky, this arrow has found a delightful prey!

Count von Sporck, who reputedly brought the French hunting horn back to Bohemia, founded a hunting order (1723), whose anthem was a *Jagdlied* called *Aria Sancti Huberti*, which began, "Pour aller à la chasse faut être matineux, pour prendre son cerf en guet faut être vigoreux"—you have to be up early to go hunting; you have to be vigorous to keep your stag in sight (Zuckerová 1983, 10).

Rather disappointingly, however, the eighteenth-century hunting party set out much later than dawn, after the masters of the limiers had reported to the hunt's main sponsor and a quarry had been selected. Gaffet pictures the huntsmen encountering their quarry at "ten or eleven in the morning" (Gaffet 1742, 42).

In spite of this, the association of hunting with the early morning is recalled in the first movement of Haydn's *Le Matin* Symphony, as already mentioned, and Leopold Mozart added a piano piece called *Die Jagd* to the collection *Der Morgen und der Abend* (1759), written in conjunction with Johann Eberlin.

The idea of morning was enough to make composers think of the topic, without any suggestion of hunting. The first morning, viewed by the newly created Adam

Figure 5.2.

and Eve in Haydn's *Schöpfung*, is heralded by a tiny fanfare of two horns, unaccompanied (part 3, no. 29: "Aus Rosenwolken bricht"); later on, in the duet, no. 32, Adam praises the dewy morning ("Der tauende Morgen, o wie ermuntert er!") and again the two horns, this time doubled by clarinets, play a short fanfare. There is a long horn solo in Haydn's other late oratorio, *Die Jahreszeiten*, to illustrate the shepherd gathering his flock in the early morning (in "Summer," no. 10, "Der muntre Hirt"). The style is pure hunting, though there is no huntsman in sight. Mendelssohn's song *Morgenlied* (Op. 86 no. 2) does not mention the hunt, the horse, or the forest, but the idea of a brilliant dewy morning inspires a subtle little fanfare in the piano opening (fig. 5.2).

This association was still remembered later, with or without actual huntsmen. In the first act of Dvořák's opera *Rusalka* (1901), morning light fills the woodland and a horn is heard in the distance, with a chorus of huntsmen, in preparation for the prince's entrance. Hunting horns, with birdsong, are also heard in a portrayal of dawn at the beginning of Dvořák's oratorio *St. Ludmila*.

The association of the hunt with the season of the fall needs a little more explanation. Vivaldi's *l'Autunno*, third of the *Four Seasons* concertos, ends with a hunt, and the "autumn" movement from Haydn's *Jahreszeiten* contains an exhilarating hunting scene, quoting various Dampierre melodies including the "halali" and the *vol ce l'est*. Ringer mentions a *caccia* by Gregor Josef Werner, which represents the month of October in an *Instrumental-Calender* published in 1748 (Ringer 1953, 155). Leopold Mozart, too, composed a little keyboard piece called "Die Jagd", specifically "für den Herbstmonat" (Pöschl 1997, 77). Much later, Tchaikovsky, in his piano suite *The Seasons* (Op. 37b, 1876), illustrates the month of September with a piece called "The hunt" with hornlike *bicinia* in 6/8 time.

Yet most of the sources assure us that hunting took place all year round, including in the depth of winter. However, there were certain seasons when hunting was less appropriate or sporting. During March and April the stags have soft and tender new antlers, and are to be seen in open country, for contact with trees and forest growth is painful to them. During May and June the antlers grow stronger, and the animals enter the woodland, using the branches to scrape off the remaining woolly casing of the new-grown "head". But hunting is unfavorable at this time, because of the heavy dews which make the verdure uncomfortably wet. During high summer the ground becomes too hard for the limiers to pick up the scent; hunting is difficult at this time. This is the time when the antlers, now cleaned, acquire their characteristic brown hue; "Les cerfs de dix cors brunissent leur tête à la fin de juillet et au commencement d'août," explains Gaffet (1742, 44). In September begins the rut. The stags chase the does and fight over them, they bray and scratch the ground and, losing caution, rush from wood to wood and across open country. They are, however, much more dangerous at this time; "they are furious, and turn and charge the huntsmen" (56). There is another disadvantage; as the rut progresses, the scent becomes so strong that some limiers refuse to follow it. Nevertheless, this is the season when the craft of hunting is best learned; it is now "that the young hunts-men can learn, and most profit in their knowledge of the stags, because they can see all sorts, old and young, and assess them better than in any other season" (64).

For ceremonial purposes, the season ends with St. Hubert's Day (3 November), when there are celebrations and banquets. This is, perhaps, the chief reason for the association of hunting with the fall. This description of the hunting year is taken from Gaffet, but it is confirmed by the other writers; the Latone poet praises the fall, in his limping verse.

> Entre les jours heureux dans l'année enchaînés,
> Qu'à ses nobles plaisirs Diane a destinés,
> Il en est un fameux dont le nomme renouvelle
> De tous les spectateurs le courage et le zèle,
> L'Automne tempérée offre mille douceurs. (Serré de Rieux 1734, 267)

> Among the happiest times of the year, destined by Diana to noble pleasures, there is one whose name refreshes the courage and zeal of all onlookers, the temperate fall, of-fering a thousand sweetnesses.

A further connection of the hunt topic is with the noble horse of the warrior, the *destrier*. The knightly horse is always portrayed as galloping, its characteristic motive proceeding in 6/8 time like most Dampierre-style hunting calls. Sometimes, the horse is so obviously a hunter that it is hard to decide whether the topic of the hunt, or that of the noble horse, is meant. This other important topic, with its dysphoric counterpart, is discussed more fully in *Sense* (45–65).

Like the horse, the hunt is always a noble and heroic topic. Of course, most con-temporary horses were draft animals or simple personal conveyances. Most hunts, likewise, were not especially heroic; quite the reverse. But all hunting had a sugges-tion of glory and adventure, of noble prestige, coats of arms, and manly swagger. This myth, with its ancient origins, is the signified of the hunt topic, the cultural unit that formed hunting semantics.

(d) The decline of the hunt

Culture, however, was forsaking the hunt at the end of the eighteenth cen-tury. The bourgeois man of feeling resented the exclusivity of the aristocratic hunt, and the new worship of nature and the landscape viewed hunting with some un-easiness. Christoph Christian Sturm's influential *Betrachtungen über die Werke*

Gottes in der Natur of 1772, a book usually dominated by philosophic rapture, suddenly flashes with anger on the subject of hunting.

> Hunting is one of the chief amusements of a certain order of people . . . , but it is to be wished they do not set such value upon it; for the power man has over animals, and the pleasure he takes in subduing them, is too often mingled with cruelty. Sometimes, it is true, there is a necessity that animals should be put to death. . . . But even then their death ought to be made as easy as possible; and unfortunately this law prescribed by nature is little attended to by sportsmen. Men, in this respect, shew themselves more cruel tyrants than the fiercest beast. Is not the way of hunting a hare or stag dreadful to every feeling heart? Can it be an innocent pleasure to pursue with rage and fury a poor animal, which flies from us in violent anguish, till at last, exhausted with terror and fatigue, it falls and expires in horrid convulsions? . . . To purchase a pleasure by the death of an innocent creature, is purchasing it too dearly. (Sturm 1819 [1772], 3:161–162)

In Germany, Aus dem Winckell's hunting manual of 1805 is already speaking of an entirely different world; a world where hunting was parforce, but parties were small (he lists the members of a hunting party, adding up to eighteen persons—Winckell 1898/1805, vol. 1, 148) and there was much concern for conservation of stock; the prodigious abundance that had fed the *chasse aux toiles* was evidently drying up. This writer gives a few pages of "French parforce signals" (1:167–170), and offers some indications of when they should be sounded (1:162–165), but most of the calls can be found in earlier French sources.

Since the hunting call was not revived in Germany until the time of Fürst Pless, it seems remarkable that the topic survived strongly in concert music. When Brahms composed his Horn Trio in 1865, the revival of hunting music in central Europe was only beginning (the definitive Austrian collection, Josef Schantl's *Die oesterreichische Jagdmusik*, was not published until 1886). In any case, the new repertoire of hunting tunes differed in many ways from the classic hunting calls, just as the new horns—particularly the Fürst-Pless Horn—were different from the great trompe de chasse, as Josef Pöschl explains (Pöschl 1996, 1314). Many of the new calls are recorded in Reinhold Stief's nine-volume *Handbuch der Jagdmusik*, published by BLV Verlagsgesellschaft of Munich. By 1900, the signifier of the musical topic was probably independent of the music of the hunting field; its aristocratic associations adhered it to ancient memories of princely huntsmen, while modern German sportsmen are generally bourgeois. The popular sport of hunting—in 1996 Pöschl numbered 5,000 huntsmen, including 100 horn players, in the South Tyrol alone—is associated with jaunty hats, good beer, and healthy bank balances. It is little relevant to general culture, as little an inheritor of the noble and ritual hunt of Gaston Phoebus as the British yacht club embodies the world of the first-rate man of war.

6 Musical Hunts

(a) Hunts in vocal music

The Dampierre-style horn call and simpler styles of call are unquestionably the main signifiers of the hunt in music from about 1700. We may examine, first, music with a specific reference to hunting, either in a vocal text or in a title. Some of these works quote actual calls that can be identified from the standard collections; others offer horn calls that evoke the general style, some of which may be field calls that have not been recorded in published sets. "Musical hunts" have been examined by other writers, notably by Fehr (1954) and Pöschl (1997).

The earliest musical hunts, in fact, antedate the *trompe de chasse*. Some of these echo the single-note calls of the oxhorn (*Hifthorn*); others show simple triadic figures which may indicate the *cor à plusieurs tours*, for which no field calls have survived.

Jannequin's four-part chanson *La Chasse* of 1529, published in 1537, contains in its second part a graphic representation of a hunt. The hounds are called by name, there is a clamor of barking and shouting huntsmen, and in the closing bars the horns are heard, sounding each one its own note, to the syllable "tronc", very close to the sound used by du Fouilloux ("tran") in his quotations of hunting calls (1573).

Much later, a call listed by du Fouilloux is copied by a prominent composer, as I hinted in chapter 4. Near the beginning of the second act of Purcell's opera *Dido and Aeneas* (1689), Aeneas returns from a hunt bearing the trophies, and holds up the huge head of a wild boar. After his words, "Upon my bending spear a monster's head stands bleeding", the orchestra repeats a rhythm notated by du Fouilloux. This, says the hunting writer, is the call played "quand la curée sera mangée", after the eating of the curée, the hounds' formal meal of parts of the dead quarry, when the head of the stag is shown to the hounds (du Fouilloux 1606 [1561], 51V). There is an odd vocal piece in Thomas Ravenscroft's *Briefe Discourse of the True Use of Charact'ring the Degrees* (1971 [1614]). The author divides human delights into five categories, "hunting, hawking, dauncing, drinking and enamouring", each illustrated with music. The section on hunting begins with John Bennet's part-song "The Hunt Is Up", and then appears a strange item, based on a series of hunting calls and cries set in four parts by Edward Piers. Among these, the cry "Boy winde the horne" gives rise to a pattern of repeated notes in all parts. The natural oxhorn is still, then, the typical instrument of the hunt.

In spite of this, there are a few traces of calls with many notes, perhaps suggesting that the helical *cor à plusieurs tours* was used in the hunting field from an early date. The *caccia* "Tosto che l'Alba" of Gherardello da Firenze (ca. 1320–ca. 1362) has been mentioned above; in it, the voices imitate a horn call spanning a fifth,

Figure 6.1.

Figure 6.2.

perhaps played by a *cornet de chasse*. This piece dates from a period long before the earliest extant horns.

Contemporary with the first surviving horns is a German part-song describing a hunt, *Das Gejaid* by Ivo de Vento (1540-75). Vento, perhaps Flemish in origin, studied in Venice and spent most of his career in Munich, working at the Bavarian court. *Das Gejaid* is one of his *Neue teutsche Lieder* of 1570 or 1571 (Mönkemeyer, *Antiqua Chorbuch*, Mainz, 1951, cited by Pöschl 1997, 57-58). It is in four sections; in section 3 the hounds get the scent, bay with delight ("mauf, mauf"), and the hunt sets off in pursuit. The descending triad in all voices seems to imitate horn calls (fig. 6.1, from Pöschl 1997, 58; the word *Förd* is presumably *Fährte*, scent). There is a similar trace of contemporary horn calls in the hunting madrigal, "Ein edler Jäger wohlgemut" by the German organist Melchior Schramm (ca. 1553-1619). This number was published in Frankfurt in 1589. The imitative opening of the piece sounds like a simple triadic hunting call; its inversion in the second and fourth voices is merely a formal procedure (fig. 6.2). The madrigal describes the search for a stag, the taking of the scent by the hounds, the excitement of the chase, and finally—rather significantly—the driving of the quarry before the *Schirm*. This is, then, a *chasse aux toiles*, as it would probably have been in the Germany of a century later.

Apart from the dubious witness of these vocal imitations of hunting calls, no evidence has been given of the widespread use of the *cor à plusieurs tours* in the hunting field. Nevertheless, composers sometimes required horns for hunting pieces in the theater. Could it have been the case, then, that the little helical horns, probably capable of all notes up to the sixteenth harmonic, were embraced by the theatrical hunt before the real hunt? The later contempt of huntsmen for the brass horn might suggest that its true home was in the theater, and that it was really an instrument of display rather than practical use.

It was first used, apparently, by Francesco Cavalli in his festa teatrale *Le Nozze*

Chiamata alla Caccia

Figure 6.3.

di Teti e di Peleo (1639). In act 1, scene 1, there appears a *chiamata alla caccia* for four horns in C, with bass. At this early period, these must have been the small helical horns, sounding in C alto—that is, at the written pitch. It is interesting that the parts ascend into the fourth register, but remain triadic at this pitch, although the horns could play diatonic tunes in this register; apparently, the hunt was associated at this early date with triadic, not diatonic tunes (in Goldschmidt 1900–01, 73; fig. 6.3).

Lully is presumably thinking of the same instrument when he writes a passage for five horns in the comédie-ballet *La Princesse d'Elide* (1664). The text of this piece mentions "several hunting horns and trumpets", and the composer responds by introducing a group of *cors de chasse*. As in the Cavalli score, they are required only to play the notes of the triad.

It is reasonable to think that the horn required in Morin's cantata *La Chasse du Cerf* (1708), described above, was a *trompe de chasse* in C of the new design, single wound, the sort of unwieldy instrument we see in the famous portrait of the Marquis de Dampierre, which appears as a frontispiece to the 1776 volume of hunting calls. If this little work was staged, as seems apparent from the stage directions, then it may have been the first theatrical representation of a hunt using the new kind of horn, rather than the *cor à plusieurs tours*.

It was quickly followed by others, including Keiser's pastoral *Die entdeckte Verstellung oder Die geheime Liebe der Diana* (1712), Fortunato Chelleri's favola pastorale *La Caccia in Etolia* (1715), Caldara's dramma per musica *Sirita* (1719), and Fux's festa teatrale *Elisa* (1719). The "bruit de chasse" in act 4 of *Les Eléments,* an opéra-ballet by Destouches and Lalande (1721), requires hunting horns. There are hunting fanfares in scene 4 of André Campra's tragédie-lyrique *Achille et Déidamie* (1735). An extensive study would be necessary to decide exactly which instruments were expected in each of these cases.

(a) Corni da Caccia in F

(b)

(c) voice

Ja - - - - - - - - - - (gen)

Figure 6.4.

Bach's secular Cantata no. 208, *Was mir behagt*, known as the "Hunting cantata", presents a little classical drama, with Diana, Endymion, and Pan as characters. It was written for a hunting enthusiast, Christian of Saxe-Weissenfels, and was Bach's first secular cantata, probably performed in 1713. The first aria, sung by Diana, extols the hunt as a divine pleasure.

> Jagen ist die Lust der Götter,
> Jagen steht den Helden an!

> Hunting is the gods' pleasure, and is becoming to the hero.

Two *corni da caccia* in F play triadic calls in the ritornello, resembling the simple calls in Flemming. However, Bach is writing for virtuosic players, and the first horn soon plays a florid elaboration of the simple hunting style. The voice copies the triadic motives, developing them into a vocal melody (fig. 6.4). Within a few bars, three kinds of hunt evocation are presented: the simple triadic horn call (a), the association with the hunt through timbre alone (b), and a triadic vocal tune (c). The horns that played this piece at Weissenfels, even at this early date, were presumably not hunting horns but orchestral horns with crooks.

A word about the "Peasant Cantata" or "Cantate Burlesque", no. 212, *Mer hahn en neue Oberkeet*, dating from 1742. This has certain hunting associations; Fehr believed that the duet, no. 2 ("Es nehme zehn tausend Dukaten"), is based on a Czech hunting song (Fehr 1954, 20; the tune is at fig. 6.5). This might explain the reappearance of the tune in Leopold Mozart's later *Sinfonia di Caccia*, described below. The tune also resembles a French hunting call listed as "La Dampierre" by Gaffet (see appendix 1). Item no. 16 is marked "Aria col corne de chasse", though the orchestral horn player has very little material of any interest; the theme of the piece resembles a rustic song. Nevertheless, there are figures in the horn part that resemble single-note horn calls in the manner of du Fouilloux. This work is per-

Horn in G

Figure 6.5.

vaded by a bucolic simplicity that precludes, perhaps, brilliant melodic horn calls or virtuosity.

In spite of the Caldara opera mentioned above, thoroughgoing portrayals of the hunt must have seemed too naïve for *opera seria*, where hunting references are usually more oblique. The aria "Va tacito e nascosto" in Handel's *Giulio Cesare in Egitto* (1724) is a simile aria, in which the singer compares his cunning actions to the stealthy movement of a huntsman. This kind of sententious comparison is typical of the genre, and one would expect little effort to picture an actual hunt. What one encounters is a piece with brilliant horn obbligato in common time, a virtuoso number in which only the timbre of the horn suggests the topic of hunting.

Opéra comique was less prim than opera seria. An extended hunting scene is inserted in *Tom Jones* (1765) by François-André Philidor (son of the chronicler of early horn calls). This takes the form of a big choral number, filled with horn *bicinia*, one of them vaguely reminiscent of Dampierre's "le debuché"; the scene culminates in the Dampierre "halali", marked "fanfare", the singers crying, "Et nos chasseurs chantent tous a l'envi". Paradoxically, Philidor is picturing a hunt in the English countryside, since his opera is based on the novel by Fielding, but his Parisian audience would expect something in the French hunting style.

Other works incorporated actual quotations of hunting calls. One of the most popular hunting pieces of all time was the *Chasse du Jeune Henri* by Etienne-Nicolas Méhul, which began life as the overture to Méhul's opera *Le Jeune Henri* (1797). In spite of the composer's espousal of the revolutionary cause, and his many political compositions, this work, far and away his most popular and successful, is about the youth of King Henri IV; and its copious hunting calls, with their obvious reference to kingship and nobility, bear witness to the continuing fashion for hunting music and the old world of the aristocratic hunt. It was arranged and copied countless times and was performed everywhere; Ringer informs us that the young Beethoven played it at his first Vienna concert, with the horn player Punto, on 18 April 1800 (Ringer 1953, 159).

The coming of dawn (*Morgenröte*) is pictured in a slow introduction, and the hunt itself then begins, with horn calls both imitated on strings and played by the two orchestral horns. The climax employs the usual "halali" tune, but two other real calls appear in slightly altered form, "la retraite" and "pour l'eau" (or "le bat l'eau"). Clearly Méhul believed he was quoting real hunting calls; "pour l'eau" closely resembles the version of Serré de Rieux quoted in appendix 1, but "la retraite" is significantly different. The closing figure (at the end of the exposition in sonata form) is, apparently, an original tune in hunting style.

The most magnificent presentation of real hunting calls, rather than mere pas-

(a) **Vivace** 4 horns in D

(b)

Figure 6.6.

tiches, comes in the chorus, "Hört das laute Getön", from the third section, "Herbst", of Haydn's *Die Jahreszeiten* (1801). Several authentic calls are used, all of them part of the greater Dampierre canon, though Fehr thought that there were also German calls (Fehr 1954, 26). Daniel Heartz has compared the calls in this chorus with those recorded in the article "Airs de Chasse" in the Encyclopédie, written by Charles Georges le Roy, concluding that Haydn did not specifically use the le Roy source (Heartz 1975–76). It seems likely that the composer knew the calls from the hunting field, since his versions do not exactly match any of those in the published collections. As for German calls, these are largely derivative from the French; there are few original German tunes, as may be seen from the manual of Georg Franz Dietrich aus dem Winkell (1898 [1805]).

Haydn's piece begins with the four horns in D, playing alone and presenting a theme composed of repeated notes and triads, firmly in the third register, resembling the kind of simple tune which might be played for the "queste", the gathering of the hunt. It may be compared with a "queste" of 1742 (fig. 6.6a,b).

The next identifiable horn call appears at m. 16, one of the "tons pour chiens" from the collection of Le Verrier (1778). If the previous tune was a "queste", then it is appropriate that the hounds, who have now set off on the chase, be encouraged with one of these tunes, which are "uniquely made to urge on the hounds, to keep them on the course they are following, and to encourage them to pursue vigorously the animal they are hunting", according to Le Verrier. Oddly, this tune is called "le raproché" by Gaffet, suggesting that it is played when the scent, having been lost, is found again.

A similar tune is heard just afterward, which however more closely resembles Le Verrier's "relancé", which would be played after the beast has effected a "ruse" (see above), and the hounds, after some confusion, have caused it to spring forward again with the hunt in pursuit. Haydn's tune and the "relancé" may be compared in figure 6.7a,b.

At m. 50 there appears "le debuché", the call sounded when the beast breaks cover to run from one area of woodland to another. Again, it is not exactly the same as the notation of this call in Serré de Rieux (see appendix 1). Aptly, the words "schon flieht der aufgesprengte Hirsch" (breaking out, the stag runs off) have just been sung.

(a)

(b)

Figure 6.7.

Figure 6.8.

The next identifiable call is Dampierre's "le vol ce l'est" at m. 72. This signifies that the tracks of the pursued beast have been sighted; presumably it was lost after its "debuché". The tune is missing from the earlier sources, but appears in the 1767 collection and is shown in figure 6.8. Notice that this collection gives the music as sounding, not as written for the horn.

At this point the horn players perform a maneuver that would have been impossible on the hunting horn: they change crooks, the music modulating to E flat. This is considered to be the "German key", perhaps prompting Fehr's guess that some fanfares are German rather than French. This does not seem to be so, however; the figures at m. 83 do, indeed, appear in German collections, but they closely resemble the "Relancé", which we have already heard. The virtuosic passage at m. 95 is quite unlike any field call. The composer is at last making use of his players' superior abilities.

Finally, the quarry, "overhauled by its enemies, exhausted of its spirit and strength", turns to face the huntsmen, to the sound of Dampierre's "halali", the singers crying "Halali, halali! den Tod des Hirsches kündigt an" (the "halali" announces the death of the stag). Both parts of the tune are played, the "halali sur pied" at m. 141 and the "halali par terre" at m. 153. The "Latone" versions may be seen in appendix 1. The stag vanquished, the hunt returns triumphant to the sound of "la Rembouillet" at m. 189. The call is to be found in appendix 1, and appears in all the collections under that name, though Fehr assures us that it was also called "le retour de chasse" (Fehr 1954, 16).

At the opening, and frequently throughout the number, the four orchestral horns play alone. Since they chiefly play established calls, and since their tone is meant to be recognized as that of the horn (the *Inventionshorn*, played in the orchestra, being related to the hunting horn), it might almost be said that this example is scarcely a case of musical topicality; like the gramophone record of a nightingale in Respighi's *Pini di Roma*, these calls are hardly more than untreated extraneous sounds, rather than representations. It is remarkable, however, that Haydn reproduces so closely the actual field calls of the time. This chorus is a positive anthology of *sonneries*, though there are sufficient small departures from the published versions of tunes to make us doubt that Haydn was copying from a published source.

Theatrical hunts continue strongly into the nineteenth century. Schubert writes a simple version in his opera *Alfons und Estrella* (no. 7, *Chor und Arie*). The opening horn solo is tolerably "Dampierre" in style, and the female voices sing figures largely based on triads.

The hunting music in Weber's *Der Freischütz* (1821) is well known. The most famous item, the chorus in act 3 marked "Jägerchor", is less strongly representative of the musical topic, though it is clearly meant to resemble a *Jägerlied* in 2/4 time; Fitzpatrick compares it to a hunting chorus in Fux's *Elisa* (1715). The scherzando has horns in D, playing a call which, according to Fehr, resembles the German horn signal "Langsam treiben". Much more typical is the chorus "Wir lassen die Hörner erschallen", in act 1. Here the horns are crooked in F, and they alone accompany the singers, the strings being silent. To the modern listener, nothing could sound more redolent of the hunt than these horn figures; yet there is already some reason to feel that the signifier—the hunting field call—is being embroidered and romanticized. The cross-rhythms, octave doublings, and posthorn-like melodic octave figures are not typical of the field call, but evoke a picture-book hunt in an age when hunting-horn playing was in decline. The short *Jägerchor* in act 3 of *Euryanthe*, accompanied by four horns and bass trombone, takes a further step away from the authentic hunting call.

The famous huntsmen's chorus at the start of act 2 of Rossini's *Guillaume Tell* (1829) is played by the orchestral tutti. Its theme, however, was first heard in act 1, at the point where Arnold heard the approach of Gessler and his followers, and here it was played by four onstage horns. It is a typical hunting piece, in 6/8 and in E flat (the German "hunting key", according to Pöschl; however, this opera was written for a French audience).

Less authentic is the *Lied mit Chor*, no. 16 in act 3 of Marschner's *Hans Heiling* (1833). The singer announces "Ein Paar Reime", and launches into the story of a huntsman's wedding. There is a rousing call, played by four horns and two trumpets in E flat, the theme of which is later incorporated into the vocal melody. It is purely triadic, in 6/8 time, but its wide range—an eleventh—seems stagey and showy.

Lortzing's comic opera *Der Wildschütz* (1842) is full of hunting references, and is perhaps a landmark in the development of the topic, since the four horns play almost nothing that could have been heard in the hunting field, although the theme

Figure 6.9.

of hunting is constantly invoked. The overture is in D and 6/8 time (and is, incidentally, strongly evocative of the "noble horse" topic), but the subsequent horn fanfares include the double-tongued effect of the military trumpet, the "ritiriton" or "tiritiriton" of Altenburg (1795, 92), which is rare in hunting *sonneries*. This is heard even more strongly in the later *Jagdlied;* the effect, which somewhat resembles the snare drummer's "flam", "drag", and "ruff", linked to the purely triadic nature of the calls themselves, gives this passage a strongly military flavor, in spite of the 6/8 meter (fig. 6.9). Later the horns play a passage of rising octaves, like a posthorn, against the voices. It would seem that the signifier of the hunt topic is now an imaginary hunting horn, rather than any instrument that might have been heard in the field.

This confusion of military and hunting calls is compounded in Berlioz's *Damnation de Faust* (1846), where the soldiers' chorus in the finale of part 2, "Villes entourées de murs et remparts", with its brilliant trumpet calls, is in a style that strongly evokes the hunt, though there are no hunting references in the text. The later *Récitatif et Chasse* in part 4, during which Mephistopheles "hears huntsmen in the woods", continually inserts horn ensembles in hunting style, which here sound remarkably authentic.

Wagner's two musical hunts—in *Tannhäuser* (1845) and *Tristan und Isolde* (1865)—represent the high point of the Romantic signifier. The "ri-ti-ri-ton" effect of the military trumpet, and the spanning of fifths and octaves that echo the posthorn, are both apparent in the first of these (act 1, scene 3), and the horns, their crooks constantly changing to match the tonality, play almost always in ensemble. The *Tristan* hunt (act 2, scene 1) places six horns in F offstage; their atmospheric fanfares gradually grow more distant as the king and his followers recede into the forest. These figures are remarkable in several ways: first, they are basically triadic rather than diatonic, like most Romantic hunting motives, so in their major-key form might seem rather simple. But they also introduce new features; they are elsewhere dysphoric, sounding minor triads instead of major, and they combine the optimistic hunting topic with another topic, the "pianto", the mournful falling semitone which foreshadows the tragic sequel to this hunt (see *Sense,* 66–73).

Much closer to the original signifier are the hunting fanfares in Delibes's ballet *Sylvia* (1876). This little classical drama about a "nymph of Diana" is permeated by a solo horn call, infinitely atmospheric, which would be playable on a natural

Figure 6.10.

horn in E flat with the use of the unreliable seventh harmonic (this note was not normally played on the hunting horn, since the player could not correct the intonation with his hand). The number called *Les Chasseresses,* also entitled "fanfare", combines a melodic shape close to those of many Dampierre-style calls with answering figures on timpani; presumably the combination of fanfares and drum figures has its origin in the music for cavalry trumpet (fig. 6.10; see part 3, below). This number is in 6/8 time and in E flat, previously considered the key of the German hunt—now, presumably, a universal element of the hunt topic.

A somewhat surprising example surfaces at the end of the century. Fauré, commissioned to write incidental music for Maeterlinck's play *Pelléas et Mélisande,* was confronted near the start by an offstage hunt—a common stage device. As Golaud enters in Fauré's score of 1898, there is a hunting call, which may be observed near the end of the *Prélude* to the orchestral suite. Though played on the versatile chromatic horn in F, it is entirely on a single note, like one of the du Fouilloux calls; indeed, it somewhat resembles the *curée,* quoted by Purcell. It seems remarkable that Fauré could have remembered that the medieval oxhorn possessed only one sounding note, when so many composers had forgotten this.

Modern musical dramatists have been less interested in hunting scenes. But a single reference to the hunt may suggest the topic; for example, Britten encounters the following text in the Canticle III, *Still Falls the Rain,* a setting of Edith Sitwell for voice, horn, and piano.

> The blind and weeping bear whom the keepers beat
> On his helpless flesh . . . the tears of the hunted hare.

He responds with a short instrumental movement. Though the direction is "marchlike" and the horn part has a dotted pattern that might suggest the military topic, the contour and rhythm markedly evoke the gapped 6/8 character of the hunting call.

When Hans Werner Henze set out to tell the story of a young king who turns into a stag (in *König Hirsch,* 1956), he ingeniously transformed several of the features of the traditional hunt topic for his woodland scenes and parties of huntsmen. The short *Vorspiel* is in a powerful 6/8 meter; and when the curtain rises on act 2, "Der Wald", a soft horn call is heard over a long bass pedal, the atmospheric effect of the horn of nocturnal mystery (see below). Later, huntsmen approach through the forest and offstage horns are heard; the hunt then recedes into the distance, like that in *Tristan* (fig. 6.11). The simple progressions of horn motion are grotesquely altered, but retain their strong evocation.

Offstage horns (sounding)

come si allontanasse la caccia

Figure 6.11.

(b) Huntsmen and soldiers

It has been remarked several times that the hunt and military topics are often confused. Even Ratner refers to the horn, somewhat misleadingly, as a "military instrument" (19); the horn might be a component of the military band, but it was not used for military signaling.

This may be less of a problem than it seems at first, though there are undeniable examples where the two topics seem inextricable. Perhaps it should be said in advance that music, in any case, is not good at signifying what Saussure called "real terms" (1974 [1916], 120). The musical topic will tend to draw out the common thematic references of two literary and social terms. Clearly, similar predicates can be attributed to the lives of hunting and soldiering: manly heroism, adventure, the outdoors, the erotic, high social class. I have discussed the general issue of topical semiosis elsewhere (*Sense*, 14–20). To confuse the issue further, there was a family relation between hunting horns and military signaling instruments, since infantry signals, immemorially given by drums, were increasingly in the eighteenth century transferred to the *Flügelhorn*, which was in the first place a hunting instrument. This was a consequence of the recruitment of huntsmen and foresters into European armies as *chasseurs* or *Jäger* (in England "riflemen"), a development described below. This common origin leaves its trace in several military calls which appear also in the hunting repertoire; for example, the hunting call *Aufbruch zur Jagd* resembles closely the "military waking call for *Jägertruppen*" (Pöschl 1997, 247), which appears also in an English source as the riflemen's call *Rouse*, noted by James Gilbert (1804, 2). In figure 6.12, the hunting call is shown, as quoted by Pöschl, as well as the military call from Gilbert.

Nevertheless, some distinction can usually be drawn between hunting references and military. The most obvious factor is the meter. Hunting calls are almost exclusively in 6/8 time, both in France and in Germany. The signals of the cavalry trumpet, on the other hand, were often in common time. There was, admittedly, another genre, the *Jagdlied*, sung by the huntsmen at convivial gatherings like the celebration of St. Hubert's Day; while this was also commonly in 6/8 time—the *Hubertuslied*, quoted by Bretonnière (1860, 21), is typical—it was sometimes in 2/4 or 4/4 time, like the hunting song in *Der Freischütz*.

However, 6/8 meter should be considered a primary element in the hunt topic. The *Song Without Words* in A of Mendelssohn, Op. 19 no. 3, nicknamed "Hunting Song", is clearly a hunting piece, with a plausible imitation of a French hunting call. The three E-flat horns in the trio of the scherzo of Beethoven's *Eroica* play an

(a) Aufbruch zur Jagd

(b) Rouse

Figure 6.12.

Allegro (ma poco sostenuto e pesante)
Trumpets in A (written)

f   marc.

Figure 6.13.

obvious pastiche hunting call in the same meter, though in this case notated in 3/4 time.

The two- and three-part character of many of these examples recalls the fact that French calls were often *bicinia*, played by two horns in simple harmony. Since the French hunting horn played mainly in a range between the fifth and twelfth harmonics (E–G as written), a characteristic shift from the triadic third register to the diatonic fourth register gave a recognizable pattern of part-writing which has been called "horn motion" (by Rupert Thackray; see Thackray 1963, 34). This may be seen in the *Jagdlied* from Beethoven's *Musik zu einem Ritterballett* (there are, of course, no voices in this score, and the piece is really a fanfare, not a *Lied*). But the characteristic *bicinia* may appear without any other markers of the hunt topic; in the D major Quintet of Mozart, K. 593, the style is apparent although the meter is binary (and, of course, there is no timbral marker).

Trumpet signals, on the other hand, were not played in parts on the parade ground or battlefield. It is highly significant, therefore, that trumpet fanfares in concert music often assume the character of horn *bicinia* or *tricinia*. They are often in 6/8 time and betray the influence of the hunt. The final theme of Glazunov's Violin Concerto, Op. 82, is a clear example (fig. 6.13). It is afterward played by unison horns, and, alas, by bells! In a new harmonic idiom (and in, effectively, 9/8 time), Strauss's "hero" (in *Ein Heldenleben*) strides to battle to the sound of three trumpets playing in the manner of hunting horns.

It must be remembered, also, that the hunting horn is about double the length of the trumpet and transposes downward, while most cavalry trumpets transpose upward and trumpet music is basically in the next higher octave. (The *Flügelhorn* or "bugle horn", another military instrument, described later in this work, was an even higher instrument.) Hunting figures often occupy the lower part of the available range; when a hunting theme appears in the minuet of Haydn's Quartet in C, Op. 64 no. 1, it is played on the cello, at a pitch where it would lie well for the horn in C. When such themes are played by the orchestra, they are often given to the cellos rather than the higher strings (the opening of the *Eroica* is typical, and in Haydn's Symphony no. 53, *L'Impériale*, the cellos are doubled by a horn in D).

This is particularly well shown in the two songs of Schubert entitled *Ellens Gesang*, with texts taken from Scott's *Lady of the Lake*. The first of these, described below in chapter 11, is about a warrior home from the war ("Raste, Krieger", D. 837). The other (D. 838) is exactly parallel, but speaks of a huntsman ("Jäger, ruhe von der Jagd"). In style, the songs are very similar; both begin with a piano introduction in fanfare style, but the soldier's song places this in the range of a trumpet in D flat (if there were such a thing), while the huntsman has his fanfare almost an octave lower, as for a horn in E flat, the German hunting key.

The timbre of the horn may itself be an important factor; Handel's aria "Va tacito e nascosto" has been mentioned. There is a horn obbligato also—in D, the French hunting key—in the "Quoniam" from Bach's Mass in B minor, presumably to represent the nobility of God ("tu solus altissimus"), though the horn plays figures that are very little reminiscent of the hunting field (except for one detail; after playing mainly in the fourth "clarino" register, the horn descends in the very last phrase into the third, triadic register, as did many early field calls—for instance, "la sourcillade" in the Versailles manuscript, fig. 4.8).

It is, perhaps, true to say that the distinction of hunting horn and cavalry trumpet was eroded by the development of the orchestra and especially the introduction of valves to the instruments, so that both could perform similar music without limitation of pitches. The "ri-ti-ri-ton" of the trumpet often appears in military calls—for example, in the "Generalmarsch"—but is not a feature of hunting-horn playing. It turns up in Romantic horn music, however, together with the predominant leaps of a fifth and an octave of the posthorn. This has been shown above, in cases of music by Weber and Lortzing.

The posthorn may, in fact, generate a subtopic all its own. In the early eighteenth century it was a small coiled brass instrument sounding only the fundamental and its octave, its shape familiar as the symbol of the modern German postal service. Later, German posthorns were given three coils and were capable of the sixth or eighth harmonic, but still made much use of octave leaps. Posthorn music is familiar from Bach's *Capriccio Sopra la Lontananza del suo Fratello Dilettissimo*, BWV 992, and Mozart's Serenade, K. 320.

A further word is necessary with regard to octave leaps, however. Bourgue has mentioned the "whoop" of the horn in approaching a note from below, which sounds somewhat like the howl of a dog. True hunting calls do not incorporate the "whoop" of a rising octave in their notation, but it sometimes appears in topical themes in the repertoire. As an initial gesture in a horn melody, it reappears in Strauss's *Don Juan* and, according to Philip Tagg, in the *Kojak* television show theme, which Tagg compares to many tunes from concert and popular music (Tagg 1979, 127–132).

Figure 6.14.

(c) Hunts in instrumental music

Often a title is enough to identify a work as a hunting piece. Thus, there are hunting sonatas, hunting symphonies, "chasses" for keyboard and for violin. The style is unmistakable, and the title is seldom needed.

"Chasses" for violin and for keyboard

"Hunts" for solo instrument, popular in the eighteenth and nineteenth centuries, seldom tell the story of a day of hunting, but merely adopt the style of the hunting fanfare in a characteristic piece, often as a vehicle for virtuosity. J. B. Cartier collects a number of violin "chasses" in his *l'Art du Violon*, published in 1803. He gives pieces for violin and continuo, by Mondonville, Leclair, Guillmain, Guignon, Chabran, and Leblanc. The time is consistently 6/8 or 12/8 throughout these works, which are more or less display pieces. Often "horn motion" is presented (for example, in Mondonville's Op. 4 of 1733, the opening of which could well be played by two horns in F), and there are many passages of repeated notes— easy to play on the violin, but also perhaps redolent of the old single-note hunting calls. One such passage in Leclair's *Sonata 9* (1734) adds a *tremblement serré* to a series of double stops; one wonders if the *roulé* effect is imitated, the horn vibrato produced by rapid soft tonguings. Many features are illustrated in a brilliant passage from J. P. Guignon's sonata, Op. 8, of about 1746 (fig. 6.14). The passage shown is Dampierre-like, but overall the piece is chiefly composed of triadic shapes. The violin "chasses" collected by Cartier are by no means the whole repertoire. There is a notable example by Wilhelm Cramer, son of the pianist and composer J. B. Cramer, mentioned by Ringer (1953, 157).

A later violin piece may be mentioned at this point. Paganini's Ninth Caprice in E, for solo violin, is written largely in "horn motion", though the time is 2/4. When the music descends on to the two lower strings, the composer writes "imitando il corno sulla IIIª e IVª corda", imitating the horn on the D string and G string. The lower register makes him think of the pitch of the horn; this passage could, indeed, be played at this pitch by two horns in E (fig. 6.15).

The earliest hunting pieces for keyboard were written by the clavecin composers. These little movements might not be noticed as manifestations of the topic, were it not for their titles; they are simple triadic tunes in 6/8 time, little different from

Figure 6.15.

other simple dance movements. Couperin's "Fanfare Pour la Suitte de la Diane", from the second *Ordre,* is a good example; we may note that it is in the French hunting key of D. The melody could be played, perhaps, one octave lower on a horn in D, though the style is at one remove from that of Dampierre. Much later, Kirnberger presents a little keyboard piece in rondeau form called "Fanfare", also in 6/8 time and in D, as I have noted elsewhere (*Sense,* 33–34).

More obviously intended as an evocation of the hunt itself is Wilhelm Friedemann Bach's *Imitation de Chasse,* listed by Fehr. This is followed by the little piece of Leopold Mozart, *Die Jagd,* mentioned above, which appears in the collection published with Johann Eberlin in 1759, called *Der Morgen und der Abend oder 12 Musikstücke für das Clavier.* Mozart's piece in 6/8 time appropriately represents the time of the morning. Wolfgang, too, began a keyboard *chasse,* but it survives only as a fragment (K. Anhang 103).

Clementi's *La Chasse,* Op. 16, published by Mills of London in 1786, is a much more considerable piece, essentially a three-movement sonata in D. The opening allegro is not markedly in hunting style, though full of triadic figures. The finale is the site of most of the hunting effects; this sonata rondo in 6/8, marked *allegro assai,* has the triads and repeated notes which have come to act as signifier of the topic, though none of its melodies could be conveniently played on the horn. But the keyboard *chasse* is already beginning to sound like a toccata, far removed from the hunting field.

The *chasse* quickly became the "favorite musical topic" of the time (Ringer 1953, 157). Among the dozens of keyboard hunting pieces which followed in successive decades, an example by J. L. Dussek stands out, called "La Chasse, for the piano forte", and published as part of the *Musical Journal,* no. 1, edited by Pleyel, Corri, and Dussek in 1797 in London. It is a single movement, with a slow introduction (perhaps the coming of dawn) and a sonata-form allegro in 6/8 time. Between them comes a short link in octaves, entirely triadic, entitled "The chase begins" and marked "French horns". Horns could, and did, play far more than these naïve empty triads (fig. 6.16), but triadic movement had now come to stand as signifier of the topic, without need for diatonic melodies.

Stephen Heller (1813–88) wrote several hunting pieces, but his concert study *La Chasse,* Op. 29 (1844) was the most celebrated and was played by Liszt. It shows the final decay of the keyboard *chasse*; though in 6/8 time, it is much too fast (*prestissimo*) for any hunting fanfare and begins as a pure toccata. The second strain is more hornlike (or at least more triadic) but the whole piece makes no positive reference to the hunt. It could be said that the dominant topic in such a piece is not the hunt but the noble horse, also indicated by 6/8 time and a close relative of the hunt topic, though the German hunting key survives. Subsequent piano *chasses* sel-

The Chase begins.

Figure 6.16.

dom evoke the hunt and its associations. Liszt's *Wilde Jagd*, though in 6/8 time, probably pictures a witches' ride rather than a hunt, as I have suggested elsewhere; such a reference is a kind of "dysphoric horse", nothing to do with hunting (*Sense*, 63).

The hunting symphony

In the field of instrumental music the topical references of the hunt begin to recede. Just as the heroism of the huntsman turns into the mere adroitness of the pianist, so the many *chasse* symphonies are just fodder for the pageantry of venatorial courts, at least in the eighteenth century.

Thus Jean-Joseph Mouret's *Symphonies Mêlées de Cors de Chasse* of 1729 were presumably written for the court of the Marshal of Noailles, where Mouret was *maître de musique* between 1707 and 1736. The horns in question were hunting horns, according to Pöschl (1997, 72), playing brilliant fanfares "based on hunting signals". Telemann, also, wrote his overture-suite *La Chasse* for an aristocratic court, that of Darmstadt; more precisely, for festivities in the hunting lodges of Kranichstein, Mönchsbruch, and Fürstenlager (Pöschl 1997, 71).

The same could be said of Leopold Mozart's *Sinfonia di Caccia* (1756), though the court for which it was intended was that of an archbishop, Colloredo of Salzburg, in whose service Mozart was at that time merely an orchestral violinist. Leopold was much respected as an intellectual, later a friend of Wieland. Yet some of his compositions betray a throwaway levity, even a contempt for the concert world; the "Peasant Wedding" cantata incorporates whistles and pistol shots, and this hunting symphony is inscribed: "Die Jagd Sinfoni/4 Violini/4 Corni ex G/2 Violi/eine Kugel Bichse/et Basso" ("Kugelbüchse" means "musket" and not, as Grove's author thinks, "ammunition boxes"). The composer adds: "At first, the horns in G must be blown very roughly, as is normal in hunting, and as loudly as ever possible. Also, an oxhorn (*Hifthorn*) may be used. Then, you should have several hounds to bark, and the rest of the people should shout together, ho ho etc., but only for 6 measures." It is not clear where the barking and shouting should begin and end, or where the gun should be fired.

Only the first of the three movements is truly a hunting piece. It begins with eight measures for horns alone (presumably the passage played "roughly"), based on the same melody as the aria in Bach's "Peasant Cantata" which resembles the

Horns in D (written)

Figure 6.17.

Allegro   4 Horns in D (written)

[*f*]

Figure 6.18.

call "la Dampierre" (see above, fig. 6.5). Mozart scores in 12/8 time, though the hunting spirit is obvious. The horns are later crooked in D. Remarkably, the figures are French in style, utilizing (especially later) fragments of diatonic scale as well as triads (fig. 6.17). Perhaps the Bohemian horn players employed at Salzburg had inherited the tradition of von Sporck, derived from the court of Versailles (Pöschl 1997, 77). The violin parts, however, resort to the routine triadic figures, extended upward in a way that would be impossible for horns.

Among the many hunt symphonies composed from the 1760s onward, two Haydn symphonies, nos. 31 and 73, are the most sophisticated. The first of these, composed in 1765 and usually called the "Horn Signal", is entitled "Auf dem An-stand" in the Mandyczewski edition. It was intended for the *Tafelmusik* or for the twice-weekly "academies" (concerts) at the court of Eisenstadt; the court would move to Esterhaza the following year. The very conspicuous horn call on which the first movement is based is something of a mystery. It is played by four D horns in unison, in triple time (fig. 6.18), but it bears no relation to any of Flemming's calls, or to any later German calls with the "Anstand" title, which is the equivalent of the "halali à pied", sounded when the stag stands at bay. Fehr believes that it "refers to the German type" of hunting call but does not support his view (Fehr 1954, 22). In fact, it resembles much more closely a military signal; indeed, it is not unlike the "Generalmarsch", quoted in Symphony no. 100, the "Military", where it is played by a trumpet in C.

There is, however, another, simpler call (at m. 9, fig. 6.19), based on an octave figure, which Hoboken identifies as a "south Hungarian, Croatian, and Rumanian signal", played on small horns "mostly made of animal material"—in other words, oxhorns (Hoboken 1957, vol. 1, 35). Since this call is composed of three pitches (the first three harmonics) it could not be played on oxhorns, in fact, but perhaps would be suited to crude metal horns of the *Halbmond* variety. Hoboken's source

Horn in D, solo

Figure 6.19.

of information is a personal communication from "Dr Ernst Paul of Weidling bei Wien". He quotes a signal from the Buckligen Welt, "the neighborhood of Aspang and Seibenstein, east of Semmering, in close proximity to the Esterhazy estates", which resembles Haydn's call.

None of this seems especially convincing, and in any case Hoboken's informant cannot explain the earlier "horn call" which gives the symphony its name. The connection of this work with hunting seems tenuous. The motive in question, being triadic, can easily be played on the cavalry trumpet in D, and it sounds distinctly like a cavalry call. As for Mandyczewski's "Anstand" title, this is surely fanciful. Incidentally, one manuscript of the symphony (which was in the possession of Alan Tyson) has this call marked "alla posta", so it must have suggested a posthorn to a contemporary listener.

In the same year, 1765, Theodor Schmidt quoted the "halali" in one of his *Symphonies in Eight Parts* (Fehr 1954, 20). This particular call became uniquely significative of the hunt. Gossec's *Simphonie de Chasse* of about 1773, which Ringer finds a monotonous work, also uses the "halali". In the early 1780s Carl Stamitz wrote a *Sinfonia la Caccia*, a three-movement piece which is consistently in hunting style, finally quoting the "halali". Ringer notices the same hunting call in symphonies of Wranitzky, Hofmeister, Sterkel, and others (Ringer 1953, 156).

A different call, however, is quoted in Haydn's *La Chasse* Symphony of 1782. The first three movements of this work have apparently nothing to do with hunting, though the andante quotes the song "Gegenliebe" from the second book of *Lieder für das Clavier*, no. 16, of 1781–84 (Hob XXVIa/16). The symphony takes its name from the finale, itself originally the overture to *La Fedeltà Premiata* (1780), a *dramma pastorale* about the goddess of the hunt. The passage for two horns in D, with oboes, at m. 29 of this movement reproduces "la sourcillade" from the "La-tone" collection (see appendix 1). The editor of that collection assures us that the call is not by Dampierre. Typically, Haydn does not copy the call exactly from the collection; as usual, we must assume that he had heard it in the field, inaccurately recalled by living huntsmen. Furthermore, if Haydn had wished to take a hunting call from a published collection, he might surely have made use of the fine Dampierre publication of 1776, which does not include "la sourcillade". It seems clear that he used his ears in the open air. It should be noted that his call is not the same as the "sourcillade" quoted by Philidor in the Versailles collection.

We may pause for a moment over this splendid movement, as it is very revealing of the hunting style in concert music. "La sourcillade" is not its only theme. The unison opening is an invented melody that evokes the style without being a true field call. It demonstrates two important melodic features: repeated notes and triadic formulae. Of course, both were typical of hunting calls, but the French call of the eighteenth century was above all a diatonic melody played mainly in the fourth register. Such melodies, being diatonic and scalic, might lose some of their hunting character when played on other instruments (the "halali" is a good example of this). Thus Haydn, devising a melody for the opening orchestral tutti, begins firmly with repeated notes and a triad in 6/8 time, which even to modern ears sound clearly redolent of the hunt. The subsequent development of this theme returns constantly to the motives of triads and repeated notes, obviously components of the hunt signifier. In fact, the "hunt style" in concert music was simpler than the field calls themselves.

We shall encounter other traits of melody that typify the hunting style in concert music, rather than reproducing the style of recorded field calls. We may conjecture that real huntsmen often played simpler calls, perhaps avoiding the fourth register and echoing the older single-note calls; that the popularity of the older style of call, recorded by Philidor l'aîné and Flemming, continued far into the Dampierre period. If this was not the case, then composers extrapolated a number of stylistic features from the hunting calls, which served as signs of the hunt for symphonic and operatic audiences. "Stylized hunting motifs in classical music are very simple, to the point of naïveté" (Pilka 1972). Vivaldi's Concerto in B flat for violin, Op. 8 no. 10 (RV 362) is called *La Caccia;* the finale has a brisk triadic theme in 3/8 time, but the atmosphere is profoundly violinistic. We might not guess that this theme resembles a hunting call were it not for the title.

The hunting symphony continued into the next century. Jan Bedrich Kittl (1806–68), a Bohemian composer with a considerable reputation, composed in 1837 his Second Symphony in E flat. Each of the four movements has a programmatic title, with the first marked "Aufruf zur Jagd" and then "Beginn der Jagd", then a slow movement marked "Jagdruhe", a scherzo called "Gelage" (revelry), and a finale, "Schluss der Jagd". Horn calls permeate the work, though they do not strongly evoke the hunting topic, sounding often military in flavor. This symphony had a great success and was conducted by Mendelssohn at Leipzig in 1840.

To modern ears, the best-known hunt symphony is Bruckner's Fourth, also in E flat (second version, 1878–80). The scherzo of this work, with its hunting fanfares, dates from 1878, when Bruckner radically revised the symphony. On 9 October that year he wrote to Wilhelm Tappert: "Only the new scherzo remains to be finished, which represents the hunt, while the trio pictures a dance tune, played by the huntsmen during their meal time" (Nowak 1985, 158). Horn calls are prominent also in the first and last movements, though—significantly—the horns are always in F, not in the "hunting" key of E flat in which much of the music is written. Bruckner's imagination embraces the key of the old field horns, but he scores resolutely for modern horns that can play in any key. The famous *tricinia* of the scherzo are scored in 2/4 time, though largely in triplets; as usual, the four horns in F play mostly triads, but almost incidentally they sometimes interpose bits of diatonic scale in "horn motion" that recall Dampierre (for example, in m. 36). The atmospheric opening of the symphony, *Ruhig bewegt,* illustrates the branching point of

p *legg. scherz.*

Figure 6.20.

another topic, the "horn of nocturnal mystery", which is described below. This topic takes on some of the associations of the hunt, especially the mysterious depth of the woodland, but abandons others. There is a similarly atmospheric horn in the finale; and both the hunting scherzo and the theme of the nocturnal opening return in this final movement (at mm. 23 and 79). Max Auer sees the whole symphony as a hunting scene: "The woodland Romanticism of the other movements tends formally towards a description of a hunt. . . . [This is] real program music" (quoted in Krohn 1955, 84).

Pöschl finds a hunting symphony as late as 1915. The *Lovska Simfonija*, by the Slovenian Fran Gerbic (1840–1917), has not been published, but it was performed by Radio Ljubljana in 1941 to mark the composer's centenary. Its four movements carry titles and the work requires a mixed chorus (Pöschl 1997, 130).

Symphonic poems, too, may adopt the topic to illustrate hunting themes. Franck's *Le Chasseur Maudit* and Smetana's *Vltava* spring to mind. An engaging late manifestation is to be found in Respighi's *Fontane di Roma* (1916). A specific fountain is chosen to illustrate each time of day; for morning, the Fountain of the Triton, by Bernini, blows its conch in Piazza Barberini in the middle of the city (the tritons, sons of Poseidon and Amphitrite, were supposed to make the roaring of the ocean with their blowing). Respighi is aware that the conch normally sounds only the fundamental (though with effort, some conches can play up to the fourth harmonic) and he accurately reproduces this with four horns in unison playing middle C. Later, he cannot resist a *tricinia* of flutes and clarinets, the triplets suggesting hunting meter. This is Tennyson's "horns of elfland faintly blowing" (from *The Princess*); however, the time of day is right (fig. 6.20). Today, the triton's conch would scarcely be heard amidst the roar of the Roman traffic.

(d) Songs about huntsmen

In a song for voice and piano, there is clearly no possibility to represent the hunt through timbre. Schubert's solution is usually quite simple. He is content to structure a vocal melody almost entirely on the triad, evoking the notes of the *trompe de chasse* in a routine way, as we see in *Jägers Liebeslied*, Op. 96 no. 2. Almost as simple is the horn motion in the piano part of *Der Alpenjäger*, D. 524, where the voice merely copies the piano melody.

Slightly more authentic is the piano introduction of *Trost* (the Mayrhofer version, D. 671), where the horns of the right hand are for the moment unaccompanied. An excellent example of horn motion is found in *Die böse Farbe*, the seventeenth song of *Die schöne Müllerin*, where the words "Horch, wenn im Wald ein Jagdhorn schallt" prompt a rhythm in sextuplet sixteenth notes which enclose passages of horn *bicinia*.

An earlier song of this set, *Der Jäger* (no. 14), displays an important feature. The meter is appropriate to the subject, but the song is in C minor; the anticipated triads are thus minor, and the topic becomes dysphoric. There is another dysphoric song, the *Lied des gefangenen Jägers*, D. 843. The D minor horn figures of this song scarcely resemble hunting calls; they sound more like military trumpet signals, in a *fandango* rhythm. Exceptional also is *Ellens Gesang II*, in which the opening solo horn call and the beginning vocal melody (to the words "Jäger, ruhe von der Jagd") are triadic in the hunting key of E flat, but the rhythm, in common time, is not at all evocative of the hunt.

A *Jagdlied* of Mendelssohn (Op. 84 no. 3) presents an interesting picture. The text is from *Des Knaben Wunderhorn*, where it is called *Nächtliche Jagd*. It is not, in fact, a *Jagdlied* (in the sense of a convivial song of huntsmen), but a love song of a huntsman who rides in the greenwood by night, hears three girls singing, and recognizes one of them as his true love. The poem mentions the forest, the moonlit night, the huntsman's ride, and the "Jubelhorn", and it describes the girls' singing as birdsong—a cluster of topical references to which the composer responds with an unequivocal Dampierresque *bicinia*, initially playable on two horns in E. However, with its 6/8 rhythm this is heard at first within the associative world of the noble horse, as the words begin:

> Mit Lust tät ich ausreiten
> Durch einen grünen Wald . . .
>
> I rode out with delight through a greenwood . . .

The horn is not mentioned until the third stanza.

> Ins Jubelhorn ich stosse,
> Das Firmament wird klar,
> Ich steige von dem Rosse
> Und zähl die Vögelschar.
>
> I blow my horn joyfully, the sky becomes clear, I dismount from my horse and count the flock of birds.

Initially, Mendelssohn's horns sound in an *andante con moto, piano*, suggesting that, though *Jubelhörner* (horns of triumph), they have some of the features of the nocturnal horn (see below in chapter 7). At the end of the song the *bicinia* break into fragments, leaving snatches of "horn motion" in the still of the night.

Mendelssohn, like Mahler, is a composer very sensitive to topical reference. The *Jagdlied*, Op. 120 no. 1, for four-part male voices, which sets a Germanized version of Walter Scott, is firmly in 6/8 time, *presto*, with triadic melody figures, apt for the morning, horse, and hunt of the text. Like the solo song, Op. 84 no. 3, mentioned above, it is not really a *Jagdlied* but a poetic song about the hunt.

Schumann's Hunting Songs, Op. 137, for male voices with *ad lib* accompaniment for four horns, are nearer to true *Jagdlieder*. The texts, by H. Laube, are rousing tributes to the hunting life, and the first number thrills to the chase of the "noble red stag", in 6/8 time, *sehr lebhaft*, with fanfares in D major. The final item is a shameless piece of nationalism in march tempo, praising the German hunt in preference to the French and the English.

> Wo giebt es wohl noch Jägerei
> Als wie im deutschen Land!
>
> Where is there such hunting as in Germany!

Of course, Schumann also wrote a *Konzertstück* for four horns and orchestra, though it does not much suggest the hunting manner, except for the timbre of the instruments.

By the mid-nineteenth century hunting in Germany—or anywhere else—was no longer *aux toiles*. Perhaps Laube was eager to rid the "German hunt" of its unpleasant historic associations. The song is a good pastiche *Jagdlied* in 4/4 time and ends with a showy fanfare in triplets.

Rather strangely, Mendelssohn could on occasion choose the hunt topic for a song which makes no mention of any hunting associations. Goethe's *Sommerlied* mentions the fields, the vegetation, the sunshine, the breeze, without any reference to horses or hunts. It might be thought of as a pastoral. Yet Mendelssohn's setting for male voices (Op. 50 no. 3) resembles a *tricinia* for horns in G, playing a typical Dampierre-like fanfare. Perhaps the mention of "Thau" (dew) led the composer to think of the morning; or perhaps it was possible for a musician to introduce topical reference for its own associative sake in a song, just as he would in an instrumental piece.

The late Romantic songwriters show much less interest in the topic of the hunt, or in verses about huntsmen, in the decadent age of the Fürst-Pless horn. When Wolf selects two poems of Mörike—*Jägerlied* and *Der Jäger*—there is very little trace of the topic, though the first of these, in 5/4 meter, has a certain equestrian feel. The tenacity of the topic is shown, however, when Strauss scores brilliant fanfares in triplets for clarinets and bassoons, *feurig bewegt*, in the orchestral song *Pilgers Morgenlied*, Goethe's lay about the pilgrim leaving town who sees the castle of his beloved enveloped in morning mist (the poem was merely a compliment by the twenty-three-year-old Goethe to a lady of the Darmstadt court). Somewhere within the consciousness of the urbane Strauss lurk the matutinal hunting horns of Haydn's day.

Throughout our history, mention of the hunt, of the morning or the fall, tends to suggest the sound of hunting horns to musicians setting verses or writing to a program. The whole panoply of the Dampierre horn call, with its meter, its timbre, and its character, may be present; but the hunt topic is also regularly evoked by means of simple triadic tunes, or merely by the timbre of the horn. It was natural that the topic might surface also in music without words or evocative titles, bring-ing with it certain associative significations, but not necessarily referring to the hunt itself. Beethoven's horn call in the *Eroica,* apparently to compliment Napo-leon, who was soldier rather than huntsman, can only be explained in this way. For this is how topics work.

7 The Topic Established

(a) Hunts without words

It is our task, then, to seek manifestations of the hunt topic in music without any specific reference to hunting in a picturesque title or text. Almost all the examples in the previous section were cases of music which evoked hunting, either by presenting a theatrical hunt, by setting words which were about hunting, or by representing a hunt in a symphony or instrumental solo. But a musical topic has the power to express certain associated sentiments and dispositions in instrumental works identified only by genre.

Manliness, nobility, adventure, risk, and exhilaration; youth, the overcoming of danger; the outdoors, the morning, the woodland, the fall; the exotopic and unforeseen. Along with these indexicalities goes a firm commitment to the male gender, and a tone that is strongly euphoric. In vocal music, as we have seen, there are a few dysphoric hunts. But it is harder to identify a dysphoric hunt in a sonata or string quartet. As for the dysphoric aspects of the *chasse aux toiles,* these are nowhere present in the musical topic, for the signification of the topic is a myth, a cultural convention that lives not in social life but in the imagination.

Dampierre-style horn calls

Since the true horn call in the style of Dampierre is largely diatonic, rather than merely triadic, it is harder to recognize unless actually played on the horn. There are, however, sufficient examples to show that it had life as a topic.

Most prominent of these is, of course, Siegfried's horn call in Wagner's *Der Ring des Nibelungen.* Admittedly, Siegfried becomes a huntsman in *Götterdämmerung,* act 3, scene 1, and in any case a primeval hero who carries a Hifthorn must be considered a huntsman among his many personae. The horn motive, however, first appears in *Siegfried,* act 1, scene 1, at Siegfried's first entrance. It seems that his horn is itself a symbol of his character even before it is illustrated in music, and that the cultural theme embodies courage, youth, virility, and strength. Incidentally, Siegfried's instrument is described as a *silver* horn; this seems unlikely, since the setting is mythical and thus prehistorical. There were no metal horns before the fourteenth century of sufficient length to sound a set of harmonics, unless one goes back to Roman times. Oxhorns, however, were often elaborately set and bedizened in precious metals, with inlaid gems.

This leitmotiv enshrines all the features of the topic, except that its call is a monody, not a *bicinia.* Since Siegfried actually blows the figure on his horn (in *Siegfried,* act 2, scene 2), the fiction must be maintained that the leitmotiv is a real

(a) Brahms

Allegro

(b) Dampierre

Figure 7.1.

Allegro con brio

Figure 7.2.

diegetic musical event. For it must always be a fiction: "The hero onstage puts an oxhorn to his lips," writes Josef Pöschl, "while, behind the scenes, a horn player blasts forth the resounding melody on a modern orchestral horn in B flat. This Siegfried-call clearly could not be played on an oxhorn" (Pöschl 1997, 125). Ox-horn calls on one note, à la du Fouilloux, are not unknown in modern music, but they do not carry the associations of the hunt topic, which requires the brilliant third- and fourth-register melodies of the *trompe de chasse*. Siegfried's call is not merely the sound of his horn. It is the voice of his character, a reckless, noble young hero, at home in the forest.

Brahms twice wrote a horn call in Dampierre style. The scherzo of the Serenade, Op. 11, begins with a tune for horn in D which, though scored in 3/4 time, somewhat resembles several Dampierre tunes—for example, "la retraite prise" (Dampierre 1776, 37) and "la Saint Hubert" (1776, 43). It lies at the junction of the third and fourth registers and is, of course, playable on the natural horn (fig. 7.1 shows Brahms's melody, with "la retraite prise"). The tune in the trio, played on horn in E, is even closer to the Dampierre style.

The appearance of the valve horn made it possible to extend diatonic movement downward into the third register, and the opening of the finale of Brahms's Horn Trio shows how the Dampierre spirit could be slightly adapted on the new instrument. Beginning in pure Dampierre style, this melody, played on a horn in E flat (the German hunting key), descends to written A (sounding C) and then leaps a fourth downward, as though the instrument had suddenly mutated into a horn in C (fig. 7.2).

In the absence of its true instrument, the Dampierre style is harder to recognize.

Allegro

Figure 7.3.

(a)

(b)

Figure 7.4.

The third strain of the scherzo of Brahms's Piano Quintet in F minor, Op. 34, has many of the features of hunting style, and would be playable on the natural horn (an octave lower), though its second note, a high A, never actually appears in real hunting calls (fig. 7.3). The tune appears later in E flat, the hunting key, in this movement in C minor.

It is remarkable that the diatonic style of the hunting tune is still just discernible in a figure distorted almost terminally by the resources of the modern horn. The theme of Strauss's *Till Eulenspiegel,* one of the most celebrated orchestral horn themes, is (ignoring its rhythmic oddities) very like a Dampierre fanfare, except for its intrusive D sharp (written; the passage is for horn in F), which must signify the irreverent cheek of Till. Indeed, one wonders why this noble, euphoric topic is thought suitable for the little trickster; apparently he is meant to be a noble soul at base. One may compare this passage with a "ton pour chien" recorded in the "La-tone" anthology (see appendix 1).

An ingenious modern work demonstrates several features of the Dampierre style. In his Trio for Violin, Horn, and Piano, a companion piece for Brahms's simi-lar work, Ligeti often specifies the positions of the valves in such a way that groups of notes can be played as though on a natural horn. In the following passage from the quick second movement, written for horn in F, the first group of notes is played as for "horn in A flat", making use of the out-of-tune seventh harmonic, and the next group for "horn in A" (fig. 7.4a). Although the time signature is 4/4, the con-tinual triplets give a sense of a hunting 6/8. This impression is to be found also in the first movement, where the "hourvari" effect (a "whoop" upward across the har-monics) is carefully notated (fig. 7.4b).

The Topic Established 97

Horns in E flat (written)

Figure 7.5.

Horn bicinia *and* tricinia

The two-part and three-part horn call, with instruments on adjacent harmonics and thus playing in thirds, fourths, and fifths (in "horn motion"), is much more common as a topical signifier. The effect is familiar from the trio of the *Eroica* scherzo, and from another scherzo, that of Brahms's Second Piano Concerto. The two natural horns used by Haydn in many of his symphonies so commonly echo the hunting *bicinia* that it almost becomes an aspect of orchestral expression; the very presence of the horns in the orchestra suggests the nearness of the hunting field, as well as being an aspect of timbral color. The ensemble of horns and trumpets at m. 344 of the finale of Symphony no. 98 in B flat closely resembles a two-part arrangement from the late edition of Dampierre, in a rousing hunting meter. An earlier symphony, no. 22, has a finale in hunting style which converges on a little fanfare for two horns, very Dampierre-like.

The "horn motion" that comes from playing adjacent harmonics may itself be a thematic resource. A figure for two E-flat horns commences the finale of Symphony no. 103, immediately to be given a violin countersubject (fig. 7.5). A similar effect appears, familiarly, in Beethoven's overture *Leonora no. 3.*

The effect of "horn motion" is sufficiently distinctive to be recognizable even in the absence of horn timbre. The hunting finale of Haydn's Symphony no. 23 in G is scored for violins, but the *bicinia* is clear, in 6/8 time. It reappears in the minuet of the String Quartet, Op. 54 no. 2 in C, in the finale of the Quartet, Op. 64 no. 1, and in Mozart's String Quintets in E flat, K. 614, and in D, K. 593, where both figures lie in the register of the horns, and both are in hunting keys, the first in 6/8 time but the other in *alla breve*. Brahms, also, favors the hunting *bicinia* for the first movement of his String Quartet in B flat, Op. 67, the low-lying parts (for second violin and viola) perfectly right for two horns in B flat basso, if only they were available.

Perhaps the most celebrated horn ensemble calls in concert music are those of the scherzo of Bruckner's Fourth Symphony, described above. But these seem to be a specific evocation of the hunt; the composer is so clear about this that the work has been included in the section on programmatic references, though no such indication appears in the score itself.

A similar evocation is found at the start of Mahler's First Symphony, though these fanfares are played on clarinets and offstage trumpets. The famous nature scene of this introduction is full of topical references: the wide-ranging pedal, the descending fourths, the two sorts of fanfare, the musical cuckoo all come from the stockroom of musical topics. The whole is marked "wie ein Naturlaut", like a natural sound, and the slightly military-sounding *bicinia* are presumably suggestive of the Romantic forest.

Horn timbre as signifier

It has been shown above in the case of items by Bach and Handel that the hunt may be evoked merely by the timbre of the horn, without much suggestion of hunting meter or melodies. The same may be true of real topical references, in the absence of specific mention of hunting. Strauss was especially enamored of the horn; it might almost be said that the heroic Strauss is particularly typified by horn timbre, while Mahler, constantly lamenting the fate of doomed soldiers, is more obviously associated with the trumpet, and the solemn, ceremonious Bruckner is particularly linked to the heavy sound of trombones and Wagner tubas, recalling the old brass ensemble of the *Stadtmusikanten*.

The first part of *Don Juan* has many of the associations of hunting. It is active, dashing, vigorous, unbuttoned. But the hunting topic is not obviously present, in spite of the throbbing triplet accompaniment. It is not until the protagonist enters, in the form of a heroic theme *molto espressivo e marcato*, that the four horns are permitted to step forth in unison (m. 314); their theme, though it begins with the rising octave of the hourvari and would be almost playable on a horn in C basso, makes no direct reference to hunting style. The timbre of the instruments is enough.

The effect of unison horns, playing a figure in quadruple time that begins with the whoop of an octave, is discussed at length by Philip Tagg in connection with the *Kojak* television show theme. He points to a number of items of popular music that have the same characteristics: the horn theme-tunes of the radio series *Gunsmoke* and *The Saint* both begin with an octave leap, to evoke a heroic and successful detective (Tagg 1979, 125–131, summarized in *LSM*, 287–290). Tagg considers that the horn, having been "less commonly used in military circumstances", is chiefly associated with "hunting and postage" and evokes "men on horseback galloping though woods and fields, hard on the heels of hounds in pursuit of game". As Tagg says, the hunting horn was never used as a military signaling instrument (unless one thinks of the *Flügelhorn*), though horns were present in the military band. As for the posthorn, this quite distinct instrument was normally limited to the octave and the fifth. Its calls are thus easy to recognize.

Triadic tunes

As Jiři Pilka comments, the most common form of the hunting signifier is a simple triadic tune, playable in the third register and perhaps reminiscent of the earlier type of hunting call, like those written down by Philidor and Flemming. These are so common as scarcely to need illustration. The minuet tune of Haydn's Quartet in E flat, Op. 50 no. 3, may suffice (fig. 7.6). In fact, the quartets of Op. 50 are full of hunting tunes, perhaps because the set was presented to the King of Prussia. Even Op. 50 no. 4 in F sharp minor has triadic tunes, which in this form are apparently dysphoric. Minor-mode fanfares, to represent grotesque or satirical heroism, are heard in the first movement of Bruckner's Second Symphony. They are common also in the military topic.

Figure 7.6.

More interesting, perhaps, than these simple evocations is the case of the hidden reference, where the connection with hunting or its associations is not initially obvious, but is later clarified. Haydn's Symphony no. 6, *Le Matin,* has already been mentioned, with its hornlike tune that is initially played on the flute, but reprised momentarily on the horn. The same device occurs, as everyone knows, in the approach to the recapitulation of Beethoven's *Eroica.* Here, the hunting theme was originally played by the cellos, whose tenor tones are able to place it in exactly the register of an E-flat natural horn, native to the German hunting field. Its premature return on the horn, out of harmony with the accompanying violins, has attracted many interpretations, which are summarized by Scott Burnham: "Most of the programmatic critics interpret the famous horn call as a bold reminder, a recalling to duty, an *Ohrfeige* for the exhausted hero," and A. B. Marx hears the horn as "drifting entirely out of a lost distance, strange, a summons not at all belonging to the present moment but which augurs and heralds those to follow—namely, the return of the heroic theme after the struggle seemed extinct" (Burnham 1995, 13–14). But if the horn call marks a return of heroism, why was it not played on the horn in the first place? It seems insufficient to interpret this witty effect of style as a mere programmatic fairy tale. It may, admittedly, be a sign of some extraneous narrative, but more profoundly it is a sign of the playful engagement between music and listener.

This gesture—the presentation of a horn call on other instruments, and the later confirmation of its true nature—is common enough. It appears in Strauss's *Don Quixote,* where the opening "ritterlich und galant" fanfares are played by flute and oboe in triplets, and are mixed with double-tongued trumpet fanfares that are distinctly military. Later, the hunting fanfares are played by four horns in unison; and finally, the two calls are juxtaposed, a nice illustration of the different natures of hunting and military fanfares, and a reminder that a nobleman may be characterized by both topics, since he may be both huntsman and warrior (fig. 7.7). Throughout the work, the double-tongued fanfare is limited to trumpets; horns are favored for the triplet fanfare.

(b) The pastoral horn

The vitality of a topic cannot be more strongly shown than by recording its development, the growth of subtopics, and its changes of meaning. It has been remarked that the sound of a hunting horn could evoke the atmosphere of woodland. E. T. A. Hoffmann commented that "certain horn tunes transport us instantly into

Figure 7.7.

Figure 7.8.

the forest" (*Allgemeine musikalische Zeitung*, vol. 3, 1800, 48). The word forest, *forêt*, recalls the exotopic nature of hunting, since it comes from *forestis*, a late Latin word related to *foris*, outside, and referring to the area outside the city and castle walls. Clearly, the forest is situated in the countryside and contributes to the pastoral image of rustic innocence, as well as possessing a mysterious and bosky atmosphere that would contribute to Romantic-era evocations of magic and danger. But no shepherd is ever portrayed playing a brass horn. The horn is normally a huntsman's instrument.

There are horn tunes in pastoral movements of the eighteenth century, but it is hard to conceive that the hunting horn was being chosen as a pastoral instrument, though it may evoke the distant woodland atmosphere of hunting. Such a passage occurs in the slow movement of Haydn's Symphony no. 31 (the "Horn Signal"). The opening of this movement, in a slow 6/8, played by solo violin with pizzicato accompaniment, is incontrovertibly pastoral in flavor. In m. 4, however, the two horns in G echo the violin tune in their own style, *piano*. It is a Romantic moment, but the "horn motion", the mobile harmony, and the Dampierre-like contour distance this kind of passage from the true pastoral horn (fig. 7.8). There are other examples of this sort of passage: as early as Symphony no. 5, horns play soft melodic figures in the slow movement, and in Symphony no. 48, horns in F echo the string theme, as they do in the "Horn Signal".

However, there is another "horn" that was, in fact, played by shepherds: the *Alphorn*. This wooden instrument appeared in many countries: not only in the Alps of Austria and Switzerland, but also in Norway and Sweden, the Baltic countries, Russia, Slovakia, Hungary, Romania, and in some of the German highlands. It is a straight tube, cut from a forest tree, and between 5 and 17 feet in length, but commonly about 6 feet (185 cm); typically, it can achieve the fifth or sixth harmonic. This makes it capable of triadic tunes like many military signals.

Alphorn tunes, however, are different in character from military calls. They are, apparently, influenced by the Swiss vocal style of *Jodel*, and by tunes that are con-

Figure 7.9.

nected with this, like the various versions of the *ranz des vaches*. Famously, this traditional tune is quoted by Beethoven in the *Hirtengesang* of the *Pastoral* Symphony, where its association with the alphorn is stressed by the horn passage in the short introduction. The master may have heard something like a *ranz des vaches* in Haydn's *Seasons*, at the onset of "Summer", to illustrate the words "Der muntre Hirt versammelt nun die frohen Herden", the cheerful shepherd gathers now his joyful flock (see Jones 1995, 12–13, whose translation from the German this is). An alphorn tune from Rigi, Switzerland, is shown in figure 7.9 (from Baines 1976, 53), showing an obvious resemblance to Beethoven's melody. Other versions may be heard in the overture to Rossini's *Guillaume Tell*, and in the "Scène aux Champs" from Berlioz's *Symphonie Fantastique*, where the instruments are cor anglais and oboe.

Very long alphorns may reach the twelfth harmonic; transcriptions of their music usually show the eleventh harmonic (the F atop the stave, as written) as sharp. Such an instrument would be needed to play the alphorn tune in the last movement of Brahms's First Symphony, which the composer had transcribed on his visit to Switzerland in 1868 (Bachmann-Geiser 1981, 93). We may notice the sharpened fourth in this tune (i.e., the eleventh harmonic, if an alphorn were used).

Occasionally, the alphorn is echoed in concert music to suggest mountainous country. A tune from the "Serenade d'un Montagnard des Abbruzes" in Berlioz's *Harold en Italie* resembles a *ranz des vaches*. It is played initially by cor anglais, but afterward by horns in G.

This association is too rare to suggest a subtopic with an Alpine evocation; provisionally, this evocation will not be considered a component of the pastoral horn. But since the connection of the horn with the pastoral spirit becomes standard, the influence of the alphorn must be recognized.

Some examples may be given of the pastoral horn. Consider the opening of Brahms's Serenade in D, Op. 11. Here is a work with no text or evocative title, but in which the pastoral sentiment is obvious. The horn melody at the beginning is accompanied by violas and cellos playing drones on D and A; the drone accompaniment is a definitive marker of the pastoral (see below, part 4). At m. 66 two horns play this theme in "horn motion". The *alla breve* meter distances the work from hunt music, though the 6/8 movement of the hunt appears strongly later, notably for the *bicinia* at m. 177 (it is effectively a brisk 6/4 within the *alla breve* meter of

Figure 7.10.

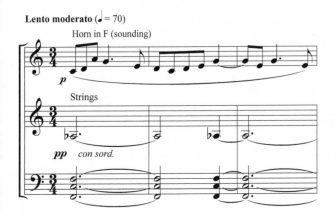

Figure 7.11.

the movement). Notice that the piece is in D, the key of the French hunt. The hunting character of the scherzo and trio has already been mentioned.

The beautiful "Prélude" to Delibes's ballet *Sylvia*, after its processional opening, moves into a piece of pronounced pastoral character with a soft oboe melody, "bien soutenu", over slowly moving harmonies. This piece is prefaced by an unaccompanied horn call which later reappears throughout the work. It is atmospheric and a little mysterious, and would be playable on a natural horn in E flat, taking in the unsatisfactory seventh harmonic (fig. 7.10). The ballet, telling of a "nymph of Diana", with shepherds, huntresses, and "divinities of the woods", marries two topics, the hunt and the pastoral (the movement "Les Chasseresses" has been cited above), so we may assume that the passage in question refers to the pastoral topic, as well as "transporting us into the forest". It ends with the coming of day, expressed with a musical sunrise. The pastoral horn, then, may also have a nocturnal reference.

Another example comes from a work that declares its pastoral character more explicitly. The slow movement of Vaughan Williams's Symphony no. 3, the *Pastoral*, presents a soft and slow horn melody over an unmoving low string chord, a very typical effect (fig. 7.11). Later, this movement is especially interesting in making much of the seventh harmonic, both of natural trumpet and natural horn, which is not normally used as it is very audibly flat (in C, 969 cents, about halfway between B flat, 1000 cents in equal temperament, and A, 900 cents).

Natural horn in F (written)
molto tranquillo

p   *non pp*

Figure 7.12.

Later in the movement a natural trumpet in E flat plays a cadenza, *senza misura*, which is by no means military in character, and in which the seventh harmonic (here written as B flat) is touched on again and again. This melody is repeated at the end on a natural horn in F, *molto tranquillo* (fig. 7.12). The effect in performance is extremely strange.

The chroniclers tell us that Vaughan Williams thought not of pastoralism or of strangeness, however, but of a real experience during the First World War. "Lodged in the composer's mind was a recollection of camp life with the R.A.M.C. [Royal Army Medical Corps] at Bordon in Hampshire where the bugler hit the seventh as a missed shot for the octave" (Howes 1954, 23). This engaging detail does not explain the evocation of the natural horn; no listener to this tranquil, meditative movement, presumably, would think of a bugler in an army barracks. But the seventh harmonic—or at least its "corrected" version, played on the valve horn—is common in pastoral evocations, like the Delibes example just mentioned. It is even suggested that Vaughan Williams's grotesquerie is a kind of double metaphor: the plangent seventh harmonic sounds primitive, immemorial, as though echoing from a distant time when simple huntsmen and shepherds knew nothing of the tuned diatonic scale. But of course, these simple musicians would not have possessed a horn capable of overblowing any harmonics at all; this passage can be played only on an instrument capable of at least the tenth harmonic. Actually, it may simply recall the alphorn, a very ancient instrument indeed, and its association with the *ranz des vaches*.

There is no suggestion of the alphorn in Honegger's *Pastorale d'Eté* of 1920. This movement for small orchestra is particularly topic-governed, however. The opening pastoral horn solo is accompanied by a suggestion of "forest murmurs", over a stationary (if not droning) bass, and later there is birdsong on flute and clarinet.

It was suggested that the horn solo from *Sylvia* contained an evocation of the night, a very different reference from that of the hunting horn, which indicated the morning, as has been shown. Another specific evocation of the night is found in Berlioz's *Roméo et Juliette*. In the love scene, which is a purely instrumental number in this work, the exquisite cantilena of horn in D and cellos evokes a "nuit sereine—le jardin de Capulet, silencieux et désert", a peaceful night in the Capulet garden, silent and deserted.

Another nocturnal evocation is to be found in Mendelssohn's incidental music to Shakespeare's play *A Midsummer Night's Dream*. Shakespeare sets the play mostly in "a wood near Athens", and the time of day is made clear.

To-morrow night, when Phoebe doth behold
Her silver visage in the watery glass,
Decking with liquid pearl the bladed grass,
A time that lovers' flights doth still conceal . . . (act 1, scene 1)

This is, moreover, a *magic* wood, full of fairies and sprites led by their king and queen, Oberon and Titania. The darkness of the nocturnal forest, with its un-tracked mysteries, is an apt context for magic. Nevertheless, the play is classified as a pastoral by an authority on the genre, Richard Cody, who writes of "a conscious community which exists among Poliziano . . . , Tasso . . . , and Shakespeare in 'A Midsummer-Night's Dream'" (Cody 1969, 14).

Thus, in Mendelssohn's *Nocturne,* the solo horn in E combines all these evoca-tions, the forest, the night, and the supernatural, which now appear to be aspects of the pastoral horn. This was, perhaps, the first evocative cantilena for solo horn; it had many successors, most of them in instrumental works where the associations have unfortunately been overlooked.

Another early Romantic horn solo is precisely associated with magic: it opens Weber's opera *Oberon,* a piece which shares some of its characters and situations with *A Midsummer Night's Dream.* Sir Huon, the hero, is given a magic horn to assist him in his quest to rescue the lovely Reiza from captivity (it is later lost in the sea). It is well known that magic instruments were a popular ingredient in Viennese *Singspiele* in the late eighteenth century: as well as a magic flute, there was a magic bassoon and a magic zither. But this magic horn of 1826 has a particular impor-tance, because a particular magic horn—*Des Knaben Wunderhorn*—became one of the dominant formative themes of German Romanticism. This collection of Ger-man "folk" poetry by Achim von Arnim and Clemens Brentano came out between 1806 and 1809. It contains verse of many kinds, of course, but the opening poem, which gives the collection its name, tells of a magic horn. A handsome youth rides up to the castle of the Empress, to present her with a magnificent horn, the gift of a sea-nymph.

A horn was in his hands,
Enringed with golden bands.

With many a precious stone
The costliest ever known,
Rubies and pearls were there;
It made the people stare.

From elephant that horn
So splendidly was born,
So beautiful a thing;
And overall a ring.

With silver gleam it shone;
And many bells thereon,
Of finest gold enwrought,
From deepest ocean brought. . . .

Then spoke the lovely youth:
"I tell a wondrous truth:
O touch that horn so featly,
O touch that horn so featly—

And all the bells shall ring,
The horn with joy shall sing,
No harp was e'er so bright
Nor maiden's voice so light. . . .

O touch that horn so featly,
And hear it sound so sweetly!"

It would seem that the magic horn was an *oliphant,* made from an elephant's tusk, the most expensive kind of medieval signaling horn. But for all its great value, it would have sounded just a single note. Nevertheless, its "Süssen hell Geklinge" resounds through many ravishing orchestral melodies, played on a brass horn with a complex valve system.

The enormous popularity and prestige of the *Knaben Wunderhorn* collection may have reinforced the magic evocation of the horn. At any rate, the solo horn in the nineteenth century, playing a fragrant cantilena with a soft accompaniment, turned into a signifier quite separate from the hunting horn; the new topic may be called the *horn of nocturnal mystery.*

There is a faint air of sadness and regret about many of its appearances; the poetic opening horn solo in Bruckner's Fourth Symphony, the *Romantic,* is a memorable example. This may be associated with a very ancient tradition. When the hero Roland was cornered by Saracens in the pass of Roncevaux in the Pyrenees (the year was 778), he is said to have blown his horn (like the *Wunderhorn,* an oliphant) to inform his master, Charlemagne, of his plight. But no help came, and Roland's whole squadron, including its greatest knights and Roland himself, was slaughtered. This sad story was known throughout French history and is the subject of an elegiac poem by Alfred de Vigny, *Le Cor* (1826). "The writer evokes the dismal sound of a horn reverberating in the stark mountain passes and wonders whether the ghosts of the knights slain at Roncevaux ever return" (Redman 1991, 80). At the close of his elegy, Vigny exclaims, "Dieu! que le son du cor est triste au fond des bois!" (Lord! how sad is the sound of the horn in the depths of the woods!) The poet seems to echo a French folksong, "Le son du cor":

Le son du cor
Exprime encore
La plainte et les regrets,
Quand son soupir
Fait retentir
L'écho de nos forêts.

The sound of the horn expresses our laments and regrets, when its sigh echoes in our forests.

This lyric was set to music, in a German translation, by Friedrich Silcher ("Wie lieblich schallt durch Busch und Wald", 1816; see Redman 1991, 79–80, 227). Later, the poet Jules Laforgue evoked "Les cors, les cors, les cors mélancoliques, mélancoliques" (in *L'Hiver qui Vient*). Night, mystery, and sadness come together in this most Romantic of expressions, which may also have connections with medieval lore.

The horn of nocturnal mystery is heard in the second subject of Dvořák's Cello Concerto, where the context of national themes suggests a pastoral atmosphere; in the slow movement of Tchaikovsky's Fifth Symphony, perhaps more languid and nocturnal; and even in the opening of Brahms's Second Piano Concerto. A cold northern forest, ubiquitous in Sibelius's music, is strongly suggested by the horn solo at the start of the Fifth Symphony. There are countless examples.

It may be objected that the entry of the horn into the ranks of the orchestra's melodic soloists was brought about not by a need to express elegy and mystery, but merely by the invention of the valve mechanism, which made it possible. This is a vain objection; the valve mechanism was, perhaps, needed to meet the demand of the developing musical topic, and of course it made many other things possible, like the bleating of chromatic sheep in Strauss's *Don Quixote* (who would guess they were horns?). Yet Mendelssohn's melody can almost be played on a natural horn in E. It seems clear that the frequent manifestation of the mysterious, poetic horn in Romantic music has much to do with its evocations of magic, darkness, and the forest. Stoelzel's two lever-valves (1815), and later the four valves of the chromatic double horn, facilitated this. The Romantics dreamed, but their dreams were aided by technology.

We have come a long way from the hunt *parforce de chiens*. Yet the course we have followed is clear. The hunt was exotopic, and took place in the forest. The danger and gloom of the forest gave a sinister and threatening sensation (we remember Mime's vain efforts to scare Siegfried), and this made people think of sorcery and mystery, and perhaps of sadness and regret for the calamities that might befall therein. Yet the forest was also a place of innocence, a limitless space where men could be free and alone like Virgil's shepherds. All of this complex narrative is packed into the Romantic horn of nocturnal mystery.

(c) Britten's four horns

In conclusion, some of the many-sided evocations of the hunting horn can be illustrated from a single work, Britten's *Serenade for Tenor, Horn, and Strings*, Op. 31, first performed in 1943 with the soloists Peter Pears and Dennis Brain. Britten was peculiarly sensitive to topical reference; he writes for Brain a horn part that is a virtual anthology of topical significations, embracing at least four types.

The work begins and ends with an invocation for horn alone. With its open fifths and fourths it sounds unquestionably pastoral (fig. 7.13a) and suggests the *ranz des vaches* (fig. 7.13c). Britten specifies that the whole passage be "played on natural harmonics", and he prominently includes the seventh harmonic (fig. 7.13b).

(a)

Figure 7.13.

All these features suggest pastoralism rather than the mysterious and nocturnal side of the horn.

These other sides are prominent in the later "Elegy", a setting of Blake's *The Sick Rose* from the *Songs of Experience*.

> O Rose, thou art sick!
> The invisible worm,
> That flies in the night,
> In the howling storm,
>
> Has found out thy bed
> Of crimson joy;
> And his dark secret love
> Does thy life destroy.

There is no attempt to suggest the storm. Instead, the string orchestra throbs quietly on a bleak fifth, E–B, while the horn plays an intense *espressivo*, a chromatic cantilena composed entirely of *pianti*, mournful falling semitones (fig. 7.14). Although the layout resembles Honegger's *Pastorale d'Eté*, described above, pastoral sentiments have now flown away; the horn's mystery, at first a metonym from the forest in which the horn was played, now hints at the dark labyrinth of the mind, the death of innocence in the face of experience and sin. Both Blake and Britten are concerned with darkness, the dark night of the soul.

Last in the cycle comes Ben Jonson's radiant invocation of the moon as "queen and huntress". Britten's "Hymn" naturally seizes on the reference to hunting, and returns to the horn of the Marquis de Dampierre, in 6/8 meter, *leggiero*, the pizzicato accompaniment perhaps recalling the hooves of the riders (fig. 7.15). The

Andante appassionato ($\quad$ ($\quad$) = 42)

Figure 7.14.

Presto e leggiero ($\quad$ = 168-176)

Figure 7.15.

sharp fourth reminds us that the eleventh harmonic is sharp (almost exactly half-way between B flat and B in equal temperament, as sounding on a horn in F).

It seems odd that this analysis has overlooked two earlier movements, since they are respectively called "Pastoral" and "Nocturne". But Britten is elusive; the first of these, a setting of Cotton's "The day's grown old, the fainting sun", with all its pastoral references ("the little, little flock"), illustrates *evening* more strongly than pastoral sentiment. The horn is not topically equipped to evoke the evening (the right time for a "serenade", to be sure), though its range of expression includes both morning and night. Brain therefore repeatedly plays gentle descending triads, setting comfortably with the sun in a gesture of simple madrigalism.

The "Nocturne" is one of Britten's paradoxes, for there is no suggestion of the nocturnal horn. The text is from Tennyson's *The Princess*.

> The splendour falls on castle walls
> And snowy summits old in story:
> The long light shakes across the lakes,
> And the wild cataract leaps in glory.
> Blow, bugle, blow, set the wild echoes flying,
> Blow, bugle; answer, echoes, dying, dying, dying.

Later the poet conjures that most famous couplet about the horn, which I have already invoked in an earlier discussion of Respighi.

p *accel.* *rit.* Figure 7.16.

> O sweet and far from cliff and scar
> The horns of Elfland faintly blowing!

With all its technical deftness and romantic fragrance, this poem is at a lower emotional temperature from the Blake that follows it. Britten elects to use the horn for one purpose only: to become a substitute bugle, and to imitate military calls. It is a foreshadowing of the *War Requiem,* where the whole brass department gets to illustrate Wilfrid Owen's line, "Bugles sang, saddening the evening air", and in the process to suggest that the bugles of the First World War were a foretaste of the *tuba mirum.* The elfin bugle of the *Serenade* (fig. 7.16) should be compared with the bugle call on soft solo horn in the *War Requiem,* answered by fantastic curling echoes on flute, clarinet, and oboe.

Thus, the horn of the *Serenade for Tenor, Horn, and Strings* is, topically, four instruments: the horn as poetic substitute for the bugle, the horn of the huntsman, the pastoral horn, and the horn of nocturnal mystery. Such was the expressive range of the horn and its music, even in the mid-twentieth century.

Part Three.   *Soldiers*

8   The Military Signifier:
1. The March

(a) Marching in step

The ubiquity of military evocations in our music betokens a wide-ranging, varied, and very complex topic. As for the signifier, the two main aspects—the military march and the trumpet call—each has its own history, though they are closely intertwined. The signification of the military topic, also, is complex, since the traditional myth of the heroic warrior was moderated by a realistic knowledge of contemporary soldiers. It will be necessary to survey first the signifier, however.

"Without the march, military music is unthinkable. The two are inseparably bound together. . . . It is the purest and truest music of the soldiers . . . [with] its purpose, to regulate the steps and raise the spirits of the soldiers" (Panoff 1938, 141). The image of a band on foot, playing for a squadron of troops marching in step, is our idea of the march. The march tells of heroism and victory. This comes through strongly when composers tell us that we are hearing a march, as in Wagner's *Huldigungsmarsch* or Elgar's *Pomp and Circumstance* marches. Even when no title is presented, in the slow movement of Schubert's "Great C major" Symphony or the scherzo of Tchaikovsky's "Pathétique", it is easy to recognize the rhythm and sentiment of the march.

Yet most of the familiar associations of the march are modern. Armies did not march in step, at least in Germany and Britain, until the eighteenth century. March tunes were not played in time with marching troops, anyway; they were originally ceremonial pieces, played by small ensembles in a rather sedate style. When early writers speak of the march, they usually mean a drum rhythm beaten as a command to march—in other words a *signal*. Until very late (the last decade of the eighteenth century, for the Prussian army) troops marched, mainly, to the beat of the drum, or without any accompaniment. And again, not all marches were military; marches were played by civilian bands, to accompany state occasions, entries into cities, proclamations, and assemblies. The military march as a signifier of armies on the march, of heroism and victory, is therefore a relatively modern feature, as is the Dampierre-style hunting-horn call.

Admittedly, marching in step was known from a very early date. According to Duffy, it had been "characteristic of the Swiss and the landsknechts [mercenaries] during the Renaissance, and the Dutch and Swedes in the 'pike and shot' era of the early seventeenth century" (Duffy 1987, 111). This is questioned by Panoff; "We cannot think in terms of modern marching in step," he surmises. "The landsknechts knew little of that. The column did not march on the same foot or with

(a)

(b)

Figure 8.1.

the same step, as the skirling musicians seemed to decree. . . . Perhaps they set off on the left foot, but each man subsequently changed the step as it suited him. The drumbeat must have merely set the speed of the march and preserved a certain order" (Panoff 1938, 30).

Marching in step, however, was described in detail, with its drum accompaniment, by Arbeau in the sixteenth century, though the minuteness of his description suggests that it was not especially familiar. The accompanying drum rhythm is a simple repetitive figure in common time, which he writes as five minims (fig. 8.1a; fig. 8.1b shows a modern equivalent).

> During the sounding and beating of these five minims and three rests the soldier makes one step, i.e. he steps and extends his two legs such that on the first note, he places and sets down his left foot, and during the other three notes, he lifts the right foot and places and sets it down on the fifth note, and during the three rests which are equivalent to three notes, he again lifts his left foot to begin another step as before. (Arbeau 1588, quoted by Hofer 1988, 69)

As well as this simple beat of five equal notes, Arbeau lists other rhythms, all of them literally repeated every two or four beats. The accompanying drum was sometimes joined by fifes (small transverse flutes) playing in unison.

Some military writers positively rejected this style as unwarlike. Francis Markham, in *Fife Decades and Epistles of Warre* (London, 1622), reports a view that men should not be "so nice or curious in the beatings of the drumme, proportioning the body, legges, head, hands and every motion so exactly to every stroke or doubling of the drumme." There were, of course, numbers called "march" in keyboard and lute music, as we shall recount below, but these may have nothing whatever to do with the military.

In Germany and Britain, soldiers marched quickly or slowly, the order being given by a drum, but we cannot assume that the soldiers' steps were synchronized. "Our owne [marches are] swift or slow as he shal be directed by the Dromme Major of the regiment" (Leonard Digges, *An Arithmetical Warlike Treatise,* London, 1590, 85; quoted by Hofer 1988, vol. 1, 61). Sometimes it is not clear whether writers are referring to the command signal, or to the march itself. "March: to open order in rank, shouldere muskets and pikes, and direct your march either quicker or slower, according to the beat of the drum" (William Bariffe, *Military Discipline, or the Young Artillery Man,* 1643; quoted by Hofer 1988, vol. 1, 67).

PLATE 1. French hussar of the Napoleonic period (painting by François Fleming). Note the pelisse, slung over the left shoulder and hanging down the back; the *sabretache*, hanging almost to the man's ankles; the sword dragging along the ground. *Used by permission of Peter Newark's Military Pictures.*

PLATE 2. Antoine Watteau, *The Shepherds* (ca. 1719). Schloss Charlottenburg, Berlin. The peasant character of the scene is contradicted by the pastel satins and lawn of the costumes. The girl's dress is gold, her sash sky-blue; the man wears silver breeches and a cherry jacket. The painting is an essay on love. *Used by permission of Stiftung Preußische Schlösser und Gärten Berlin-Brandenburg.*

PLATE 3. Bartolomeo Pinelli, *Shepherd Musicians Before a Shrine* (1807), detail. Watercolor: Florence, Uffizi. The two instruments, especially the zampogna, are portrayed rather inaccurately. *Used by permission of the Soprintendenza Speciale per il Polo Museale Fiorentino, Gabinetto Fotografico (017).*

PLATE 4. Player of the double *aulós*. Red-figure painting on a drinking bowl, ca. 480 B.C. The two instruments make a V-shape as held by the player. *Staatliche Antikensammlungen und Glyptothek München.*

PLATE 5. Titian, *The Three Ages of Man*, detail. The two instruments held by the young woman make obvious reference to the double *aulós*, but they are actually recorders. *Duke of Sutherland Collection, on loan to the National Gallery of Scotland.*

PLATE 6. The angel's visitation to the shepherds. From the Book of Hours of Jeanne d'Evreux (fourteenth century). *Metropolitan Museum of Art, The Cloisters Collection, 1954 (54.1.2), New York.*

Bagpiper, enlarged from Plate 6. The instrument has a chanter, but is without drone pipes.

PLATE 7. Pieter Bruegel the elder, *Dance of the Peasants* (ca. 1568). The bagpipe as a peasant instrument. There are two immense drones and a single chanter, and the cheeks are blown out, the eyes half-closed, by the effort of blowing it. The dancing is heavy and clumsy. *Used by permission of the Kunsthistorisches Museum, Vienna.*

Marching in step took a very long time to establish itself across Europe; its introduction into Germany by Prince Leopold I of Anhalt-Dessau, around 1700, was only the beginning of a long process. It was promoted, in the middle of the century, by Marshal Saxe and Frederick the Great, and adopted by the British army in 1748. By the time of the Seven Years War (1756–63) it was everywhere established on the parade ground, though even then it probably did not last long on the battlefield (see Duffy 1987, 111–112).

(b) Early bands and marches

The term "march", originally meaning a maneuver, was metonymically applied to the drum or trumpet signal that commanded the movement. It did not, in the first place, apply to a musical number. The earliest musical marches date from the mid-seventeenth century. Some modern collections, however, present marches of the landsknechts—mercenary soldiers—of the sixteenth century, but these collections were all compiled and written down in the Romantic period. Their authenticity is dubious.

In fact, the "military march" as a genre is first noticed in the eighteenth century; especially after the French Revolution, marches were distinguished for various evocations and purposes. Gossec wrote a "Marche Lugubre", a "Marche Religieuse", a "Marche Victorieuse", and a "Marche Funèbre" (Hofer 1993, 42–43). The term "marche militaire" then yielded its German equivalent *Militärmarsch*.

It seems that the earliest marches—in the sense of musical numbers—are art music rather than military pieces. This, according to Hofer, explains the sudden appearance of marches for the military; army marches were copied from a repertoire of domestic and chamber music, just as the hunting horn was, perhaps, carried out from the theater on to the hunting field.

The first collections of march arrangements, in the sense of musical numbers for ensemble, are those of Philidor and Lully in the France of Louis XIV, composed for a band of shawms, pommers, and dulcians, and preserved in the Bibliothèque Nationale. They are not distinguished as "military", although some of them are clearly intended for army units. One of these marches, Lully's "La Marche Française", is partly shown as figure 8.2a. It is a sedate piece, but there are also dance-like marches, like the "Marche des Dragons du Roy", which resembles a bourrée (fig. 8.2b). These items were not suitable for actual marching, of course; this is illustrated by occasional changes of time signature; in the "Marche des Fussillier", the interposing of a 3/2 measure would infuriatingly wrong-foot any marching troops (fig. 8.2c).

The German regiments established similar oboe bands between 1680 and 1720, and Flemming (1726) tells us that the normal band consisted of "zwey Discante, zwey la Taillen, und zwey Bassons". This was the type of wind ensemble, without percussion, which was afterward called *Harmonie*. Its purpose, according to Flemming, was not to control the march but to "cheer up" (*aufmuntern*) the soldiers (Rameis 1976, 17).

The little six-piece military band, consisting chiefly of oboes, without percus-

Figure 8.2.

sion, was standard for the infantry unit of the early eighteenth century. Flemming tells us that it was augmented in Saxony with two horns, in Brandenburg-Prussia and England by a trumpeter "on foot" (that is, not mounted, since trumpeters normally served the cavalry; Rameis 1976, 17). An Austrian illustration of about 1725 shows a band of this type, with horns and a trumpet; it seems that the players are not marching—or if they are, they are not in step (fig. 8.3).

The earliest known manuscript march collection specifically meant for military use, ten marches of the Saxon Electoral Army (1729), contains arrangements for two oboes, two horns, and bassoon. Quite clearly, such a group would be useless for controlling the march; its modest tones would not be heard over the sound of marching feet, especially at the distant end of the column. Most of the marches are like contemporary Italian opera, and do not lend themselves to playing on the march. The intrusion of syncopes and echo effects suggests concert performance: part of the tenth march from this series is shown in figure 8.4.

This brings us to a paradox: if march tunes were to be used to accompany real marching, they would need the weight of trumpets and drums, yet the earliest ensembles of trumpets and drums were affiliated to the cavalry, who, of course, could not march in step. Military and court trumpeters were musicians of high standing, and would not wish to lower themselves to playing with the infantry. This will be explained later in the section. There was thus a class distinction that kept the trum-

Figure 8.3.

Figure 8.4.

pet out of infantry use until the eighteenth century; in its capacity as a signaling instrument, the trumpet has *never* been adopted by the infantry.

The chief genre of the mounted trumpets was the "flourish" or "fanfare", which was normally improvised. This is described in the next chapter. The word "fanfare" came eventually to mean any piece for trumpets, even the solo signal; indeed, it was also used for the signals of the hunting horn. But the cavalry trumpeters, like the oboists of the infantry, might play ensemble arrangements of marches. Part of a "Marche Royale" for three trumpets and drums is shown in figure 8.5, taken from the same French collection mentioned earlier. The style is reminiscent of the improvised fanfares described by Bendinelli (see chapter 9). Naturally, the cavalry march was not for marching, but was a ceremonial piece.

(c) The "Turkish music"

The introduction of percussion instruments into the military band came about through Turkish influence. The encounter of European culture with the Ottoman military ensemble had a political origin. The second siege of Vienna by the Turks (1683) was decisively repulsed, marking the end of Turkish power in Europe after several centuries of aggressive advance. The European terror of the "Grande Turke", conceived as a brutal and dangerous warmonger, began to give way to a fascination with Turkish styles of dress, decoration, and music. At the same time,

Figure 8.5.

Turkish society, chastened by its military setbacks, started to adopt European manners. French clothing, furniture, and architecture were imitated.

A period of political engagement with Europe now began. Ambassadors were sent to European courts. At the same moment when the Ottomans ceased to be a real threat, Europe began to see them as picturesque orientals, barbaric rather than barbarians (this account based on Shaw 1976 and McCarthy 1997).

After the failure of the Vienna siege, the sultan presented to the emperor a Turkish military band or *mehter*. This noisy ensemble was a stock-in-trade of the janissaries, slave soldiers who had been seized as young boys from Christian families, raised as Moslems, and commited to celibate service of the state. *Mehter*s were not entirely unknown in Europe before this date; a Turkish envoy to the court of Vienna entered the city through the Kärtnertor in 1665 to the accompaniment of a full mehter. A band had been presented to King John Sobieski of Poland in 1673 (this ensemble visited Dresden in 1697). Later Russia acquired a band (in 1725). Other courts constructed artifical Turkish bands; the Berlin mehter was manned by local musicians, with the addition of a few Africans.

The mehter, partly marching and partly mounted, was a different kind of military band from the little European *Harmonie*. With penetrating reed instruments and powerful brass and drums, it was deafening. Based on the *zurna*, a conical oboe, and the *boru*, a single-wound natural trumpet, it contained an impressive display of percussion, notably the *davu*, a two-headed drum held across the body and played on both heads, the *nakkare*, small kettledrums, and the *zil*, pairs of cymbals held horizontally or sometimes vertically. The *cagana* or "Turkish crescent" (a frame held upright and carrying many little bells; it was also called "bell tree" and "jingling Johnny") was characteristic as well. The largest instrument was the *kos*, a copper single-headed drum, sometimes played on horseback, with a drum at each side of the player (Jäger 1996, 1318–1319).

Where true Turkish instruments were not available in the European centers, they were copied with the use of bass drum, large cymbals, tambourine, and tri-

118 *Soldiers*

angle. This produced the kind of ensemble heard in Haydn's "Military" Symphony and the march in *Die Entführung aus dem Serail*. There developed, as is well known, a whole *alla turca* topic, which lasted for about seventy years from 1760 and is excellently described by Matthew Head (2000). Turkish items appeared in opera and concert, and "Turkish" stops were introduced on the harpsichord. But most important to us is the adoption of a heavy percussion section in the military band, which was called "Turkish music". Though real Turkish bands used small drums (the davu and nakkare) as well as the mighty kos, the military snare drum was at first excluded from European bands because it was established as a *signaling* instrument in the West. Kettledrums were used, though not as a standard component, as they were, of course, cavalry instruments in the West, and the "Turkish music" was an *infantry* phenomenon in Europe. The bass drum was considered the essence of Turkish percussion.

Paradoxically, as this Turkish influence came to bear on the European military scene, successive sultans were trying to destroy the janissaries. They were dissolved in 1826. In 1828 Giuseppe Donizetti (brother of the composer) was brought to Istanbul to create a European-style band.

Naturally, the little oboe bands of the Western military were overpowered by this powerful battery, and they were quickly augmented. The clarinet, a new instrument, was added along with flutes, trumpets, and more oboes. By the end of the century, there were piccolo, contrabassoon, trombones, and serpents; in the early nineteenth century, bands had been enlarged to 25–30 players (Rameis 1976, 19–20). They were to expand beyond this. A great French parade of 1833 deployed a band of 88 clarinets, 12 flutes, 10 oboes, 20 horns, 20 trumpets, 16 trombones, 18 bassoons, 15 ophicleides, 22 bombardons, 3 kettledrummers, 2 bass drums, and 6 side-drummers, 232 players in all (Kastner 1848, 317–318). A military commission was given the task in 1845 of reforming French military music. It judged the ideal band to contain 74 players; there should be at least 55 players in an infantry band, 36 in the cavalry, and 36 in the chasseurs (Kastner 1848, 262–282). Such were the "Turkish" bands of nineteenth-century Europe. They were amply able to accompany marching troops. They typified the military topic for Romantic composers.

(d) The pace of marching

These bands were now used to accompany marching troops. In fact, it seems that the Turkish percussion instruments were at first *only* used on the march; when bands played for ceremonial purposes, they reverted to the traditional sound of the *Harmonie*.

It is possible to ascertain the speed of eighteenth-century marching troops. Early in the century the "ordinary march" was as slow as 60 to 80 steps to the minute. Hofer gives evidence that in 1759 the "common step" in the British army, and probably in Germany also, was 60 steps to the minute; there was also a "quick step" of double this, 120 to the minute. In 1778 a Prussian drill manual specified 75 to the minute, and in 1788 a quicker march, the *Deployirschritt*, later called *Geschwindschritt*, was introduced at 108 to the minute. By 1786 the British march had

Figure 8.6.

increased to 70 to the minute, quickening further to 75 by 1794 (Hofer 1988, 481). It has been considered that the quick march was imported into Germany from Britain, but this is now questioned. The modern quick march (the standard march is quick nowadays) is between 100 and 120 steps per minute.

The French march was also originally slow. A document in Darmstadt (called *Ordonnance pour la Mussique de la Legion Corsse 1772*) gives the *pas ordinaire* at 70 to the minute, the *pas de route* at 90, and the *pas redoublé* at a very fast 140. The same manuscript gives examples of "redoublé" marches, some in 6/8 time.

A later Austrian commentator, Joseph Fahrbach (*Organizzazione della Musica Militare Austriaca*, 1845) declares that there are three tempi, the *Ordinair-Marsch*, at 95 steps to the minute, the *Manövrier-Marsch*, 108 to the minute, and the *Dopplier-Marsch*, at 120 to the minute (Rameis 1976, 127).

Quantz, in his book on flute playing (1752), instructs that "a march should be played solemnly. If it is in alla breve meter or bourrée rhythm, two pulses [*Pulsschläge*] come in each measure" (quoted by Hofer 1988, 482). It is clear that some marches require four steps to each measure, others only two, and composers, with some regularity, indicate the latter with the split common signature (¢) or with a 2/4 marking. But they are not consistent, and they never specifically identify their tunes as quick marches or *pas ordinaire*. It is sometimes difficult to guess which is intended. This is an important matter, for when concert composers use the march rhythm, they presumably echo a contemporary march type. This will be discussed a little later.

Most of the documents that give us tempi for the march are drill manuals; that is, they speak of marching soldiers, not of music. As the eighteenth century progressed it became normal to play marches for actual marching, so the speed of the music, considered by Quantz, and that of the drill, specified in military manuals, become one and the same. Hofer considers that the spread of the quick march necessitated the composition of a whole new repertoire. Some eighteenth-century marches do, indeed, lend themselves to the quicker tempo, as shown by a tune preserved in Darmstadt, which sounds effective at 100 steps to the minute, 4 steps per measure. Its authorship is attributed to Princess Anna Amalie of Prussia (fig. 8.6). Other marches sound quick from the musical standpoint, but at the marching speeds of the day could only have been played for the *pas ordinaire;* for instance, a "Marche Turke", in the Berlin library, which, in spite of its signature (and its name!) would probably have been played *alla breve*, with two steps to the measure, 75 steps to the minute (fig. 8.7).

This last example shows a feature which became common: the presentation of a fanfare-like unison before the main tune begins. This is a survival of the command signal; even before the time of marching in step, infantry moved off in re-

Figure 8.7.

(a)

etc.

(b)

etc.

Figure 8.8.

sponse to a drum signal that determined roughly the speed of the step. With the developments in marching, and the introduction of the bugle as a signaling instrument, the pace of the march was precisely indicated by the prefacing signal.

Thus, some drill manuals—notably those of the Imperial armies—specified exact tempos for signals. An *Exercier-Reglement* of the nineteenth century (in Rameis 1976, 182–194) specifies "115 steps per minute" for the drummer's *Generalmarsch,* other commands being played "in march tempo". The trumpet *Beschleunigung,* the command "to order the speeding up of an activity", was played at 125 steps to the minute; the *Laufschritt* (running step) of the infantry proceeded at 160 steps to the minute. Even calls that did not command movement, like the *Ganzer Ruf* or the *Retraite,* were marked "etwas langsamer als im Marschtempo", somewhat slower than march tempo.

British manuals of military signals were extremely precise about tempos. The 1909 list of "Trumpet and Bugle Sounds" distinguishes the marching speeds of different regiments; the first brigade of Foot Guards marched at 106 to the minute, the Fourth Hussars at 108. More important still, battle calls were played much faster than parade calls: the "Charge", for example, at 160 to the minute.

Thus, the short triadic signal prefacing the march originally had an important

Figure 8.9.

function. It appears in a very early Prussian grenadiers' march (fig. 8.8a, from Panoff 1938, 142, based on Kastner), and in a march by G. von Pirch, preserved in
Berlin (fig. 8.8b). With the enlargement of military bands, the trumpets were often
used to blow fanfares in the midst of the texture, as they do in the aria "Non più
andrai" from *Figaro*. A fine "March for a German Volunteer Corps" by F. X. Süss-
mayr, preserved in the British Library and arranged for two oboes, two clarinets,
two horns, trumpet, and bassoon, illustrates this (fig. 8.9). The prefacing signal is
echoed in *Eine kleine Nachtmusik* and in Schubert's *Marche Militaire*, Op. 51 no. 1.
One is sometimes aware that the first strain of a march tune is itself akin to a signal;
the modern *Florentiner Marsch* of Julius Fučik (fig. 8.12) and Kenneth J. Alford's
march *The Standard of St. George* begin with tunes of this kind. They bear witness
to the kinship of the march and the military signal.

(e) Modern bands and their marches

It is usually considered that the French Revolution caused a change in military music, and that our modern bands date essentially from this period. The little
oboe ensemble—the *Harmonie*—quitted the parade ground and was restricted to
chamber music. Meanwhile, military bands grew larger, with the introduction of
instruments like the serpent, bass horn, ophicleide, bombardon, cornet, and flugel
horn. The new enlarged bands could march in step with the music; their chief tasks
were now to play for parades and social occasions, but also to give public concerts
in the street, in parks, and on promenades. "Military music left the barracks and
went out to the people" (Panoff 1938, 140). Already, the signifier was mingling with
the signified, and military bands became a means of invoking the cultural myth
of soldierly splendor, as well as merely a part of military life. They played marches,
but were also acquiring an extensive repertoire of arrangements: symphonies, overtures, serenades, selections from operas, and music of all kinds. The practical aspect of military music might even fall away, leaving the band to evoke an imaginary
army; John Philip Sousa, having been conductor of the U.S. Marine Band, resigned
in 1892 to form his own concert band, which later toured the world.

This new "orchestral" band was rendered more flexible by technological im-
provements, notably the introduction of valves on the trumpet and horn and later
the invention of the euphonium and the family of saxhorns. The way was led by
the fruitful co-operation of J. G. Moritz, a Berlin instrument-maker, and the bandmaster Wilhelm Wieprecht, an opera musician who was put in charge of the band

of the Berlin Guard Dragoon Regiment. Eventually he became Director of Music of the Guard Army Corps, comprising cavalry, infantry, and artillery regiments. This talented Prussian arranger developed a large band of mixed keyed and valved instruments, directing Moritz to produce appropriate modifications. In 1838 he directed a mass spectacular in Berlin, with 1,197 bandsmen chosen from 32 bands. During the nineteenth century it became established that the best bandmasters came from Germany; many German musicians served faithfully in this capacity in the British army.

But these new bands almost lost touch with army life. Their bandmasters were civilian conservatoire students. To the end of his life, Wieprecht "conducted the band of the regiment in frock coat and cravat" (Murray 1994, 91).

The year 1817 was a vital moment for the development of the military march. It was then that the first large official collection of marches was printed, by authority of King Frederick William III of Prussia: the *Sammlung von Märschen fur türkische Musik zu bestimmten Gebrauch in der Königlich Preussischen Armee* (collection of marches for Turkish bands for the particular use of the Royal Prussian Army). The reference to "Turkish" music merely meant that the arrangements contained parts for percussion. Although it was not issued in score or bound into volumes, but rather in separate parts of each march, there were three sections:

1. Slow marches for infantry
2. Quick marches for infantry
3. Cavalry marches

Part 1 contains *Präsentiermärsche*, marches for the inspection, at 72 steps to the minute; part 2, *Parademärsche*, for the march past, 114 to the minute. Part 3, the cavalry section, contains "marches at 72 for playing at the walk, tunes in the double time of 140 or so for ranking past at the trot, and in rollicking 6/8 for the gallop past" (Murray 1994, 85). In fact, part 3 did not begin to appear until 1824. It is, of course, for brass only, without the oboes and flutes of the *Fusstruppen*. The association of compound time with the cavalry is clearly connected to the topic of the noble horse; 6/8 time is an important ingredient of the equestrian motive, as it is the standard meter of the hunting call. Many modern marches adopt 6/8 meter, notably Sousa's *Washington Post*, an evocation of the messenger "riding post".

The Prussian collection was often reissued and enlarged; by 1914 there was a total of 537 marches. These, then, were the paradigms of the military march for musicians of the nineteenth century. At last, the type of march is specified, quick or slow, and since we know the drill speeds for this period, we can be fairly sure of the tempo of each march, at least those for the infantry. A couple of marches from the original series is shown in figure 8.10.

The military march of the nineteenth century is musically very different from its forebears. It had adopted the reprise form of the dance, with two binary units, the second called "trio". This form was enlarged and varied to give elaborate structures with a variety of melodic ideas. The brilliant color, produced by the large body of brass instruments, and the vigorous rhythm, contributed by the "Turkish" percussion, make the march a stirring, purely musical item. It is, of course, a quick

(a)

(b)

Figure 8.10.

march, but many tunes are scored in a fast *alla breve* time (sometimes in 2/4 time), two steps per measure, with a bass note on every step and accompanying chords dividing the beat in the middle of the texture; the *Radetsky March* of Johann Strauss the elder exemplifies this. With a beat underlined by the heavy weight of bass trombone, ophicleide, and bombardon, supported by the bang and rattle of snare drum and bass drum, the music can acquire a vigorous lift and swing. Typical is Karl Komzák's *Erzherzog Albrecht* march of 1888 (shown in fig. 8.11, without its four-measure introduction). This kind of march is probably paradigmatic for modern audiences. Many of the best-known marches—Carl Teike's *Alte Kameraden*, John Philip Sousa's *Hail to the Spirit of Liberty*, and Kenneth J. Alford's *Colonel Bogey*—are of this type. The style, with its lilting off-beat harmonies, is imitated in a veritable concert number, Chabrier's *Joyeuse Marche*.

The irrepressible, self-sufficient marching rhythm of the new bands made it possible for composers to write trio sections with cantabile melodies, contrasting with the vigorous main section of the march. Many famous marches, notably Sousa's *The Stars and Stripes Forever* and Elgar's *Pomp and Circumstance No. 1*, are chiefly remembered for their trio melodies. Bandmasters sometimes interpret the two parts of the modern march as symbols of war and peace. This may be illustrated from Julius Fučik's *Florentiner March* of ca. 1910, where the first section is like a military signal, the trio a lyric cantabile with answering figures in the countermelody, the swing of the rhythm maintained throughout by a big percussion section (fig. 8.12a,b).

Figure 8.11.

(a) first strain

(b) trio

Figure 8.12.

(f) Other types of march

There are evidently marches not primarily military: funeral marches, wedding marches, marches of priests, huntsmen, pilgrims. We know this mainly from opera scores and incidental music for the stage. In order to understand this, and its relevance to topic theory, we need to know a little about the ensembles of ceremonial musicians of the fifteenth to eighteenth centuries in Europe east of the French border: the German-speaking lands and the Slavic countries.

Aristocratic courts funded groups of *Hoftrompeter*—trumpets and trombones, using modern terminology—and *Hofmusiker,* using a wider variety of instruments including shawms. The trumpeters in these bands were usually guild members, highly paid and splendidly uniformed, and they mostly used broad mouthpieces which made them specialists in the low registers of the instruments. "The broad-sounding, bourdon-like music of the *Hoftrompeterkorps* was considered an acoustic symbol of aristocracy" (Lackner 1993, 101). Some were also *Feldtrompeter,* skilled in playing military signals on parade and on the field of battle. The court bands, in any case, formed the basis of military bands when these became common in the eighteenth century; the *Harmoniemusik,* which has already been described, was the descendant of these groups that were part of the establishments of noble courts, just as military uniform began as the livery of great nobles.

Alongside these bands were the civic ensembles, *Stadtmusikanten,* that included *Turmmusiker* (one of whose duties was to sound signals and alarms from the towers of the city walls) and *Stadtpfeifer,* players usually of several instruments, who might include skill on the trumpet with playing the shawm, cornett, or pommer. Town trumpeters were seldom members of the great national guilds; they were despised by the guild players. There were, it seems, ceremonial wind bands both at court and in the towns, and their repertoires and duties were not dissimilar. According to Detlev Altenburg (a modern musicologist, not the eighteenth-century authority on the trumpet) these included:

1. Military signals, in the case of Feldtrompeter in the court establishments. In civic groups, the corresponding function was *Turmblasen,* signals from the battlements of the city.
2. At court, tournaments, and *Reiterballetten,* grand displays on horseback using trumpets and drums; ceremonial entries of the prince. In town, meetings of the town council and sessions of the law courts.
3. Court and civic balls.
4. Playing for opera and the stage. The *intrada* that begins Monteverdi's *Orfeo* is a splendid reminder of the sound of the *Hoftrompeter.* In civic life, playing for concerts and general musical life.
5. Playing for meals (*Tafelblasen*).
6. Playing in church, normally for special occasions. These might include coronations, baptisms, weddings, masses, Te Deums, and psalm-settings, especially if there were important visitors.
7. Funerals. Brass players normally played with mutes on these occasions (based on Lackner 1997, 82–92, and Lackner 1993, 85–127).

Before the time of the march arrangements of Lully and Philidor, there are some records of march tunes for fifes. The earliest of these are the little melodies quoted by William Bariffe (*Military Discipline, or the Young Artillery Man,* 1643; see Hofer 1988, 90), not called "march", but apparently intended to be played with the drumbeat of the march. In this early period, it must be remembered that "march" in the first place meant a drum or trumpet signal, a command for a column of troops to begin marching. When Fantini (1638) lists the "marciata", he is referring to a trumpet signal, not a musical piece (Baines 1976, 130). There were, however, musical pieces called marches very early in the field of *art* music; the first of these may have been *Thomas King's March* in the Egerton Manuscript (about 1590). There are marches by William Byrd in *My Ladye Nevell's Booke:* "The Earl of Oxford's March" (which reappears in the *Fitzwilliam Virginal Book*), and a sequence called "The Battle" that includes a "March of Footmen" (i.e., infantry), a "March of Horsemen", "The Irish March", and "The March to the Fight". The last of these is in triple time. In the somewhat later *Elizabeth Rogers' Virginal Book* (1656) we find "Sir Thomas Fairfax's march", "The Scots March", and "Prince Rupert's March"; the first two of these are in (editorial) 6/4 time. The numbers in this list that are in 4/4 time—for example "The Earl of Oxford's march"—are perfectly acceptable marching pieces, not much different from the earliest eighteenth-century marches. We may, perhaps, assume that they resemble some of the band music of the time (Hofer 1988, 95, 97).

All these marches come from a period before the column marched in step, of course, if we ignore Thoinot Arbeau's evidence to the contrary. But it emerges from this survey of ceremonial practices before 1700 that the march was not, in the first place, a military phenomenon alone. Assumedly, marches might be played for the entry of a visiting aristocrat, for the procession of the town council, for an orderly processional in church, or for a state funeral. The "military march" that we have been discussing in this chapter was a special case of a general ceremonial style that might be adapted for many different occasions. It may be that we should identify another topic, that of the *processional march*, with references to ceremony, solemnity, or high occasions. This is not primarily a military signification, and so it will not be developed in the present work.

However, the topic of "processional march" is assumedly in play in many operatic marches: marches for priests (in *Die Zauberflöte*), for pilgrims (Berlioz's *Harold in Italy*), for guild leaders (*Die Meistersinger*). Such pieces tend to be slow, as were most marches before about 1770; the *pas ordinaire* might be regarded as a primary ingredient of this amorphous topic.

We may dismiss these types as representing separate genres, however. They are merely the application of a ceremonial style to stately moments in operas and symphonic poems. The wedding march has more pretensions to separate existence. It has famously materialized in Mendelssohn's *Midsummer Night's Dream* incidental music, in Meyerbeer's *Les Huguenots*, in Wagner's *Lohengrin*, and in Grieg's piano piece *Wedding Day at Troldhaugen*. It would be impossible to imagine a group of pieces more different from each other than these. There are no musical determining features of the wedding march. It would also be impossible to invoke the topic "wedding march" in an instrumental piece, sonata or symphony. There is, in fact, no such thing as a wedding march: merely marches provided for fictional weddings.

Only the funeral march remains as a proposed topic. In the seventeenth century, Lackner thinks, it was the preserve of the *Trompeterkorps* and drummers. If a prince had died, "as a sign of national mourning, the trumpets were played exclusively with mutes, while the kettledrums were covered with black cloths" (Lackner 1997, 86). The earliest surviving example, says our authority, is Purcell's march for the funeral of Queen Mary. This is specifically marked "The Queens Funerall March Sounded Before her Chariot". The funeral occurred on 5 March 1695. It is written for four "flat trumpets" (slide trumpets), which makes it possible for Purcell to give the melody to a player specializing in the middle range, where the instrument is more sonorous, instead of the clarino specialist, whose tone would have been more brilliant. Clearly the "bourdon-like" tone of the old brass ensemble is considered apt for funerals. It is basically in C minor (though starting with a C major chord), very simple, homophonic, with only two rhythmic values, and is only fifteen measures in length, a lugubrious piece. One would certainly not recognize it as a march without Purcell's title. Its status as ceremonial music was slightly vitiated by its reuse, later the same year, in the music for a play, *The Libertine*.

After this, the next funeral marches date from the 1790s. There are, of course, marches in operas and oratorios that occur in funereal circumstances, like the *Dead March* in Handel's oratorio *Saul* (1738). If we study this example we find that it is a *pas ordinaire* march in C major, very simple in style. The marking "grave" would give it a tempo of about 60 beats to the minute, the normal *pas ordinaire* pace, with four steps to the measure. There are three trombones and a pair of timpani in the orchestra, which give a "sacred" flavor to the piece. The death of King Saul in the Battle of Mount Gilboa is lamented in this march. Oddly, it is followed by a short instrumental interlude in C minor, chromatic, spasmodic, much more funereal in tone than the march, and then a chorus in the same key, "Mourn, Israel", marked *largo assai*. Presumably, if the composer had wished to compose a funeral march in the modern sense, he would have done so, but there is little to identify this march as anything more than a sedate *pas ordinaire* piece. It is not so much evidence of the existence of the topic "funeral march" at this time, as quite strong evidence for the topic's absence.

There are no "funeral marches" in the military collections of the eighteenth century, but nevertheless slow marches were presumably played at funerals. The turning point seems to come with the first performance of François-Joseph Gossec's *Marche Lugubre*, on 20 September 1790. There had been an army rebellion against Royalist officers in which a number of soldiers had been killed. The Revolutionary government mounted a celebration on the Champ de Mars in memory of "soldier brothers who died for the maintaining of the law".

The novelty of Revolutionary music is less apparent today than it must have seemed at the time. New ceremonies were needed for the religion of Reason and the Supreme Being, and Gossec, above all other composers, provided the music for these; he became "the only real master to be inspired by the Revolution. . . . In the composition of Revolutionary hymns, Gossec scarcely met with rivals of his stature" (Dufrane 1927, 115). Funereal celebrations were a particular cult of the Revolutionaries, and Gossec subsequently wrote a *Marche Funèbre* in E flat for the death of General Hoche (1794), a *Chant Funèbre sur la Mort de Ferraud* (1794), and a *Cantate Funèbre pour la Fête du 20 Prairial An VII* (1799)—not to mention the lost *Chant Funèbre en l'Honneur de Simoneau* (1792). There was a whole genre of revolutionary funeral music; Cherubini wrote a funeral hymn in memory of Hoche, which begins with a slow march in D minor with powerful explosions of the bass drum and soft timpani rolls. It strongly echoes Gossec's *March Lugubre*.

The *Marche Lugubre* had a devastating effect at its first performance. It is a short piece, only 48 measures in length, plus reprises, entirely in D minor, and is almost bereft of melody. Scored for wind and percussion, it begins with soft timpani rolls answered by plaintive phrases for brass, with bass drum. There is a long silence, suddenly interrupted by a crash of the tam-tam and a fortissimo outburst of the full band. It is more an effect than a musical number. Such naked sensationalism was new to music. "The lacerating harmonies, broken up by silences and marked by veiled beats of the tam-tam, truly chilled the public and 'spread a religious terror in the soul,'" proclaimed the *Moniteur*. Another pamphlet, the *Révolutions de Paris*, wrote that "the notes, detached one from another, crushed the heart, dragged out the guts" (Dufrane 1927, 121). The march became a standard at funerals; it was played at the funeral of Mirabeau and even at that of Méhul (1817).

This seems to have set the standard for future funeral marches. Henceforth, these will be concert pieces evoking the grandeur and terror of death, rather than merely slow marches suitable for entries and exits. The Gossec type of gloomy but sensational tone poem is revisited by Berlioz, for example, in his *Marche Funèbre pour la Dernière Scène d'Hamlet* of 1848. This has an offstage chorus, with snare drums, bass drum, cymbals, and tam-tam, and an offstage troop of soldiers who at one point fire their guns.

In the piano repertoire, the *Marcia Funebre Sulla Morte d'un Eroe*, the third movement of Beethoven's Sonata in A flat, Op. 26, resembles Gossec's march only insofar as it has very little melody. It is scored in the irrational key of A flat minor, visibly the tonic minor of the sonata's home key, although it modulates very soon to B major (not C flat major) and D major. Without anything you could call a theme, the piece relies on changing harmonies within the hands that strike out a stately rhythm in thick chords. In the middle section, Gossec's soft timpani rolls and perhaps also the rolling of "kettledrums covered with black cloths" are heard. The piece is manifestly an evocation, not music for use. If the "hero" was Napoleon, as was originally the hero of the *Eroica*, then the connection with post-revolutionary France is reinforced.

Published in 1802, this sonata is contemporaneous with the composition of the *Eroica* funeral march, a much more complex piece. If marched, it would clearly require four steps to the measure, in spite of its 2/4 signature, and it is usually played slower than Beethoven's marking of 80; the natural speed in *adagio assai* seems to be in the region of 70 to 75, firmly in the *pas ordinaire* range. This march is obviously not meant for marching, however. It is extended in a symphonic narrative, embracing a prolonged episode in the major with rippling triplets, and a double fugue based on a related theme. The lengthy coda (at m. 209), after referring to Haydn's Symphony no. 101 in D ("The Clock"), breaks the march tune into tragic shreds. All is noble and affecting; nothing is practicable for marching troops.

However, there are signs of military sentiment: the *military* topic is present, even if we cannot yet acknowledge a topic called "funeral march". And in contrast to Handel there is a self-conscious feeling of tragic solemnity. The drummer's *Wirbelschlag* is repeatedly imitated by the basses (unlike Berlioz, Beethoven had no snare drummers to hand), and the "ritiriton" is heard in the string parts, though not in the parts for horns and trumpets where it might be more at home. Instead, the brass instruments give shape and character to the episodic theme at m. 90, and thus, retrospectively, to the first major-key theme, played by the oboe at m. 69; the trumpets blow a fine cavalry-style signal at m. 96.

But this march is not suitable for practical use. If Napoleon had died and somebody had wanted to use Beethoven's march, it would have needed simplifying. It is, however, part of the new repertoire of overtly grim marches called "funeral march". In other words, "funeral march" is a *signified* of this piece. In the sense that "signifier" has been used in the present work, there is almost no signifier for this topic; it *begins* as an evocation. Naturally, the nineteenth century would see many such funeral marches and would use them for marching to funerals. But the "funeral march" topic was never truly *Gebrauchsmusik*; it was always an evocation. When fully fledged (in the first movement of Mahler's Third Symphony, for example) it feels monumental, immemorial. This is because of its involvement in heroic tragedy, the noble deaths of Roland and Hector, not because of any ancient pedigree of the musical genre. Beethoven's funeral march is similarly involved in a heroic past.

Other famous funeral marches are clearly expressive evocations. Chopin's *Marche Funèbre*, included in the Sonata in B flat minor, Op. 35 (1840; the march dates from 1837), cannot be used for marching as it is a piano piece (though it has been many times orchestrated, and indeed has been marched to). The funeral march on the death of Siegfried in *Götterdämmerung* is an extended symphonic poem, quite unmarchable in any form. If "funeral march" is a topic—a subtopic of "march"—then it is one of those topics that originate, broadly speaking, as expressive habits, not as aspects of social music. And like the "noble horse", it dates from the 1790s.

(g) Concert marches by mainstream composers

It will be noticed that modern troops march to music that is the work of specialists, usually military bandmasters, like Komzák, Fučik, Sousa, and Alford. This was not the case in the eighteenth and early nineteenth centuries. Apart from the marches of Haydn for military *Harmonie* and the many wind marches composed by Mozart, most of which appear as movements in serenades and cassations, Beethoven wrote two marches "for the Czech army", commissioned by the Archduke Anton of Austria (WoO 18 and 19), and J. N. Hummel composed a group of military marches, one of them specified for the artillery corps of the city of Vienna (listed as no. 26 in the Supplement to Sachs's catalogue). F.-J. Gossec, of course, wrote marches for the French Revolutionary armies.

After 1820, mainstream composers wrote less often for actual military use, partly because bands were expanding to include many instruments not normal in the symphony orchestra: cornets and flugelhorns, saxhorns and saxophones, serpents, ophicleides, and bombardons. Instead, composers turned to the writing of marches that were orchestral character pieces, often as a compliment to individual benefactors or to celebrate some notable event. The symphony orchestra could not, of course, march on parade. Admittedly, Wagner's *Huldigungs-Marsch* of 1868, composed as a tribute to King Ludwig II of Bavaria, was written for the military band of the day.

With the separation of concert marches and military pieces, there was also a bifurcation of style. Bandmasters turned almost universally to the *alla breve* type of march already described, with accompanying chords on the weak parts of the measure, like *Erzherzog Albrecht* (fig. 8.11). Concert composers, on the other hand, generally favored the more solemn and heavy-footed rhythm with four steps to the measure.

Berlioz wrote a number of marches, some of them published separately (for ex-

Marschmäßig, anfänglich etwas zurückhaltene

Figure 8.13.

ample, an excerpt from act 1 of *Les Troyens* was published as the *Marche Troyenne,* 1864). Liszt, too, wrote marches, usually for piano solo, though the *Festival March* for Goethe's birthday of 1849 was twice orchestrated (by Conradi and Raff).

Wagner's marches, the *Huldigungsmarsch,* the *Kaisermarsch,* and the *Grosser Festmarsch* of 1876 (this last written for the centenary of American independence) are grand symphonic poems. The *Kaisermarsch* includes a male chorus. The *Huldigungsmarsch,* the only march of the period written for military band by a prominent composer, may serve as a paradigm of these grand ceremonial marches, not intended for parade ground use. It is a slowish, heavy-footed work, beginning with a solemn introduction marked "zurückhaltend" (held back), moving by way of brilliant fanfares into a powerful march theme of two strains, with a swaggering bass figure (fig. 8.13). The structure is truncated sonata form, the second strain returning in the tonic key, and there is an obsessive coda based on the theme. The march is clearly a symphonic number, not suitable for marching and quite unlike contemporary army marches.

Since this march is almost contemporary with the Komzák march shown at figure 8.11, there has clearly been a stylistic divorce of the concert march from the military march, even though the *Huldigungsmarsch* was actually written for band. Indeed, composers ceased to imagine their marches for real marching feet. Elgar thought of himself as one of "the old troubadours and bards . . . turned on to step in front of an army and inspire them with a song" (in the *Strand Magazine,* May 1904; see Reed 1939, 63). The soldiers he wished to lead were imaginary warriors, armed with shields and lances. His conception of the military spirit was revealed in the overture *Froissart* of 1890, an evocation of the fourteenth-century historian of the Hundred Years War. The *Pomp and Circumstance* marches, mostly written from 1901 to 1907, are a kind of appendix to *Froissart,* meant to evoke the color and heraldry of the Middle Ages. They have since been interpreted as monuments to Victorian imperialism; it was unfortunate, perhaps, that the trio tune of *Pomp and Circumstance* no. 1 was incorporated in the Coronation Ode for Edward VII (1902), with words by A. C. Benson ("Land of hope and glory").

This famous march illustrates the gulf that had opened between the parade ground and the concert hall. It is, of course, a march in four, not *alla breve,* in spite of its 2/4 marking; the four heavy steps occupy two measures of the score. Its trio section moves at about 80 to the minute. The orchestration, with harp and organ,

Figure 8.14.

proclaims it a symphonic piece. Most important of all, it is structured on the narrative system of symphonic music, not on the simple sectional pattern of the parade march. There are moments in its unfolding which would be almost as distracting to marching soldiers as the 3/2 measures in the seventeenth-century *Marche des Fussillier*. Toward the end of the first section of the march, a repeated figure suddenly quits the regularity of four-measure groups to echo its closing two notes downward through four registers, apparently collapsing into incoherence. But from the dissolution emerges a fanfare on a single note, enharmonically related, that leads forward into a new sequential pattern, which itself lapses into a chromatic

132 *Soldiers*

scale from which is conjured the full close in D that prefaces the Trio (fig. 8.14). Such a passage is the work of a symphonic imagination, absolutely irrelevant to any army that might be marching, but wonderfully evocative of some observed military scene, perhaps the passing of two bands playing different music, one succeeding the other, such as Ives pictured in *Putnam's Camp* from *Three Places in New England.*

The outstanding successors to these marches are the two coronation pieces of Walton, *Crown Imperial* (for George VI) and *Orb and Sceptre* (for Elizabeth II). Like much of the composer's output, these works have an edge of satire. The main theme of the first of them—whether satirical or not—would confuse a marching army much more seriously than Elgar's march, for it is composed in irregular groups, at first in phrases three measures in length. The positive and joyful character of the military march survives in these pieces, but it is now merely an evocation. These are sentimental, rather than naïve marches.

There is a final installment in this story of the modern march. While Sousa and Alford were creating the great marching numbers of the twentieth century, there was a new demand for marches for light orchestra; not for marching, but to furnish entertainment in bandstands and popular theaters. This was provided by composers like Eric Coates (*Knightsbridge, Calling all Workers*). Finally, marches were needed as background to movies; Coates wrote *The Dam Busters* and Ron Goodwin *633 Squadron,* both celebrating exploits of Second World War airmen. Most of these were in the lilting *alla breve* style of modern military marches, with a lyric trio, and all evoked some kind of heroic spirit, whether that of bomber pilots, workers in factories, or the busy life of London. Notice especially that marches are being used to evoke warlike heroism, not to suggest marching troops, for airplanes, assuredly, cannot march in step.

The marches composed by military bandmasters were fine *Gebrauchsmusik,* and Coates's light march style resembled them in all but their honest soldierliness. But marches by mainstream composers were character pieces or symphonic poems, already part of the signified rather than the signifier. They did not much resemble the driving, lilting marches of the bandmasters. Such is, in sketch, the story of the military march. The history of the topic itself will not be continued here, but must be reserved for chapter 11.

9   The Military Signifier:
2. The Military Trumpet and
Its Players

The march, beginning as a signal, turned into a largely ceremonial piece, but later recovered aspects of command when armies began to march in step and bands adopted the Turkish *batterie*. The trumpet call had been, from the beginning, a signal, and so it remained.

The early trumpet had many forms: at first a straight instrument, it was later wound into an S shape, afterward made on a circular pattern like the hunting horn (the *Jägertrompete*). The flat-wound trumpet, familiar to us, was born in the sixteenth century. It was sometimes fitted with a sliding crook, to form the *tromba da tirarsi* or slide trumpet, which permitted both the correcting of intonation and even the achieving of notes missing in the harmonic series (Baines 1981 [1976], 182). By the seventeenth and eighteenth centuries, the cavalry trumpet was normally a single-wound or double-wound long trumpet, about 224 cm overall and thus pitched in D. Because c′ (middle C) was played as the fourth harmonic on these old instruments (on the modern trumpet it is the second), the D trumpet sounded a tone higher than written. In the hand, the single-wound instrument was 65–85 cm in length, the double-wound between 40 cm and 50 cm (Lackner 1993, 134). Military signals lay in the second and third registers, from c (bass C) to c″ (C on the treble stave) as written, but by 1750 there were plenty of players who were expert in the clarino range (the fourth and fifth registers).

Since the fifteenth century, trumpeters had enjoyed high social status. Within the empire they were, however, divided into two main groups, the town musicians and the *Hoftrompeter*. The functions of these players, and also of the *Turmmusiker* and *Stadtpfeifer,* have been described in the last chapter. As explained, the *Hoftrompeter* had several duties: these included supplying trumpeters to the army, and in fact one could not graduate as a master trumpeter until one had served at apprentice level for seven years and taken part in at least one military campaign. The examination to pass out was focused chiefly on knowledge of the *Feldstücke,* the military signals. In spite of the long training, court players were not necessarily literate, though as the eighteenth century progressed more and more could read notation and indeed play clarino. Court trumpeters and kettledrummers were accustomed to playing on horseback. The trumpet, in the Renaissance, was "an attribute of political power" (Lackner 1993, 99).

Both classes of trumpeter had their professional societies, but members of the imperial guild of *Hof- und Feldtrompeter* considered themselves much superior to the mere town musicians. The guild was set up by the emperor in 1623, with the Elector of Saxony in Dresden as its High Marshal. Membership of the *Reichszunft* carried many rights and privileges.

Apart from the field signals, the trumpeters played chiefly in ensemble. At first, all used large mouthpieces and could play only in the low register. Later, there were mouthpieces of different sizes (though the trumpets themselves were uniform), and players specialized respectively in the high or low registers. But the predominant range of these ceremonial brass ensembles was low, and their grave, sonorous tones became part of the ethos of the European courts, a "symbol of aristocracy", as already mentioned. Later in the eighteenth century, many of their privileges were eroded, and in the early nineteenth century the guilds were suppressed. However, it has been suggested that the high dignity of the court trumpeter is preserved in one small aspect of our modern life: the placing of the orchestral wind high on the score, with the strings—originally the mere journeymen of the musical establishment—at the bottom (Lackner 1993, 140, quoting W. Ehmann, *Das geistliche Blasen*, 1950).

(a) The trumpet signal

Since the first recorded use of the trumpet for military signals (if one excludes the trumpets of ancient times) was in the twelfth century, it may seem strange that there are so few records of the signals played before the middle of the eighteenth century. Occasionally one hears signals in compositions of the day; the French *porte selles* appears in Jannequin's chanson *La Bataille*, and there are contemporary signals in "Non più guerra" from Monteverdi's *Fourth Book of Madrigals* of 1603.

Undoubtedly, the dearth of notated signals was caused by the secrecy which normally surrounded them. They were trade secrets of the trumpeters' guilds and were passed on aurally, not by means of notation. In any case, all regiments had their own particular signals. The ordinary civilian in seventeenth-century Europe can have known military signals only as a style, not as an actual repertoire. Occasionally, traces of what one assumes to be contemporary trumpet signals appear in concert music. For example, Bach quotes a horn figure in Cantata no. 127 which is identical with part of the trumpet obbligato in the aria "Grosser Herr, O starker König" in the *Christmas Oratorio* (Tarr 1970; see fig. 9.1). The same figure appears in the horn part of the second Gavotte from the First Orchestral Suite and in the horn parts of the First Brandenburg Concerto. It is found also in a violin sonata of Biber. The connection with Christmas (both in the oratorio and in the cantata) leads Tarr to think that it may be a trace of an old *intrada*, played at the entry of a great personage, and thus appropriate to celebrate a birth.

In spite of the scarcity of early trumpet signals, there are a few surviving collections. One of the earliest was written down by two Danish trumpeters, Hendrich Lübeck and Magnus Thomsen, around the year 1600. This collection has been edited in modern times by G. Schünemann and published in *Archiv für Musikwissenschaft*, Bd 17, and also *Das Erbe deutscher Musik*, 1st series, *Reichsdenkmale* vii (1936). Both players were in the Danish royal service, but they had traveled

Figure 9.1.

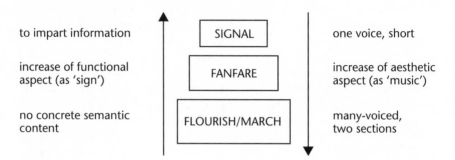

to impart information	SIGNAL	one voice, short
increase of functional aspect (as 'sign')	FANFARE	increase of aesthetic aspect (as 'music')
no concrete semantic content	FLOURISH/MARCH	many-voiced, two sections

Figure 9.2.

to Dresden and learned the Saxon trumpet calls. Their return to Denmark may have made it easier for them to write down the trumpet signals, free from the tyrannies of the German trumpeters' guilds.

We must be careful, in this early period, to distinguish the field signal from the improvised ensemble of trumpets. Cesare Bendinelli (*Tutta l'Arte della Trombetta*, 1614) describes the latter genre and gives instructions for its performance: "One player begins, and the others of the group follow, as is accustomed" (Lackner 1997, 179). It is a brilliant explosion of sound. The effect is captured well by Monteverdi in the *Toccata* that opens *Orfeo* and the Vespers of 1610. The term "fanfare" (from Arabic *anfar*, "trumpets"), though it is properly used for this kind of item, came to be freely employed for any brilliant flourish, even on a solo instrument, and thus sometimes meant a signal. Other terms for the trumpet signal were *Feldstück*, the word used in Koch's *Lexikon*, *Aufzug* or "parade," and—confusingly—*Marsch*. Achim Hofer provides a useful diagram, showing that real signals (which gave orders to the troops) and grand flourishes, with purely aesthetic and ceremonial intention, were at opposite poles of a continuum; the march might be merely a ceremonial piece, while the trumpet signal conveyed information. Between them was the "fanfare", which could have either function (fig. 9.2, Hofer 1988, 198). Since a "march", a ceremonial ensemble number, might also be a signal to march, this term might occupy either end of the continuum.

After Lübeck and Thomsen, there are a few early sources of military trumpet signals. Bendinelli, a court trumpeter in Vienna and Munich, whose description of the improvised "fanfare" has already been mentioned, included ten signals in his book. In two respects, this collection is impressive. First, the names of the calls match many later collections; the most standard cavalry signals are already foreshadowed. Bendinelli lists the "buta sella", which is clearly the *boute selle*, the command to fix saddles prior to mounting, later wrongly called "boots and saddles" in the British army; the "a monta a cavallo", the later *à cheval;* the "allo standardo", more familiar as the *à l'estendart;* the "rittirata", later the *retraite;* the "augetto", later the *guet,* the call for the mounting of the watch.

Second, the music of the calls foreshadows later calls, even as far as the eighteenth century. It seems that there was some tendency to standardization, even before the official adoption of trumpet signals. As an example we may take the *buta sella.* Bendinelli gives a long signal occupying seven lines of notation, including two "toccatas" as introduction and conclusion. His signals lie mainly in the second register, rising seldom higher than the fifth harmonic. Two extracts are shown in figure 9.3a. These may be compared with the *boute-selle* of Mersenne (*Harmonie Universelle,* book 5, 1636; fig. 9.3b). Another Italian trumpeter, Girolamo Fantini, gives a *butta sella* in 1638, which includes passages similar to Bendinelli's version (*Modo per Imparare a Sonare di Tromba Tanto di Guerra Quanto Musicalmente,* fig. 9.3c). A similar pattern is to be found in the set written down by the elder Philidor in 1705, and preserved in the library of Versailles. His version of the call is in thirteen "couplets", from which parts of numbers 7 and 9 are shown here, transposed from Philidor's bass clef into the tenor clef used in the earlier collections (fig. 9.3d). As the center of gravity of the trumpet signal moved upward, this very low call was superseded. Nevertheless, it is echoed as late as the collection of Le Coq Madeleine (*Le Boute-selle et Autres Airs de Trompettes de la Cavalerie de France,* 1720), of which part of the fourth couplet is shown in figure 9.3e, with clef transposed and errors corrected—this is a notoriously inaccurate print. None of these collections are official publications authorized by governments.

However, with the centralizing of army administrations and the decline of the guilds in the eighteenth century, official sets of trumpet signals began to appear in print, for each of the nations of Europe. The earliest set is probably that of the Prussian dragoons, 1751 (a dragoon is a mounted infantryman, who rides into battle and dismounts to fight). It was followed in 1769 by a set for the cavalry. The watershed came in 1787, when Frederick William II of Prussia ordered that his army's signals should be standardized, and commissioned Popitz, staff trumpeter of the lancers, to assemble a set of standard signals. They were published by Hermann Schmidt, superintendent of military music. A selection is shown in appendix 2, together with adaptations and new versions contained in the ordinance of 1846. Some survived in the German army of the 1930s, with the slightest modifications (Panoff 1938, 114–118). They are melodic and memorable, sometimes straying into the clarino register (notice the *boute selle* in appendix 2).

The Austrian military were hard on the heels of the Prussians. In 1751 the Austrian *Exercier-Reglements* begin to appear in Vienna, eventually containing full sets of trumpet and drum signals both for cavalry and infantry. These continue until the First World War, the signals changing very little. Lackner, working in Vienna, had sight of reglements from 1751, 1807, 1841, 1851, 1867, and 1911; Kastner gives a set of Austrian calls from 1846; a modern reglement is reproduced in Rameis 1976; I have copied a reglement from 1901. The persistence of the signals, almost in exact form, is remarkable. A selection appears in appendix 2, taken from Lackner, Rameis, and the 1901 reglement. The closeness of late calls to very early signals

(a) Bendinelli 1614

etc.

(b) Mersenne 1636

etc.

(c) Fantini 1638

(d) Philidor 1705

etc.

(e) Le Coq Madeleine 1720

etc.

Figure 9.3.

is demonstrated by comparing the *Generalmarsch* and the *ganzer Ruf,* as shown in the 1901 reglement, with their counterparts in the 1751 list, the third post of the *Marche,* and the *hocher Ruf* (from Lackner 1997, 221–223). Some of these signals are specified for infantry or artillery, but in general no distinction is made, except that the same signal may have different meanings, according to which arm of the military they command (the cavalry *Aufsitzen,* mount, shown in appendix 2, is also the infantry *Vergatterung,* change the guard, though the infantry—as we shall see— would presumably have heard it an octave higher).

The two military arms responded to very different sounds. The cavalry trumpet has been described. The infantry did not use this instrument when they began to abandon their drum signals. Their signals were played on a short, semicircular in- strument called a *Flügelhorn* (it was also called *Halbmond,* half-moon, because of its shape—see fig. 9.4, an instrument in the Edinburgh collection). Its origin lay in the *deutsches Jagen* or *chasse aux toiles;* it was used by the hunting masters who worked on the wings (*Flügel*) of the long lines, spread out across the countryside, that rounded up the game. It was the natural instrument for infantry trumpeters, since the first foot soldiers to acquire trumpet signals were the *Jägertruppen* or *corps de chasseurs,* light-armed troops recruited from huntsmen and foresters, who spe-

138 *Soldiers*

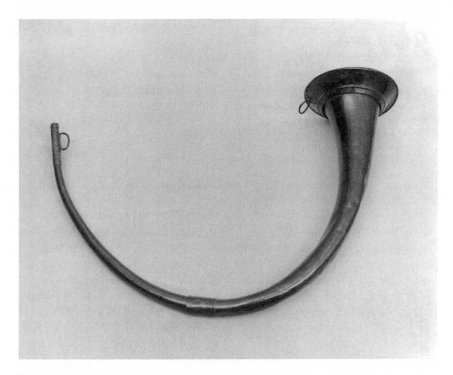

Figure 9.4.

cialized in scouting, guerrilla tactics, and fighting behind enemy lines, being accustomed to woodland and rough country. In Britain they were called *riflemen*. Dragoons seem to have counted as *Jäger*, since they acquired horn signals at the same time.

The flügelhorn seems to have been introduced first in Hanover in 1758; it was probably adopted in Prussia about 1762. In a royal ordinance of 1787, directions were issued for the use of the flügelhorn by Prussian players (Kastner gives bugle signals of the Prussian light infantry of 1846, some of which are shown in appendix 2). The Austrians acquired the flügelhorn in the late eighteenth century, the Bavarians in 1804. The British army called it "bugle horn" (recalling that "bugle", an old word for a wild ox, was one of the names for the natural oxhorn when used for signaling). In the early years of the nineteenth century the instrument changed its shape and was wound in a single coil so that it somewhat resembled a trumpet. Modern regimental bugles retain the conical bore and broad timbre of the old flügelhorn, though they are twice wound and are usually in B flat, at the same pitch as the orchestral trumpet. Somewhat confusingly, the American army calls this instrument a "cavalry bugle"; "bugle" in North America, means a kind of trumpet in G.

(The modern flugel horn, found in military bands, is a step further from the old *Halbmond*. It is a single-wound conical bugle in B flat, fitted with three valves, and

(a)

(b)

Figure 9.5.

sounds at the same pitch as the cornet or B flat trumpet, but with the characteristic broad timbre of the bugle.)

Strictly speaking, the old flügelhorn was a horn rather than a trumpet, for it was conical throughout its length. The criteria distinguishing horn from trumpet are much disputed; actually, most brass instruments have both cylindrical and conical sections, and sometimes it is a little difficult to say which form of tube is predominant. We do not need to enter this debate. Clearly, the flügelhorn was pitched much higher than the French hunting horn; the Bavarian type was in D flat, sounding a semitone higher than written, and many surviving flügelhorns are in D, a semitone higher again. The hunting horn in D sounded a minor seventh lower than written, of course, an octave below the flügelhorn. But in spite of its high pitch, the flügelhorn was rather broad in timbre, "hornlike" in fact.

The most important consequence of the shortness of tube was that middle C (as written) was played as the second harmonic on the flügelhorn (as it still is on the orchestral trumpet). On the cavalry trumpet, middle C was the fourth harmonic; the trumpeter, therefore, could play the E above (fifth harmonic) without use of valves. For the flügelhorn player, playing in the second register, the next note available was the G, the third harmonic. Thus, the instrument was not triadic in the octave above middle C, and many cavalry calls could not be played at this pitch.

Flügelhorn signals, therefore, were either specially written, or were adaptations of the trumpet signals. An English collection of calls, both for trumpet and for bugle horn (Hyde 1800), shows how this was done. The two versions of the *reveille* are largely different calls. The cavalry *retreat* is the same call on bugle horn, played one or two harmonics higher (fig. 9.5a,b). The command *turn out skirmishers* is simply played an octave higher on the bugle horn. By about 1850, lists of military calls usually include bugle calls as well as trumpet calls, distinguished by the absence of the E on the bottom of the stave; as the flügelhorn changed shape it was renamed "clairon" or even "cornet". Bugle and trumpet differed also in their characteristic range: trumpet calls usually lie between the third and eighth harmonics (an eleventh, written as G below middle C to C on the stave), bugle calls mainly between the second and sixth (a twelfth, written as middle C to G above the stave, since the bugler reads in a different register). Bugle calls are shown in appendix 2 for French chasseurs and Prussian light infantry.

Some armies mixed the calls, listing all calls together but specifying some for cavalry, some for infantry, some for both arms. Thus it was in the Exercier-

Reglements of the Austro-Hungarian army. Some, like the *Attacke*, are reserved for cavalry; others, for instance *Vergatterung* (changing of the guard), are for both infantry and cavalry (though with different functions; this particular call is the cavalry *Aufsitzen*, to horse); some are for infantry alone. In the latter category, the *Fussmarsch* (see appendix 2) could not be played on the infantry bugle as it stands. In such cases, the player probably transposed the call up an octave. The fourth (clarino) register was not much used for signaling, though early collections sometimes employed it, as does the second post of *der hoche Ruf* in the Austrian cavalry reglement of 1751 (see appendix 2). This could not have been played on the flügelhorn, of course.

The familiar "bugle call" of modern times, imitated by Britten in the *War Requiem*, is therefore rather high in pitch, because it is played on the infantry bugle. The cavalry trumpet blew signals that were, to a large degree, lower and perhaps more "dignified". This division—between rather low-lying, sonorous calls, and higher, more nervous calls—can be traced also in concert music.

To summarize: before the mid-eighteenth century, although the cavalry trumpet was used for signaling, there was no general system of calls—at least, not for a whole army—and very little record of what calls there were. Composers might quote existing calls, but we have no way of identifying these apart from guesswork. During the eighteenth century, sets of authorized signals began to appear, both for cavalry and for infantry. The infantry calls were played, however, on an instrument that came from the hunting field, the flügelhorn. They were played at a higher pitch, because the E on the bottom of the stave was missing on this instrument. However, the cavalry calls, as well as being largely lower, were also heard in a different timbre, that of the trumpet, with its cylindrical tube, as opposed to the broader sound of the conical flügelhorn.

Appendix 2 shows a collection of military trumpet and bugle calls, from French, Prussian, and Austrian collections. Calls have been chosen for their relevance to the military topic; they are either calls which have been quoted by composers of opera and concert music, or calls which demonstrate most clearly the style. All are quoted in C; the old military signaling instruments were commonly in D and sounded a tone higher. However, very early calls were published in the bass clef, with bass C as the fourth harmonic, so that the instrument sounded a ninth higher; these have been standardized and presented in the treble clef, middle C as the fourth harmonic. One should not forget that in some cases, the player also transposed the call a whole octave higher.

10 The Military Signified

(a) Chivalry

It is easy to feel stirred by the vigorous march tunes and rousing trumpet calls of the military topic. Intuitively, the signification of this topic seems euphoric, manly, heroic, adventurous, evocative of noble deeds and reckless courage. "A trumpeter should be bold and manly, skilful and honest," wrote a seventeenth-century commentator (Panoff 1938, 35). The military nobility of the Age of Reason was "brought up on fireside tales of heroic deeds" (Duffy 1987, 35). Gentlemen received a classical education, reading about Hector and Achilles. The medieval and Renaissance romances were widely read, with their extolment of warlike glory and chivalrous behavior. Stories of great fighters and heroes still lived in oral tradition.

The idea of chivalry originated in the Middle Ages. The invention of the stirrup in the eighth century permitted the use of the horse on the battlefield and created the most effective weapon of the time, the cavalry charge. "So during the eighth and ninth centuries the only fighting man of any consequence, the only *miles* who counted, was the mounted warrior, the knight. The battlefield was dominated by heavy cavalry, encased in complete armor and riding on huge heavy horses. Maintaining such a status was expensive; each horseman required an esquire, a groom, a horse-scout and one or two foot-soldiers" (Howard 1976, 3). He needed to be a wealthy man; hence military followers were granted lands in return for service. Thus the European words for "horseman"—*chevalier, Ritter, cavaliere, caballero*—came to imply nobility.

Since medieval warriors were Christians, a theory had to be found to reconcile fighting with Christian pacifism. The idea of the "just war", connected with the Crusades, demanded not only courage but, according to Aquinas, "magnanimity, confidence, freedom from anxiety, magnificence, constancy, tolerance and perseverance" (Contamine 1984 [1980], 251). The hero Bayard is described thus (in the *Histoire du Gentil Seigneur de Bayart*): "In boldness few men have approached him . . . in courage and magnanimity a second Hector, raging against the enemy, gentle, peaceful and courteous to friends."

Chivalry, the combination of courage, generosity, and good manners, was synonymous with high social class, "linked to race, blood and lineage" and a desire for "honour, glory and posthumous renown". Glory required physical sacrifice, "wearing armour day and night, fasting most of the time", according to the fifteenth-century writer Jean de Bueil. The nature of medieval warfare meant that battle was partly a set of duels between individual warriors, and so courage was linked to individual prowess, "outstanding actions . . . personally attributable to one man" (Contamine 1984 [1980], 253, 254).

This spirit is enshrined in the *chansons de geste*, chronicles and panegyrics of the centuries before 1500. The noble tone of these writings was to be diluted in the fifteenth and sixteenth centuries; for example, the story of Roland, knight of Charlemagne, was chiefly known in later times from Ariosto's *Orlando Furioso* (1516), which is reflected in many operas by prominent composers. Such Renaissance versions of the heroic stories were "seen through the distorting lenses of fifteenth-century legend, which cast upon the whole world of 'chivalry' a golden and fictitious glamour, a sunset glow from a consciously disappearing society" (Huizinga, quoted by Howard 1976, 4).

In spite of corrupting influences, the connection of arms and aristocracy survived into seventeenth- and eighteenth-century Europe. "Society was strongly permeated with a military spirit. . . . Social values were military values, and the exemplary act was . . . one of chivalry." But since the effectiveness of the mounted knight had passed, nobility had become a symbolic matter rather than a reality of battle. In France, the *noblesse militaire* became a class-within-a-class, many aristocrats preferring to live peaceably on their estates. Nevertheless, governments exploited the military traditions of the aristocracy. Both in France and in Prussia, officers were drawn exclusively from the upper class; Frederick William I of Prussia encouraged the development of a highly exclusive officer class, many of whom, being comparatively poor, were dependent on him for their status. French governments made the mistake of requiring their officers to be wealthy. The military staff was thus filled with parvenus and coxcombs, causing resentment amongst the older families (based on Howard 1976 and Corvisier 1979 [1976]).

(b) Warrior mentality, army mentality

The domination of the battlefield by cavalry had, in any case, ceased long before. The first battle at which horsemen were worsted by foot soldiers was Crécy (1346), when 1500 French knights were killed by English longbowmen. This trend was confirmed by the introduction of firearms. The new artillery was able to knock down the proud castles of the nobles, and the infantry, carrying small arms, could destroy the enemy at a distance, before they had a chance to get near. "What is the use, any more," asked a sixteenth-century writer, "of the skill-at-arms of the knights, their strength, their hardihood, their discipline and their desire for honour when such weapons [i.e. firearms] may be used in war?" (Keegan 1993, 333). Horsemen might find a way to resist this; the invention of the wheel-lock permitted the carrying of loaded muskets on horseback, and the seventeenth century developed the *caracole,* in which cavalrymen "rode up to the enemy lines, fired at point-blank range, and wheeled off to left and right" (Howard 1976, 34). But such a maneuver required a concerted discipline; no longer could each man fight for himself, concerned chiefly for his own personal glory.

Firearms made necessary for the infantry, too, a faculty of concerted movement that eliminated initiative. It required a considerable series of separate actions to fire a musket (forty-seven, according to one drill book); in order to maintain a continuous fire, ranks of musketeers advanced, discharged, then fell back while the next rank advanced, fired, and fell back, and so on. Since black gunpowder created clouds of dense smoke, it would have been easy to shoot your comrades if units did not act in perfect unison. Marching in step, which has been discussed above, was a useful skill, with the cadenced stop (in the British army, on the command "halt"). Eventually, in the eighteenth century, parade grounds were laid out for the exercise of these skills. To underline the soldier's loss of individuality, uniforms were worn.

The change in military ethos is perfectly summarized by André Corvisier as a change from the "warrior" mentality to the "army" mentality (1979 [1976], 183). The warrior-hero was largely an aristocratic myth, his high sense of honor now a mark of class rather than a military obligation: "The modern era retained some of the morality of chivalry, keeping alive the medieval romances that were still fashionable everywhere in the sixteenth century; although anachronistic, they continued to be widely read. . . . And with the Renaissance, the ideas of ancient Rome dominated military literature for three centuries" (183).

But there was little room for the individual pursuit of glory in the new armies. In many ways, the army officer had to acquire professional skills. First, soldiers had to be taught discipline and they had to learn to drill. This was necessary in order to maximize firepower on the battlefield, and, as has been said, to avoid accidents to one's own side. The drill of the parade ground owes its origin to Frederick William I, Elector of Brandenburg, who became "King of Prussia" in 1713. He was "the personification of a drill-sergeant in appearance and behaviour" and "was to provide a model for all military-minded royalty for the next century and a half" (Mollo 1972, 40).

Together with his drillmaster, Prince Leopold of Anhalt-Dessau, Frederick William I set out to achieve nothing less than perfection in the exercising of his infantry: methods of marching were improved, the pace and direction being finely adjusted by pendulum, pace-stick, and drum-tap, so that wheelings and evolutions could be performed with speed and accuracy. The king and the "Old Dessauer" managed between them to produce an infantryman who would react to orders promptly and accurately, and who could be relied on to advance on the enemy without losing the all-important dressing, loading, and firing while on the move.

On the battlefield, this kind of discipline turned an army into a command unit. Formations were introduced; the British square formation is the best known, though other nations, following the ideas of Gustavus Adolphus of Sweden, used flat formations. To coordinate the actions of the three arms, cavalry, infantry, and artillery, commanders had to grasp "an integrated structure of hierarchical control and instantaneous, disciplined response" (Howard 1976, 59). New texts on military tactics were being produced, notably the *Essai Général de Tactique* of Jacques de Guibert (Paris, 1772).

Second, officers had to master new technology. Artillery had become a vital ingredient in military actions; new types of fortification were devised to resist it, since heavy cannon could quickly dismantle a stone castle. A magnificent example of an artillery fortification may be seen at Fort George, near Inverness in Scotland. In response, complex techniques of siege warfare were developed, and the military engineers ("sappers", in British parlance, because of the "saps" or zigzag trenches they built to approach the defended position) were skilled professionals. Rifles were increasingly used; they were much more accurate than the musket, having spiral grooves inside the barrel which caused the projectile to spin rapidly and thus hold a straight course. The rifle superseded the musket finally after the invention, by Claude-Etienne Minié in 1849, of the expanding lead bullet, which made the weapon easier to load.

And third, the organization of armies was being centralized and streamlined. Medieval and Renaissance armies were raised by monarchs on the basis of military service; noblemen were obliged to contribute a certain force of soldiers in return for holding their estates. In practice, many of them paid a tax in lieu of this, and the king used the money to pay mercenaries. Most of the armies of the sixteenth century were largely composed of paid units with their own mercenary officers. The new model of political state, however, demanded a standing army, organized by a bureaucratic machine. In France, colonels of regiments had regarded their forces as their own property, private fiefs that were part of their feudal dignity. With the reforms of the Le Telliers—the father, Michel Le Tellier (died 1685) and his son, François Michel Le Tellier, Marquis de Louvois (died 1691)—the army was run by a civilian *intendance*. The control of central government was powerfully asserted, and precedence among officers became a matter of seniority, not birth.

The new method of raising troops was to be by forced conscription. The first laws of state conscription were effected in Austria in 1781. After the Revolution, French armies were raised entirely by conscription, and after the defeat of Napoleon the German states universally adopted this system also. The result was an exponential growth in the size of armies. At the start of 1792, the French army had 150,000 men. In August 1793 the *levée en masse* was passed, making service obligatory on all adult males. By the end of the year the army had grown to 983,000, and by September 1794 it was 1,169,000 (Keegan 1993, 233). In 1914, Germany had 3,400,000 men under arms (Howard 1976, 99).

(c) The pendulum of warfare

While administrators mastered the practice of controlling and supplying an army, the whole tenor of warfare was changing. It has been argued that war goes in epochs, its earnestness and brutality periodically giving way to an era of restraint. During the time of the religious wars and the Thirty Years War (1618–48), warfare had been accompanied by a general state of terrifying bloody chaos. There were "abductions and other outrages" and "the violent settling of old scores" (Corvisier 1979 [1976], 4). Armies ranged across the countryside pillaging, raping, burning, and murdering. "Warfare reached the nadir of brutality and pointlessness. . . . It was a period in which warfare seemed to escape from rational control; to cease indeed to be 'war' . . . and to degenerate instead into universal, anarchic, and self-perpetuating violence" (Howard 1976, 37).

But this was beginning to change. By 1677, Roger, Earl of Orrery, a military leader, perceived that "we make war more like foxes, than lyons, and you have twenty sieges for one battel" (quoted by Nef 1950, 156). Later Daniel Defoe commented, "Now it is frequent to have armies of fifty thousand men of a side stand at bay within view of one another, and spend a whole campaign in dodging, or, as it is genteelly called, observing one another, and then march off into winter quarters" (156). The wholesale destruction and ravishing of the countryside gave way to rational wars in which only the battlefield was bloody: "by the eighteenth century . . . the horrors of war tended to center on the field of combat" (Corvisier 1979 [1976], 6). The new centralized and conscripted armies behaved with more control and restraint when on campaign. Even on the battlefield, they showed less inhumanity; there was a tradition of chivalry and gentlemanliness toward the enemy, and officers would allow the defeated enemy to run away rather than pursuing them to destruction. "English and French officers in particular sought to outdo each other in demonstrations of chivalrous concern" (Duffy 1987, 12–13). But this was less the chivalry of the medieval knight than a modern theater of show-off, what Denis de Rougemont calls "fighting in lace cuffs" (Rougemont 1962 [1940], 257). A contemporary writer, Schertel von Burtenbach (1779), considered that you should refrain from deeds that would "occasion loss and harm among the enemy, but inflict no essential damage to hostile interests and yield not the slightest benefit for us" (quoted by Duffy 1987, 13). Armies passed the winter in retirement. They could not move until May when the grass began to grow, because the huge complement of military horses needed grazing.

Although standing armies were growing very large, generals preferred to deploy comparatively small forces on the field of battle. The largest army ever led into battle by Frederick the Great was the 65,000 men he commanded at Prague in 1757; he won the great victory of Rossbach with an army of 23,000. It was found that a very large army, in the days before the telephone and radio, could not be controlled as a unit; Marshal Saxe thought the largest effective force was 46,000. Battles were "localized episodes" (Nef 1950, 157).

Military writers taught that battles, in fact, should be avoided. The Saxon *Dienst-Reglement* of 1753 declared that "the greatest generals refrain from giving battle, except for urgent reasons. There can be no guarantee of victory, even after the finest possible preparations have been made. Some small blunder, some unavoidable accident are enough to lose you the encounter" (Duffy 1987, 190). The great Marshal Saxe proclaimed in 1732, "I do not favour pitched battles, especially at the beginning of a war, and I am convinced that a skilful general could make war all his life without being forced into one" (Howard 1976, 71). Consequently armies spent most of their time in evasive tactics. General Lazare Carnot, leader of the French armies after the Revolution, found that the old-style officers had cultivated not "the art of defending strong places, but that of surrendering them honourably, after certain conventional formalities" (quoted by Nef 1950, 157). This was the age in which the *guerre des postes,* small-scale skirmishing in the woods and hills, acquired new importance; there was a better chance of success and less to lose if you failed. For this purpose, *Jäger* battalions were raised, as already mentioned.

Armies would quite often grant armistices or truces which would astonish a modern soldier. In 1733, during the War of the Spanish Succession, the playwright Carlo Goldoni was present with the army of the king of Sardinia near Crema, facing the stronghold of Pizzighetone, held by German troops. The Germans asked for a truce, which was readily granted.

> A bridge thrown over the breach afforded a communication between the besiegers and the besieged: tables were spread in every quarter, and the officers entertained one another by turns: within and without, under tents and arbours, there was nothing but balls, entertainments and concerts. All the people of the environs flocked there on foot, on horseback, and in carriages: provisions arrived from every quarter; abundance was seen in a moment, and there was no want of stage doctors and tumblers. It was a charming fair, a delightful rendezvous. (Quoted by Nef 1950, 158–159)

Soldiering was as much theatrical as warlike. Indeed, real soldiers sometimes appeared on the opera stage, as did a squadron of cavalry, "granted by the King to make the theatrical action more interesting", at a performance of Perez's *Alessandro nell'Indie* in Naples in 1749 (Chegai 1998, 31).

This radical change in the conduct of war is attributed by Nef to the invention of the bayonet in the mid-seventeenth century. The horror of this weapon, he thinks, led men to recoil from out-and-out war. This view has been contested, but it is undeniable that warfare changed. There were plenty of wars in the eighteenth century, but nevertheless the soldiers of the time spent most of their lives doing very little. They "concerned themselves predominantly with problems of siege-craft, fortifications, marches, and supply. . . . Most of their time was passed in profoundest peace" (Howard 1976, 72). They were, in fact, more interested in ceremonial than in fighting; "ceremonial has reached a peak of development in our period", wrote H. F. von Flemming in his book on soldiering (*Der vollkommene deutsche Soldat,* 1726, quoted by Duffy 1987, 6).

This strutting, play-acting army found a focus in the new military academies. Since 1668 there had been schools for sappers (the first was founded by Louis XIV in Metz), but the new military academies were meant as general schools of civilized behavior. They began with the *Ecole Royale Militaire* in Paris in 1751, followed by the Austrian military academy (Wiener Neustadt, 1752). Cadets learned very little about warfare; the scientific programs of Sandhurst or West Point would not have been acceptable in these classy, exclusive institutions. "There existed no settled idea of what military academies were supposed to do", writes Christopher Duffy; "in most of the academies the education was better suited for a citizen of the world than for a professional soldier" (Duffy 1987, 48–49). The curriculum included French, geography, law, and history; mathematics and geometry; drawing and civil architecture, fencing and dancing. "Dancing is most necessary for the man of good education and for the officer. It makes him acceptable or even indispensable at parties when he relaxes in his off-duty hours. It is good for the officer to betake himself to such assemblies, and especially the mixed companies attended by ladies and pretty girls, which are an education for all persons of the male sex" (Major Baron O'Cahill, *Der vollkommene Officier,* 1787, quoted by Duffy 1987, 51).

The military schools were not taken very seriously, and many young officers bypassed them, going directly from their homes and country estates into the infantry and cavalry. But it seems that the officer class saw itself as elegant, fashionable, cultivated, devil-of-a-fellows. The men who talked about Hector and Roland behaved in real life as libertines.

The old heroic mythology had, in fact, degenerated into the posturing bravado of vain young men. But most people had seen through the myth long before. In many parts of Europe, the old respect for arms and their bearers had faded away. Enlightenment philosophy encouraged a skepticism about the need for armies and wars. The new wealthy bourgeoisie looked at the military, saw groups of arrogant aristocratic officers and dirty, outcast soldiery, and felt nothing but "derision and contempt" (Howard 1976, 73). In Sweden, Prussia, and Russia, rulers succeeded in upholding a feeling of respect for the army; elsewhere, it was regarded with hostility and ridicule. "Italy was the first country to manifest the decline of the profession of arms, in terms of social values," Corvisier tells us (196), but France and Britain were close behind.

The common soldiers, in spite of army reforms, remained ignorant, violent, and licentious. They were notorious for drunkenness, for keeping prostitutes in the camps, and for wild sprees. Their officers sought the good life; in the garrison towns, they frequented coffee houses, clubs, and Masonic lodges, mixing freely with the local bourgeois. Guard rooms became scenes of card playing and gambling, sometimes leading to all-night parties. A young officer might find it easy "to climb a ladder to keep a tryst with a pretty nun, to pay off a succession of trollops, or learn manners from the company of a lady of culture and standing" (Duffy 1987, 87). The great generals traveled with every comfort to hand; their baggage "could be expected to contain tents, beds, wardrobes, tables, chairs, kitchen utensils, table services and multiple changes of clothes. The whole could easily amount to 145 tons" (Duffy 1987, 85).

(d) Soldiers on the stage

Although the literature of heroic chivalry continued, a new literature grew up, presenting a much more realistic image of the soldier. The bourgeois civilian had little sympathy with the warrior myth, which was in any case a symbol of his social betters. The condition of the contemporary soldier was too obvious for more sophisticated people to be taken in by stories of noble warriors. And in the eighteenth century, the site of bourgeois cynicism was the stage.

Two of the most popular French plays of the eighteenth century were both called *Le Déserteur*. The version by M. J. Sedaine, which was turned into an *opéra comique* by Monsigny, was a slight piece. The other play, written by Louis-Sébastien Mercier and produced in Paris in 1770, was a much more significant work.

The young officer Valcour tries to seduce Clary, an innocent girl. Clary's betrothed, Durimel, is the son of an *officier de fortune,* a bourgeois who has served faithfully but who cannot achieve promotion because of his low birth. But it transpires that Durimel has previously deserted from the army, after being maltreated by a bullying colonel. The penalty for desertion is death; although Valcour tries to intervene, Durimel accepts his fate and is shot.

At the beginning of the play, the arrival of the regiment in town is greeted with dread by the local people. "Look at us! Unhappy country! Endless battalions! Infantry, cavalry, dragoons, light troops, hussars, baggage trains—a procession from hell. . . . All this is going to swoop down on our houses. This deluge will be our ruin." As for the idealism of war, it all seems pointless to these middle-class characters. "All considered, Hanoverians, Germans, Hungarians, Prussians, Frenchmen; all these gentlemen, at one moment our enemies and at another our allies, have in their turn treated us exactly the same; we don't know which to prefer. . . . What do you mean by the word 'enemy'? Since childhood I've seen warfare change direction and purpose twenty times. Outbursts of joy follow massacres, and they all become friends after having cut each other's throats."

Clary's mother sees another danger. "Here come the officers in town," she says; "it's important to get your daughters married off beforehand." Valcour's particular brand of heroism is lampooned. His courage derives, not from reflecting on the great heroes, but from thinking about a pretty girl. "I am aware that love turns me into a hero. It amuses me, it inflames me. . . . As I await the day of battle, could I have had a more fortunate meeting? Have you ever seen a prettier face, a finer waist, more elegant, better held, such a lively air; and crowned with such adorable tresses? . . . Our duty is to serve our country and beauty. The myrtles of love are enlaced with the laurels of Mars; my friend, I shall subdue this divine beauty, and then I'm going to hit the enemy as hard as you like."

The real protagonist of the play is Durimel's father, the middle-class officer, who is a man of feeling, aware of the tragedy and horror of war. In unison with the bourgeois audience, he is more aware of war's horror than of the old military ideals of heroism and glory.

> Ah, the duty of fighting! Cruel duty! When it must be obeyed, I can scarcely silence my sickness of heart; but the fatherland commands me, I must set an example to the soldiers. . . . However, during the periods between these bloody calamities, I become a man again, and I again have a need for peace. My soul longs to perform generous actions. I try, in lending succour to humanity, to make up for the hurts of which I was the fatal and blind instrument. Ah, how much does the tragic spectacle of war, offering us such painful sights, make our hearts more tender and sensitive.

This is a complex play, its characters realistic and many-sided. Yet it portrays the aristocratic officer as self-seeking and ruthless, the army as burdensome, warfare as pointless, the *officier de fortune* as most to be admired. It was enormously successful; its performance in front of the king and queen led to Mercier's being granted a pension of 800 livres.

A contemporary German play, *Die Soldaten* by J. M. R. Lenz (1775, the basis of Zimmermann's opera of 1960), portrays the army in a very similar light. The principal topic is military celibacy; commanders preferred their officers to be unmarried, and this—according to Lenz—turned them into universal lechers. As in Mercier's work, there is a middle-class girl who is courted by an officer. When she speaks to an older woman about the young man's "love", she is advised: "The love of an officer, Marie! Of a man who is hardened to every kind of debauchery and infidelity, who ceases to be a good soldier the moment he becomes a faithful lover."

The officer's touchiness on the subject of honor is ridiculed when the regimental chaplain criticizes the men's attempts to dishonor young girls. To this accusation, the major replies: "You've a damned uncivil tongue when you speak of officers, sir. God damn it, if anyone else were to talk to me like that . . . ! Do you think, sir, we cease to be gentlemen the moment we enter the service?" And finally, the commanding officer laments: "I look upon soldiers as the monster to whom from time to time an unhappy female must be sacrificed, in order that all other wives and daughters may be spared."

These plays are the best of a whole genre in which upper-class officers are portrayed as coxcombs, armies as foolish, and war as lamentable. It is a very different picture from the warrior romances. It was to this kind of army that the young Cherubino was sent (in Mozart's *Figaro*), prompting the most famous of all military arias, "Non più andrai". It is ironic that this very aria, satirizing the vanity of army officers, was itself turned into a march and played by military bands (Hofer 1988, 385).

(e) Absolute war

But things were about to change. As the eighteenth century came to an end, the age of military discretion, of small armies and officerly decorum, was overtaken by a world of violent contrasts: a new level of brutal and murderous warfare, and yet a period largely without war; a cultivated dislike for stories of inhuman butchery, yet an explosion of the glamour of soldiering and a descent of the warrior myth into popular culture.

After the French Revolution, limited warfare gave way to a new kind of mass conflict in which the brutality of the pre-1650 wars was revived. This, according to Nef, was the next era in the history of warfare, though he admits that it had its roots in the reforms of the old drill-sergeant, Frederick William I, whom we have already met. As we have seen, armies expanded to immense sizes, and these huge numbers were used to crush the enemy, exacting and suffering great losses. Before 1789, pitched battles were rare and human losses seldom exceeded 10 percent of the force deployed. Between 1792 and 1800, the French republic fought fifty battles by land and sea. At Waterloo in 1815 Napoleon lost 27,000 men out of 72,000, Wellington 15,000 out of 68,000 (Keegan 1993, 360). These terrible losses continued; in the forty-eight battles of the American Civil War (1861–65), 94,000 Confederates died out of a total of 1,300,000 enlisted. In the First World War the French lost 1,000,000 men by 1917.

Such losses were caused by a strategy of unrelenting tenacity in pursuing and destroying the enemy. Lazare Carnot, the French revolutionary general who has already been quoted, proclaimed that "war is a violent condition; one should make it *à l'outrance* or go home". Commanders would now confront their opponents with a dense column of firepower, rather than the thin lines of the previous century; they coordinated cavalry, infantry, and artillery so that no section needed to worry about harming its own side. Such centralized, single-minded focus would have been impossible with the militias and mercenary troops of the old armies. It was achieved, not on the basis of individual heroism (in spite of the introduction of medals for valor, a peculiarly Romantic idea), but by the birth of nationalism. The members of Napoleon's *Grande Armée* felt themselves representatives of a new France in which freedom and talent were promoted and respected. The rest of Europe was scarcely organized in nations at all. In 1800 there was no state called "Germany" or "Italy". The Prussia which suffered the trauma of defeat at Jena in 1806 was no more than the hereditary fief of the Hohenzollern family. Gneisenau, the Prussian general, realized that it was "necessary to give the people a Fatherland if they are to defend that Fatherland effectively" (Howard 1976, 87). The fatherland that was invented at that time eventually became Germany in 1871, buttressed by the Romantic nationalism of Bismarck, which was so much admired by Brahms.

With nationalism came militarism. Common soldiers in the old armies were outcasts, their officers noblemen by birth. In the nineteenth century, a military uniform gave rank and standing to young men whose birth was middle-class or humble. Previously, the militia member and the mercenary were seen as servile. Now, the conscript and the recruit were responsible and useful citizens. There is even a suggestion that youths, disoriented by social changes and the spread of credit capitalism, found it hard to identify themselves as adults. They joined the army to acquire status and respectability. "This judgement implies that there was a measure of infantilism in Europe's enthusiastic espousal of militarising tendencies, and that may well be: 'infantilism' and 'infantry' have the same root" (Keegan 1993, 357). The call of military duty was now seen as superior to all other calls. On the third day of the First World War Bavarian universities addressed their student bodies thus: "The muses are silent. The issue is battle, the battle forced upon us for German culture, which is threatened by the barbarians from the East, and for German values, which the enemy in the West envies us. And so the *furor teutonicus* bursts into flame once again" (quoted by Keegan 1993, 358). As John Keegan comments, the appeal to the *furor teutonicus*—the spirit of Attila's hordes that destroyed ancient Rome—seems peculiarly inept. But this was the kind of militaristic nationalism which led so many to their deaths, which, on the other side, led Basil Hood to write, for Edward German's operetta *Merrie England* (1902): "And Austro-Hungarians, and German barbarians, as foemen might curse them, the yeomen of England." The absurdity of this kind of nationalism was buttressed by a new vision of chivalry, romantic, arrogant, and trivial. This acquired its own popular literature, which is described below.

Yet the century between Waterloo and the Somme was, in fact, a period with very few wars, a "Great Peace". It was dominated, in the military field, by the ideas of Baron Carl von Clausewitz, a Prussian officer who, after Napoleon's defeat of his country, served in the Russian army. His book *On War,* published after his death in 1831, proclaimed (more or less—this famous quotation is, in fact, not quite what he said) that war was "the continuation of politics by other means". In other words, war was an expedient of the state, a rational policy to achieve comprehensible ends, not a way of life or an outburst of anger. He also made the distinction between "absolute war" and "real war". In the real world, war had been "incoherent and incomplete". War makers had changed the objectives, had held back from final destruction, had switched sides and purposes. Rational warfare, he thought, could have only one objective. "The natural aim of military operations is the enemy's overthrow, and . . . strict adherence to the logic of the concept can, in the last analysis, admit of no other. Since both belligerents must hold that view it would follow that military operations could not be suspended, that hostilities could not end until one or other side were finally defeated" (Clausewitz 1976 [1831], 579). The author confessed that his belief in this idea was founded on his observation of Napoleon, who had "waged [war] without respite until the enemy succumbed". The nineteenth century, especially the German generals of 1870 and 1914, agreed with him. Unfortunately, no one had foreseen that two immense armies, with enormous firepower based on the improved high-explosive weapons developed during this time, would simply collapse into stalemate, with the huge loss of life this would cause. The First World War was largely the fruit of Clausewitz's teachings, as well as the basis of their overthrow. It was meant to be the "war to end all wars". The disillusionment of the Second World War took these words out of people's mouths; nevertheless, this may have been the "abiding effect" of the two conflicts, as John Keegan surmises (Keegan 1997 [1989], 498). Just as the era of limited war, of the aristocratic officer and the outcast army, ended after 1789, so that of absolute war, with national armies inspirited with a sentiment of militarism, died perhaps after 1914, and certainly after 1945.

(f) Heroes of *The Boy's Own Paper*

Although many of the ruling class continued to read the warrior masterpieces, the philosophy of warfare in the nineteenth century was cruel and realistic, and this, to a large degree, caused people to avoid wars. The heroes of the ancient world and of the medieval epics were still admired in some quarters, however. Yet the old texts were interpreted in new ways.

The story of Roland is a particularly telling example, for the original text of the epic had been lost. The basic tale was known from the Italian Renaissance writers, though they had added fantastical stories of magic and love. The basic tale told of a valiant knight of Charlemagne who traveled with his master on a warlike expedition to Spain in the year 778. On their return, Roland was treacherously given command of the rearguard (his enemy at court had conspired with the Saracens for the attack of the rearguard as the army marched back to France). The Franks set off across the Pyrenees. The main column of the army got safely through, but in the desolate pass of Roncevaux the rearguard was set on by an immense host of Saracens and completely wiped out. So died the most "noble et preux chevalier" of the French.

It was also known that there had been a "Chanson de Roland", which was imagined to be a kind of battle song. It was traditionally assumed to have been sung by the Norman soldiers before the Battle of Hastings in 1066, and again before the Battle of Poitiers in 1356. But no copy existed of the supposed song. This did not prevent people from speculating on its nature, and indeed on the character of Roland himself, about which little was known except conventional chivalric accolades.

An enthusiast, Antoine René, Marquis of Paulmy, published a summary of the story in 1777, adding a completely fictional "reconstruction" of the battle song itself. He justified his invention by arguing that, since Roland must have possessed all manly virtues, we are permitted to put these into verse. "It is natural to believe that the character of Roland was presented to the soldiers as a model to imitate, and that the paladin was shown as a brave, intrepid, passionate knight, zealous in the service of his king and the glory of his fatherland; to add that he was humane after victory, a sincere friend to his comrades, gentle with townsmen and peasants; that he was not quarrelsome, avoided excess in drinking, and was not a slave of women" (quoted by Redman 1991, 25). Paulmy then offers a lengthy "song", with the following refrain:

> Soldats françois, chantons Roland;
> De son pays il fut la gloire:
> Le nom d'un guerrier si vaillant
> Est le signal de la victoire.

French soldiers, sing of Roland; he was the glory of his country: the name of a warrior so valiant is the signal for victory.

After 1789 there was a demand for patriotic and revolutionary songs. Since Roland had evidently been a poor respecter of social divisions, he was now seen as a proto-revolutionary. For example, Rouget de Lisle, two weeks after writing the *Marseillaise,* composed a song called *Roland à Roncevaux* (1792). Here Roland's highest quality was his egalitarian treatment of the great and the humble, and he introduces the word "patrie"—the new revolutionary byword. His refrain is typical:

> Mourons pour la patrie,
> Mourons pour la patrie,
> C'est le sort le plus beau, le plus digne d'envie.

Let's die for our country: that's the finest destiny, the one most worthy of envy.

Roland had been a Frank, not a Frenchman, and German writers also claimed him as their military model. Uhland produced three works on the theme: *Klein Roland* (1808), *Roland Schildträger,* and *Roland und Alda* (both 1811). It never occurred to anyone that the "Chanson de Roland" was not, in fact, a battle song but a long verse epic, giving a less corrupt account of the hero's career. The true manuscript was discovered in the Bodleian Library, Oxford, and at last published in 1837. It was then realized that the original tale contained no magic and precious little romantic love; Etienne Jean Delécluze, in *Roland ou la Chevalerie* (1845), discovered therein a pre-medieval age when "chivalry was still purely heroic. In this narrative, there is no fantastic event, no amorous adventure". In spite of this, Auguste Mermet composed the opera *Roland à Roncevaux* (1864): this contained a story of love rivalry; Roland died in the arms of his beloved, and there was even a "chanson" in the old sense of a battle song. The work was a smash hit and became the most successful opera of the age.

With the growth of nationalism—and especially after the disaster of the Franco-Prussian war in 1870–71—the story became a militaristic rallying call, focused on the glory of French arms. Joseph Fabre's modern version of 1901 was dedicated "to the national army, this translation of the epic of patriotism". After the First World War, the popular lecturer Maurice Bouchor even attributed the story to the French people themselves: "It is the sentiment of the masses which created the legend, imposed the subject on the poet and inspired the tone" (all these references from Redman 1991).

But while the nationalistic consciousness was transforming Roland into a patriotic Frenchman, sophisticated taste was moving away from tales of valor and chivalry. It is true that two serious British authors had much success with tales of medieval derring-do: Walter Scott's adventure novels proved popular with opera composers (on this subject, see Mitchell 1977), and Tennyson produced his Arthurian poems (*Morte d'Arthur* in 1842, *Idylls of the King* in 1859). But the new sphere of imaginative literature was the domestic scene, with sensitive insights into personal life and individual psychology. Jane Austen wrote miniatures of provincial life. Gustave Flaubert subjected the dreams of Romanticism to a satirical eye. Fyodor Dostoievsky examined moral and political life with a grim psychological realism. These were the most advanced artists of their era; stories of high adventure were pushed to the margins.

"One of the most characteristic features of a modern age . . . is the banishment of the ensigns of war and bloodshed from the intercourse of civil life," wrote Matthew Arnold (Rutherford 1978, 6), and another writer could speak in 1866 of "the withering of the hero and the flourishing of the private individual . . . the almost entire subsidence of historical painting." Robert Southey wrote, "We admire Homer deservedly . . . but if Homer were living now, he would write very differently. Book after book of butchery" (quoted by Rutherford, 1978, 13).

For the person of education and sensitivity, heroism and chivalry had been betrayed. Some thought that the process began as early as 1615, with the completion of *Don Quixote* by the retired soldier Miguel de Cervantes. This was a scurrilous critique of the imaginary exploits of chivalry. Its true hero is the lower-class Sancho Panza, a comic figure. "The deflation of specifically chivalric folly . . . has been extended to the whole profession of arms . . . and thence to all varieties of courage and self-sacrifice", writes Andrew Rutherford (1978, 1). In the later age of heroism, when the *Chanson de Roland* was being translated and admired, some realized that chivalry had become hollow, a cloak for cynicism. John Ruskin bitterly accused Cervantes of destroying man's sense of honor; "he, of all men, most helped forward the terrible change in the soldiers of Europe, from the spirit of Bayard to the spirit of Bonaparte, helped to change loyalty into licence, protection into plunder, truth into treachery, chivalry into selfishness" (quoted by Rutherford, 1978, 5). Many currents ran through nineteenth-century culture; alongside the pomp and swagger of patriotic soldiers, there was a disillusionment with arrogant militarism, even when it was classically expressed in noble epics.

Instead of inspiring masterpieces, heroism was now espoused by the masses. A brand of trivial heroics became the dream of the schoolboy and the lending library.

Chivalry was downgraded to "a favourite theme of popular art, which often re-asserts values out of fashion with a literary public alienated from the culture as a whole" (Rutherford 1978, 9). It was "abandoned to a sub-literature, often of best-sellers, extending from *Westward Ho!* and the works of Marryat and Lever to Charlotte M. Yonge's *Book of Golden Deeds,* James Grant's *Romance of War,* and straightforward adventure stories for boys" (16). (The novelists mentioned are Charles Kingsley [1819–79], author of *Westward Ho!*; Captain Frederick Marryat [1792–1848], author of many maritime stories including *Mr Midshipman Easy* [1836]; and Charles James Lever [1806–72], whose Irish tales include *Charles O'Malley, the Irish Dragoon* [1841].) There was a new interest in works of popular history. Macaulay's *History of England* (1849) was immensely popular and "Sir E. S. Creasey" 's *Fifteen Decisive Battles of the World, from Marathon to Waterloo* became a best-seller. Serious authors looked scornfully on this craze for the warlike. "Time out of mind strength and courage have been the theme of bards and romances; and from the story of Troy down to today, poetry has always chosen a soldier for a hero. I wonder is it because men are cowards in heart that they admire bravery so much, and place military valour so far beyond every other quality for reward and worship?" (Thackeray in *Vanity Fair,* quoted by Rutherford 1978, 14).

This cultural trend was reflected most strongly in the popularity of books for boys. R. M Ballantyne (*The Coral Island; The Gorilla Hunters*) and G. A. Henty (*St George for England; Under Drake's Flag*) wrote adventure tales that passed into many editions, the latter enormously popular in spite of being a mediocre writer. These authors, and their imitators, wrote also for the many boys' magazines. *The Boy's Own Paper,* targeted at boys of the middle and upper classes, first appeared in 1879 and was soon the definitive title. It was strongly monarchist, full of moral lessons and the spirit of noble heroism. Its diet of historical adventure, school stories, and sport prepared its readers for breezy exploits in which all danger was imaginary. Many of them were to die in the First World War.

The spirit of this kind of writing is typified by a short entry on May 31, 1879. The lady poet noticed a news feature about the defeat at Isandlwana in the Zulu War. A young lieutenant, Standish Vereker, having lost his horse, pinched the horse of an African trooper. Learning that its owner was still around, he "heroically" returned the horse, was overtaken by the Zulus, and met his death. The author describes this as "an incident of unselfish generosity, worthy to be named with Sir Philip Sidney's passing the water to the dying soldier." Her thirteen stanzas of stumbling doggerel reveal the cultural country occupied by primeval chivalry in the nineteenth century, many miles from the high tone of Roland and Bayard.

> Down in the wild south country
> The English flag lay low,
> And English troops were sorely pressed
> By fierce, exulting foe.
>
> Was each man for his neighbour?
> Or each man for his own?

In bitter stress and struggle
A nation's soul is shown.

God only knows all secrets,
But women's hearts reply,
"Living, our men were heroes,
And heroes they would die."

And there was one among them,
A gallant soldier boy,
Before whom life lay golden,
A very dream of joy.

The battle it was over,
The struggle had been vain,
And life's one chance remaining
The river was to gain.

His horse had fallen 'neath him,
And he the way must tread:
A mounted comrade met him,
Another horse he led.

"Mount, Vereker!" he shouted,
"The Zulus press behind!
Thank God for this good charger,
And race him like the wind!"

He asked no second bidding,
God knows his life was fair!
With all the hopes and memories
Which rose before him there.

He scarce had reached the saddle
Before a trooper came,
And loud, in piteous accents,
Pleaded a prior claim.

Cried he, "The horse you've mounted
Is mine, this moment lost."
Down came the gentle Vereker,
And did not count the cost.

There was no time for parley,
For question or reply,
He owned the claim undoubting,
And stayed behind to die!

He could not seize another's:
He could not dream a lie:
These were the hard things for him,
The easy was to die!

Three cheers for merry England,
Nor can her day be done,
For she has many like him,
Her just and gentle son! (Isabella Fyvie Mayo)

(g) Military uniform

The changing image of the soldier, from liveryman to Romantic braggado-cio to scientific killer, was reflected in the clothes he wore as well as in cultural tradition. During the Renaissance most fighters wore whatever clothing they felt comfortable in; there was little to distinguish military from civil dress. Uniforms, originally merely the livery of the nobleman who was colonel of the regiment, came to be standardized during the seventeenth and eighteenth centuries. Different regiments were distinguished by the facings of their coats, those areas of collar, lapel, and frock that were turned back to reveal the lining. Colors were gradually codified, though in Austria this was not finally achieved until 1763 (Hans Bleckwenn, in Schick 1978, 16–34).

The uniforms of officers gradually became more showy. Copious extra buttons were added, in brass, pewter, or even silver and gold. There were trimmings of lace and embroidery. Most ornate were the uniforms of hussar regiments, originally ethnic Hungarian cavalry but eventually the crack light troops of every army. With their tight breeches, tall caps, and short boots, they dressed for visual effect. Over the left shoulder hung the pelisse, an elaborate jacket (it was never actually worn), and from the belt hung a *sabretache*, a gigantic pouch with ornate insignia. The sword hung so low that, when the man was unmounted, it dragged along the ground. The whole ensemble looked impressive but inconvenient; nevertheless, it was worn into battle (Mollo 1972, 57; plate 1).

The young Cherubinos who made up the officer corps began to personalize their uniforms in many ways. A satirical book published in 1782 gives the following advice: "The fashion of your clothes must depend on that ordered in the corps; that is to say, must be in direct opposition to it: for it would show a deplorable poverty of genius if you had not some ideas of your own in dress. Your cross belt should be broad, with a huge blade pendant to it—to which you may add a dirk and a bayonet, in order to give you the more tremendous appearance. . . . Thus equipped you sally forth, with your colours, or chitterlin [shirt frill] advanced and flying" (Mollo 1972, 96–97). General Mercer, who served at Waterloo, tells us, "It was the fashion of the day for boys to imitate or try to resemble women, wearing as they did such short waists, and filling out the jacket with handkerchiefs to resemble the female figure." A French officer recalls a young man who wore false calves under his breeches; there was laughter when they slid round to the front during an inspection. Mercer also speaks of "immensely long chains" which held the trousers down under the instep, and the habit of trailing the sabre along the ground, a feature seen in many military portraits, including the one shown as plate 1. Uniforms, originally distinguishing marks to tell friend from foe, became expressions of the effeminate display of foolish young men.

It seems a paradox that the new age of brutal wars was also the most spectacular period for military uniforms. Napoleon's *grande armée* was "the most colourful army ever", even when drawn up for the last time at Waterloo (Mollo 1972, 104). According to Eckart Klessmann (in Schick 1978, 100), "The uniforms worn during the first fifteen years of the nineteenth century represent the most elaborate display of pomp in the whole history of military dress."

Romantic chivalry was again reflected in military uniform after 1830. There was an increasing desire for visual impact, often absurd. Some Russian and Prussian regiments adopted the *Pickelhaube,* the enormous helmet with a tall spike. In 1854 Napoleon III re-formed the *Garde Impériale,* its uniforms based partly on the style of the First Empire, but with additional spectacle. Carabiniers and dragoons wore enormous crested brass helmets; cuirassiers had gleaming breastplates, useful against sword thrusts but no good against rifle bullets; many troops wore high jack-boots; tunics were commonly short; the hussars still sported their elaborate braided uniform with pelisse over the shoulder and hanging sabretache. But of course, these fancy-dress soldiers never did much fighting, until the Franco-Prussian War of 1870 in which they were decimated. Nor were the French the only nation to go in for such extravagant kit; in fact, the French style was copied by other nations. "Nearly every land force in the world wore at least a version of French uniform", so that the subject cannot be discussed "without frequent use of French language terms" (Thorburn 1969, 7).

On the other hand, the French army inaugurated an opposing trend, the distinction of dress and undress uniforms. French soldiers were supplied with a loose, informal outfit which could be worn in battle or in camp. This was rapidly copied, and "by 1870 the armies of Europe had almost without exception modified their previously impractical full dress into a practical dress, inspired chiefly by the example of the French" (Mollo, in Schick 1978, 178). A development of weaponry led to the final retreat of the lavish uniform. Eighteenth-century muskets were accurate only at very close range, but the universal introduction of the rifle made it possible to kill one's enemy at 200 yards or more. British troops in the First Boer War in South Africa, 1881, were still wearing scarlet coats. This made them conspicuous in the dusty landscape of the veldt, and the Boers were able to pick them off from a great distance. Somewhat earlier, soldiers in India had begun wearing khaki, a greenish-brown color that shaded into the landscape (named from the Hindustani word *khak,* dust). Gradually this was adopted for all colonial campaigns, and by 1902 it had become the standard color of all uniforms except dress. "For the first time, the design of the soldier's dress for battle was considered scientifically and to such good effect that, when war broke out in 1914, the British soldier was the most sensibly dressed and accoutred fighting man in Europe" (Mollo, in Schick 1978, 156). One by one, the European nations abandoned their brilliant uniforms. By 1914 only the French retained their colorful appearance, all other armies appearing in various shades of grey and khaki. Practical considerations—the attitudes of absolute war—had triumphed over male vanity and popular Romanticism. Now, the doctrine of absolute war was itself to be put to the test. By 1918, the heroism of the boy's serial story had given way to the tragic pessimism of

Wilfred Owen, and the drab uniforms, instead of reflecting the rigorous doctrines of absolute war, came to express a kind of melancholy.

(h) Warriors and soldiers

Warfare and soldiering were accompanied, throughout their history, by a myth of the heroic warrior. But whether the hoplites of Pericles' Athens truly manifested the spirit of Homer; whether the young cadets of the eighteenth-century military academies could match the noble selflessness of Roland; whether the readers of *The Boy's Own Paper* had any real conception of how it felt to be on the receiving end of an artillery barrage, these things are hard to say. We can, however, be sure that soldiering had a debased image in the minds of civilians, the people who made up the ranks of the musical public throughout most of modern history. The pusillanimous soldiers of the classical era, the arrogant coxcombs of Romanticism, were not objects of admiration, and presumably were not directly parts of the signification of the musical topic. Nevertheless, musicians returned continually to the military topic, almost always in euphoric vein. They expressed, not the reputation of the contemporary army, but the persistent myth of the warrior. Indeed, many aspects of military life itself, short of the actual fighting, were themselves expressions of this; the absurd uniforms of the officers, their pelisses, sabretaches, and Pickelhauben, reflected a crude delight in the swagger of the hero. Just as the brass hunting horn owed its success to its expression of the splendor of the hunt, rather than its usefulness in hunting, so the attitudes, practices, and appearance of the military reflected a dream of heroism rather than the reality of fighting. In spite of this, the signification of the musical topic can only be fully grasped in the light of contemporary warfare and its all-too-human participants. Only by observing these can we reveal the mingling of signified and signifier which seems to be an essential feature of the cultural and musical topic.

11 The Soldier Represented

(a) The explicit soldier

Both aspects of the military signifier have varied backgrounds. The march was originally a processional and ceremonial piece. It came to be more closely associated with soldiers during the seventeenth and eighteenth centuries. The arrival of the "Turkish" instruments and the use of the march for real marching reinforced the military character of the march, but even in the Romantic period one still encounters marches for slaves, priests, huntsmen, and pilgrims. Nevertheless, it becomes easier to discern the specifically military character of soldiers' marches.

Like the march, the trumpet fanfare had a double origin; it had been the signaling medium of the cavalry, but it had also been part of the repertoire of the *Stadtmusikanten*. Fanfares were played on court and civic occasions. Admittedly, the civic fanfare was normally an ensemble piece, at first improvised, while the military signal was a solo item. But the heroic trumpet figure, even in modern times, might signify civic pageantry as well as soldiering.

The contour of the military topic is different from that of the hunt. One cannot trace offshoots and developments, as one can for the hunt topic. There is nothing like the pastoral horn or the "horn of nocturnal mystery". On the other hand, both march and trumpet signal have varied backgrounds, and although the warlike flavor is usually apparent, there is always a hint of the ceremonial, of civic splendor as well as soldiering.

The military spirit may be identified if we search the literature for marches and trumpet signals explicitly connected with soldiering, either in operas or songs, or in instrumental works with titles. For clearly, concert composers thought of the march rhythm, and the brilliant trumpet flourish, as evoking a military world, even quite early in our history.

(b) Marches in opera and concert

Opera seria often contained numbers called *marcia*. For example, Metastasio's libretto *Ezio,* first set by Pietro Auletta in 1728, was performed in Berlin in 1730 in a setting by Johann Adolf Hasse. It begins with the return to Rome of the general Aetius—Ezio—with his army, after their victory over Attila's Huns. In the Hasse version, after a short scene in recitative, there is a grand triumph; Ezio enters, "heralded by warlike instruments, slaves and the standards of the conquered, followed by the victorious soldiers". The march resembles the military numbers of the time. In *alla breve* meter, it sounds effective at about half note = 60 to the minute, the *pas ordinaire,* and the musical figures are in a dotted rhythm, like marches

Figure 11.1.

in all ages. It resembles in style the "Marsch des Regiments Zweite Garde" in the Saxon collection of 1729, mentioned above (fig. 11.1a,b).

This is a standard operatic situation; another victorious warrior, with his troops, is celebrated with a *marcia* in act 1, scene 6 of Hasse's and Metastasio's *Nitteti* (1758). A very interesting example occurs in act 2 of this composer's *Il Trionfo di Clelia* (1762). It is the familiar scene of Horatius keeping the bridge against the Etruscans. The defenders rush away, surprised by the enemy, and the Etruscans advance on to the bridge "in slow order". In the Dresden manuscript of the opera, their *marcia* is superscribed *un poco maestoso*. This particular copy is full of annotations by the composer; he adds, "not too slow or too fast, but following what is demanded by the dramatic tempo [*il tempo comico*] of the scene". We deduce, first, that this was a slow march in *pas ordinaire*; second, that the pace of the troops was related to that of the music, even if they did not march in step. The march is followed by an orchestral battle scene, *presto assai e furioso,* using the trumpets and kettledrums of the orchestra.

Such a military reference may be found in operas throughout the century, in all countries. In France, a similar triumphant procession is accompanied by a military march for oboes, horns, and strings, which must have sounded much like parade ground marches. The opera *Ernelinde* by François-André Philidor, also composer of *Tom Jones,* was first performed in Paris in 1767 and is set in Norway. The generals Ricimer and Sandomir have reduced the city of Trondheim. In act 1 Ricimer enters with the victorious armies, to the accompaniment of a "marche", which on its reprise is sung by the chorus (fig. 11.2). Like Hasse's marches, this is in *alla breve* time, the two beats per measure proceeding at about half note = 60.

Mozart's operatic marches are almost all *pas ordinaire alla breve* pieces: the march to which Ferrando and Guglielmo go off to war (or pretend to) in *Così Fan Tutte* is an obvious example. There are a number of marches, also, in the serenades of Mozart, concert pieces which imitate the music of the parade ground. They are mostly in *pas ordinaire*, in 2/4, though occasionally one encounters a different tempo: the *marcia* which commences the *Haffner* Serenade, K. 249, is written with four beats per measure at a speed that approximates to 88 steps to the minute. It was written in Salzburg in 1776, and its character, marked *maestoso,* is somewhat

Marche

Figure 11.2.

Maestoso

Figure 11.3.

different from the operatic marches so far discussed. It reminds us that the old slow march was accelerating and changing during this period.

Although quicker marching speeds existed as early as the 1760s, operatic military marches are always in *alla breve, pas ordinaire*. Not until 1817 is the military spirit enshrined in an operatic quick march, with four steps to the measure. The famous opening to Rossini's *La Gazza Ladra* commemorates the protagonist Fernando, a soldier just returned from the war. Beginning with a snare drum roll, the march tune, *maestoso marziale*, is usually played a little faster than quarter note = 100. If marched in *alla breve*, the resultant 50 steps to the minute would be slower than any known drill speed. By this time, troops are almost certainly marching in step, so the speed is all-important. The very loud dynamic, the rattle of two snare drums, and the presence of piccolo, clarinets, and trombone suggest the influence of "Turkish music"—and Turkish marches, of course, were always quick.

Although Schubert's marches for piano duet are mostly contemporary with this example, many of them are in the old *pas ordinaire*. The second of the *Trois Marches Héroiques,* D. 602, composed about 1818, is presumably such a piece (fig. 11.3). The composer marks it, correctly, in *alla breve* time, two steps to a measure. The famous *Marche Militaire* in D, however, with its opening fanfare and *allegro vivace* instruction in 2/4 time, seems a *Geschwindschritt* march, needing a tempo nearer to 108 to the minute.

Schubert frames in march rhythm a song about soldiering, the *Romanze des Richard Löwenherz*, the king's song from Scott's *Ivanhoe* ("Grosser Thaten that der Ritter"). There is a suggestion of trumpet calls in the piano part and the voice sings a fanfare-like melody, though in the minor. The entire song is in a dotted march style, and the fanfares move eventually to the major. The tempo is questionable; it is marked *mässig* and sounds slow, but if the time signature is correct in giving four beats to the bar, this is too quick for *pas ordinaire*, about 88 beats to the minute.

Henceforth, the marches of nineteenth-century concert and stage music are mostly quick. The offstage wind band prefacing the chorus of soldiers in Berlioz's *La Damnation de Faust* plays a march which, written in 2/4 time, is presumably just one step to the measure, and seems to sound well at half note = 76 or so, a quickish *pas ordinaire*. The same composer's "Marche au Supplice" from the *Symphonie Fantastique* has a 4/4 signature; if we are to accept this, then the resultant quick march must proceed at about 120 steps to the minute, fast for that time. The character of the music seems to confirm this, though of course an *alla breve* step would yield a pace of quarter note = 60, exactly the old *pas ordinaire*. When a later composer writes a march in *pas ordinaire*, as Dvořák does in the second movement of the Second Symphony, the slowness of the pace is particularly noticed: this piece is marked *adagio molto, tempo di marcia*, although the pace is no slower than 88 to the minute (there is an eighth-note beat in 2/4 time).

Marches in operas tend now to be quick, as we saw in *La Gazza Ladra*. The famous march tune that concludes the overture to Rossini's *Guillaume Tell* (1829) resembles a French bugle call written down in 1831, the *pas redoublé*, marked at 130 steps to the minute by a French bandmaster (shown in appendix 2). Equally famous is the Grand March from *Aida*, with its onstage trumpets unmistakably warlike in character. It proceeds at about quarter note = 100. It is not in *alla breve*. Of course, Verdi's operas are full of march rhythms, many of them in arias or choruses, like the choruses "E bella la guerra" in *La Forza del Destino* and "Viva Italia" in *La Battaglia di Legnano*. The epitome of the march number is the duet "Dio, che nell'alma infondere" in *Don Carlo*, a magnificent piece for tenor and baritone in which the focus is on the two voices; there is no "Turkish" orchestra to add its noise.

The many marches of Romantic and modern music are mostly quick. Only marches specifically designated funeral marches, or which imply a funereal spirit (like Chopin's piano Prelude in C minor, Op. 28 no. 20), proceed at slower speeds, though a spirit of great solemnity, found in the trio section of the first *Pomp and Circumstance* march of Elgar, may go as slow as 80 to the minute. Much more typically, the Romantic concert march goes very fast indeed: the fifth *Pomp and Circumstance* number is usually played faster than 140.

(c) Quotations of trumpet calls

Trumpet signals, like marches, could be associated with civic ceremony. For example, the trumpet of the herald—still today a feature of ceremonial life—is sometimes heard in opera. Gluck's tragedy *Alceste* (1767) begins with a scene in which the people mourn the coming death of their king Admeto; his death is then proclaimed by a herald, introduced by a fanfare of two trumpets in D. Much later, at the arrival by ship of the Venetian ambassadors in act 3 of Verdi's *Otello* (1887), there is a brilliant herald's call for two trumpets. The herald's fanfare seems to be endemic in our history.

There is good evidence, however, that trumpet calls, all things being equal, normally carried a military reference. Above all, some of the calls in concert music and opera were literal quotations of items from the military repertoire, always associated with soldiers on stage or titles that betrayed a military context. They prove the soldierly evocation of the trumpet fanfare, which surely persists in similar gestures in untitled and unworded items. Almost as persuasive evidence are the trumpet calls in military style that lie very close to real army signals without being actual quotations, and are sounded in vocal works that identify them as representations of the world of the soldier.

Haydn's "Military" Symphony (no. 100 in G) was popularly so-called in its own day. It must have been so intended, for it quotes a signal of the Imperial army. The slow movement presents an *alla breve, pas ordinaire* march tune, later with the paraphernalia of Turkish percussion (triangle, cymbals, bass drum), then with only oboes, clarinets, bassoons, horns—that is, a *Harmonie*. Later the trumpet in C is left alone for an unaccompanied solo, and this turns out to be the *Generalmarsch*, the command for all squadrons to march (not merely a particular squadron, which would have its own signal). This signal was first recorded in 1751 (Lackner 1997, 332) and remained standard for the Austro-Hungarian army throughout the next century. Two versions are found in appendix 2.

Lackner (1997, 350) asserts that the rudimentary trumpet calls in Beethoven's *Battle of Vittoria* Symphony are real English and French signals. He does not support this view; and indeed, it seems unlikely, since the two nations are given exactly the same signals. These simple calls do not appear in standard collections. Probably Beethoven invented them in an idle mood, as idle as that in which he composed the rest of the symphony.

However, there is an exact quotation a few years later. It comes in the overture to Auber's opera *Fra Diavolo* (1830). In this case, the signal is not one of those in the national collections, but a regimental march command, that of the Austrian Infantry Regiment No. 59 of Salzburg (Lackner 1997, 403–404). The army signal is shown at figure 11.4a; Auber's quotation, for trumpet in F, follows at 11.4b. It announces the military element in the drama; the tenor Lorenzo is an officer of *carabinieri*.

It is easy to guess that the offstage brass band in part 4 of Berlioz's *La Damnation de Faust* plays an arrangement of a true military call, prefacing a chorus of soldiers. It is the French cavalry *retraite* of 1825 (see appendix 2). The same signal, approximately, is heard at the beginning of Tchaikovsky's *Capriccio Italien* (1880); conceivably, there was an Italian signal that was closely related to the French one.

The short trumpet blast in the third movement of Mahler's Symphony no. 3 is an absolutely literal quotation. This occurs at an oddly disorienting moment; there is an episode for posthorn (at rehearsal figure 14), marked *sehr gemächlich* (very leisurely), *frei vorgetragen* (performed freely), *wie am weiter Ferne* (as though in the far distance), *wie die Weise eines Posthorns* (like a posthorn tune). Mahler must have known that posthorn tunes were brilliant, rhetorical affairs. Heinitz reproduces a

Figure 11.4.

whole page of these, taken from a posthorn tutor of Mahler's time (Heinitz 1928, 69; see also Lackner 1993, 243–244). Yet Mahler's other instructions confirm that this languid, plangent melody, accompanied by a high chord for violins, is pastoral; indeed, it is surely a kind of *ranz des vaches*. Lackner compares it to two folksongs, "Es zogen drei Burschen" and "Freut euch des Lebens" (Lackner 1997, 370). Why did Mahler choose a posthorn for this pastoral nuance, an instrument which would have to be specially obtained for the performance? The composer's resources of irony and enigma are in play. As the posthorn episode comes to a close (just before fig. 17) the scene suddenly focuses on a military trumpet call, "schnell und schmetternd wie eine Fanfare, ohne Rücksicht auf das Tempo," quick and ringing like a fanfare, without respect for the tempo. The original pace of the movement then returns, *comodo* and *scherzando*. The intruding signal is the *abblasen* (the fallout; Mahler's version is identical to the army call, shown in appendix 2), and the instrument is the trumpet in F.

A further example of literal quotation is to be found in a much slighter work, the overture to Franz von Suppé's operetta *Die leichte Kavallerie* (1866), which has a contemporary Austrian military setting. This quotes at length the cavalry call *la retraite* (see appendix 2). It is worth noting that Suppé rationalizes the free rhythm of the call, which, since it is not a command to march, is played *senza misura*.

A word should be said about the rather simple Austrian call *habt acht!* (see appendix 2). In various forms—chromatically altered, with minor third, rhythmically adjusted—this signal is ubiquitous in concert and stage music. It is played many times by onstage trumpets in Wagner's *Lohengrin,* where the quotations are virtually exact—as they are, for example, in Kreutzer's opera *Das Nachtlager in Granada,* second act finale, in Liszt's symphonic poem *Hungaria,* just before letter G, and in the penultimate measure of Mahler's song *Revelge.* So common is this signal that it may easily be overlooked as an example of true quotation; it becomes a mere orchestral cliché. Nevertheless, it often lurks behind instrumental figures in familiar music.

There is a theoretical issue in the passages just mentioned. They are literal quotations, and thus are poor examples of the musical topic. The topic is a musical convention whereby a certain stylistic habit refers to an aspect of the social and cultural world, independently of the actual context, and through that aspect to changing historical facts and finally to universals of human behavior and feeling. The topic is most fully at work when it forms a pointer to the semantic of an instrumental piece without words or title. A quotation is an intrusion; it introduces into the semantic of the text another semantic, that of another text. This is excellently shown in the example from Mahler's Third Symphony, which is irrelevant in terms of its surroundings but might acquire sense if the movement were a kind of programmatic lantern show of extraneous allusions, like those faded salon-medleys of Albert W. Ketèlbey, *In a Monastery Garden, In a Persian Market,* and others. A topical reference that says, in effect, "Here a cavalry trumpeter blows a signal", is not really functioning as a topic. Neither the pastoral reference nor the fanfare is a direct key to the semantic of the symphony.

Most important of all, an exact quotation cannot be adapted to convey expressive truths, because it is inseparable from social truths. The *Generalmarsch* initially signifies the contemporary soldier; since it is a real signal, it reflects chiefly the modern army's euphoric portrayal of itself, in spite of the civilian's discomfort with this. Change a note or two, and it may suggest the might of ancient Rome and the valor of Roland and Bayard, or on the contrary it may turn into satire of the debased army world, or even invoke the tragedy of men who must fall in battle. The literal quotation cannot embody these changing expressions.

Literal quotations, nevertheless, are quasi-topics. They are chosen because of their topical reference, though they remain intrusions. In this respect, they differ from other quotations, like the fragment of *Tristan und Isolde* in act 3 of *Die Meistersinger.* Topical quotations are not integrated in the semantic of the work. They prove, paradoxically, the reference of the topic, without truly functioning as topics.

(d) Imitation trumpet signals

If the literal quotation is merely a proto-topic, we would expect composers to invent realistic pseudo-quotations when they wish to evoke soldiering. And indeed, most trumpet calls in concert music and opera evince not so much the "direct adoption of authentic military signals", but rather "signal-like contours or signal motives" (Lackner 1997, 332). These calls, although soldiering is still central in their signification, have a more direct access to the cultural unit; they evoke warfare and soldiering, but—if euphoric—they begin to glorify it with the aura of the primeval warrior. Eventually, the military topic, like the hunt tradition, may offer a direct channel to the manly and active associations of idealized soldiering, without pretending to be an actual military signal. Finally, the intermediary reference to soldiering falls away, and the topic directly evokes moral character: heroism, adventure, manliness, courage, strength, decision.

There is a formula to secure a kind of instant soldier. First write a figure using the notes of the harmonic series, between the third and eighth harmonic, and preferably within the range of the old cavalry trumpet. To this basis, add a double- or triple-tongued effect. It is worth noting that this rhythm, often written as three notes, two shorts and a long, double-tongued, may have been played differently in the eighteenth century. Altenberg tells us that the three-note motive, with two

Ausdruck:

ri - ti - ri-ton   ti - ri - ti - ri-ton

Abgekürzte
Bezeichnung:

Figure 11.5.

short notes, should be played as "ritiriton", with three short notes triple-tongued, or as "tiritiriton", with four short notes (fig. 11.5; Altenberg 1795, 92–93). It is sometimes written in this way, of course; for example, the fanfares in the minuet of Haydn's Symphony no. 93, and the flourish that starts the Wedding March from Mendelssohn's *Midsummer Night's Dream* music are written with three short notes, "ritiriton". Perhaps the ubiquitous written figure, showing only two short notes, should be played as "ritiriton" or "tiritiriton".

For the moment, then, let us consider trumpet signals, or copies of trumpet signals on other instruments, which retain an expressly military association. The famous offstage trumpet signal in *Fidelio*, and in the overture *Leonora No. 3*, sounds like a true military call, though it is not an actual quotation. It can easily be related to real signals: beginning like the Austrian *abblasen*, already mentioned, it then rises in a shadow of part of the *Generalmarsch* and concludes with a fragment of the *Alarme* (see Nowak 1955, who relates it to several further Austrian cavalry signals). This may be an example of a heralding fanfare (it announces the arrival of Don Fernando and thus the salvation of Florestan and Leonore); we are told that it is a signal of the *Turmmusikanten,* posted on the battlements to watch for the liberator's appearance.

The fanfare that introduces the final section of Rossini's overture to *Guillaume Tell* (1829) is a textbook example of the formula, without reproducing a real army signal. It represents one of those march commands that are played at the pace of the march, and introduce a march tune played by the whole band. The march itself, since it resembles the *pas redoublé* trumpet call, may be assumed to proceed at 130 to the minute, as already explained. It is often wrongly heard as equestrian because of its use in a radio and television series, *The Lone Ranger,* but the equestrian topic is quite different, of course (see *Sense*, 45–65). The opera that follows is largely concerned with personal rivalries and vengeance, but Kobbé considers, very credibly, that the trumpet signal represents "the call to arms and the uprising of the Swiss against their Austrian oppressors" (Kobbé 1987, 353).

Countless operas of this period introduce trumpet signals in military style. Lackner lists Weber's *Euryanthe* and *Oberon,* Meyerbeer's *Les Huguenots* and *Robert le Diable,* Halévy's *La Juive,* Wagner's *Rienzi,* Maillart's *Les Dragons de Villars,* Bizet's *Carmen,* and others (Lackner 1997, 405–411). When we survey these signals, it becomes clear that there is a theatrical type of trumpet signal which avoids certain crude habits of the cavalry trumpeter and adds a sophistication alien to the parade ground. Most important, the true signal is normally confined to the third register, occasionally taking in the note below (the fifth of the second register). It is thus

Figure 11.6.

purely triadic. Stage trumpet calls, however, often ascend into the fourth register, but treat it as though it were another third register; that is, they remain triadic in a region where the instrument is actually diatonic.

An initial example, which does not, however, rise into the fourth register, is the signal announcing the great song contest in act 3 of *Die Meistersinger*. This begins with a quotation from an old Prussian cavalry signal, *remettre le sabre* (Kastner 1848, 44). The continuation, with its introverted rapid figures, somewhat difficult to play, would have been quickly simplified by a military player. The signal for the changing of guard in act 1 of *Carmen* is played on the trumpet, of course, and could not be played on a bugle because it utilizes the E on the bottom of the stave, sounded as the fifth harmonic. The trumpet would not be appropriate for Don José's unit, since they are dragoons, an arm commanded by the bugle, which lacks this note. However, it can easily be adapted for the bugle; rather surprisingly, it almost exactly matches a later British army bugle call, the regimental call of the First Brigade of Foot Guards (*Trumpet and Bugle Sounds* 1909, 24, fig. 11.6). Perhaps a British bandmaster had visited the opera house. There are a few slightly similar calls in the French army repertoire; for example, the *pas accéléré* of the Chasseurs d'Orléans, recorded in a French royal ordinance of 1845 (see appendix 2), though this is in simple duple time, rather than the 6/8 of Bizet's tune. It is not the French *à cheval*, as Grove's authors appear to claim; such a familiar cavalry call would have sounded out of place. Bizet's tune perfectly delineates the difference between repertoire music and the military; as a bugle call, it could not descend to the low E, and as a trumpet call, it would be mostly in the fourth register, seldom entered by the cavalry trumpeter because here the instrument is diatonic. Significantly, the chorus of children who follow the marching troops sings a caricatured bugle call, playable on the bugle in D and thus lacking the low E (sounding F sharp; of course, this note would not do, since the music is in the minor mode). It echoes some such signal as the *marcher par le flanc gauche* of the French carabiniers, from the 1845 royal ordinance, shown by Kastner (1848, 28). Somewhat further from any identifiable model is the trumpet signal in Donizetti's *La Fille du Régiment*, though this is peculiarly convincing. It bears a passing resemblance to *l'instruction*, a French cavalry signal of 1825 (Kastner 1848, 22). Though the opera is set in the Tyrol, the "regiment" of which Marie is "daughter" is a unit of French grenadiers.

A further departure from the parade signal is the framing of trumpet calls in homophonic parts, like the *bicinia* and *tricinia* of the hunting horn. Some military sources give arrangements of trumpet signals in three and four parts. For example, a French cavalry ordinance of 1825 (Kastner 1848, 21–23) presents arrangements of several calls for three and four trumpets. But such arrangements cannot be considered typical of the military trumpet signal; they clearly could not be accomplished in battle. In general, the harmonized arrangement must be thought of as a huntsman's resource. Sometimes one suspects that harmonized signals in repertoire music are echoing the *civil* call, which may be the case with the blast of trumpets that introduces the entry of the singers in Wagner's *Tannhäuser*, act 2 scene 4. However, the aria "Celeste Aida", near the beginning of Verdi's *Aida* (1871), starts with a brilliant fanfare for four trumpets. The singer, Radames, hopes that he may be able to marry Aida after returning victorious from a campaign against the Ethiopians. This will depend on his being chosen to lead the army; and it is to this choice that the fanfares refer. The reference, then, is military. The three-part trumpet calls characterizing the hero's going to battle in Strauss's *Ein Heldenleben* have been mentioned in chapter 6.

It will be perceived that each one of these synthetic military signals is positive and strong in character. There is no irony, no recognition of the low and shabby nature of the modern soldiery, nor is there any use of the topic to refer to the lamentable fate of many soldiers or the swindle of the recruiting officer, glamorizing the military life in order to lead young men to their deaths. These unheroic references are not available so long as the fanfares are evocations of military scenes on the stage.

(e) Toward the topic

Unquestionably the military march and trumpet call, as well as their signaling function, had the aim of "cheering up" the soldiers (*aufmuntern*, Flemming's word, in Rameis 1976, 17). Perhaps the soldiers were cheered up by the cultural mythology of the hero; even the decadent soldiers of the day liked to think of themselves as little Rolands. Yet the concert composer was placed in an awkward position; if she simply copied the military signal, audiences might think also of the decadence of contemporary armies. To situate her composition in the heroic world of the cultural unit, the composer had to depart a little from exact reproduction. This was so *a fortiori* when satire or dysphoria was meant, but all expressive use of the topic, euphoric or dysphoric, had to adapt and distort the army signals. The distortion of the march and fanfare was necessary in order to move away from a mere picturing of soldiers to an invocation of the cultural theme. Signaling and marching are then less in evidence than imaginative representation, moving from a generalized vigor and optimism toward the theme of the warrior hero. The warriors invoked had lived long before any of these marches or signals could have been heard, of course.

A subtle example is to be found in Schubert's *Ellens Gesang I* (D. 837), based on Scott's *Lady of the Lake*. There is a specific military reference, for the song is about a soldier home from war ("Raste, Krieger, Krieg ist aus"); yet the topical themes in the music are all negative, since the text consistently tells of a war that is over. The lyrical opening is laid over an accompaniment in a serenade-like triple time. Yet the accompanying figure has both the "tiriton" and the triadic contour of a fanfare, and the melodious vocal theme is not only fanfare-shaped, but virtually quotes the *abblasen*, the cavalry call that marks the end of a parade, appropriate for a war that

Allegro mosso con brio

Figure 11.7.

is finished. Later the text speaks both of drumbeats and trumpet signals (though calling them "deathly horns"):

> Nicht der Trommel wildes Rasen,
> Nicht des Kriegs gebietend Wort,
> Nicht der Todeshörner Blasen
> Scheuchen deinen Schlummer fort.

No furious drumming, no commanding word of war, no blast of deathly horns shall frighten thee from sleep.

The piano thrums with a repetitive tattoo, and the voice again sings a triadic shape, this time a little suggestive of the *habt Acht!*

A simple and very characteristic example of a military reference without text or title is heard at the opening of the last movement of Dvořák's Eighth Symphony. Two trumpets sound a brilliant call in unison, unaccompanied. It resembles those many military signals that are virtually confined to a single note. But instead of remaining on one note—the eighth harmonic—it digresses upward to the ninth harmonic, and down to the seventh. The out-of-tune seventh was never utilized in cavalry calls; here, of course, its intonation is corrected with the use of valves. The intruding note turns a typical signal into a poetic idea.

Similarly poetic is the opening fanfare of the *Marche et Cortège de Bacchus,* the finale of Delibes's ballet *Sylvia.* A trace of the seventh harmonic gives an archaic tone, perhaps apt for these "bacchantes guerrières armées de javelines", warrior girls armed with javelins.

The progressive departure from the style of the parade ground may be observed in Liszt's symphonic poems. *Festklänge, Hungaria,* and *Hunnenschlacht* are heroic pieces, full of marches and trumpet calls. However, the first of these, with no historical reference, deploys fanfares and marches that are near to the military repertoire of the day, including a signal for two trumpets which strongly suggests a contemporary march command (fig. 11.7) and a rousing march that might have come from a military bandsheet. The victorious battle pictured in this piece may be, in fact, that of Liszt himself against the opponents to his marriage with the Princess Carolyne Sayn-Wittgenstein. His triumph was short-lived; the pope later revoked his sanction of the lady's divorce (Ramann 1887, 309). *Hungaria* is permeated with march tunes—the opening dynamic is *quasi andante marziale*—yet the military features are distorted, played in minor keys with the coloring of Hungarian traditional music (with the exception of the *habt Acht!* already mentioned). A fanfare for three trumpets in F, marked *allegro eroico,* has the shifting harmonies made possible by the valve instrument, sounding poetic and rhetorical (fig. 11.8).

Allegro eroico

Figure 11.8.

Figure 11.9.

Hunnenschlacht, a musical translation of a painting by Kaulbach, portrays the battle of the Catalaunian Plains (A.D. 451) at which Attila's pagan Huns were defeated by a force of Christian Goths (Ramann 1887, 268–270). It is dominated by a fanfare tune that begins in cellos and bassoons and progresses across the whole orchestra; it is later marked *schlachtruf*, battle cry, confirming its warlike reference. It is, however, in the minor key and obsessively sequential, an expressive idea rather than an imitation army signal (fig. 11.9). In this piece the cultural evocation of the heroic warrior is being accessed through musical ideas with roots in contemporary military music, distorted for the purpose of expression.

It is surprising that the truest paradigm of the military topic, the "sword" leitmotiv in the *Ring*, is sufficiently altered for a great musicologist, Carl Dahlhaus, to miss the point completely and describe it as resembling "the action of drawing a sword" (Dahlhaus 1979 [1971], 116). It suggests, in fact, the ubiquitous *habt Acht!* except that it spans a tenth, a little too much for a cavalry trumpeter. It perfectly exemplifies how the modern cavalry signal can be slightly modified to evoke an individual warlike hero from myth. The slight modification is enough to bypass the reference to contemporary armies and, apparently, to deceive Dahlhaus.

One of the repertoire's most rousing marches, in the third movement of Tchaikovsky's "Pathétique" Symphony, has plenty of signs of the military topic, including the "ritiriton" in the brass, though its speed (about quarter note = 150) is faster than the fastest pace ever known on the parade ground. But it exhibits another feature of the art repertoire: the movement begins as a scherzo, the dance topic being progressively overrun by the march. This composer likes to mix topics: in the Fifth Symphony the topic of the noble horse merges into a waltzing ballroom (*Sense*, 54–55).

In this piece the mediating factor of the military topic, the reference to contemporary military music, has disappeared. It is not possible to know whether the composer thought of marching soldiers. The topic is therefore working in its true sense, evoking its associations without the listener having to bring armies to mind. The

The Soldier Represented 171

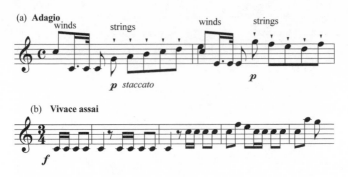

Figure 11.10.

music is virile, active, warlike, powerful, heroic, but purely on the level of representation. The indexicality at the heart of the topic, through which these associations are accessed by a showing of another musical repertoire, is now hidden. Do soldiers march in Tchaikovsky's brilliant march? Perhaps their ideals, their imagination, their pride are marching in this piece, rather than their feet.

At one further step from this we may find melodies in the shape of trumpet fanfares, with no explicit reference to army signals. It will be recalled that the "Horn Signal" Symphony of Haydn (no. 31 in D) contains a figure, played on horns, that somewhat resembles the *Generalmarsch*. If this is a true perception, its playing on horns is easily explained, for trumpets are not employed in Haydn's earlier symphonies. This may have led hearers to assume that it was a hunting-horn signal and to make those assertions about its background that we have already questioned.

Hence the many military references in Haydn may be sought at first in horn parts or elsewhere. A passage for two horns in D in the very early Symphony no. 1 is clearly military. The little fanfares at the start of Symphony no. 7 (*Le Midi*), played by the wind instruments, perhaps indicate that military parades took place at midday (fig. 11.10a). Two horns in G stand in for trumpets in the fanfares of Symphony no. 47. When trumpets at last become available, they are boosted by horns in C alto (sounding at the same pitch as the trumpets) in the military slow introduction to Symphony no. 50; drums, also, enhance the cavalry evocation. Horns and trumpets, playing in octaves, characterize the minuet as a military piece too. Symphony no. 82 ("The Bear") presents trumpet fanfares in triple time that recall the "Horn Signal" (fig. 11.10b), though the finale of this work is clearly a pastoral number. A London symphony, no. 97 in C, again presents fanfares in triple time, played by the orchestral tutti in unison, which turn into a symphonic theme.

Mozart, too, derived themes from fanfare motives, like the snatch of military sentiment at the start of the E flat Piano Concerto, K. 271, played by strings, oboes, and horns. The minuet of the *Haffner* Symphony (no. 35, K. 385) presents a rising triad employing trumpets and horns, echoed in immediate diminution by the strings.

Indeed, the strings may themselves offer fanfare-like themes in the absence of brass. The opening of Haydn's String Quartet in C, Op. 54 no. 2, is typical; unsuited

Figure 11.11.

Figure 11.12.

to any brass instrument, it unmistakably has the brilliant self-confidence of the military topic. The finale of the Quartet in B flat, Op. 50 no. 1, is similar, turning a snatch of fanfare into a contredanse. Strings give out both an introductory fanfare and a march in *pas ordinaire* in the opening of Mozart's *Eine kleine Nachtmusik*.

Finally, the triadic shape of the trumpet call may be almost imperceptible. Who would guess that the gentle triadic opening violin theme of Mozart's Piano Concerto in B flat, K. 595, is hiding a snatch of the military spirit? It is more obviously an example of the "singing allegro" topic. Yet the tiny fragment for wind that echoes the first phrase recalls the *abblasen;* with its march-style slow movement and its triadic finale, this is surely an elegant *concerto guerriero* (fig. 11.11).

It will be recalled that the early march was usually slow, and marches appear so frequently as slow movements that it would be wearisome to list them. Haydn's "Oxford" Symphony, no. 92, and Mozart's *Haffner* Symphony will suffice. Marches, like fanfares, may appear in disguise: Mozart's Piano Concerto in C, K. 415, begins with a soft, unharmonized string figure in a typical march style (and, in this *allegro* tempo, at a plausible *pas ordinaire* pace, if the signature is changed to *alla breve*) that later blossoms into fanfares both for trumpets and for strings.

(f) The topic within the narrative

As with other musical topics, the military topic is functioning typically when it occurs as an episode or brief reference during the course of a narrative, especially in a piece with no program or text.

Chopin's music has a heroic and chevaleresque side, much demonstrated in the polonaises. His Fantaisie in F minor, Op. 49, begins in the tempo of a reflective

Figure 11.13.

funeral march. Much of the piece echoes the march topic to some extent, and this tendency culminates in two stirring march episodes. They are preceded by virtuosic flourishes resembling fanfares, combining the topic of the military signal with brilliant pianistic display in motives that are doubly defiant, as though illustrating W. S. Gilbert's "piano's martial blast" that rouses "the echoes of the past" (m. 109, fig. 11.12). The march that follows is in an awkward tempo, however. It is played at about 85 to the minute, which is a rapid *pas ordinaire,* not a *pas redoublé,* assuming that they are conceived in *alla breve.* Yet the spirit is vigorous, furiously exciting, as though these marches were, in fact, marched at four to the measure (fig. 11.13). This would yield a march at 170 to the minute, impossible for a marching squadron. As in Tchaikovsky's Sixth Symphony, the marching is imaginary, designed for minds and spirits rather than feet. The climactic position of these episodes—as though the latent march spirit of the whole Fantaisie were suddenly released into the daylight—requires a celestial, rather than an earthly march.

When Weber, in two of his overtures, unfurls the march topic shortly after the outset, you guess that he is prefiguring marches from the body of the opera. Thus the march of Charlemagne's court in act 3 of *Oberon* is played very quietly at m. 10 of the overture. There is a similar number in march time, the trio and chorus "Ich bau' auf Gott" from act 1 of *Euryanthe,* prefigured at m. 8 of that opera's overture. These may be considered operatic as well as topical gestures. But when the same procedure appears in concert overtures, the military topic is uniquely in play. Brahms's *Tragic Overture,* Op. 81, is written in a darkly military spirit, more inward and profound than the constantly lurking marches of the choral *Triumphlied,* Op. 55, which was dedicated to the kaiser. The march topic asserts itself at m. 5 of the overture. Its working out leads, during the development section, to a kind of nocturnal march for muffled wind and bass pizzicato, a highly evocative moment that suggests an army of silent ghosts (fig. 11.14). Brahms was thrilled with the military; he had an extensive collection of toy soldiers, according to Albert Dietrich (Dietrich & Widmann 1904, 37–38).

The military signal can work the same kind of magic. Mendelssohn's overture *The Hebrides* was, famously, written after a visit to Scotland, and especially to the island of Staffa where the composer saw Fingal's Cave, an immense cavern into which the waves perpetually swirl. The work's principal theme evokes the surge of

Figure 11.14.

Figure 11.15.

the sea. One would hardly notice that it is built on a descending triad, initially in the minor mode. But the topic of the military signal emerges later as an important reference. At a still point in the development, trumpets and horns blow a powerful fanfare, answered softly by the "sea" motive in the strings. The fanfares continue, each time answered by the "sea", sometimes in its major form (fig. 11.15). This mysterious moment at the center of the overture illustrates the power of music to link and merge topics. Somewhere in the sound of the Scottish sea, which surrounds the nation and everywhere penetrates its heart in sea lochs, is echoed the martial glory of her past.

(g) Soldiers ironic and dysphoric

A few dysphoric *hunting* calls have been mentioned above, but it cannot be said that dysphoria was a common resource of the hunt topic. It is different with the military topic. As the plays of Lenz and Mercier attest, everyone in the late eighteenth century was aware of the debauched nature of the contemporary soldiery. Above all, the young men who enlisted as officers were sometimes empty-headed braggarts, adding fancy bits to their uniforms and swaggering and strutting to fascinate the girls. They were a laughingstock, and Mozart laughs heartily in *Figaro*. The aria "Non più andrai", already mentioned, parodies the military topic in a diminutive march, with off-the-peg trumpet signals. This march is really *too* military; almost every note is related to the triad of the fanfare. It contains nothing that is not "military topic"; it is an example of the "quantitative exaggeration" which Esti Sheinberg considers to be a component of musical satire (Sheinberg 2000, 120). More military than anything in the military repertoire itself, it achieves only caricature, but the satire is affectionate.

"Non più andrai" is a kind of toy-soldier march. Comic opera sported other such marches: the air "Quel plaisir d'être soldat", from Boieldieu's opera *La dame blanche,* characterizes the charming Lieutenant George Brown, an Englishman just returned from war who finds himself at a christening party in the Scottish Highlands. Although he had been wounded and nursed back to life by a charming girl (who, of course, turns up later in the opera), Brown is not a hero but a breezy, devil-may-care fellow who is evidently the toast of the ladies. Marches for toy soldiers have persisted; they appear in Tchaikovsky's *Nutcracker,* in Vaughan Williams's incidental music to *The Wasps* (the *March-past of the Kitchen Utensils*), and in Prokofiev's opera *The Love for Three Oranges.*

The *Lied* repertoire contains a number of dysphoric marches. Indeed, the intimate circumstances of song performance make it harder for the military topic to appear in its euphoric form, since this is connected with a popular expression that is too crude for the refinement of the salon. Thus, lieder are usually about the woman's loss of her sweetheart or husband or the impending death of the soldier. Wolf's "Sie blasen zum Abmarsch" (from the *Spanish Song Book*), in which a girl laments the departure of her fiancé to war, though marked *im Marschtempo,* has grinding harmonies in G minor, sounding cold, dejected. There are tiny bugle calls; he is an infantryman (the "Fussvolk" are mentioned).

Sheinberg describes the process when a military march is satirized. "A march is a musical topic that correlates with the military. If some elements of this topic are presented in a way that is incongruous with its stylistic norms, e.g. by their exaggeration, then not only the musical topic of the march will be satirized, but the whole ethics correlated with the military . . . will be highlighted in a derogatory light" (Sheinberg 2000, 25). She is here concerned with a different sort of exaggeration, the transgression of "musical norms" like the norm of pitch: music that is "too high", like the roulades of the Queen of Night, can seem ironic. She refers to "the use of the piccolo for the musical topic of 'a military march'" (26); she is surely referring here to Prokofiev's music to the movie *Lieutenant Kizhe* (1933).

This was based on a story by Yury Tynianov, "a charmingly dry and absurd tale that was perfectly suited to Prokofiev's own satirical sense of humor" (Robinson 1987, 277). A tsarist clerk makes a clerical slip, writing the unlikely name "Kizhe" on a list of officers. When it is assumed that such a man exists, the clerk is too cowed to admit his error and Kizhe advances through the ranks, being finally made a general by the tsar. Tynianov's tale is "a witty attack on official stupidity and the profoundly Russian terror of displeasing one's superior", satirizing "the stupidity of royalty" (Robinson 1987, 277, 280).

The orchestral suite which Prokofiev adapted from the film score begins with "The Birth of Kizhe". A trumpet signal (actually a cornet; Kizhe was, perhaps, an officer of infantry), is heard in the distance; it is not very much like the military

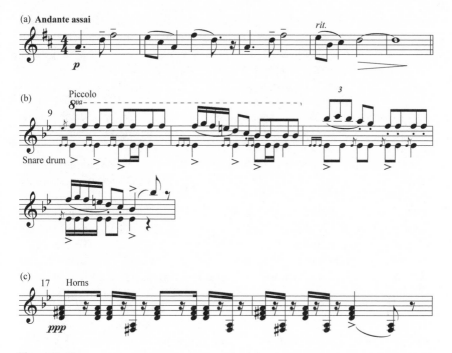

Figure 11.16.

repertoire, but almost suggests a *ranz des vaches*. A snare drum begins a childishly copybook march rhythm, and the piccolo plays an absurdly banal tune, followed by a trite fanfare-like figure for four horns (fig. 11.16, a to c; the piccolo is shown as written, and of course sounds even higher). The high register of the piccolo, a transgression of the "norm", is only one aspect of the level of irony in this music. The drum rhythm and the faceless march tune are studied variants on the musical signifier, because they are too much the topic, not enough themselves. A veritable military march identifies itself not solely because of the signs of the topic, but also because of other signs, the signs of its individuality as a musical item. There are no such signs in "The Birth of Kizhe", only banality. Banality-for-individuality represents an aspect of *expression,* and so this music accomplishes satire by means of an adaptation of topical signifiers. Another banal march by this composer, in the opera *The Love for Three Oranges,* has been mentioned above as a "toy-soldier" number.

Another military march, that of the first movement of Shostakovich's Seventh Symphony, is similar in its semantic structure, but very different in its tone and its level of dysphoria. As in *Kizhe,* it rehearses some of the signs of the military topic in a context of utter banality. There is the over-simple tattoo of a snare drum. Each phrase repeats the same vacuous rhythm. And as the tune is itself repeated, the fragments are echoed between oboe and bassoon, they are played in a limping canon of clarinets and oboes, and they are eventually blasted by a powerful brass

The Soldier Represented 177

ensemble, a "military" bass figure joining in and finally rising to dominate the texture. Always the tune, in its full vacuity, is played complete and unvaried. This episode is a "universalised image of stupidity and crass tastelessness" (according to the conductor Yevgeny Mravinsky, quoted by Sheinberg, 2000, 91). This music is much more alienated than *Kizhe*, evidently because the military pomp of the Soviet Union is being attacked, rather than the absurdity of tsarist days, long past and in any case open to ridicule in a changed world. The Soviet state had threatened and constrained Shostakovich; in Stalinist times, life was dangerous for everyone. The composer guessed, however, that the political leaders would be crass enough to overlook the satirical content of his music and accept its "overt meaning" (Sheinberg's term, 2000, 58). This was risky; the march is a black and angry protest against oppression.

Many composers have turned to dysphoria in the military topic, but instead of satire they have chosen tragedy. Mahler's military songs are all about soldiers who go to their deaths: from the *Knaben Wunderhorn* songs, *Revelge* is about a drummer, killed on the battlefield, who joins a macabre roll call of the dead outside his sweetheart's house, and *Der Tamboursg'sell* is about another drummer, condemned to hanging, presumably for desertion. *Wo die schönen Trompeten blasen* pictures a soldier knocking on his sweetheart's door; before returning to her for their marriage, he must go off to war, "where the fine trumpets blow, and where I will find my home under the green grass". These songs show how the composer mixed drumbeats with trumpet signals, all within the meter of the march, and how march tunes and trumpet figures were bent into dysphoric forms.

These motives are seldom exact quotations, though *Revelge* ends with the *habt Acht!* literally played on trumpet in C. An earlier passage in the song (the orchestral interlude between strophes 5 and 6) shows how this simple shape could be progressively soured. The whole song is based on the rhythm of the quick march, snare drum and orchestra constantly echoing the drum figures of the *Exercier Reglement*. The opening roll, answered by three trumpets, is in the spirit of the drummer's version of the *Generalmarsch* (drum signals for the infantry bear absolutely no relation to the cavalry trumpet signals, of course), and the relentless beat later in the song surely copies the "drag" or "ruff" (called *Wirbelschlag* in the reglement). However, at this point the snare drum itself joins the strings, so that we hear the "drag" itself along with its imitation (after the words "so liegen wie gemäht", fig. 11.17).

This string figure, with two or three crushed rising notes before the arrival on the beat, is a universal imitation of the *Wirbelschlag*. It may be observed in the funeral march of Liszt's *Grand Solo de Concert*, and orchestrally in the opening of the *Eroica* funeral march and in the *Jupiter* Symphony. A similar imitation appears at the start of *Wo die schönen Trompeten blasen*, where it is answered by a trumpet call that is in triplets and thus effectively in 6/8 meter like a hunting horn. It might be thought that Mahler had become careless about the distinction of huntsmen and soldiers; but compound meters are common enough also in cavalry signals. A later form of Mahler's trumpet figure near the end of the song is akin to part of the *Attacke*, a signal in 9/8 meter (see appendix 2). When the words of the song's title ("Allwo dort die schönen Trompeten blasen") are sung, it seems again that

Figure 11.17.

Figure 11.18.

hunt and warfare are being confused. This phrase is illustrated not by trumpets but by a horn *bicinia,* very hunt-like in style though much too high for hunting players. Yet the song ends in clear military style, with a soft minor-mode trumpet fanfare akin to many cavalry signals, though not suggesting any particular call.

The chromatic, minor-mode nature of many of the marches and signals in these songs evidently matches the dysphoric message of the texts. We may assume that the nameless soldiers who march in Mahler's symphonies are similarly doomed. Even when the march seems vigorous and stirring, as in the *Allegro energico* in the finale of the Sixth Symphony, there is an air of parody. This is one of Mahler's stilted, blind, spectral tunes, its face set against mere effectiveness.

Bruckner's soldiers, on the other hand, retain a certain poetic heroism in an atmosphere of reflective seriousness. Real cavalry calls sometimes descend into the second register, where only the fifth is available; the *Kirchenruf* of the Austro-Hungarian army is a section of the *Retraite,* coming just after the passage quoted by Suppé. It is marked *langsam, feierlich* (slow, solemn) in an *Exercier Reglement* of 1901 (fig. 11.18b). The solemnity of this call to church, played before funeral services, is echoed in the sonorous and solemn theme that opens Bruckner's Third Symphony, played on the long trumpet in D (with valves, of course; only the first three measures could be played on a cavalry trumpet)(fig. 11.18a). But one senses the romantic fantasy of this music, recalling the woodland horn of the Fourth Symphony. Bruckner has no stomach for Mahler's grim realism.

In fact, the period of "absolute war" brought forth very few dysphoric soldiers.

The Soldier Represented 179

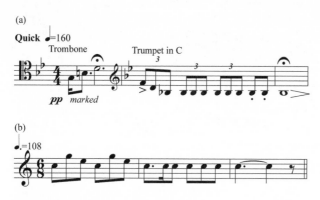

(a)

Quick ♩=160

Trombone

Trumpet in C

pp marked

(b)

♩.=108

Figure 11.19.

Warriors were either picturesque, like Bizet's dragoons, or heroic, like Wagner's Siegfried. And when signal-like themes appear without any military context—thus as true topics—there is the sunny confidence of similar references in the previous century. Schumann's song "Er, der herrlichste von allen" (from *Frauenliebe und -leben*) has the careless zest of the fanfare that gives it shape; the opening theme of Brahms's First Piano Concerto bespeaks a kind of neurasthenic drama; and the swooping cavalry signal that initiates Mendelssohn's Octet is rapturously poetic. Even Mahler's elegies fail to capture the horror of war, but merely reflect bitterly on its sad consequences.

Yet two British composers portrayed the ferocity of war, at a time when Clausewitz's teachings were being discredited by wars that drifted into murderous stalemate. Holst's orchestral piece *Mars, the Bringer of War*, from *The Planets*, parodies the military march by making it unmarchable, like those very early marches with odd measures in triple time. Along with the serpentine chromatic melodies that overlay this ferocious rhythm in 5/4 meter, there are wretched mockeries of military bugle calls. The piece is black, angry, grotesque. Completed before August 1914, it presages the collapse of Romantic heroism.

Finally, the dysphoria of Britten's *War Requiem* is more elegiac, more resigned, in tune with the poems of Wilfred Owen which trope the text of the requiem mass. There are several march rhythms, notably the spiky motive that accompanies the tenor solo "What passing bells" (in the *Requiem Aeternam* at rehearsal figure 9), and the tune resembling a popular war song for "Out there we've walked", with its chilling imitations of the screaming of shells (*Dies Irae*, rehearsal figure 33). From the start of the *Dies Irae*, this economical work is largely dominated by two bugle calls, played at the outset on trombone and C trumpet (fig. 11.19a). The first, in a snap rhythm, is scarcely matched in the army literature. It is, perhaps, merely a setting of Owen's opening words "Bugles sang". The other one—ubiquitous in the work—is more interesting, first because it is played so fast; regimental and parade calls, many of which were in compound time like this motive, were mostly played at the more sedate 108 to the minute, while "war calls", played in battle, were very rapid, marked at speeds like 160 to the minute (like the *Charge,* in *Trumpet and Bugle Sounds* 1909, 51). This is exactly Britten's marking. However, his tune does not much resemble the *Charge;* it slightly echoes a regimental call, that of the Dorsetshire Regiment (*Trumpet and Bugle Sounds* 1909, 36; fig. 11.19b). And indeed, Owen's soldiers are turning in for the night, rather than fighting.

> Voices of boys were by the riverside,
> Sleep mothered them, and left the twilight sad.

Britten is reminding us, perhaps, of the soldiers' eventual fate (they are "bowed by the shadow of the morrow") rather than evoking the atmosphere of a sad evening. One feels, however, that Britten's melodies are impressionistic. He can have had little knowledge of the military, and the ethos of the bugle call must have reached him through culture, not through direct experience. The frenetic, curling woodwind figures that echo his bugle call (for example, after rehearsal figure 24) situate the whole passage in an area of irony.

(h) Soldiers on the map of culture

It cannot be pretended, however, that the military topic is naturally ironic or parodistic. Marches occur throughout the repertoire, from the seventeenth to the twenty-first centuries, without any trace of irony; in Handel's *Deidamia,* in Rameau's *Les Indes Galantes,* in Beethoven's *King Stephen,* in Meyerbeer's *Le Prophète,* in Mendelssohn's *Athalie,* in Grieg's *Sigurd Jorsalfar,* in Coleridge Taylor's *Othello* suite, as well as in works without evocative titles like Schubert's "Great C major" Symphony, Mendelssohn's G minor Piano Concerto, Tchaikovsky's Second Symphony, and Rachmaninov's Second Suite for two pianos. Movie composers regularly turn to the march to supply military weight, as Howard Shore does in the soundtrack of *The Lord of the Rings.* Like the trumpet signal, the march rhythm is absolutely ubiquitous in our repertoire.

Whatever the views of civilized sophisticates, military heroism has been fundamental to our culture and has occupied the imaginations of everyone, even those, perhaps, who felt at home in George Eliot's world of quiet country towns or Henry James's refined drawing rooms. We may sneer at the foolish young officers, the absurd uniforms, the saber-rattling militarism, the juvenile puffery of the nineteenth century, but musical semantics shows the military theme still central to culture. For culture is infallibly mapped by musical topics.

Part Four.   *Shepherds*

12 The Pastoral Signified: The Myth

(a) The poetry of illusion

Pastoralism is one of the most ancient, and longest lived, of all literary and cultural genres. With its offshoots in the *locus amoenus* and the *fête galante*, it can be traced from the poetry of Hesiod (eighth century B.C.) to that of Verlaine (1844–96). In music, apart from the reputed pastoral songs of antiquity (*boukoliasmoi*), the tradition encompasses the whole of the notated repertoire, beginning with the troubadour *pastourelles* and Adam de la Halle's *Jeu de Robin et Marion* (thirteenth century), and leading, through the madrigal, early opera, the Arcadian movement, and Romantic nature worship, to the songs of Debussy and Strauss's *Daphne*. Yet this is the most profoundly mythical of all topics. Never at any time did it bear much relation to social realities. It is important to understand how it came to have such power over the imaginations of people in all eras.

It is still common to find the pastoral genre dismissed as vapid and childish. Like many literary views, this began with Johnson. It is expressed by W. W. Greg in a seminal book on pastoralism. "Pastoralism came to its fairest flower amid the artificiality of a decadent court or as the plaything of the leisure hours of a college of learning, and its insipid convention having become 'a literary plague in every European capital', it finally disappeared from view amid the fopperies of the Roman Arcadia and the puerile conceits of the Petit Trianon" (from *Pastoral Poetry and Pastoral Drama*, London, 1906, quoted in Loughrey 1984, 77). Contemporary psychology-oriented writers, too, have seen pastoral as mere wish-fulfilment. Laurence Lerner comments on Pope's description of pastoral as "illusion". "An illusion, Freud concludes, is a belief in which 'wish-fulfilment is a prominent factor in its motivation.' The wish to find in country life a relief from the problems of a sophisticated society formed itself, in Renaissance times, into a set of poetic conventions. . . . These are the conventions of pastoral. Pastoral is the poetry of illusion: the Golden Age is the historiography of wish-fulfilment" (from *The Pastoral World: Arcadia and the Golden Age*, 1972, quoted in Loughrey 1984, 154).

The prejudice against pastoral has made it harder for modern writers to understand the prevalence of the genre throughout Western literature, and above all to see that the pastoral was an allegory of music; to understand that music was for Europeans simply the pastoral without its shepherds.

(b) The classical pastoral

Essentially, the convention begins with Theocritus's *Idylls*, written in Alexandria in the third century B.C. But readers of these little poems will find many familiar clichés missing. They are studiously simple, written in dialect, and they present the musical shepherds of Sicily, Theocritus's birthplace, engaged in singing competitions. There is a touch of elegy; the first idyll bemoans the death of Daphnis, a hero-shepherd who may have represented nature itself. But there are no gods or demigods, no fauns, no talk of the Golden Age, no explicit nostalgia or sense of cosmic regret. It is not obvious that Theocritus saw his pastoral world as an allegory.

It was the Roman poet Virgil who, in the *Eclogues*, took Theocritus's world as a vehicle for allegory and nostalgia. He turned the pastoral into a hymn to love: "All-conquering is Love", he wrote (in the translation of C. Day Lewis), "no use to fight against him". The shepherd's typical state is one of lost love; Corydon, in the second Eclogue, longs for the beautiful Alexis with a "futile passion", his laments echoed by the cattle, lizards, and cicadas, his sadness expressed in the music of a seven-pipe syrinx.

Theocritus might have been reminiscing about his own land of birth, but Virgil wrote of Arcadia, a place in the mountains of the Peloponnese traditionally inhabited by Pan. The historian Polybius was born there, and he described it as a home of musical peasants, who, in spite of their inspired flute playing, lived crude and unlettered lives in a harsh landscape. Virgil seized on the idea of the musical shepherds, and ignored their crudity and the harshness of the landscape. For him, Arcadia became a happy Utopia where it was always springtime.

But this willful departure from truth turned the shepherds into imaginary figures; they do not quite ring true. One is consciously distanced from Virgil's shepherds. Their pastoral simplicity is something one cannot possess; its appeal lies in its difference from the sophistication of the reader. Both Theocritus and Virgil are townsmen, writing picturesquely about the countryside. But Virgil no longer needs a real countryside; his pastoral is within his own mind, a state of being that he can imagine but can never attain, which is delineated precisely by that which is excluded from real life. In the notorious Fourth Eclogue this is called the "Golden Age", a period of history in which justice reigned, wickedness was washed away, and men were like children, innocent and happy, occupied only with love and song, responsible to the gods of music, Apollo and Pan. So powerful is this piece that medieval critics considered it a Christian prophecy, and it earned a place for Virgil on the facades of cathedrals.

But this pastoral is a myth of loss. The Golden Age, the state of simplicity, has been lost and can never be recovered. In the Ninth Eclogue the farmer, Moeris, has been thrown from his farm and is making his way at last to the town. He sings as he goes, but it is the song of regret, loss, abandonment, the praise of the good old days, which have been borne away by time almost beyond the bounds of memory. With his friend Lycidas, he disappears into the twilight, into "that vesperinal mixture of sadness and tranquillity which is perhaps Virgil's most personal contribution" (Panofsky 1957, 299).

> Time bears all away, even memory. In boyhood
> Often I'd spend the long, long summer daylight singing.
> Lost to memory, all those songs; and now my voice too

Is not what it was: the wolves ill-wished it before I could spot them. (Translation by C. Day Lewis)

"Nicht hell eracht' ich das heilig Alte" he might well exclaim with Wagner's First Norn, I do not clearly recall the sacred times of old.

(c) The Italian Renaissance

The Renaissance writers embraced eagerly this tone of lament, and they extended the pastoral in various ways. First, they introduced an element of narrative; second, they created the pastoral drama.

The *Arcadia* of Jacopo Sannazaro, written in the late fifteenth century, is in effect a novel. It is made up of a mixture of prose and verse in Italian, telling an episodic and disjointed story about a group of amorous shepherds, and its influence quickly spread far and wide, to France, Spain, Portugal, and England. The predominant emotions are melancholy and despair, but there is no trace of hatred or resentment in a society which is devoid of social distinction. The lyrics which punctuate the story are said to be accompanied by the *zampogna*, actually a type of bagpipe, though Sannazaro may have intended the classical double *aulós*, and the trees and mountains are continually invoked as listeners to the action.

Sannazaro enjoyed the patronage of the court of Naples. It is extremely significant that the shepherds of *Arcadia* can mostly be identified with personalities of that court: Sannazaro himself appears under the name of Sincero. The conceit of linking pure fantasy with real people would become a standard aspect of pastoralism. Not only were the countryfolk of the pastoral myth figments of the cultivated imagination, they were also mere masks for the cultivated readers to whom the verse was addressed. For "shepherd" always read "courtier in disguise".

The pastoral drama has a somewhat different history, particularly important to musicians because of its connections with opera. Its first important manifestation in Italian was *La Favola d'Orfeo* by Angelo Poliziano (1480). The poet called this work a "favola pastorale"; the word "favola" did not mean "story", but was simply the Latin word *fabula*, a play. Pirrotta thinks the poet wished to invoke his dependence on the Florentine religious theater (1969, 22). His subject comes from Ovid, but he utilizes the form and meter of the *sacra rappresentazione*. The play is in two parts, the first a tale of three shepherds, thus a pastoral episode in the old sense; the second, however, tells the story of Orpheus's encounter with Pluto, Minos, and Proserpina in his doomed attempt to recover his wife Euridice from the underworld. The Christian element of the sacred play has been replaced by a drama involving pagan gods. In the process, the pastoral has been extended to embrace the supernatural—in particular the story of Orpheus, which was to become a recurrent theme.

Poliziano was working in Florence, but the definitive canon of pastoral plays had its origin in Ferrara. Early in the sixteenth century many short dramatic pastorals were produced there. They were often called *egloghe*, "eclogues", Virgil's term. In 1545, however, there appeared a play which represented a distinct change of view. *Egle*, by Giambattista Giraldi, is in five acts like a tragedy; its *dramatis personae* are not shepherds but demigods—nymphs, fauns, and satyrs. In other words, this was a conscious attempt to imitate Euripides's *Cyclops*. In classical dramatic theory there were three genres, tragedy, comedy, and satyr-play, *Cyclops* being the paradigm of the last of these. To confirm the derivation, Giraldi also wrote a treatise, the *Discorso Sovra il Comporre le Satire Atte alla Scena* (Discourse on the writing of satyr-plays for the theater). Henceforth, pastoral dramas would often have fauns and satyrs among their characters, interacting with the shepherds and shepherdesses who quickly returned in the work of Giraldi's colleagues and successors. The satyr—a sexually free forest spirit in Greek tradition, half-man, half-goat—came to be identified with the faun, a Roman tutelary spirit of the countryside.

For example, Agostino Beccari's five-act *Il Sacrificio* (about 1555) tells the story of three pairs of pastoral lovers, but also presents a satyr whose passes at the girls have to be repulsed. It led to the shorter, but much more influential, *Aminta* of Torquato Tasso (1573). This piece is almost consistently lyric, the action limited to the pursuit, and eventual surrender, of a nymph called Silvia (connected with *selva*, forest, and *silvestre*, rustic). There is also a satyr, whose harassing of Silvia has to be repelled. The gentle melancholy of the pastoral and the languidly amatory atmosphere are everywhere present, but there is also a discreet eroticism, an ingenuous invocation of sexual freedom ("s'ei piace, ei lice" sings the chorus—if it is pleasing, it is allowed). Tasso's peculiar qualities equipped him especially to be the focus of a genre which allegorized music, for he believed that music was the soul of poetry. As a piece of theater, *Aminta* is so profoundly discreet that it almost resolves into a series of exquisite poetic narratives, without any action at all (the lovers, Aminta and Silvia, never actually meet on stage). As verbal music it is perfect; Tasso's verse invokes "fleeting sensations and the subtlest of vibrations, trusting all to suggestion, distilling meaning to a minimum" (Anthony Oldcorn, in Brand & Pertile 1999 [1996], 267). The pure and limpid lyricism of Tasso set a standard for more than two centuries of Italian verse, and established the union of poetic musicality with the pastoral genre.

At least as influential was *Il Pastor Fido* by Battista Guarini (1589). Although probably too long for actual staging, this famous work demonstrated that the pastoral ambience could accompany real action and dramatic tension. The love of Mirtillo and Amarilli triumphs in the end, but only after the designs of the wanton nymph Corisca have been foiled, and a satyr, pursuing Corisca, has been put to rout. There are elaborate choruses of shepherds, huntsmen, nymphs, and priests. Guarini's style is less perfect than Tasso's, but the pastoral cadence is still present in his verse, foreshadowing Marini, Chiabrera, and Metastasio.

The appearance of the *Pastor Fido* led to an exchange of polemics, and these crystallized in Guarini's *Il Compendio della Poesia Tragicomica* (ed. Brognoligo, 1914). In this very significant document, the poet implied that his shepherds were not real countrymen at all, but were the prototypes of artists, and especially of musicians. His echoing of Polybius is probably intentional.

> It is no marvel that the Arcadian shepherds, noblest of all, embellished their speeches with poetic ornaments, being more than any other people in the greatest intimacy

with the Muses. . . . All the Arcadians were poets; . . . their principal study, and their principal activity was music: . . . they learned it as children; . . . their laws required them to do so. (Guarini, quoted by Pirrotta and Povoledo 1983 [1969], 264–265)

Music, true music, from which all mankind profits, is indispensable to the Arcadians. . . . This is known and believed by everyone, that amongst the Arcadians the youths, almost without exception, are accustomed from early years to sing songs of praise and thanksgiving to certain tunes, with which they honor the native heroes and gods, according to ancestral custom. Afterwards, having learnt the tunes of Philoxenos and Timotheus, they celebrate with great zeal the Dionysian mysteries, with dance and flute-playing, each year in the theater. (Polybius, *Historiae*, IV, quoted by Jung 1980, 21)

The extraordinary enchantment and the perverse unreality of the pastoral mode are explained in this essay. Pastoralism is an allegory of the imagination, and the unmeaning lyricism of pastoral verse is an allegory of music. In pastoralism, as in music, there is no conceptual "real". Emotion and desire are utterly free; the imagination is responsible only to the text, not to the world; time is suspended in a lyric present. Musicians are familiar with this state, but it has been more difficult for literary commentators, even the most sophisticated, to grasp it.

The meaning of "pastoral", then, has changed substantially since the time of Virgil. The Golden Age is now less of a moral idea, a time when justice was observed, than a dream of freedom, "the wishful dream of a happiness to be gained without effort, of an erotic bliss made absolute by its own irresponsibility" (Renato Poggioli, in Loughrey 1984, 108). Along with shepherds and shepherdesses we now encounter the satyrs and fauns of the classical satyr-play, and even Apollo, Proserpina, and other veritable deities. There may be tension, conflict, and denouement. But the centrality of lyricism—the constant reversion to timeless lyrics—is still evident, and the suggestion of melancholy, of lament, which we found in Virgil has become a pervasive feeling, even though shepherds are still said to live in a state of innocence and happiness in a perpetual springtime countryside. There is a delicate investigation of feelings, "a sensibility always refining itself, a scrutiny of sentiments always looking deeper into itself, introducing that element of languor, intimacy, passion, which is usually called elegy" (Carrara 1909, 3). Pastoralism has approached the condition of music.

It is at this point that the origin of opera supervenes. The *Euridice* of Rinuccini, set to music by Peri and Caccini, was unquestionably influenced by Tasso, while Monteverdi's *Orfeo* (1607) mingles the pastoral play with the choruses and ballets of the court *intermedium* or *festa*. The meters of the pastoral play, *endecasillabo* and *settenario* (eleven- and seven-syllable lines), remained standard for Italian recitative throughout the history of opera. For two centuries, Italian verse and music worked together in tandem. It was a condition foreshadowed only in the antique world.

(d) French pastorals

It is a familiar jibe of the *canaille* that pastoralism showed its true and final colors when the French courtiers played at being shepherds and shepherdesses while the real peasantry of France was starving, and the *hameau* at Versailles is still surveyed by mocking and horrified tourists. This prejudice has already been revealed in the words of W. W. Greg. It is important, therefore, to cast a glance at French pastoralism, which had a different history from the pastoralism of Italy. Beginning with adaptations of the *Aminta* (by Maurice Scève) and loyal copies of Theocritus and Virgil (by the poets of the Pléiade, Vauquelin de la Fresnaye and Jean-Antoine de Baïf), the French pastoral took root in the courtly and occasional poems of Ronsard, in which great personages were praised in the guise of shepherds, often repeating the myth of the shepherd-king; "in a distant past, shepherd and king were one" (Gerhardt 1950, 239, on the dedication of Ronsard's *Eglogues*). In spite of the artificiality of this verse, the musical elegance of language and the frequent references to music preserve the allegorical character of the style. Ronsard writes, in an epithalamium for Charles of Lorraine and Claude de Valois:

> De ce beau mariage entonnez vos Musettes,
> Monstrez-vous aujourd'huy tels sonneurs que vous estes . . .
> Car il vaut mieux, Enfans, celebrer ce beau jour,
> Qu'user vos chalumeaux à chanter de l'Amour. (Gerhardt 1950, 236)

> For this great marriage intone your bagpipes; show yourselves today the fine players that you are. . . . For it's worth more, my children, to celebrate this fine day, than to use your reed pipes for singing of love.

And in an encomium for Cathérine de Médicis:

> De mon flageol un jour puissé-je tant apprendre
> Que je chante a l'enuy les honneurs de Catin . . . (p. 238)

> If only I could say clearly enough, with my pipe, that I sing endlessly in honor of Cathy . . .

But the definitive French pastoral was still to come. All previous pastorals had been set in an undefined locale, usually called "Arcadia". The aristocratic Honoré d'Urfé had the idea of writing a novel in prose about shepherds and shepherdesses who inhabited a real place, the district of Forez, between Lyon and Clermont-Ferrand on the edge of the Massif Central, where he had been born and had grown up. The story of his 5,000-page novel *Astrée* was set in the fifth century, in a mythical kingdom of ancient Gaul. It appeared in three parts between 1607 and 1619, and seemed to have a realism which all previous pastorals had lacked. It was easy to recognize great ladies in his nymphs, people of high society in his shepherds, and clergy in his druids. They were not crude and filthy peasants, he explains, because "the condition of shepherd is for them the result of free choice, of the decision taken by their ancestors to live in peace" (Gerhardt 1950, 258).

In truth, he had taken the idea from a Spanish pastoral novel, the *Diana* of Jorge de Montemayor. There were no mythical gods in Forez; no satyrs, no fauns, no magic. D'Urfé's readers, accustomed to the marvels of the Italian pastoralists, found *Astrée* overwhelmingly realistic, not least because the writer himself had a sort of "pastoral" temperament, candid, serene, civilized, gracious. He was the only pastoral author who was a true countryman, albeit a nobleman. None of the Parisian dreams of an imaginary Arcadian countryside for him, but a realistic picture of the valley of the Lignon in central France.

Nevertheless, his novel is entirely occupied with the shades and refinements of love, with the neoplatonic praise of *honnête amitié*, and there are endless speeches that analyze the loves and longings of his characters in painstaking detail. It seems perverse that he was admired for his realism; he even felt he should apologize for avoiding the conceits and unrealities of the older pastoral, saying that realism was permitted "because I represent nothing to the eye, but only to the ear, which is a sense that touches the soul less forcefully" (quoted by Gerhardt 1950, 261). The comment must surely be ironic; the whole force of the pastoral rested on the intimate power of the ear, the charm and freedom of music, both the music of the language and the music of song and pipe. This novel became the main and sole point of reference for later French pastoralists. When Fontenelle, late in the century, came to write his *Poésies Pastorales* (1688), there was no echo of the ancients or the Italians; his pastoralism is almost entirely that of *Astrée*. This work was avidly read for a century, and even in the 1700s it still claimed its enthusiasts, who included Marie Antoinette. It was the pastoral best known to the French rococo painters, and, indeed, to those who frolicked at Versailles.

(e) Arcadia and Metastasio

It used to be acceptable to condemn most Italian poetry of the seventeenth century, including that of Chiabrera and Marino. If something of a revaluation has taken place, there is still to be observed a muddying and complication of the limpid style of Tasso; there was "an endless number of poets, mostly mediocre or frankly bad" (Cherchi, in Brand & Pertile 1999 [1996], 304) who cultivated far-fetched analogies and undignified language, often morbid and gory. This "baroque" tendency was deplored by the savants, and in 1689 they founded an academy in Rome. The leader was Giovanni Maria Crescimbeni, and the group had formed originally around the exiled Queen Christina of Sweden. They took the name "Arcadia". The chief purpose was to restore good taste. They referred especially to Theocritus and Virgil, to Sannazaro, Tasso, and Guarini, and they saw the pastoral as the most felicitous and lofty form of verse. Their emblem was the syrinx, portrayed with Pan and two satyrs, and each of them adopted a pastoral name. This led to a number of "colonies" in other Italian cities. Many of the significant poets of the later seventeenth and early eighteenth centuries were members of these academies and sported names which sounded like those of shepherds and shepherdesses. These, naturally, included the authors of important opera libretti.

Crescimbeni wrote a lengthy history of Italian poetry in which, in a passage on the "eclogue", he explained the essentially allegorical character of pastoral verse. "But with regard to its material, although this style of composition seems incapable of noble subjects . . . nevertheless at the same time under the woodland semblance they can conceal the most noble and lofty allegories; amidst naturalness and simplicity they can reveal the most significant insights, in their most pure and open-hearted beauty" (Crescimbeni 1731 [1698], 276).

The Arcadians wrote sonnets and *canzonette,* full of shepherds and satyrs, the style clear and musical, the content slight. Their importance would be marginal if they had not directly influenced the central poetic tradition of the eighteenth century, which centered on the opera libretto.

One of their number was Gian Vincenzo Gravina, a theorist and author of still-born classical tragedies; and it was Gravina who discovered and adopted the child Metastasio. In truth, the pedant Gravina, who had fallen out with the Arcadians, tried to discourage the boy from reading the Ferrarese pastorals, but in vain. In 1718 the young poet entered the Arcadian Academy under the name of Artino Corasio.

Metastasio became the leading poet and librettist of eighteenth-century Italy, and his style was firmly founded on Tasso's *Aminta.* The "line Tasso-Metastasio", according to Walter Binni, is the pivot of the "Arcadian enterprise to restore the course of Italian poetry to the height of the second *cinquecento*" (Binni 1963, 320n2). Thus Metastasio, as well as writing limpid, musical verse of the utmost simplicity and clarity, is also a fundamentally pastoral poet. At the beginning of his career he wrote a group of pastoral *feste teatrali* and *serenate,* beginning with *Endimione* (1721). The Tassesque spirit is apparent, but there is also a pathos, a sensuality, a caressing tenderness which mark this verse as popular. Metastasio, like D'Urfé, seemed realistic to his contemporaries; but it is not the Frenchman's realism of place and action, but that of the comedy, justifying De Sanctis's famous judgment on the later *drammi:* they were "superficially tragedies, at base comedies". In the following dialogue of shepherd and shepherdess (from *Angelica,* 1722) the pastoral tone is unmistakable and the musicality is suitably Tassesque, but the fragile teasing of the two speakers is closer to comedy (Tirsi is the shepherd, Licori the shepherdess).

Tirsi	La mia bella pastorella,
	Chi mi dice ove n'andò?
Licori	Tirsi, Tirsi, ove sei? dove ti ascondi?
Tir.	Ovunque Tirsi sia,
	È teco, anima mia . . .
Lic.	Felice preda, e per me cara! Intanto
	Questo da me tu prendi
	Di bianchi gelsomini
	Artifizioso ramo; ad uno ad uno
	In ordinata filza
	Paziente io gli adattai sul finto stelo;
	Ed erano pur dianzi
	Bagnati ancor dal mattutino umore.
	Prendi; vinca tua fede il lor candore.
Tir.	Caro dono e gentile,
	Alla mia fede, al volto tuo simile!

My lovely shepherdess, who will tell me where she has gone?
—Tirsi, Tirsi, where are you? where are you hiding?
—Wherever Tirsi is, she is always with you, my love . . .
—Happy prey, and dear to me! Meanwhile, take from me this artful branch of
white jasmine; one by one, I attached them to the feigning stem; not long ago
they were bathed in morning dew. Take; may their purity overcome your heart.
—Dear and kind gift, as pure as my heart, as your face!

The poet returned to pastoral *feste* often during his career. But his great *drammi
per musica*, basis of the whole genre of *opera seria*, were also full of pastoral themes
and language, although the "reform" dramas of Zeno and Metastasio were meant
to be historical. In *Demetrio* (1731), the eponymous king is at the start disguised
as the shepherd Alceste. The Cretan lady Argene, in *L'Olimpiade* (1733), is disguised
as the shepherdess Licori. In *Achille in Sciro* (1736), Achilles, exiled to Scyros, is
disguised as a girl and sings in a pastoral chorus of nymphs. And in a late text, *Il
Re Pastore* (1751), the King of Sidon is disguised as a shepherd called Aminta, while
the Princess Tamiri appears as a shepherdess. It is hardly necessary to recall that
Mozart set an adaptation of *Il Re Pastore*, also *Il Sogno di Scipione* and an altered
La Clemenza di Tito, as well as many separate arias and ensembles by the master
poet.

Apart from these details, Metastasio's dramas are full of pastoral arias, either
referring to clichés like the shepherd-king ("Nasce al bosco in rozza cuna", in *Ezio*)
or simply referring irrelevantly to shepherds and pastoral scenes ("Il pastor, se torna
aprile", in *Semiramide*).

There was, in fact, another genre called *dramma pastorale*, though Metastasio
did not specifically write any of these. The dramas *Atalanta* and *Asteria* by S. B.
Pallavicini, set by J. A. Hasse in 1737, are three-act operas based on Arcadian subjects.

Of course, Metastasio's texts are written specifically for music; he tells us that he
composed them at the harpsichord. Like Tasso, he believed profoundly in the power
of music and the natural musicality of man. "Who could ever doubt," he asks, "the
power of music on our souls? Who does not feel it and does not observe its effects
on himself and on others?" (from the *Estratto dell Arte Poetica di Aristotile*, in *Op-
ere*, ed. Brunelli, 1947, vol. 2, 976). But he stops short of casting pastoral as an allegory of the imagination, or pastoral verse as a kind of music, as Guarini apparently did.

For contemporaries, then, the pastoral element of Metastasio's work was connected with good taste, clarity of expression, musicality, pathos, tenderness, emotional truth. The lofty allegory proposed by Guarini is, perhaps, scarcely present,
and D'Urfé's praise of neoplatonic love is beyond Metastasio. But the inconsistency
of young, happy, silken shepherds appearing on stage when in the surrounding
countryside real shepherds were dying of starvation did not disturb contemporary
audiences. On the contrary, Metastasio's comic spirit seemed extraordinarily true
to life. It became common for apologists of the pastoral genre to classify dramas
simply according to the social class of the protagonists. "The pastoral play . . . [is
concerned with] the fortunes of peasants alone [*soli rustici*]. From it are excluded

kings and heroes, who appear in tragedy, and bourgeois and townspeople [*popo-laraschi*] who make up comedy" (Quadrio 1739, vol. 5, 364). Of course, everyone knew that contemporary peasants were not like the characters in pastoral plays. But people were more interested in the realities of genre than those of the squalid outside world.

(f) The final idylls

Before the French Revolution intervened to transform much of European culture, two final pastoralists appeared on the scene. One, Salomon Gessner (1730–1788), was German-Swiss; the other, André Chénier (1762–1794), was French. After them, the *rustic pastoral* would gain sway, based on the volkslied and its embodiment of an idealized European peasantry. The old "high pastoral" portraying classical shepherds in idyllic landscapes, had its last tour of duty in the work of Gessner and Chénier.

The career of Salomon Gessner makes one think of artists like "Namby pamby" Philips and Ludwig Spohr. Enormously successful in his lifetime, translated into most European languages, popular in every country, his work is now utterly forgotten. The Mozart family (Leopold considered himself a man of culture) had Gessner's works in their library (Sisman 1997, 78). His pastorals are small in extent: they include the novel *Daphnis* and two books of *Idyllen*, short vignettes in a kind of "poetic" prose, peopled with shepherds and shepherdesses, fauns and satyrs, telling of love, song competitions, the worship of Pan and the nymphs, the sacrifice of victims. Gessner is "more antique than most of the idyllists who came before him" (Van Tieghem 1930, 224). It is as though he wanted to distill the entire pastoral tradition and present it in concentrated form. His prose is light, simple, apt, and verges so nearly on verse that he sometimes hides several pentameters, one after another, in the prose continuum. Some of the idylls are moralistic, some merely sentimental. In truth, there is neither real innovation in these works nor a real sensitivity to the classical. They are spuriously refined, purveying an idealized and innocent world that merely reflects the happy and peaceful family life he enjoyed in Zürich. There is much of *Daphnis and Chloe* in Gessner, though without Longus's sly sensuality; some of Theocritus, without the smell of the countryside (he found "too much of nuts and cheese" in the ancient author). The antique pastoralism of these pieces, though laid on with a trowel, is no more than surface decoration; his Hellenism is a "very thin varnish" (Van Tieghem 1930, 225).

Chénier's *Bucoliques*, on the other hand, are delicate, discreet, enormously cultured, though no more than a haphazard notebook of fugitive ideas, contained in a body of poems, long and short, interspersed with sentences and paragraphs in prose, written over much of the poet's short life. They illustrate, perhaps, how the classical pastoral could be modernized and could become relevant to Romantic sensibilities, for they are not universally idyllic. As well as childish innocence and young love, they thematize premature death, murder committed by jealous lovers, and many of the darker and more dramatic emotions. But Chénier reverts continually to simple love scenes, often involving young children.

This artist is able to combine sensualism, a belief in human fickleness, with a disarmingly simple naturalness that is as reminiscent of Rousseau as of Theocritus. But the classical shepherds remain, a gloss of ancient culture in an age of refined Hellenism, the age of Le Brun and Winckelmann. The poet can be seen as part of the continuity of French culture, backward to Fontenelle and the pastoral painters, Watteau and Boucher, and forward to the Romantics. "His love scenes recall in miniature the *fêtes galantes* of his century. Undoubtedly, Chénier's evocation of young love in a pastoral setting had a marked influence on Victor Hugo, who, in removing all vestiges of ancient shepherds . . . , nonetheless evoked the same expansiveness, the same naturalness that resulted from . . . [the love of young people], love quick to bloom and quick to fade" (Smernoff 1977, 76). The fame of Gessner, and the comparative obscurity and brief career of Chénier, illustrate the power of popular taste in elevating the ephemeral. For this exquisite poet, and the pastoralism he cultivated, both perished in the Paris of the Revolution. The idyll would die for three-quarters of a century in Europe.

(g) The meaning of pastoral

Before leaving the "high pastoral", it is worth looking at some of the profounder interpretations of this genre, apparently so slight, and reviewing its associations with music, visual art, and the imagination.

Peter Marinelli, for example, finds pastoral associated with *time* and with *nature*. The pastoral milieu is always separated from the poet by time; it invokes an opposition of nature and art, and nature is situated in the lost pastoral realm, which was lost at the time of the Fall. Arcadia is "from its creation the product of wistful and melancholy longing"; the poet longs to return to nature, to primitive simplicity. "The Fall is . . . the major pre-condition of pastoral poetry, the greatest loss of all. . . . All pastoral poetry, initially at least, expresses a preference for Nature over Art" (Marinelli 1971, 23). A return to the state of nature, characterized as the Golden Age, takes two forms: it is either a state of innocence in the sense of an absence of tumult and strife and a freedom from passion, or, in the erotic tradition, of another kind of innocence, that of sexual freedom.

For time and place are equivalent in the pastoral world. In the idyll you can be "in" a time, just as you can be in a place. Bakhtin writes of "the special relationship that time has to space in the [literary] idyll: an organic fastening-down, a grafting of life and its events to a place . . . where the fathers and grandfathers lived and where one's children and their children will live" (quoted by Will 1997, 317). Since nothing changes in the pastoral world, time is not experienced as a historical or developing process. Only the cycles of the seasons and the hours of day and night are markers of time, which thus repeats itself constantly. This prelapsarian sort of time can be observed in some of the societies studied by anthropologists, and in early modern Europe (see *Sense*, 84–86 and 93–96). Nothing seems to change. There are no goals, no ambitions, no disappointments; "This unity of place in the life of generations weakens and renders less distinct all the temporal boundaries between individual lives and between various phases of one and the same life,"

Bakhtin continues. It is the time of children; David and li'l Em'ly, as four-year-olds in the early pages of Dickens's novel *David Copperfield,* had "no more thought of growing older, than we had of growing younger". This is the time of lyric verse, and also of the musical lyric, as I have claimed elsewhere (*Sense,* chapter 4).

Art is paradoxically situated in this pattern. On the one hand, art and artifice have built civilization and separated mankind from his original simplicity (the male pronoun, since it is invariably used by the sources quoted here, is adopted throughout this section); on the other hand, for the sophisticated artist the pastoral paradise is a creation of the imagination, the purest kind of artistic vision. "The poet comes to Arcadia for a clarification of his artistic, intellectual and moral purpose" (Marinelli 1971, 45). Removed from moral and political responsibility, he can explore the purely aesthetic, in a language that is essentially lyric.

The pastoral world is full of love and melancholy. The artist, envisioning himself as a shepherd, becomes "a despairing lover who, in withdrawal from grief in love, finds himself a poet in recompense". "It is not strange therefore to find a constant thread of allusion . . . to myths of unhappy lovers who were also connected with the origins of poetry: to Orpheus, who by the power of his poetry communicated a sympathetic spirit to even inanimate nature; to Pan . . . ; to Apollo. . . . Disappointed lovers, gods or humans, become either patrons of poetry or poets themselves" (Marinelli 1971, 49).

Frank Kermode reaches a conclusion very close to that of Guarini. The shepherd, "a natural piper and singer, . . . is easily made to stand for the poet" (Kermode 1952, 18). "He became the type of the natural life, uncomplicated, contemplative, and in sympathy with Nature as the townsman could never be. . . . [Shepherds'] craft endows them with a kind of purity, almost a kind of holiness" (Kermode 1952, 16–17).

Singing and making music, then, are amoral (or pre-moral) activities. They arise from a freedom from responsibility, but they lead to melancholy and despair, because the lyric world in which they flourish has been lost. Time has intervened to condemn man to activity and business. Yet before *negotium* there was *otium* (leisure), a state of contemplation that was out of time, in which time stood still. Now, after the Fall, time stands still only in music and in the most musical verse. It is especially significant that the eighteenth century, when pastoral verse was revived and then abandoned, was a time when the universal timelessness of music was placed alongside a new sort of musical time, the progressive time of classical transitions and development sections (see *Sense,* 81–114).

But perhaps the true poetry, like the true music, is that in which the lyric is most effectively realized, in other words the poetry and music which most "aspire to the condition of music". If this be the case, then the pastoral enclosure is the poem itself. "To make 'poetic' is in part to 'pastoralize'" (Toliver 1971, 12). The shepherd is, unconditionally, the poet; he "represents man neither as *homo sapiens* nor as *homo faber* [man the craftsman], but only as *homo artifex* [man the artist]: or more simply, as a musician and a poet" (Poggioli 1975, 167). "This association of the poet with the shepherd and of the poem with Arcadia comes about partly because when shepherds retreat to an enclosed and harbored world of song they are in a privileged position to indicate the nature of aesthetic distance and poetic transfor-mations of reality" (Toliver 1971, 12). The poem is another place, into which one withdraws for refreshment or enlightenment, and "whole books of verse in the Renaissance are taken to be bowers of bliss in which a reader can browse for idyllic or erotic pleasure". The poem itself, then, is the pastoral paradise; its shepherds sing all day, because they do not have to improve the landscape with "the georgic arts of the gardener or the home economist" (Toliver 1971, 13).

Richard Cody, in his book on Poliziano, Tasso, and Shakespeare (Cody 1969), goes further. The Renaissance pastoralists used the Arcadian ambience to enclose a ritual of neoplatonic theology, based on Orphic religion. The pastoral drama was a narrative of the inner life, a reconciliation of desire and truth, a hymn to the "erotic dualism of 'this-worldliness' and 'otherworldliness' ". Shepherdliness was an allegory of innocence, an innocence that could only be envisioned by one who has loved most purely, who has, indeed, entered into "the fourth and inward-turning stage of erotic ascent, as described in [Plato's] *Symposium*" (Cody 1969, 29). Unlike tragedy, pastoral drama incorporated the satyric and the playful; the lightness and wit of pastoral were a kind a *serio ludere*. In fact, the Orphic spirit brought all op-positions and dualities into a unity in diversity, just as Orphism was believed to be monotheistic in a pagan world that elsewhere believed in many gods.

Since poetry and poetic drama become a ritual, "the difference between phi-losophy and poetry disappears". The poet's song is less of a discourse on love than an acting out in sacred words of the "death and new life of the rational soul, lost and found again in the flames of intellectual love". The familiar themes of courtly love, "the wilful mutual suffering", the purifying fire of unhappy love, the lover's yearning for death, the "indifference to social and Christian sanction, the sense of a mystical initiation", the "death swoon" in which the lover dies, or seems to die, and is resurrected either in body or in spirit, are pastoralized by these artists. Every-thing is dominated by the power of love, which is the passionate, idealizing love of Plato; "Nell'Aminta domina l'amore passione", declares Croce (Cody 1969, 44). Po-etry (and indeed music, since it is lyric singing that is meant) becomes "part of the religious discipline of contemplation" and is "traditionally . . . a magic practice".

This interpretation of pastoralism helps to explain the centrality of the myth of Orpheus in Renaissance pastoralism (mythic or supernatural beings had not fea-tured in the antique pastorals). For Cody, the pastoral tradition begins definitively with Poliziano's *Orfeo* (1480), and of course Orpheus figures largely in the origins of opera. Orpheus is able, through his music, to control the trees, rocks, and wild beasts, sway Hades, and even survive death; his songs reputedly formed the liturgy of the religion known as *Orphism*, which was known to have influenced Plato in his philosophy of love. As the archetypal musician (he had received his lyre from Apollo) Orpheus consecrates all music and poetry as mystic actions.

Orpheus was the original artist, who mysteriously influenced the world with his songs. Through participation in the "Orphic melody" we can reconcile the world's dualities into "a condition of music". As a model for all poetry, Orphism is "her-metic", "veiling sacred truth from the profane". The uninitiated, therefore, cannot see the most profound truths within Orphic texts. The greatest pastoral dramas,

Poliziano's *Orfeo* and Tasso's *Aminta,* are allegories of the inner life, fables of the soul, in which the pastoral figures are merely emblems in an utterance in which "the poet, himself, in his own person everywhere in the poem, is the only voice that is Orphic".

(h) The religious pastoral

It was considered from an early date, with some justification, that Scripture contained numerous pastoral themes. The Song of Songs was read as a pastoral (Quadrio 1739, vol. 3, part 3, 364). Many leading characters of the Bible—Jacob, Isaac, and Abraham—are described as shepherds; Saul is a "shepherd king"; David, who began as a shepherd but became a harper, parallels Orpheus. Christ, descendant of David, calls himself the "Good Shepherd" (John, x, 11).

Most important of all, the nativity was revealed first to shepherds, "abiding in the field, keeping watch over their flock by night" (Luke, ii, 8). This justified the many pastoral references in Christmas music, both vocal and instrumental. Since shepherds were traditionally considered to be musicians, it came to be assumed that they celebrated the birth with music and dance, singing lullabies to the infant. In Christmas plays of the fourteenth century the people sang and danced in front of the crib, as Georg Wizel describes in 1550. "In many places, on Christmas eve and on the evening of Christmas Day at Vespers, the holy birth of our savior Christ was shown, with a representation of the stable at Bethlehem, the angels, the shepherds, the three kings etc. and even the Christ-child, sounding forth in song, springing up and down, clapping their hands, to express the great joy that everyone feels, or should feel, at this birth" (quoted in Jung 1980, 150–151). Somewhat later another writer, Enoch Widman, describes choral dances, which he associates with the dance-like and lullaby-like character of most Christmas music ("proportion" is explained by Jung as meaning "proportio tripla", triple time).

> At Vespers on Christmas Day, when from olden times the infant Jesus is rocked in the cradle, as people say, and the organist plays *Resonet in Laudibus, In Dulci Jubilo, Joseph lieber Joseph mein,* the choir also sings, and several groups betake themselves to dance to the tunes, according to the proportion, and the young men cause little girls to stand up in church and to dance around the high altar, and elderly people also dance in front of the young ones, thus to commemorate the happy and joyous birth of Jesus Christ after their outwardly rough manner. (Quoted by Jung, 1980, 151)

The familiar tunes mentioned by Widman are, indeed, all in a rocking triple meter.

Italians also celebrated Christmas in this way, singing and dancing around the crib during the Nativity services. These occasions were particularly notable for the "suoni pastorali", the racket of flutes, shawms, and bagpipes played by shepherds, who came down from the Abruzzi to Rome, and from the Calabrian highlands to Naples, to perform before the churches and wayside shrines, and in the inns. These performances of "pifferari" or "zampognari" (a reference to the *zampogna* or bagpipe, which is described below) were especially associated with the Novena of the

Feast of the Immaculate Conception (December 8; a "novena" is a period of prayer lasting nine days). This was a time of special musical celebration that generated a repertoire of "novena songs", one of which is cited by H. Möller (quoted in Jung 1980, 152). This "spiritual folksong, that goes to a pifferari-tune", seems to be the number quoted by Handel in "He shall feed his flock" in *Messiah*; the original text begins "Quando nascette Ninno a Bettelemme", and Jung quotes the tune later (on p. 242) (see chapter 13 of the present work, below). I reproduce the last of its three stanzas.

> Guardavano le pecore lu pasture;
> E l'Angelo, sbrennente chiù de lu sule,
> Comparette,
> E le dicette:
> Nò ve spaventate, nò!
> Contento e riso.
> La terra è arrenventata Paradiso!

The shepherds were watching over their flocks; and the angel, shining like the sun, appeared and said to them: do not be afraid! Be happy and laugh. The earth has become paradise again!

These traditions persisted into modern times. Friedrich Theodor Vischer, writing in 1839, furnishes a graphic description.

> A shrieking, melancholy sound of shawms arose, and some pifferari came up, peasants from the mountains with red-edged jackets of sheepskin, brown cloaks, pointed hats, sandals on their feet. . . .
> They are always in twos, one playing a monotonous but pleasant accompaniment on the bagpipe, the other playing short passages on a small shrill-toned flute, with pauses in which he sings some words of a prayer. From a certain distance, this music sounds very good, inherited as it is by tradition from ancient times, and having a distinctly pastoral character. At present you cannot go far in the streets without hearing this noise from one side or the other. (Quoted in Jung 1980, 153–154)

The word "flute" (*Flöte*) betrays the usual confusion of terminology, for the "shrill tone" was produced by a reed instrument, of course. A watercolor of the period portrays the scene; two musicians play before a wayside shrine, their costumes not exactly corresponding to Vischer's description (plate 3).

Travelers often thought of the pastorals of antiquity when encountering these musicians. A German scholar found their instruments "even today as primitively constructed as the tibia and avena of which Virgil sings in his *Eclogues*", and Berlioz, listening to the Roman *pifferari*, felt himself "a contemporary of those ancient peoples, in whose midst the Arcadian Evander, generous host of Aeneas, took his ease" (both quoted in Jung 1980, 154). Evander was the Arcadian who founded a colony on the Tiber, subsequently incorporated into Rome.

Such were the associations of the pastoral tradition with Christmas within popular culture. But the connection was also firmly established in literature. As early as the fourteenth century, Boccaccio combines a story of nymphs (in the

Comedia delle Ninfe Fiorentine, 1341–1342) with "Christian allegory and religious moralising" (Stewart 1999 [1996], 76). In Petrarch's *Bucolicum Carmen* (1346), the story of the Nativity is told in pastoral terms, the Virgin being described as a "nymph". A similar work is the *Parthenice Mariana* by G. B. Spagnoli, called Mantuan (1481); here the sacred story is mixed with classical deities and mythology, though the author was later canonized (in 1883). The painter Mantegna illustrates the Nativity in classical surroundings in his altar piece for the church of San Zeno in Verona, and again in frescoes in the Capella Ovetari in the church of the Eremitani in Padua.

The most significant of all these religious pastorals is Sannazaro's *De Partu Virginis* (the Virgin's confinement), a Latin poem published in 1526 that gives a Virgilian account of the Nativity. It was extremely popular at the time, passing through many editions and translations. Full of allegory and classical device, it evokes the shepherds at Bethlehem in a style that exactly resembles that of the poet's celebrated *Arcadia.* They gather foliage, laurel, palm trees to decorate the cave in which the child has been born. "They enter the cave and Sannazaro, as the shepherd Lycidas . . . together with Aegon, who is thought to represent St Augustine . . . , hymn the child to the sound of the panpipes. They echo Vergil's famous fourth eclogue in which the birth of a child brings about the renewal of the world. . . . The goats voluntarily return home with full udders . . . , the lion lies down with the lamb . . . , the oak trees ooze honey" (Kidwell 1993, 153).

This work cost Sannazaro enormous pains, and it was much admired by contemporaries. Its comparative obscurity today is caused, perhaps, by its Latin text, less accessible than Italian to modern scholars.

Even Guarini's *Il Pastor Fido,* surely a paradigm, with Tasso's *Aminta,* of pastoral plays, has been seen in Christian terms. It concerns a curse that has been laid on Arcadia on account of a female misdeed; it can only be raised by the fidelity of a good shepherd (a Good Shepherd, perhaps), yielding obvious echoes of the redemption of Eve's misdeed by the mission of Christ. "A Counter-Reformation allegory may therefore underlie, and give moral sanction to, what is in detail just another tale of amorous pastoral fantasy" (Andrews 1996, 297).

(i) The European poor

"Pastoral is an image of what they call the Golden Age. So that we are not to describe our shepherds as shepherds at this day really are, but as they may be conceiv'd to have been. . . . We must therefore use some illusion to render a Pastoral delightful; and this consists in exposing the best side only of a shepherd's life, and in concealing its miseries." These words of Pope (from *A Discourse on Pastoral Poetry,* in Loughrey 1984, 51) show that the artificiality of pastoralism was as clear to contemporaries as it is to us. He was not the only writer to stress the difference between the shepherd of the idyll and the contemporary peasant. Gottsched (in the *Critischer Dichtkunst* of 1730) commented that "our country folk are mostly wretched, depressed and troubled people. They are seldom the owners of their flocks, and even when they are, they are burdened with so many taxes and duties that they can hardly earn their bread with all their bitter labour" (quoted by Schneider 1988, 16).

It is misguided to attack the pastoral for ignoring the hardships of the peasant of the time. It was not meant to have any relation to the peasant of the time. Contemporaries, finding in pastoral a discourse on neoplatonic love and an allegory of music, would have found any critical reference to contemporary country people crassly vulgar.

For indeed, if we examine the real peasantry of Europe during the time when poets and musicians were developing the pastoral theme, we find a different picture. The peasant who "tastes the sweets of life" is hard to find. As we know, there were to be fundamental changes in the social and political structure, beginning in France in 1789. The soil from which these changes grew was already being laid down in the two previous centuries. Between 1600 and 1750 Europe experienced a long depression, partly caused by the collapse of the Spanish economy (Spain, with its New World riches and enormous power, had fueled the trade and industry of Europe in the sixteenth century), partly by the ravages of wars. This led to a steady fall in prices; and this meant that those elements of society dependent on the land—notably the landowning nobility—found their revenues diminishing.

All over the continent, they were adopting various measures to support their income. In Britain they resorted to enclosures, fencing off common land and devoting it to sheep rearing. This deprived the ordinary people of their rights of common, making it hard for them to rear their livestock, and sending many of them off the land into the towns or overseas to America. In mainland Europe, landowners abused the rights of *corvée* (labor service); where these were limited by statute, loopholes were found enabling the lord to occupy more and more of the peasant's working time, and where they were not, the common people found themselves entirely occupied on the lord's demesne during periods of sowing or harvest. Naturally, where peasants paid land dues or rents, these were steadily increased, especially as many were paying dues several times over. "Thus, together with the miseries of the times and the latent weaknesses of agricultural science, the burdens which weighed on the peasantry—seigneurial, ecclesiastical and state—became unbearable; the levies of the landowner taking 1/4, 1/3 of their income, sometimes more" (Léon 1970, 87).

Of course, there were better-off country people; in France and western Germany, the prosperous peasant, owning his smallholding, called a *Bauer* in Germany, could survive times of hardship almost without suffering. Also, there was a division between northern Europe—Britain and the Low Countries, and parts of France—which has been called "Europe bien nourrie" (well-nourished Europe), and the south and east, the "Europe de faim" (hungry Europe; Léon 1970, 49). But as the eighteenth century progressed, more and more found themselves in the ranks of the rural poor, men who paid rent on their house, owned no land, and worked as laborers. In *ancien-régime* France, for example, the rural laborer's condition was "pretty wretched".

If we consider his living quarters, we see that they were entirely insufficient. Most houses were made of clay, covered with thatch; there was just a single low room, without a floor, little windows without glass; . . . you could say that the peasant lived "in water and mud." . . .

With regard to furniture and clothing, we must distinguish better-off peasants from the poor. The former had simple, primitive, but adequate furniture. . . . The others could hardly satisfy the most rudimentary needs. (Sée 1921, 48–49)

But this was the best of it. The real weakness of this social system was revealed when there was a time of crisis. At regular intervals during the eighteenth century there were periods of bad harvest and rising prices which drove the peasantry to the edge of famine.

The crises [were] constantly repeated: a succession of two or more bad harvests, . . . scarcity of cereals in the markets, an astronomical rise in prices to dizzy heights . . . reduced whole populations to conditions of shortage, even of famine. . . .

In a normal year, life was just about assured for peasants of moderate means; it became impossible in periods of alimentary crisis, when indebtedness took its toll of the countrypeople. . . . Small laborers and handworkers were never able to relax and their wretchedness became tragic in periods of crisis. Condemned to famine and to death, they were the great suppliers of the cemeteries. And these constituted the majority of the peasant masses of the west. (Léon 1970, 49, 87)

These wretched conditions led to terrible epidemics. Smallpox, measles, and typhoid claimed thousands of victims. The people were helpless. There was little medical care, and most peasants were illiterate, unschooled, superstitious. When life became unlivable, many turned to theft and brigandage; "vagabonds inspired real terror in the countryside; the law and the police were powerless against the bands of thieves" (Sée 1921, 50).

Broadly speaking, things were worse the farther east you traveled, and there were plenty of regional variations. But the above presents a thumbnail sketch of peasant conditions before the great revolutions of the eighteenth and nineteenth centuries.

(j) The sacred landscape

It would seem that Gessner and Chénier were the last creators of pastoral poetry in the old sense. Classical shepherds and shepherdesses, fauns and satyrs, disappear from the poetry of the 1790s and the nineteenth century (though see chapter 15, below; they reappeared later in a new form). In place of the languorous, elegiac nostalgia of the classics, a new kind of pastoralism emerged. It too idealized the peasantry and shepherds, but they were not center stage; the protagonist was now the landscape, the woods and fields and brooks, the mountains, sunshine, moonlight, and distant vistas that formed the setting. There was a new kind of religious vision, but instead of adapting Virgil's Golden Age as an image of the Christian heaven, these writers found God in the landscape itself. They were animists and pantheists. Pastoralism, therefore, lost its lightness and charm and gathered a kind of moral tension.

This movement was connected with an interest in folksong and the spirit of the *Volk,* which is described in the next chapter. But the interpretation of nature as God-in-landscape was an essentially new pastoral semantic. A milestone in its development was the publication in 1730 of James Thomson's poem *The Seasons,* which later became the basis of Van Swieten's libretto to Haydn's oratorio. This was "a major aesthetic turning point, establishing the possiblity of new relations both between man and the natural world and between the sister arts" (Kroeber 1975, 101). The poem acknowledges its pastoral heritage, its return to the "rural scenes, such as the Mantuan swain [Virgil in the *Eclogues*] paints in the matchless harmony of song" (*Spring,* ll. 456–457), and its address, with "Doric reed" (Theocritus wrote in the Doric dialect) to the "pastoral banks" of the River Tweed (*Autumn,* l. 890). Thomson's vision, however, is intellectual and abstract. He can be observant of detail and he can notice common objects amid the grandeur of the scene. But his description is always general: his scenery is exemplary, an imagined paradigm on which to reflect.

> See, where the winding vale its lavish stores,
> Irriguous, spreads. See how the lily drinks
> The latent rill, scarce oozing through the grass
> Of growth luxuriant, or the humid bank
> In fair profusion decks. Long let us walk
> Where the breeze blows from yon extended field
> Of blossomed beans. (*Spring,* ll. 494–500)

Thomson's purpose is didactic. He wishes not to preach a theological message, but to marvel at the manifold workings of nature as viewed by a scientific eye, enraptured with the symmetries and consistencies of the natural world.

> O Nature! all-sufficient! over all
> Enrich me with the knowledge of thy works:
> Snatch me to heaven; thy rolling wonders there,
> World beyond world, in infinite extent
> Profusely scattered o'er the blue immense,
> Show me. (*Autumn,* ll. 1352–1357)

Alongside Thomson's rationalistic contemplation of the landscape as a revelation of the marvels of physical nature is the holding up of nature as a manifestation of the glory of God, in the *Betrachtungen über die Werke Gottes in der Natur* (Reflections on the works of God in nature, 1772) by Christoph Christian Sturm, a Lutheran pastor. This popular book meditates piously on the grass, the plants, the animals, the hills, the sun and moon, on storms and birdsong. It was translated into many languages; an English translation appeared in 1819.

Sturm provides a short reading for each day of the year, some of them topical ("snow" in January; "winds and tempests" in March), some merely general. The style is asphyxiatingly prosaic and moralistic. Nature is generalized, rendered abstract, and interpreted consistently in a spirit of sanctimonious pulpitry. On March 1 we are admonished, "In general, it is a noble employment, and well worthy of man, to study the book of nature continually; to learn in it the truths which may remind us of the immense greatness of God, and our own littleness; his blessings, and the obligations they impose on us" (Sturm 1819, vol. 1, 142). The book is intellectual and rationalistic, often retailing "scientific" truths about the stars, the human body, the blue sky, the sun and moon. Reflecting on "grass" on May 18, the writer has no thoughts for the beauty or poetry of a fresh meadow, but tries to guess how many blades of grass are growing in an ordinary field. The large total is then considered evidence of the prodigality of creation.

Nevertheless, even amid this chilling prose there are traces of pastoralism. Enumerating "the pleasures which summer affords to the sense" on June 23, he mentions flowers, plants, the stately oak, the beautiful verdure, "winged songsters", the murmuring of brooks, the flocks, trees, and groves that "afford us a delightful shade"; his thoughts are clearly guided by the tradition of the *locus amoenus* (Sturm 1819, vol. 2, 122–123). The third volume of the English edition shows a pensive shepherd with his crook as its lithographic frontispiece.

This rationalistic and positivistic nature worship was a poor successor to the neoplatonic vision of Renaissance pastoralism. But it contained the seed of a new vision that would nourish Romanticism. Reflections on God's greatness and man's littleness were not likely to thrill the world into a new consciousness. But a mysterious discovery of the divine in the commonplace, the infinite in the local, would inspirit a whole new age. This discovery happened far from the centers of European music, in the English Lake District and the valley of the River Wye.

The poet William Wordsworth was aware of his pastoral heritage. His poems are full of references to the old pastoral, to Theocritus, Virgil, Spenser, Milton, and Pope (see Broughton 1920). But he also made a stand against the Theocritean tradition.

> And shepherds were the men who pleas'd me first.
> Not such as in Arcadian fastnesses
> Sequester'd, handed down among themselves,
> As ancient poets sing, the golden age . . . (*The Prelude*, Book 8, ll. 128–131)

Peter Marinelli considers *The Prelude* "of distinct importance to the pastoral tradition" (Marinelli 1971, 1). In this work Wordsworth "draws a line, apparently for ever, between the classical and the modern pastoral" (4); it witnesses to the death of the old pastoral "and its rebirth . . . under quite a different aspect" (3). Yet the essential features of the pastoral tradition remain; pastoral is always, as Empson said, the "process of putting the complex into the simple", and is about a "return" of some kind, "to nature . . . to primitive freedom from passion" (13).

Instead of turning away from the modern world to speculate about some lost Golden Age, Wordsworth fixes his experience in a particular contemporary time and place. Yet he always implies that his experience is not merely an observation of the physical world, but a mysterious seeing through the surface of reality to a spiritual dimension. His nature poetry has all the observant description of Thomson, but it is made local and particular. The famous piece which we call "Tintern Abbey" is fully titled: "Lines written a few miles above Tintern Abbey, on revisiting the banks of the Wye during a tour, July 15, 1798". Having identified exactly the date and place of the poet's experience, it begins by highlighting the importance of this moment in his life:

> Five years have passed; five summers, with the length
> Of five long winters! and again I hear
> These waters, rolling from their mountain-springs
> With a soft inland murmur.

The nature description is pastoral, but it is not idealized; fruit is "unripe", hedge-rows are "run wild"; as the poem proceeds, it becomes clear that the level of description overlays a level of spiritual experience. Instead of an air of refined reminiscence, full of clichés learned from high culture, this poetry is intimate, confidential, coming from the center of the poet's heart. During the time since he last saw the Wye, Wordsworth has benefited inwardly from the blessed memory of this scene.

> The day is come when I again repose
> Here, under this dark sycamore, and view
> These plots of cottage-ground, these orchard-tufts.
> Which, at this season, with their unripe fruits,
> Among the woods and copses lose themselves,
> Nor, with their green and simple hue, disturb
> The wild green landscape. Once again I see
> These hedge-rows, hardly hedge-rows, little lines
> Of sportive wood run wild: these pastoral farms
> Green to the very door; and wreaths of smoke
> Sent up, in silence, from among the trees. (*Tintern Abbey*, ll. 9–19)

The writer is not merely describing nature; he is "seeing into the life of things" with "an eye made quiet by the power of harmony" (ll. 47–49). This power to instill harmony into the wildness of nature is something like the power of music:

> The mind of man is fram'd even like the breath
> And harmony of music. There is a dark
> Invisible workmanship that reconciles
> Discordant elements, and makes them move
> In one society. (*The Prelude*, Book 1, ll. 340–344)

Music, of course, cannot specify familiar localities. But very clearly, music can appeal to the listener with a voice of intimacy, injecting into its topical content a visionary insight that transcends the conventional meanings of its melodies and rhythms, and which overcomes the lapse of time. Wordsworth achieves this feeling of intimacy by particularizing and familiarizing his scenery in time and place. But this is no more than a trick of apodeixis. Even the precise dates and times he furnishes for his poems are no more than invocations of a poetic present; Wordsworth's landscape is not viewed *sub specie aeternitatis*, like Thomson's, but in the immediacy of direct experience, focused at the central crossing point of time. Nature speaks a language of revelation because it enters the experience of the reader; we are not invited to reflect on its majesty or beauty, but we find ourselves living within it, enabled to realize its divinity because it brings to life the divinity within ourselves. This was the end product of Wordsworth's Wye valley; it does not matter that, living in Edinburgh or San Francisco, we have never seen the River Wye, or if we have, it was as a strange and exotic sight. We feel it as familiar because the text tells us to, and its familiarity is the foundation for a feeling of intimacy, spiritual focus, a mysterious life within the bosom of the common.

Where Thomson generalized nature, inventing paradigmatic scenes, Wordsworth specified actual locations and made them seem commonplace and familiar. And where Sturm divinized the landscape by willfully seeing the hand of God in it, Wordsworth turned nature into an inner experience in which nature teaches secrets to the mind, but at the same time the mind imparts a divinity to nature. The subject is no longer God, but the poet himself, and the landscape, far from being a mere portrayal, becomes an experience. "Experience . . . is the method used by Romantic poets to organize their explorations of the natural world. Because Wordsworth's relation to nature is interactive instead of observational, his poetry is not simply more subjective than Thomson's but also conveys the impression of being truer to nature. . . . It is a way to better understanding of the objective universe. . . . A Wordsworthian landscape is inseparable from the history of the poet's mind" (Kroeber 1975, 99, 103).

Clearly, the texture of the Wordsworthian semantic is different from that of the classical pastoral. The landscape and its inhabitants are signifiers of an inner vision. But rather than being a Platonic allegory of artistic creation, conceived as a lyric innocence viewed in the *locus amoenus,* this vision glimpses the infinite in temporalized and particularized scenery, especially the pastoral scenery of the English countryside. Karl Kroeber speaks of a "topographical line of development from pastoral" (Kroeber 1975, 83). The older pastoral was "organized aesthetically and psychologically, and [was] based upon deliberately transparent disguise"; it was "antithetical to entanglements of realistic topographical poetry". Notably, the old pastoral was usually set in a warm Mediterranean landscape. The new scenery is not only northern and realistically observed, it is also subject to wind, storm, and flood. The older writers—including Thomson and Sturm—represented "the natural through the supernatural. Wordsworth's poetic chiaroscuro depends upon his determination to represent the supernatural in the natural" (84, 89).

Tintern Abbey (1798) and *The Prelude* (1805) are neatly contemporary with the works of Beethoven in which the pastoral signified underwent a similar development. Such is the synchronicity of culture, even when one can argue no direct influence. Similarly, Beethoven is bound to employ the old pastoral signifiers, the musical habits that once brought to mind piping shepherds and their flocks, in his evocation of a new vision, the mysticism of nature as an experience of the soul.

13 The Pastoral Signifier

(a) Pastoral instruments

The shepherd with his pipe is the classic image of pastoral music. And indeed, the classical authors spoke constantly of the shepherd's pipe, using the Greek word *aulós* and the Latin *tibia*. Much confusion has arisen from early translations that render these words as "flute". For example, the fifth epigram of Theocritus begins:

Λῆς ποτὶ τᾶν Νυμφᾶν διδύμοις αὐλοῖσιν ἀεῖσαι ἁδύ τί μοι . . .

Francis Fawkes, whose translation was published in 1767, writes:

> Say wilt thou warble to thy double flute,
> And make its melody thy music suit? (Fawkes 1767, 272)

Even the modern translator Anthony Holden has:

> Come on now, by the Nymphs, let's have a song,
> Play something pretty on your double-flute (Holden 1974, 217)

The word αὐλοῖσιν, *auloisin*, is simply the dative/ablative case of "*aulós*." So "flute" is quite incorrect. "Oboe" would be closer to the truth, or even better "shawm", for the *aulós* was a double-reed instrument of great power, made of bone, wood, metal, or ivory, and usually played in pairs (plate 4, a painting from about 480 B.C.). It was so hard to blow that players are often depicted with a leather band, passing over the mouth and tying at the back of the head, with another band over the top of the head to hold it in place, the whole harness designed to maintain the pressure of the lips against the instrument (this is illustrated in *The New Grove*, vol. 1, 699).

The *aulós* was undoubtedly played by country people, but it was also an art instrument in ancient Greece. Indeed, the tuning of *auloi* played its part in determining the Greek modal system, according to one commentator (Schlesinger 1939). The technique of half-covering the finger holes, in fact, may have given rise to the enharmonic genus. It seems to have had an oriental origin, and was known all over the Near East. It is the instrument referred to in Isaiah 31:29 ("One goeth with a pipe to come into the mountain of the Lord"). Used for religious ceremonies, to lead processions, at banquets, in the theater, it was the most familiar musical instrument of the ancient world.

It would seem that the *aulós* mouthpiece had originally been simply a split straw, such as a child may blow in the modern countryside. Writers sometimes call it *avena*, oat-straw. But this was soon replaced with a made-up mouthpiece, two halves of cane being pressed together to form a reed like that of the oboe, which was stored in its own separate case (Howard 1893, 25–26). The narrow bore of the pipe made it possible to overblow harmonics, giving a single pipe the range, according to Aristoxenos, of two octaves and a fifth, using a "speaker" hole near the mouthpiece, like the speaker keys of an oboe.

There were two varieties of double pipe. In some portrayals the two pipes are of equal length, but other pictures show pipes of different lengths, the longer curved at the end and terminating in a narrow bell like that of a clarinet. The latter sort were called Phrygian pipes. It seems likely that the two pipes were played together in some kind of polyphony; "it was on the *aulós*", judges Howard, "that music in two parts was first performed" (1893, p. 45). The final development of the instrument, found in Pompeii, was fitted with a series of silver rings that encased the ivory shank and controlled finger holes that were covered or uncovered by turning the rings. Thus, the pipe could be adjusted to play different modes. This sophisticated instrument must have possessed great beauty.

The syrinx or "pan-pipes" is also connected with the pastoral theme. This was, indeed, a shepherd's instrument. It was never used in art music. Homer says, "Behind the sheep, piping on their reeds, they go"; since the *aulós* was normally constructed of wood or other hard substances, this was clearly a reference to the syrinx, made from a group of 5 to 13 reeds tied together in a raft, each reed stopped with wax at a different level so that, when end-blown, they sounded a scale. The myth of a nymph, pursued by Pan but miraculously turned into a reed to save her from his molestations, stresses the material with which the instrument was made. At first the reeds of the syrinx were of equal length, the difference of pitch being achieved solely by the wax stops; later they were trimmed, giving the instrument a wing-like shape.

But the popularity of the syrinx in Renaissance and modern iconography is probably a reflection of its being played, in ancient paintings and statuary, by satyrs and fauns. There is an air of the supernatural, a gust of the nature-spirit, about the syrinx. "Wherever there are pan-pipes", says Sachs, "in Greece or in primitive countries, they are connected with love charm" (1940, 143).

There has been much confusion about the two ancient instruments. When Mallarmé wrote of the "flute" played by a faun, with its "two pipes" (*deux tuyeaux*) that evoke "the visible and serene artificial breath of inspiration" and "dream, in a long solo", forming a "sonorous, vain and monotonous line" (in *L'Après-midi d'un Faune*), he is obviously imagining a soft and caressing sound; Debussy echoes this in his illustration of the poem. But if there were only "two" pipes, and not the five-plus of the syrinx, then the instrument must have been the double *aulós*, the sound of which would have given Mallarmé an unpleasant surprise. This confusion was of long lineage. Titian, in the *Three Ages of Man* in the Edinburgh gallery, portrays a young woman with two pipes, clearly echoing the theme of the double *aulós;* but the instruments shown are *flauti dolci*, recorders (plate 5). The identity of the *aulós* was not properly understood throughout most of modern history, and this left its mark on the musical topic.

Since the most pervasive signifier of the pastoral topic is the drone bass, one could be forgiven for thinking that the immemorial pastoral instrument was the bagpipe. But in fact, the earliest mention of the bagpipe in Europe is by Suetonius

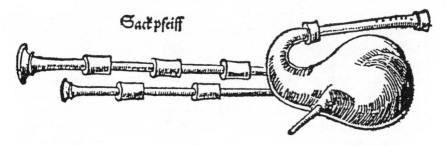

Figure 13.1.

in the first century A.D., who cites his Greek contemporary, Dio Chrysostom, with a description of the Emperor Nero playing a wind instrument with a pipe in his mouth "and the bag thrust under his arms". This instrument had long been known in Egypt and Asia, but it was not played in ancient Greece, and even when it appeared later, there was nothing to suggest that it was associated with shepherds. It was used, apparently, by the Roman legions. It has reappeared as a military instrument at different periods; a Swiss illustration of 1484 shows troops in armor, with players of fife and drum, oxhorn and bagpipe (Panoff 1938, 34), and the Prussian artillery in the eighteenth century had bagpipers (79). Of course, its most notorious association with the army is in Scotland, where the great Highland bagpipe is still the standard regimental instrument.

In modern Europe, however, the chief evocation of the bagpipe has been pastoral. An illustration of the Annunciation to the Shepherds in the Book of Hours of Jeanne d'Evreux (about 1325) shows, in the bottom left corner, a shepherd playing a reed pipe of some description, and within the initial of the word "Deus", another shepherd playing a bagpipe (plate 6). This particular instrument has only a chanter, without drones, but another illustration in the same manuscript shows a bagpipe with a long chanter and an enormous drone ending in a huge bell (see Winternitz 1967, 129). This was, perhaps, an innovation at the time; there is no reference to bagpipe drones before about 1300. So the connection is established, at this early date, between the bagpipe and shepherding, and indeed the conventional association between the piping shepherd and the Nativity is apparent. Even the drone bass—epitome of the later pastoral topic—is already in existence.

Bagpipes of various kinds have been played by shepherds and peasants throughout Europe, East and West, at all times since the Middle Ages. Iconographic evidence convinces us that it was usually a popular instrument, not normally used in aristocratic or art music. It is shown in paintings of peasant festivals, like the *Dance of the Peasants* (about 1568, plate 7) of Pieter Bruegel the Elder, and its players are commonly beggars, like the ragged *Bagpiper* of Dürer (1514). The earliest music encyclopedia, Sebastian Virdung's *Musica getutscht* (1511), gives a clear illustration of a bagpipe with a single chanter and two drones (fig. 13.1), but says nothing about the technology or use of the instrument. Later, Michael Praetorius, in chapter 19 of volume 2, part 2 of *Syntagma Musicum* (1618–1619), describes and illustrates a variety of bagpipes (see fig. 13.2, which also shows shawms and pommers), including the "grosser Bock" with its two enormous drones with large bells (no. 6 in the illustration) and the "Schaper Pfeiff" or shepherd's pipe (no. 7). In the Vienna of Mozart's time, the Bock had become a crude and macho instrument with flaring bells made of horn and with long black hair left uncut on the bag. It was played by street musicians.

On another page Praetorius gives the first-ever picture of a French *musette* (fig. 13.3), called a "Sackpfeiff mit dem Blassbalg," bagpipe with bellows. Probably this instrument and the Italian zampogna represent the two outstanding signifiers in the background of the musical topic. The zampogna is native to central and southern Italy including Sicily, and was the chosen instrument of the shepherds in the mountains of the Abruzzi and Calabria. It is one of the largest of the bagpipes. Winternitz gives a photograph of an instrument with a huge drone, about 5 feet (1.5 m) in length (his plate 27c). The zampogna has two chanters and two drones, all four pipes mounted in the same stock, with the chanters at a slight angle to each other. The right-hand chanter plays higher notes than the left; normally the two chanters are played together, the lower providing a rudimentary accompaniment to the higher. The two drones are normally an octave apart. All pipes are furnished with double reeds, giving the powerful nasal tone of the instrument; with its two melody pipes, it has much in common with the double *aulós* of antiquity.

It was usually played in a duo with a separate melody instrument, a *ciaramella* or *piffaro*, which it accompanied largely in thirds and sixths; "but when the ciaramellist breaks off to sing a verse, to rest, or to pass the hat round, the bagpiper is able to continue a semblance of the melody on the R. chanter, accompanying himself on the other" (Baines 1995 [1960], 95). The descent of the zampognari to Rome and Naples at Christmas and the time of the Novena has been described above.

The zampogna was not the only European bagpipe with a double chanter. Baines gives examples of Slovene and Basque bagpipes, for example. Apparently, its distinguishing feature—and the factor that made its music so attractive to visiting musicians—was the sweetness of the harmony cultivated by Italian players. This sweetness is illustrated by a passage from a modern performance, which Baines transcribes from a recording (fig. 13.4, from Baines 1995 [1960], 96). In this passage, the right-hand chanter plays largely in thirds with the soloist, the left-hand rocking back and forth in a simple paraphrase of the melody. The two drones, on tonic and dominant, often serve to create full triads, even five-note chords. The two players together generate an almost orchestral effect.

The delicate little musette could not have presented a greater contrast. Indeed, Winternitz shows a zampogna and a musette side by side, the Italian instrument with the longest pipe of 4 feet (1.2 m), the French with a chanter of just 9½ inches (24 cm). There are no ordinary drone pipes on the musette, as we shall see (Winternitz 1967, plate 24b).

Like the brass trompe de chasse, the musette demonstrates a mingling of the discourses of signified and signifier. It was developed for the French nobility at the end of the sixteenth century, specifically because of the fashion for pastoral literature. It was never played by peasants, though it is sometimes portrayed by painters

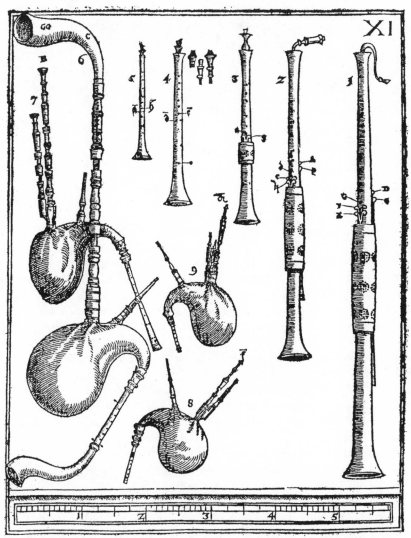

1. Bas-Pommer   2. Basset oder Tenor-Pommer.   3. Alt Pommer.
   4. Discant Schalmey. 5. Klein Schalmey. 6. Grosser Bock
        7. Schaper Pfeiff. 8. Hümmelchen. 9. Dudey.

Figure 13.2.

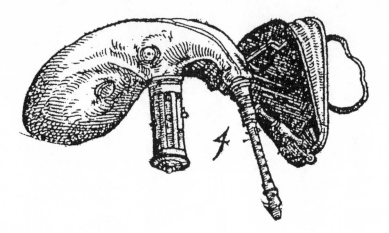

Figure 13.3.

in the hands of idealized shepherds (see plate 2). Because the effort of blowing into a mouth-pipe was not considered refined, the musette was provided with a small bellows strapped to the arm. Thus, "it produces no grimaces on the player's face, and in no way hinders freedom of voice or of speech" (Pierre Trichet, *Traité des Instruments de Musique,* ca. 1640, quoted by Leppert 1978, 11). At first it had one chanter only, as can be seen in Praetorius's illustration. The small scale of the musette brought the finger-holes and keys closer together so it was easier for ladies to play. In place of drones it was given a bourdon cylinder, an adaptation of the old *rackett,* a reed instrument consisting of a stubby cylinder of wood or ivory, drilled with a long bore which turned back on itself many times, giving a comparatively long tube within a small space. The musette version had several tubes—as many as six—and these could be brought into action, or silenced, with ivory slides called *layettes,* which were also used to tune the drones. Thus it was possible to adjust the drones to play in several keys. A second chanter was introduced in about 1650, the two chanters—called *grand* and *petit chalumeau*—being low and high and joined in a single stock, like those of the zampogna. The higher chanter was played with keys (the other had a mixture of keys and holes).

Its tone was sweet and intimate. It was "far more refined, far more dignified, far sweeter, and less shrill [than the folk bagpipe], so that it is played in chambers and in studies without offense to the ear" (Trichet, quoted by Leppert 1978, 11). It could be an exquisite *objet d'art.* "Nothing was spared in decorating the musette with the finest material. The leather bag was covered with brocade or velvet; rosewood and ivory were used for the pipes; ribbons and tassels were added" (Winternitz 1967, 81). This is the instrument portrayed in pastoral paintings of the eighteenth century. Watteau, Boucher, Fragonard, and others showed it in the hands of idealized peasants, and it was sometimes held by aristocrats when they sat for portraits, as a sign of refined delicacy.

Since players of the musette were literate, treatises on its technique began to

Figure 13.4.

appear, beginning with the *Traité de la Musette* of Charles Emmanuel Borjon, published in 1672 in Lyon. "For a few years now," he proclaims, "nothing has become more commonplace than to see the nobility . . . numbering among its pleasures that of playing the musette. . . . And how many women take pains to add to their accomplishments that of playing the musette?" (quoted in Leppert 1978, 36).

The *grand écurie,* the French royal musical establishment, contained musettists from early in the seventeenth century. These were professionals, some of them great virtuosos; there were two dynasties, the Hotteterres and the Chédevilles. Jean Hotteterre was a member in the 1650s. His son, Martin, was also a musette builder and was credited with the introduction of the second chanter. Martin's son, Jacques, published a *Méthode pour la Musette* in 1737. A contemporary of Jacques, Nicolas

Chédeville, was both builder and composer. He published an undated *Les Deffis ou l'Etude Amusante, Pièces pour la Musette.* Thus the musette, unlike the zampogna and most other bagpipes, acquired an extensive published repertoire.

The royal players performed in *bergeries,* court pastoral ballets that were already under way in the time of Louis XIII and flourished under the Sun King, his successor. Pastoral scenes soon appeared in operas, too, sometimes as an integral part of the plot, as they were in Lully's *Isis* and *Roland.* "The pastoral and rustic spectacles cannot do without them," comments Borjon of the musettists, "and we see them almost every year in the King's ballets" (quoted in Leppert 1978, 36).

A curious sidelight on this royal and aristocratic passion for the musette is provided in a book called *Observation sur la Musique,* by Ancelet, published in Amsterdam in 1757. "[The musette] never quits the notes C sol ut, and G ré sol: is this persistence not a symbol of the constancy of shepherds?" (quoted in Leppert 1978, 59). Thus the drone pipes, a token of the instrument's true humble origin, are seen as linking the musette with those idealized personnel who inhabited only literature and the imagination.

A word should be said about the hurdy-gurdy or *vielle,* which was almost equally patronized during the late seventeenth and early eighteenth centuries, and which, musically if not technically, bore much resemblance to the musette. It was a stringed instrument, often converted from a guitar or a lute, in which the strings were bowed by a wheel turned by the right hand. There were chanter strings which could be played with keys operated by the left hand, and drone strings. It had been associated for centuries with vagrants and beggars, but it was suddenly elevated to court use about 1680. Like the musette, it was played by noble amateurs, like Maria Leszczynska, Louis XV's queen, and beautiful exemplars of the instrument were built from ivory and expensive woods. It is often seen in pastoral paintings and engravings of the era.

In one respect, the hurdy-gurdy differed musically from the musette. The bagpipe, since it was fed from a reservoir of air over which the player had no control, possessed a level monotony of tone without any of the effects of phrasing or tonguing that characterize mouth-blown instruments. The hurdy-gurdy's tone, on the other hand, could be inflected and modified somewhat by a cunning handling of the bowing wheel, which itself transferred a kind of whirring effect to the sound. In later concert music, it may be possible to hear still the unevenness of tone that was the outstanding property of this instrument.

Also, the vielle is distinguished from the musette in that it never ceased to be played by the lowest classes of society (the musette was, of course, an aristocratic instrument from the start, in spite of its kinship to mouth-blown bagpipes). Because of the grinding poverty of the peasants of Savoy, in the north of Italy, some of the menfolk would travel across Europe during the winter months, when there was no work in the fields, becoming street entertainers, with lantern shows and music. These "Savoyards" were often portrayed by painters. There was even a certain fashion for showing aristocratic children, fancifully pictured as Savoyards. Their chosen instrument was the hurdy-gurdy. Thus, starving paupers were playing in the street the same instrument that occupied the most privileged in their

Ch'a - mu - ri è un   truf - fa - riel - lu

Figure 13.5.

courts and drawing rooms. Nothing could illustrate more vividly the separation of the idealized pastoral spirit from the misery of real peasants, at least in the imaginations and consciences of the wealthy.

(b) The Siciliana

The gentle 12/8 or 6/8 meter of the siciliana seems fundamental to the pastoral spirit. It would be satisfying to show that composers adopted a dance measure from the traditional culture of Sicily, the birthplace of pastoralism's leading poet Theocritus, and to find in the languorous rhythm of the siciliana a suggestion of the warm airs and sensual mores of this beautiful island. Unfortunately, it is extremely hard to trace the origin of this style, or to associate it reliably with Sicily. By the era of the great baroque composers, everyone knew what constituted a siciliana, but its emergence as a topical signifier is almost impossible to trace.

Two scholars have examined this question in much detail (Tiby 1954; Jung 1980, 145–150). They tell a complex story, but the outcome is inconclusive. There was an early verse form, the *strambotto,* which was associated with Sicily and often formed a basis for numbers called "aria siciliana" in the early seventeenth century. But these arias were most commonly in simple duple time, not in compound time. When Orazio Vecchi wrote a part song for male voices entitled "Imitatione del Siciliano", in the *Veglie di Siena* of 1604, the reference may be to the text, which is in dialect, not to the music. This piece is, however, in triple time with dotted rhythms, making it possible to hear it as a 12/8 siciliana (fig. 13.5, from Jung 1980, 146). Yet the rhythm is ubiquitous in this early period. It had appeared, for example, in a madrigal by Marenzio that imitates the drone of a bagpipe, "Strider faceva le zampogne a l'aura". Apparently, the anonymous poet grafted a reference to the shepherd with his bagpipe onto a conventional Petrarchan verse, presumably because Marenzio wanted to imitate the instrument and its style. Oddly, the words refer conventionally to springtime, though Marenzio, living in Rome, would have heard the zampognari mainly at Christmas. There is a triple rhythm with dotted notes, similar to the Vecchi item (fig. 13.6). But the term *siciliana* does not appear.

This madrigal is apparently a pastoral number, however, and it is easy to find other examples of this rhythm in pastoral contexts. The aria "Nel pur ardor" in Peri's *Euridice* (1601) groups the 3/2 bars in pairs, so that the score resembles somewhat more closely the later pastoral style. Thyrsis, we are told, "viene in scena suonando la presente Sinfonia con un Triflauto," comes on stage playing the present sinfonia on a triple flute. The sinfonia is, indeed, played by three flutes (the singer would have mimed this to some kind of fanciful instrument, one assumes). The

Figure 13.6.

idea of a "triple flute" is of great interest; if the reference is to the *aulós,* then it is exaggerated, for *auloi* were played in pairs, never in threes (though a modern version, the Sardinian *launeddas,* has a drone pipe attached to the longer of the two mouth pipes, making three pipes in all: Baines 1983). Later on, composers often wrote flute trios for the pastoral topic. Somebody, somewhere, had dreamed up the idea of a triple *aulós.* The rhythm of the sinfonia is, effectively, in 6/8 time, with the usual dotted notes.

Again, this is manifestly a pastoral piece, but there is no mention of the term *siciliana.* Indeed, it seems to require a faster tempo than the familiar Sicilian evocation of a century later. It recalls, perhaps, the *moresca* that concludes Monteverdi's *Orfeo,* which was certainly a vigorous dance. Most early operas contain a number or two in this meter, either quick or slow.

The siciliana is occasionally mentioned by writers. Garzoni lists it alongside dances like the pavan and galliard in an encyclopedic work of 1599 (Little 1995 [1980], 292), but does not describe it. There is no record of the traditional dance itself and almost no trace of its music. There are, however, possible fragments of traditional material in instrumental works. A "capriccio pastorale" of Frescobaldi, published in 1637, is an organ piece notated in 6/2 time (though not with this signature), like the Peri aria. The "pastoral" appellation may refer to the drone bass; perhaps Frescobaldi, like Marenzio, was remembering the sound of the *pifferari* in the streets of Rome. Much more important than this, he quotes an old Christmas song of south Italy, "Siam pastori e pastorelle" (fig. 13.7, from Jung 1980, 156). The same tune is used by Giuseppe Aldrovandini, a Bolognese composer, in an instrumental "Pastorale" of about 1700, also with drone bass. The age of this tune is not known, but its echoing by two composers at a distance of sixty years would seem to place it in the popular repertoire. The tune is quoted again in 1718, in the Concerto Grosso, Op. 3 no. 12, by Manfredini, "fatto per la notte di natale", where the first movement is a largo siciliano with two solo violin parts, the traditional melody coming several measures after the beginning.

While on this topic, we may also recall the "old Neapolitan Christmas song" quoted by Jung (1980, 242), "Quando nascette Ninno a Bettelemme" (fig. 13.8), of which the text was quoted in part in chapter 12, and which is clearly the basis of the air "He shall feed his flock" from Handel's *Messiah.* But none of these examples

Siam pas - to - ri e pas - to - rel - le, a - do - ria - mo il Re - den - tor

Figure 13.7.

Quan - do na - scet - te Nin - no a Bet - te - lem - me,

Figure 13.8.

really reveals anything about the siciliana; they are examples of *pifferari* music, with its rocking meters, its drone basses, and its Christmas texts in dialect.

It is usually considered that the importance of the siciliana as pastoral signifier was established by the Sicilian composer Alessandro Scarlatti, who was born in Palermo in 1660. But Scarlatti left Palermo at the age of twelve and spent the rest of his life in Rome and Naples. His operas are full of arias in a slow or moderate 12/8, though only two of these (one in the opera *La Donna è Ancora Fedele*, the other in the cantata *Una Beltà ch'Eguale*) are actually titled "aria siciliana" (Dent 1960 [1905], 147). Quoting the whole of "Bella, se vuoi per te" from *Una Beltà*, Dent finds that it has a "decidedly Sicilian character", attributing this information to a librarian of the Palermo conservatoire with whom he corresponded (1960 [1905], 151). This kind of information will scarcely pass muster. Grout maintains that "the relation of this type of aria to the dance tunes called *Siciliana* . . . is not clear" (1979, 58). Most commentators notice that these pieces often have flatted seconds in the cadences, generating the harmony called "Neapolitan sixth". Jung observes that many of them are in minor keys. An example is given from *La Caduta de' Decemviri* of 1697, an opera especially rich in numbers of this type. Appio's G minor aria from act 3, near the end of the opera, "Se tu della mia morte", is a *basso continuo* piece, unusually well wrought. The character has just attempted suicide, but has been prevented by Valeria, who loves him though he has rejected her. "If I cannot die by my own hand," he proclaims, "may your eyes kill me." It is a moment of despair and poignancy (fig. 13.9a). In the middle section of this da capo piece, the cadence is approached through a Neapolitan sixth (fig. 13.9b). The sweetness of Scarlatti's style may be illustrated also with a major-key aria from the same opera, Icilio's "S'io non t'amassi tanto" from act 2. Icilio loves Virginia, to whom he sings this piece, but believes that she has betrayed him. "If I did not love you so much," he sings, "I could fear the less." The accompaniment is played by solo viola and cello, producing a very choice trio in close harmony, the voice at the top, in a melting adagio (fig. 13.10). The sophistication of this music is patent. It is aesthetically rather distant from the skirling of the *pifferari*.

(a)

Figure 13.9.

Figure 13.10.

Whether truly Sicilian or not, these arias of Scarlatti realize the mature style of the siciliana, as the eighteenth century understood it. They are always in 12/8 (Scarlatti's favorite marking; he also writes quick arias in this meter), in slow or leisurely tempi, with dotted figures, and they do not have the drone basses of the *pifferari* pieces, or their sacred words; the texts are usually emotional, lamenting, or melancholy.

With the success of Scarlatti's operas, the Sicilian pastoral manner becomes widely known and is described in the musical encyclopedias. As early as 1703, the "canzonetta siciliana" is described, in Brossard's *Dictionnaire de Musique,* as a kind of gigue in 6/8 or 12/8 (Little 1995 [1980], 292). Mattheson, in the *Neu-eröffnete Orchestre* of 1713, attributes two tempi, slow and fast, to this style, suggesting that he heard Scarlatti's quick 12/8 arias, also, as part of the picture: "The Neapolitan and Sicilian style derives especially from a particular negligent way of singing. Its principal type is either a slow English gigue or a slower tempo that has an unadorned *tendresse;* the other type, however, in allegro or more joyous tempo, embraces usually a song in barcarolle style" (quoted in Jung 1980, 148).

However, this writer notices that modern composers favor the slower type, which has "a certain seriousness", suited to "tender and moving subjects"; "nowadays it serves more often to express sad and touching affects".

Walther's *Musicalisches Lexicon* of 1732 also places this style in the vocal category and calls it a "slow gigue", but is more specific about the time signature, "almost always 12/8 or 6/8". Quantz, on the other hand, in the *Versuch* of 1752, is already speaking of the siciliana as an instrumental piece; like Mattheson he considers that the style resides chiefly in a manner of performance. "An 'alla Siciliano' in 12/8 [*Zwölfachttheiltacte*], mingled with dotted notes, must be played very simply and almost without trills, though not too slowly. Thus few embellishments are permitted, except a few scalic [*schleifende*] sixteenth-notes and *Vorschläge,* since it is an imitation of a Sicilian shepherd's dance" (quoted in Jung 1980, 148).

As for the "not too slow" tempo, Quantz groups the instruction "alla Siciliana" with slowish tempi like *cantabile, larghetto, poco andante,* and *adagio spirituoso,* but adds that the tempo should be governed by "the expression of the passions that dominate in each piece". These, according to Mattheson in the *Vollkommene Capellmeister* (1739), are characteristically feelings of "tenderness" and "noble simplicity" (Jung 1980, 150).

Of course, these theorists are already speaking of the siciliana meter *in the concert repertoire,* not of preexistent traditional material. It seems surprising that there is so little surviving evidence for the Sicilian origin of the siciliana. There is some trace of *pifferari* music, which bears a close relation to this style. But unquestionably, baroque composers distinguished the music of the street musicians from the "Sicilian shepherd's dance" which was supposed to lie at the root of the siciliana. Above all, the siciliana did not normally reproduce the drone of the zampogna.

We may, perhaps, envisage the sort of mingling of signified and signifier that we observed in the case of the hunt and military topics. Baroque musicians, wishing to evoke the happy simplicity of the shepherd, or of the souls in heaven, echoed a kind of music associated with Sicilian peasants, whose relaxed and languid style suited the warm airs of their homeland. Except that there were never such peasants; there was never such a style; the sweet and lilting siciliana was an invention, already an aspect of the signified. It was related, admittedly, to a kind of music that sophisticated Romans and Neapolitans heard in the street at Christmastime, but it was at one remove from the *pifferari* repertoire. Thus, it could be employed in circumstances far removed from Christmas, and indeed it was more fragrant, more courtly, without any suggestion of the rough men who descended from the Abruzzi on the Novena of the Feast of the Immaculate Conception. This, if true, would be typical of the processes of topical signification.

(c) The simplicity of countryfolk

The quality of simplicity was from the very first associated with pastoral. It was rightly thought that country people expressed themselves in simple words; take away the crudity, the obscenities, the triviality, and you might attain a distilled simplicity from which the cultivated person could learn. The earliest pastoralists, Theocritus and Virgil, wished to evoke a style and a diction that was the voice of unreflecting innocence, with the "emphasis on brief, disconnected sentences; the stress on things rather than the relations between them; the reluctance to project into them feelings and modes of existence that are analogous to human feelings and modes; and the perception of a world that is not continuous, but a series of discrete units, each to be savored for its own sake" (Rosenmeyer 1969, 46–47).

It seems unlikely that the ancient poets learned this style from a study of traditional verse. The process was rather the reverse; they had imagined an ideal peasant, conceived a simple diction for her, then imputed to her a simplicity of expression that they had invented. Nevertheless, when it became fashionable to study real folksong, the admiration for idealized simplicity persisted. The lyrics of Burns and the volkslieder of Brahms continue to rehearse the love of brevity, objectivism, repetitiveness, childlikeness, that informed the earliest artists. For our purposes, and in spite of its rather heavier connections, the interest in folksong is an aspect of pastoralism.

Indeed, the first opera composers affected a kind of musical simplicity that had nothing to do with folksong research. Jung points out that Monteverdi's pastoral style in *Orfeo* is contrasted with the style of the Underworld: acts 1, 2, and 5 are pastoral, but acts 3 and 4 inhabit a different sound world, dominated by wind and brass. The melodic and harmonic styles change also; in the pastoral acts:

1. the range of the vocal line seldom exceeds a fifth,
2. the melody proceeds stepwise, seldom in leaps,
3. periodically framed songlike phrasing and melody are preferred,
4. the rhythm is limited to constantly repeated stress-patterns and dance-like schemes, often in triple time with characteristic dotted effects,
5. the harmony is not expressive, distant scale-degrees are entirely missing,

6. in the instrumental and vocal dance numbers, the tonality operates principally in the major area. (Jung 1980, 124, slightly paraphrased)

This is best observed in the concerted numbers. For example, the act 1 chorus of
nymphs and shepherds, "Lasciate i monti", demonstrates briefly all the points made
by Jung, except that it is largely in minor keys; the second-act chorus "Dunque fa
degn'Orfeo" is in a major key, but in duple time. These should be compared with
the chorus of infernal spirits in act 4, "Nulla impresa per uom", which differs in
most of the respects listed by Jung.

It is impossible to know whether "Lasciate i monti" resembles in any way the
sort of songs sung by Italian country people in Monteverdi's day. Actually, the final
strophic chorus, "Vanne Orfeo felice", seems a more convincing imitation of rustic
music, though it is in duple time. But this is no more than a guess. Very little rustic
music was written down in the seventeenth century, or in any century until the
nineteenth, of course.

Undoubtedly, Monteverdi's listeners responded to the technical simplicity of
this music, which is easily associated with pastoralism, rather than to a recognition
of some contemporary rustic style. The same is perhaps true of another period of
"simple" music, that of the Berlin Song Schools, and the associated idea of "folksong". The Berlin lawyer Christian Gottfried Krause published a manifesto of
songwriting, *Von der musikalischen Poesie,* and collaborated with the poet Karl
Ramler on a collection of songs, *Oden mit Melodien,* published in 1753. In the preface to this collection, Krause laid down a set of rules for song composition. German
songs must be simple in form, preferably on the model of French chansons; they
must depend entirely on melody, so that they can be sung as one strolls through
the countryside. Later he added that the melodies must be catchy (*eingänglich*), able
to be learned without difficulty, there must be no "theatrical traits", fioriture, and
so on, and the melodies must be framed so that they are complete and pleasing
without bass, "so that, in the absence of bass, nothing is missed" (Friedlaender
1902, vol. 1, part 1, xliii). Krause was himself an amateur composer, and the music
journalist C. F. Marpurg also added some songs. Marpurg had something to say
about the style in his *Critische Briefe* (1761): "The range of the voice must not be
too great in the Lied, since it must be easy for all throats. Thus it is best to remain
within the limit of a sixth, or at most an octave. Even within these limits, difficult
passages and leaps should be avoided" (quoted in Wiora 1971, 108). These writers
often refer to "nature"; the simple song style is more "natural", less subject to
"Verschnörkelung und Kunstelei", flourishes and artiness (Friedländer 1902, vol. 1,
part 1, p. xliii). Johann Adolf Scheibe proclaimed that "a song melody must be free,
flowing, pure and above all natural, so that it can be sung at once and without
special trouble even by someone inexperienced in music" (quoted by Wiora 1971,
112). Wiora notices that the *Kunstlied,* the composed song of literate society, was
prevented from developing or becoming more complex during the two centuries
before 1800. It remained strophic, harmonically and phrasally very simple, narrow
in range, formulaic. Quoting Heinrich W. Schwab, he speaks of the "kunstlose
Kunstlied", the artless art song (Wiora 1971, 109).

An even more important connection was with the ideas of Johann Gottfried Herder, the philosopher who derived nationalism and the "spirit of the people" from a study of traditional verse. He had been impressed with Percy's *Reliques of Ancient English Poetry,* published in 1765, which contained Scottish material as well as English. He believed that the soul of a people lay in its traditional verse, an idea expounded in the essay *Von deutscher Art und Kunst* (1773). In primitive societies, he thought, language and music were closely united; the oldest languages, Greek and Hebrew, were essentially lyric in nature, and primitive man was "poet, musician, thinker, historian and priest all in one" (Marks 1971, 53). Like many German intellectuals of the time, Herder was impressed by recent publications of Scottish traditional material, especially the *Ossian* forgeries of James Macpherson, said to be translated from the Gaelic. Ossian's songs, Herder asserted, were "songs of the people, songs of an uncultivated, sensuous (that is, sense-perceptive) people" (quoted in Marks, 1971, 54). It was, of course, Herder who originated the term *volkslied;* Herder is much quoted in Krause's pamphlet. According to Paul Marks, he was influenced by "Rousseau's philosophy of the unencumbered man, the return to the preternatural spirit of unfettered expression" (Marks 1971, 54). This doctrine was essentially pastoral in nature.

As well as the "Ossian" forgeries, there had been several collections of Scottish songs that were published in the early eighteenth century, beginning with Allan Ramsay's *Tea Table Miscellany* of 1723 and James Oswald's *Caledonian Pocket Companion* of 1745 (see Monelle 1997b, 88). The authenticity of the songs in these publications was variable. Nevertheless, it was partly in imitation of them that Herder published his *Alte Volkslieder* (1774–78), containing songs of many lands, and this inspired a large collection of German folk verses, *Des Knaben Wunderhorn,* assembled by Achim von Arnim and Clemens Brentano and published in 1806–1809. The items in this famous collection were taken largely from earlier published sources, some as old as the sixteenth century though many quite recent and part of the same revival that powered the *Wunderhorn* itself. All were adapted, added to, and made to conform to a "folk" style that was part of the current myth. In some cases, the modern annotator of this work, Heinz Rölleke, discreetly announces that the source cannot be found, beyond the editors' own manuscript, or even suggests that the given source is a "fiction." We may assume that a level of original composition went into the collection (see Arnim and Brentano 1979 [1806–1809]).

In his afterword, "Von Volksliedern", to volume 1, Arnim tells the story of his first becoming interested in folksong, striking a distinctly pastoral note. "When I first understood the full, characteristic power and sense of folksong, it was in the country. I was awakened on a warm summer night by lively cries. Looking out of my window, I saw amid the trees farm servants and villagers, singing together. . . . I then realised, when the sound fell on my ears, that I was uplifted most of all by the singing of people who were not [professional] singers" (Arnim and Brentano 1979 [1806–1809], vol. 3, 235)

The texts are often pastoral in flavor. There were, then, at this stage two traditions of German song, the *Hausmusik* of the Berlin Song Schools and the volkslieder of *Des Knaben Wunderhorn*. The outstanding difference was that the Berlin songs were always, of course, published with both music and words, while the collections of Herder and Arnim/Brentano were of words only. Were Arnim's readers able to guess the sort of tunes that his "farm servants and villagers" sang?

Some "traditional" tunes had already been published. The first collection appears to have been the satirically titled *Eyn feyner kleyner Almanach vol schönerr echterr liblicherr Volkslieder*, compiled by Christoph Friedrich Nicolai and published in 1777–78. But in general, musicians were lazy in distinguishing between "real" folksong, collected scientifically from country people, and *volkstümlich* songs written in an imitation folk style. The composers of these songs were the same people who wrote *Hausmusik* songs—or rather, they were their successors, the so-called "Second Berlin Song School", figures like J. F. Reichardt, J. A. P. Schulz, F. L. A. Kunzler, and C. F. Zelter. They showed considerable confusion about what constituted folksong. On one side, the volkslied was treated almost as a genre, parallel to the operatic aria, and the *volkstümlich* style was a manner in which sophisticated composers could work, if they wished. On the other side, the volkslied was strictly a song of the people, anonymous, very ancient, and learned orally. This inconsistency did not trouble anybody. Friedrich David Gräter declared that "real folksongs . . . are sung by the people, widely known and passed on only by mouth. . . . A distinguishing feature is their transplanting for centuries from mouth to mouth" (quoted in Pulikowski 1933, 32). Reichardt, though he took the view that "genuine folksong" was monodic, not needing harmony or bass, was nevertheless able to speak of the odes of J. A. P. Schulz as "wahre Volksgesänge" and "schönen vortrefflichen Liedern im Volkstone" (beautiful, admirable songs in folk style). The much-admired Schulz was named by H. G. Nägeli a "lovely folksinger" on account of his "naive folk-like songs" (Pulikowski 1933, 18). Schulz himself, in the preface to his twenty "Liedern im Volkston bey dem Clavier zu singen", boasted of composing "mehr volksmässig als kunstmässig". Repeating the practical considerations of the bourgeois song composer—whatever the voice or the experience of the singer, it should be easy to learn and perform these songs—he implied that these were best met by composing in folk style. "To this end I have chosen only those texts from our best poets, that seemed ideal for these folksongs, and tried to affect in the melodies the greatest simplicity and intelligibility—indeed, to give every tune the feeling of familiarity . . . [for] in this sense of familiarity lies the whole secret of the folk style" (quoted in Pulikowski 1933, 20). Thus the folksong has inherited the simplicity of the Berlin songbooks. Schulz aimed for "the feeling of being un-sought-out, artless, familiar, in a word the 'Volkston'" (Pulikowski 1933, 21).

The apparent carelessness of these musicians in distinguishing real traditional material from synthetic seems very surprising to an English or a Hungarian reader. In some parts of Europe, the style of rustic song was radically different from anything sung by the bourgeois, or indeed anything that was published until very modern times. Scottish and German readers find this situation rather less surprising. The term *volkslied* really means "song of the people" or merely "popular song"; "folksong" is an English neologism invented merely to sound like its German equivalent. Perhaps this paradoxical situation is explained by the greater homogeneity of

Figure 13.11.

Scottish and German society. In the absence of a ruling class devoted to foreign music, people of all kinds sang the same songs, which thus developed in unison with other music. The ancient modal songs in sixteenth-century songbooks had altered and developed in time with the stylistic changes in European music, because they were sung by everybody, including the literate and the educated. In England, rustic song was despised and ignored. It was thus preserved almost unchanged, and when Vaughan Williams listened to country singers in the early years of the twentieth century he heard tunes that might almost have been sung in the time of Elizabeth. By this time, English folksongs sounded strange and exotic to modern listeners. German folksongs have kept pace with changes in global style. This is a guess; but whatever the case, German traditional song developed stylistically while English song remained static.

One can trace the development of an old tune within the repertoire of popular song. *Herr von Falkenstein* appears first in a Netherlandish songbook of 1539. In 1843 a version of the tune was collected in the German countryside. There is no special reason to think that the later version has been reworked by a sentimental urban composer, though the collector may have rationalized it a little. At any rate, we find it published in 1935 by the Deutsche Volksliedarchiv, in their great and impeccably scientific collection *Deutsche Volkslieder.* Figure 13.11 shows the 1539 and 1843 versions (from Wiora 1971, 19). A tune that is rhythmically plain, in the first mode, becomes a dance-like number in D major. "In many other cases," adds Wiora, "the melodies seem at first distinctly modern, but comparative research shows that they descend from the earliest times and have taken on modern stylistic features, like triadic melody in major keys, in the structural changes from period to period."

It is true that the earlier Berlin songs, like their predecessors (the songs of Heinrich Albert and the *Singende Muse an der Pleisse* of Sperontes), were sometimes quite unlike folksongs. An example from the original set of *Oden mit Melodien* (1753) is Quantz's setting of a poem by Ramler, "Wenn ich mir ein Mädchen wähle" (fig. 13.12, from Friedlaender 1902, vol. 1, part 2, 86). It is a rudimentary minuet, the first section (shown) having three four-measure phrases that exactly follow the prosody of the verse. The bass supports the tune somewhat artfully; the second section (not shown) begins as a canon. The text is not pastoral. The singer

Figure 13.12.

Figure 13.13.

imagines his ideal girl, doubtless to the approval of his comrades drinking and smoking around the table.

It was natural that the Herderian emphasis on the spirit of the common people should bring together rustic song and *Hausmusik*. Composers like Schulz felt themselves part of the rustic tradition, in spite of being urban bourgeois. Schulz's rustic love song *Liebeszauber,* with words by Gottfried August Bürger, is included in *Erk's deutscher Liederschatz* along with songs by Weber and Reichardt and many folksongs (fig. 13.13).

Naturally, collections of folksongs—in the proper sense of traditional songs, learned orally—proliferated. The level of authenticity of these collections, like that of the verse collections, was variable. Important were the *Deutsche Volkslieder mit ihren Original-Weisen,* edited by A. Kretzschmer and A. W. F. von Zuccalmaglio and published in Berlin, 1838–40, and *Musikalischer Hausschatz der Deutschen,* by

Figure 13.14.

G. W. Fink, Leipzig, 1843. Both these publications tended to "romanticize" the songs, correcting their oddities and sentimentalizing the melos. The first collection to aim at authentic representation was the immense *Deutscher Liederhort*, collected by Ludwig Erk and Franz M. Böhme and published in Leipzig in 1893–94. This adds critical commentaries to most of the tunes and gives some of them in differing versions. But most editors refined and improved the tunes "so that the cliché of the 'country idyll' was not destroyed" (Bröcker 1998, 1736). This "romantic coloring" of the tunes (the phrase is Walter Wiora's) stresses anew that people were not interested in scientific authenticity. German listeners knew what a folksong sounded like; they did not need an ethnomusicologist to tell them. However, their impatience with authenticity demonstrates that the *Volksseele*, the immemorial spirit of unlettered country people that embodies the wisdom of the ages, is really an imaginative mythology, since the country people in question live chiefly in the minds of sophisticated listeners.

Brahms, as is well known, composed collections of "folksongs". His favored source of "true" folksong was the slightly fishy Kretzschmer-Zuccalmaglio collection. But quite apart from actual folksong arrangements, composed music is full of echoes and snatches of these "folksongs", demonstrating their centrality to the culture of Germany and their familiarity to most listeners. Composers often echo old tunes, apparently without thought. Friedlaender gives as an example the famous "Lorelei" tune, with echoes in melodies of Haydn, C. H. Graun, Kirnberger, Beethoven, and Robert Volkmann. But composers were echoing old tunes almost from the start. In the second set of *Berlinische Oden und Lieder,* Leipzig, 1759, a song by C. G. Krause, a setting of a poem by Hagedorn, clearly refers to the "Lorelei" melody. In Figure 13.14 Krause's song is compared to a version of "Lorelei" from 1837–39. The words are a typical *ländliche Idylle*, about the singing of birds in May (Krause's song is shown in Friedlaender, vol. 1, part 2, 98; the tunes are compared in vol. 1, part 1, 381–384).

It is not suggested that the German folksong is closely linked to a pastoral text, though there is a body of *Hirtenlieder*, along with the songs of soldiers, huntsmen, sailors, children, and heroic ballads and love songs. Yet undoubtedly, there was envisaged a connection between innocent simplicity, the anonymous voice of the people, and the spirit of the nation. These early enthusiasts—Herder, Arnim and Brentano—sought a mysterious wisdom in the utterances of simple folk, the singing of "farm servants and villagers", which was to inform a world tired of the teachings of the great. The myth of primal innocence is familiar to us; it is a *pastoral* myth.

As Romanticism came in, the magical innocence and purity of the Volk was extolled with more enthusiasm. As early as 1804, an anonymous writer in the *allgemeine musikalische Zeitung* identified folksongs as "old, true-hearted songs. . . . Products of a fresh fantasy, an intimate, tender, bold feeling, a free, joyous-childlike-naive mood . . . products of that feeling for nature, which seldom errs" (quoted by Pulikowski 1933, 39). Writers continually extolled the "noble simplicity" of folksong, and Kretzschmer, later Zuccalmaglio's collaborator, wrote in 1828 of folksong as "true song", which is an "outpouring of the unbridled soul . . . something holy, noble and elevating" (Pulikowski 1933, 56). In 1835 Franz David Christoph Stöpel wrote in the *amZ* of "a folk music . . . in which the most naive, the most lovely songs of nature from valleys and fields, from festivals, and in the tranquil family circle, ring out harmoniously and penetrate deep into the sensitivity, without giving the slightest offense to the artistically educated mind" (Pulikowski 1933, 74). The "educated mind" had, of course, been prepared for the folksong explosion by the simplicity of Hausmusik, the songs of Albert, Sperontes, and Krause. It was a remarkable coming together of two different but related cultural strands.

(d) The high and low pastoral

In spite of the high-minded elevation of folksong by these idealistic writers, the kind of sentiment indicated by a folk style, in song or dance, when it became established in the nineteenth century as a pastoral signifier, was less dignified than the old pastoral tradition. The old traces of Orphic religion, of Neoplatonism, of ideal love and mystic vision disappeared in the pastoral spirit of elevated folksong, being reserved for the old signifiers, insofar as these persisted: the siciliana, the imitations of the *aulós*, the evocations of noble innocence. There was, apparently, a poetic pastoral and a rustic pastoral in the Romantic period.

Certain aspects of the topic might appear equally in the low as in the high pastoral. For example, the pedal points, evoking the sound of the rustic bagpipe, persisted in every kind of pastoral nuance. But there was another reason for the different aesthetic status of the folksong. Of course, the connection of the siciliana with traditional music was so dubious as to be no more than a well-understood convention; "high" pastoralism was aristocratic, and there was no pretense of any real interest in the peasantry. The bourgeois, however, liked to imagine that his cultivation of the folksong betokened a true love of the ancient, the simple, the collective, and a sentimental respect for the unlettered rustic. Unfortunately "folksong", both in Germany and in Scotland, was vitiated by a desire to civilize and tame its oddities. Bourgeois dreams of the *Volksseele* were disingenuous. The dreamers of the Romantic salon had no more desire to get to know the country people of their time than had the courtiers of fifteenth-century Ferrara. The high regard for folksong, so much a component of Brahms's aesthetic, was based on a pretense. The aristocratic pastoral was purely conventional, and came clean about this. The bourgeois pastoral was earnest, spiritual, and a little dishonest.

14 The Pastoral in Music

(a) Pastoral genres

There have been specifically pastoral genres in music. The *pastorela* of the troubadours, the pastoral *intermedium* of sixteenth-century courts, the instrumental *pastorali* of Francesco Fiamengo (1637), Lully's operatic *pastorales,* the *dramma pastorale* of the opera-seria age, the Austrian *missa pastorale,* the popular south German *pastorella,* all were pastoral repertoires associated with certain forms and styles (see Chew 1980; Jones 1995, 15–16). In addition, Koch, speaking of classical instrumental music, distinguishes the pastorale as a separate genre from the musette and the siciliano. "*Pastorale* indicates . . . a piece of rustic, simple, but tender character, in which the singing of the idealized world of shepherds is expressed. It is generally in a fairly slow 6/8 meter . . . [and] is very similar to the musette and the siciliano, except that it is played more slowly than the former, and has fewer dotted eighths than the latter" (Koch 1964 [1802], 1142). However, this work is not concerned with the pastoral as a genre or type of musical piece, but with the pastoral topic insofar as it intrudes into music of all kinds.

(b) The *pifferari*

It has been commented that exact quotations represent only proto-topics. There are a couple of quotations in the world of pastoral music which have already been described: the song "Siam pastori e pastorelle" in works by Frescobaldi and Aldrovandini, and the Neapolitan Christmas number "Quando nascette Ninno", quoted in *Messiah*. But generally, there is no question of actual quotation.

However, it seems that the common pastoral meter, in 12/8 or 6/8, may be associated with the playing of the Abruzzi shepherds who descended to Rome at Christmastime; that, indeed, the siciliana itself may be no more than a refinement of the music of the *pifferari*. Occasionally a composer will do more than merely write music in a graceful slow compound meter; she will apparently copy the sound of the *pifferari* in other ways. Such copies may be thought of in the same way as quotations of military signals; they are, as it were, too picturesque to be considered true manifestations of the topic.

Corelli's "Christmas concerto", the *Concerto Fatto per la Notte di Natale,* Op. 6 no. 8, though in the key of G minor, ends with a semi-detached item marked *pastorale ad libitum,* in G major. It is in 12/8 time, largo, with bass drones and violins moving in thirds in sweet harmony. Admittedly, at m. 8 the drones disappear and the piece begins to resemble an ordinary siciliana. But the opening of this number clearly imitates the music of the *pifferari,* even though the drone is quitted for the cadence in m. 2, and the keen timbre of wind instruments is missing from this

Largo

Figure 14.1.

piece for string orchestra (fig. 14.1). But the music says: "Do not think first of pastoral emotions, innocence, nobility and simplicity; think, instead, of Christmas, and the rough Christian men who play in the streets of Rome".

The most familiar *pifferari* number is, of course, the *Pifa* in *Messiah*. Like Corelli's pastorale, it is a close imitation of the Abruzzi mountaineers, without wind tone; the piece is for strings alone. But the long pedal points, the leisurely improvisational tunes in thirds, the 12/8 meter with dotted rhythms including trochaic effects, these all closely reproduce the *pifferari* style as far as we know it. The pastoral topic, with its literary pedigree, is a gesture of high refinement. But these pieces, bringing to mind the Abruzzi shepherds, are rustic rather than pastoral.

There is another copy of *pifferari* music, coming from another era and proving that the tradition continued through many centuries. Berlioz, we know, heard the *pifferari* in Rome. In *Harold in Italy*, he composed a "Serenade d'un Montagnard des Abbruzes à sa Maitresse," serenade of an Abruzzi mountaineer to his mistress. The piece is marked *allegro assai* and is in 6/8 meter, but in other respects it is a clear attempt to evoke *pifferari* style: there are drones on oboes and clarinets; the melody on oboe and piccolo is harmonized on violas; the chords are dense and warm, and the piece is naïve, simple, and popular in tone. The flavor is rustic; it is an evocation of the *pifferari*, not a reference to pastoral emotions (fig. 14.2).

(c) The pastoral topic in baroque music

If the above examples are proto-topics, there are plenty of examples of the true pastoral topic in baroque music. The evocation of the *aulós* and *syrinx*, using modern wind instruments; the drones of the bagpipe; the sounds of the *pifferari* and zampognari, and their courtly equivalent, the siciliana—these are the foundations of the pastoral topic in baroque music. The simplicity of folksong is also to be found with a pastoral signification, though its heyday was the Romantic period.

Vivaldi occasionally gave titles to his concertos. There are two such pieces that illustrate the difference between rustic and pastoral, between "real" country people and ideal shepherds. The string concerto in G called *Alla rustica*, RV 151, has no compound meters and no drones, but it is in a studiously simple style. The first movement sounds like a peasant tune in square six-measure units, with the sharpened fourth degree that evokes modal scales. It is very un-Vivaldian (fig. 14.3).

On the other hand, *La Pastorella*, a chamber concerto for recorder and oboe,

Figure 14.2.

Figure 14.3.

RV 95, contains a sunny, leisurely siciliana in D major, the recorder playing above a bass that does little more than descend by step from the D above middle C to the C sharp below the bass stave. The soloists have most to do during the first movement. One is tempted to hear them as echoes of the *auloi*, but they sound more like birdsong. This concerto is a delicate, artful piece, with a fugal finale in 12/8 time.

But Vivaldi did not need a pastoral title to write in this style. The solo violin concerto in C called *Il Piacere*, RV 180 (no. 6 from *Il Cimento dell'Armonia e dell'Invenzione*), contains as its slow movement a distinctive E-minor siciliana in 12/8 time, the orchestra playing throughout in unison, the soloist adding a melody of much character, both participants playing consistently in dotted rhythm.

Bach's cantatas, secular and sacred, present a varied picture. We may investigate Bach's pastoral vein by examining first a couple of secular cantatas with specifically pastoral themes, both derived from Greek mythology.

Cantata 249a, "Entfliehet, verschwindet", has been lost, though the text remains. Fortunately, several of the items appear as contrafacti in the Easter Oratorio, so the work can be partly reconstructed. The other pastoral cantata has already been mentioned in connection with the hunt: it is no. 208, "Was mir behagt".

It is striking that no siciliana appears in either of these works (though, of course, we do not have the whole of Cantata 249a). Instead, the pastoral reference is indicated by duets and trios of wind instruments, the mythical shepherds' pipes. Most famous is the chorus "Schafe können sicher weiden" (Sheep may safely graze) from Cantata 208. The absence of siciliane from these cantatas may be merely a matter

Figure 14.4.

of chance, since the evidence is so scanty. It may, on the other hand, be due to Bach's association of the siciliana meter with the Christian heaven; it was, perhaps, a "sacred" meter. It also had a close connection with the season of Christmas. The sinfonia that opens part 2 of the Christmas Oratorio, employing a duet of flutes, is typical (fig. 14.4). Without drones, and with the dotted rhythms so common in Scarlatti, the piece is far from the world of the *pifferari;* these are classical shepherds, not *abruzzesi.* Or rather, they are the shepherds who attended the Nativity; the recitative that follows begins, "Und es waren Hirten in derselben Gegend", and there were shepherds abiding in the fields. "It represents the angels and the shepherds making music together", comments Schweitzer (1911 [1905], vol. 2, 307). The connections of Virgil's Golden Age with the Christian heaven, and of Polybius's piping shepherds with the world of biblical pastoralism, are brought together in this kind of piece. Handel knew of no such refinements; he illustrates the same biblical text in *Messiah* with the famous *Pifa,* already mentioned.

The belief in heaven as the destination of human life led to an unexpected connection, that of pastoralism with death. This may bring to mind the association of Platonic love with death, the theme of the "funerary Eros", in modern times the *Liebestod* (see Wind 1967 [1958], 152–170). Bach's cantatas about death are largely lacking in a sentiment of sadness or lament. Cantata no. 8, "Liebster Gott, wenn werd' ich sterben", opens with an exquisite chorus in siciliana meter, with horn, flauto piccolo, and two oboes d'amore. The strings play detached chords while the two heavenly shepherds concertize with each other. The cantata ends with a brilliant gigue with flute obbligato. But there could also be lament; the immense chorale chorus that begins the *St. Matthew Passion,* "Kommt, ihr Töchter", is in siciliana time with recurring bass pedals, though it portrays the wailing of the daughters of Zion over the sacrifice of Christ, recounted in the chorale sung by the boys' choir: "O Lamm Gottes unschuldig, am Stamm des Kreuzes geschlachtet", O blameless lamb of God, slaughtered upon the cross. Each of the accompanying orchestras has a duet of flutes. The theme of death is much darker in this piece; nevertheless, its meter evokes a Virgilian heaven.

Significant for the future are the siciliane in 6/8 time, rather than 12/8. Since Virgil's shepherds often become angels in this Lutheran world, the tenor aria "Bleibt, ihr Engel" in Cantata 19, "Es erhub sich ein Streit", can presumably be interpreted as a pastoral piece ("Stay, ye angels," appeals the singer, "stay with me, be my guides on either side"). The dotted rhythms and the languorous *adagio* tempo suggest this strongly, but the signature is 6/8. There is, of course, no doubt about the pastoral character of Cantata 112, "Der Herr ist mein getreuer Hirt" (The Lord is my faithful shepherd), in which an alto aria, "Zum reinen Wasser er mich weist", accompanied by oboe d'amore solo, is in gentle 6/8 time, without dotted rhythms.

Bach's wind instruments often become pastoral signifiers. It is hard to know whether flutes (especially *flauti dolci*, recorders) or oboes are more typical; recorders play in some of the most celebrated examples—paradoxically, for oboes would have sounded more like the classical *auloi*. We may think of the two recorders in "Sheep may safely graze". The connection with classical tradition is perhaps made clear by the recurrent trios and duets. Only the *aulós* was played in pairs, and the trios bring to mind Peri's *triflauto*, a fanciful exaggeration of classical organology. The opening recitative of Cantata 184, "Erwünschtes Freudenlicht", contains a reference to Christ as the Good Shepherd: "Longed-for light of joy, that breaks through, with the new Covenant, in Jesus, our shepherd". Over a stationary bass, the tenor soloist's phrases are divided by ornamental figures in triplets for two transverse flutes. There are three flutes (in this case *flauti dolci*) in the recitative which begins Cantata 175, "Er rufet seinend Schafen mit Namen" (He calls his sheep by their names), and this is followed by an aria in a smooth 12/8 meter (that is, without dotted rhythms) with the three recorders playing garlands of thirds and sixths. "Komm, leite mich", sings the alto soloist: "Come, lead me, my soul longs for green pastures, my heart languishes and groans, day and night, for my shepherd, my friend".

Like the meter of the siciliana, ensembles of flutes and oboes are often connected with death. The two oboes d'amore in Cantata 8, enclosing the idea of death in a sweet heavenly atmosphere, have already been mentioned. There are two recorders in another cantata about death, no. 161, "Komm du süsse Todesstunde", shining a sweet and joyous light on the opening aria and playing in thirds and sixths in a bright C major. The piece is not a siciliana, but resembles slightly "Sheep may safely graze", without the throbbing pedal point of that number.

Since flutes and oboes are commonplace in Bach's orchestra, it may be thought precious to highlight them as topically significant. Yet occasionally the pastoral reference is made obvious. In part 4 of the *Christmas Oratorio* the scene of the Nativity is described. The angel announces to the shepherds, "You will find the child wrapped in swaddling bands and laid in a manger" (no. 16). The chorus sings a chorale, "Behold him, lying there in the dark stable" (no. 17). No. 18 is a recitative, "So geht denn hin, ihr Hirten"; "Go then, ye shepherds, and you will find the child laid in a hard manger; then sing to him, in his cradle, with a sweet sound, and with the chorus of angels, this song of peace!" Just as the shepherds are commanded to sing, the two oboes d'amore and two oboes da caccia of Bach's orchestra enter with rich repeated chords. The shepherds, having tuned up, then accompany the "song of peace" itself—the aria, no. 19, "Schlafe, mein Liebster", in which the two oboes d'amore are featured as duettists, with their distant echo of Polybius's rustic musicians. However, this number is imported directly, with its text intact, from the secular Cantata 213, "Lasst uns sorgen, lasst uns wachen", where it is *accompanied by strings only.* It seems clear that the use of oboes in the *Christmas Oratorio,* and their deployment in this aria are directly prompted by their pastoral evocation. It may be noted also that the duet in part 3, "Herr, dein Mitleid", is accompanied by two oboes d'amore and bass only; in its original form in Cantata 213 the instruments were violas rather than oboes. A study of the oboes' participation in this popular oratorio is very illuminating of their pastoral signification.

One finds the same devices in the operas and oratorios of Handel: *pifferari*-like numbers, the siciliana meter, bagpipe drones, duets of oboes and flutes. The cosmopolitan and highly professional Handel deploys many and various effects, derived from his experience of Italian and French music and his extraordinarily rich invention. Nevertheless, he lacks the intellectual concentration of Bach; the theological subtleties, the identification of the Christian heaven with Virgil's Golden Age, the association of the pastoral with death—this sort of thing is not a part of Handel's more public and conventional art.

The *Pifa* in *Messiah,* as an illustration of the shepherds who visit the Nativity, has been mentioned. It is not, perhaps, Handel's only *pifferari* number. The air of the First Woman in *Solomon,* "Beneath the vine, or fig-tree's shade", is clearly a pastoral piece.

> Beneath the vine, or fig-tree's shade,
> Ev'ry shepherd sings the maid
> Who his simple heart betray'd,
> In a rustic measure.

The meter is 6/8 (Handel is not always careful to write siciliane in 12/8), but the long pedals (the note C, played as *bassetto* by violas, is maintained for sixteen measures before the cadence), the simple tune in thirds and sixths with some trochees, the flute which doubles the violins and later plays an octave higher, stress the closeness of this piece to *pifferari* music. Almost as evocative is the air "The peasant tastes the sweets of life" in *Joseph and His Brethren,* a number in 12/8 meter with similarly long pedal points, though the melos of this item has an "English" feel, and there is a nonfunctional sharp fourth degree (F sharp in the key of C major) which uncannily evokes modal folk music. It is a unique and memorable piece.

The siciliana meter is ubiquitous in Handel; sometimes it is combined with pedal points, without much similarity to *pifferari* music. The air, later reworked as a duet, "He shall feed his flock" in *Messiah,* is a famous example; it has already been mentioned as a quotation of a traditional tune, "Quando nascette il ninno". The aria "Con rauco mormorio" in *Rodelinda* shares its pedal points, but is more texturally complex (it begins imitatively between violins and violas). As with the *pifferari* pieces, some siciliane are written in 6/8 time; there is a pastoral ballet in *Ariodante*—the dancers are "ninfe leggiadre e amanti pastorelle"—which starts with a sinfonia in 6/8, sweetly harmonized for an orchestra of horns, oboes, bassoons, and strings, and beginning over a brief pedal point.

The "true" siciliana lacks the bagpipe crudity of pedal points, of course. Perhaps the most beautiful of all Handel's siciliane is the air of the shepherd Acis in *Acis and Galatea,* "Love in her eyes sits playing", with its delightful text and its fragrant

Figure 14.5.

music, including an important oboe part. The siciliana is usually characterized by dotted rhythms, but these are not always present; the aria "Pastorello d'un povero armento" in *Rodelinda* freely mixes dotted and undotted figures (fig. 14.5). Somewhat melodically similar is "How beautiful are the feet" in *Messiah*, in which the dotted rhythm is more predominant. It will be recalled that Koch later found the pastorale less inclined to dotted rhythms than the siciliano.

There is no doubt about the pastoral content of "Care selve", an aria from the pastoral opera *Atalanta*. However, like Scarlatti, Handel quite freely uses the siciliana meter for emotional arias without pastoral reference. There are two of these in *Ariodante*, "Invida sorte avara", in F minor, and "Se tanto piace al cor" in E minor, both in 12/8 time. The linking of pastoralism with the elegy, with amatory sentiment, and with pure lyricism is enough to explain this habit.

If we return to the opera *Rodelinda,* we may notice a characteristic feature of the aria "Con rauco mormorio". The scene is a "luogo delizioso".

> Con rauco mormorio
> Piangono al pianto mio
> Ruscelli e fonti.

> With a hoarse murmur, streams and fountains weep to the sound of my weeping.

In the middle section of this da capo number, birds are heard to echo the voice of the singer, mimicked by three flutes, one transverse and the others *flauti dolci*. Clearly, the literary topic of the *locus amoenus* is the basis of this aria's pastoralism, with its constituent theme of birdsong.

Handel liked to imitate birds, in common with several of his contemporaries. Vivaldi imitated a goldfinch in his Flute Concerto in D, RV 428, *Il Gardellino*. Handel's most famous bird imitation is "Hush, ye pretty warbling choirs" in *Acis and Galatea*. Notable also is the aria "Augelletti, che cantate" in *Rinaldo,* in which two flutes, and later a *flauto piccolo* (a sopranino recorder), play trills and eighth-note figures in thirds, over a bassetto. The scene is a "luogo di delizie con fonti, viali ed uccelliere, in cui volano e cantano gli uccelli", a place of delights with fountains, avenues, and aviaries, in which the birds fly and sing. The theme of the *locus amoenus* is evidently present, with birdsong strongly emphasized. It seems an obvious thing to say, but the flutes in this piece are clearly not shepherds' pipes (fig. 14.6). Since the *locus amoenus* is part of the world of the pastoral, and since the mimicking of birdsong is such an obvious musical resource, we must probably identify this

Figure 14.6.

Figure 14.7.

device as a subtopic of the pastoral genre. Nevertheless, Bach's recorders generally do not ape birdsong; in "Sheep may safely graze", or in Cantatas 161, 175 and 184, the references are to heaven, shepherds, and angels. But the topic of birdsong persists throughout our history, as a moment's reflection will reveal.

Bach's flutes and oboes were shepherds' pipes. And so were Handel's, on many occasions. Like Bach, he preferred duets and trios of winds to mere solos. These could be flutes, as in the episode "He led them forth like sheep" in the chorus "But as for his people", in *Israel in Egypt*, in which the two transverse flutes repeatedly echo the singers' phrases; this passage is in 3/4 time, though the number began in 12/8. They could be oboes; the aria with chorus "Non tardate, fauni ancora" from *Il Parnaso in Festa* is in siciliana time, with a pedal point, and its two oboes, playing in thirds and sixths, might almost suggest the *pifferari*. *Il Parnaso* is a serenata, an inherently pastoral genre. Handel must have found this piece successful, since he used it again in a revival of *Il Pastor Fido* only eight months later (in November 1734), with the words "Accorete, o voi pastori", and again in *The Triumph of Time and Truth*, in 1757 (as "Dryads, sylvans, with fair Flora"). Without the 12/8 signature, two oboes provide pastoral color in the chorus "Oh, the pleasure of the plains" in *Acis and Galatea*, imitating each other and concertizing in a way that would be difficult on the double *aulós*, with its single player. There is a long bass pedal point (fig. 14.7).

Solo instruments are found, too; "Love in her eyes", in *Acis and Galatea*, with its oboe solo, has already been mentioned. A later item in *Acis*, Galatea's air "Must I my Acis still bemoan", also features a solo oboe, the part marked *pianissimo ed adagio*, in 3/4 time. In his private score, D. F. Tovey writes in pencil: "One of the most

Figure 14.8.

beautiful oboe solos in the world". Jung calls this piece "a pastoral lament" (Jung 1980, 246).

(d) The classical period

No apology is made for a sudden leap to the end of the century. Joseph Haydn's secular vocal music is so limited in scope that he must be examined as an instrumental composer. But he produced two great oratorios, *Die Schöpfung* and *Die Jahreszeiten,* at the end of his career. Both are, in a certain sense, pastoral in spirit. But by this time (1798 and 1801) the world of the siciliana, of simple pastoral convention, had been overwhelmed by the Romantic world of poetic individualism. The composer's response, however, to a simple demand for a pastoral evocation is extremely remarkable.

In the famous recitative in the *Schöpfung* in which the creation of the animals is described, the stag and the horse are portrayed with figures in a brisk 6/8 time, imitating the gallop of hooves. Thus Haydn either invents or establishes the topic of the noble horse, which was of great importance in the next century. Next, van Swieten furnishes the following text:

> Auf grünen Matten weidet schon das Rind, in Herden abgeteilt.
> Die triften deckt, als wie gesät, das wollenreiche, sanfte Schaf.
>
> On green meadows graze the cattle, separated into herds.
> The pastures are covered, as though seeded, by woolly, peaceful sheep.

Each of these lines is preceded by the same short passage for flute solo and pizzicato strings in 6/8 time; the rhythms are dotted (fig. 14.8). Unlike the galloping stag and horse, these grazing animals are represented by a musical convention rather than by an icon. A half-century after Bach's death, the siciliana and the shepherd's pipe retain their rustic evocation. Yet this musical fragment is resolutely Haydnesque. It seems to evoke not the classical pastorals and ideal shepherds of long ago, but the theme of Romantic nature worship; the contemplation of the landscape, rather than a dream of the Golden Age.

This knowledge may permit us to identify pastorals in Haydn's instrumental works, most of which antedate the *Schöpfung.* They are numerous. Slow movements in 6/8 time are often pastoral in sentiment, and on one occasion the com-

Andante: siciliano

Figure 14.9.

Allegretto
dolce

Figure 14.10.

poser makes this clear. The second movement of Symphony no. 27 in G, probably composed in the late 1760s, is marked *andante: siciliano.* Yet the piece is not very much like the siciliane of Scarlatti or Bach. Marked with a 6/8 signature, it is emphatically not a 12/8 movement in disguise, as may often be said of Handel's pieces with this signature. A lyric, expressive melody is accompanied by a rippling violin figure that breaks at the end of each measure; a cadence is reached after four measures (fig. 14.9). The music is poetic, songlike, individual, and the accompanying figure recalls evocations of water, or rustling leaves, in other music.

Usually Haydn does not identify his pastorals as siciliane. The slow movement of Symphony no. 31, the "Horn Signal", resembles closely the creation of sheep and cattle in the later oratorio. There is a lyric melody in 6/8 time, marked *adagio,* accompanied by pizzicato strings. However, the soloist is here a violinist rather than a flute player; this is one of those exquisite passages for Tomasini, Haydn's able orchestral leader. It is immediately followed by a passage for two horns in G, a pastoral evocation that has been mentioned above. The second movement of Symphony no. 89 includes two flutes in a 6/8 melody similar in spirit, with the mixture of dotted and undotted figures that Haydn likes; the marking is *andante con moto.*

The decisive establishment of 6/8 as the pastoral meter, in preference to 12/8, becomes clear when the hypermeasure is ternary. The allegretto movement of the Quartet in G, Op. 54 no. 1, has an expressive melody, marked *dolce,* accompanied by a throbbing pedal point, but the phrases are three measures long (fig. 14.10). The measures could not be grouped in twos. Nevertheless, the droning bass strengthens the pastoral association. The slow movement of the earlier Quartet in F minor, Op. 20 no. 5, has a trace of pedal point, in this case marked *staccato.* A pastoral can occur even as a first movement; such is the case in the Quartet in D, Op. 76 no. 5, and, of course, in Mozart's Piano Sonata in A major, K. 331.

Henceforth, 6/8 will be the standard pastoral meter, in preference to 12/8. It is instructive to find Beethoven, in his sketches for the *Pastoral* Symphony, writing the word "siciliano" among the early versions of the *Hirtenlied,* the last movement, which is in 6/8 time—although the symphony would contain a bona fide 12/8 siciliana, in the shape of the "Scene by the Brook", the slow movement of the work (Kirby 1970, 112).

Yet the spirit of these movements of Haydn is different from that of the older pastorals. In place of the rustic skirl of the *pifferari* or the courtly elegance of the siciliana, there is an intimacy, a personal quality that arises from the songlike melody and its affecting accompaniment. The music is more strongly subjectivized; this sort of pastoral appeals to immediate poetic experience, to the soul and emotional life of the composer and her listener.

Quite different in flavor are Haydn's references to rustic music, yet these, too, will take their place in the story of the musical pastoral. In two late symphonies, folksongs from Croatia and Hungary are used. The slow movement of Symphony no. 103 uses a tune from Sopron, near Eisenstadt, and the finale of this symphony is based on another traditional tune. Most famously, the finale of Symphony no. 104 quotes an Eisenstadt tune, in this case over a drone bass (Hughes 1970 [1950], 115–116). Apparently, the "bear dance" that concludes Symphony no. 82 ("The Bear") is not a real folk tune, but, with its droning basses, it is clearly a reference to peasant style. The same may be said of the trio of the minuet in Symphony no. 88, in which the drones shift as the music changes key, a standard effect; the melody, with its sharpened fourths, imitates the modal character of some folksongs.

The passages in Symphony no. 103 can be called pastoral only in retrospect, since they do not show any of the pastoral signifiers—notably the drone bass—that we have identified. But the spirit of folksong, at least as it was understood by composers in Vienna, was to be a central feature of the newer pastoral, and Haydn would subsequently announce this in his final vocal works, the *Creation* and the *Seasons.*

The *Creation* was based on a libretto refashioned by Gottfried van Swieten from a manuscript which Haydn may have brought back from London, and which may have been originally written for Handel (for this complicated story, see Olleson 1968). Like many of Handel's texts, it continually echoes scripture; and the composer shows his admiration for the great predecessor by writing magnificent fugues and quoting, from time to time, Handelian themes. Yet the general feeling is quite un-Handelian, and the elevated biblical narrative is continually personalized and domesticated by the songlike charm of Haydn's melos. The volkslied comes into its own in this oratorio, in a rustic form that resembles many singspiel numbers.

The 12/8 siciliana meter is to be found several times. As in Symphony no. 27, it often supports a murmuring accompaniment figure, as in the aria, no. 6, in which a brook is described ("Leise rauschend gleitet fort im stillen Tal der helle Bach", softly murmuring, the bright stream glides forth in the silent valley). There is also a pastoral in 6/8 time that closely resembles the instrumental pieces described above. The aria, no. 8, "Nun beut die Flur das frische Grün", well illustrates the intimate charm of Haydn's melody in a pastoral connection. There is no pedal point or accompaniment figure, and the harmony is bland and innocent. There are

Figure 14.11.

other pastoral effects; an evocation of the early morning in part 3, "Aus Rosen-wolken bricht", is introduced by three flutes in harmony, accompanied by pizzicato strings, the final manifestation of Peri's *triflauto* (and had Haydn heard Bach's Can-tata 175, "Er rufet seinen Schafen"?). The topic of birdsong also intrudes. The aria, no. 15, "Auf starkem Fittige"—its English title, "On mighty pens", has given much mirth—describes the singing of the lark, the nightingale, and a pair of doves, each imitated cheerfully by the orchestra.

Perhaps the most enlightening number, from our point of view, is the duet and chorus, "Von deiner Güt", no. 30. Adam and Eve marvel at God's works in the world. There are two main sections; the first is, effectively, in 12/8 time (though written in *alla breve*, with triplets; fig. 14.11). An undulant violin accompaniment supports the caressing oboe solo, which gives way to successive entries of the two voices; afterward the singers come together in thirds, in the manner of an operatic number. In spite of its traces of baroque practice—the compound meter and the pastoral oboe—the piece is very unlike a baroque siciliana: more personal, more intimate, with a simple but long-breathed cantilena. This is obviously a pastoral, yet there are no specific pastoral references in the text. Without shepherds and woolly flocks, it is more truly an example of the pastoral topic, since the final sig-nifications of this topic—innocence, naïve bliss, the world before sin—are now chiefly meant, rather than any intermediate signifieds.

> Von deiner Güt', o Herr und Gott,
> Ist Erd' und Himmel voll,
> Die Welt, so gross, so wunderbar,
> Ist deiner Hände Werk.

Allegretto

Figure 14.12.

Earth and heaven are full of thy good things, O God; the world, so great, so wonderful, is the work of thy hands.

The chorus enters with blessings of God's power, the rippling accompaniment continuing, the violins blossoming into obbligato triplet figures. Since this is the morning of the first day, Adam now addresses the rising sun.

Der Sterne hellster, o wie schön
Verkündest du den Tag!
Wie schmückst du ihn, o Sonne du
Des Weltalls Seel' und Aug'!

Thou brightest of stars, how beautifully thou heraldest the day! Thou sun, how well thou adornest it, thou soul and eye of the world!

The pastoral sentiment continues, but with the use of a new signifier; a lengthy and complex passage follows, based on an innocuous folk-like tune in short phrases bound by simple cadences. Adam, newly created, may be expected to have rustic musical sensitivities, and this tune (with, perhaps, its six-measure phrases regularized, and without its elaborate development) would do for a jolly countryman in a singspiel of J. A. Hiller (fig. 14.12).

This magnificent number may help us to accept the volkslied as a successor to the siciliana as focus of the pastoral topic. Several other items in this oratorio are witness to Haydn's idea of popular melody: the choral passage "Und eine neue Welt" in no. 2; the trio, "In holder Anmut stehn", no. 18; the sturdy march tune "Mit Würd' und Hoheit", no. 24, which celebrates mankind as king of nature. There are traits of folk style everywhere in the work. Since it was performed in Vienna thirty-three times between 1798 and 1808 (Jones 1995, 10), and was afterward heard everywhere in Europe and has remained in the repertoire ever since, it is seminal for the development of the pastoral topic in the next century.

The *Seasons*, written as a sequel, is important chiefly because of its classic text—an adaptation of James Thomson's pastoral poem—and because it confirms certain trends of its predecessor. The opening chorus of "Spring", "Komm, holder Lenz", is a melting example of the "new siciliana" in 6/8 time, with a trace of bass drones. When a real countryman needs a song, Haydn produces something in the same spirit as "In holder Anmut", though even simpler (the aria "Schon eilet froh der Akkermann", no. 4). Somewhat similar is the "Freudenlied" sung by the country girl Hanne, "O wie lieblich ist der Anblick", though this piece illustrates the kinship of Haydn's folk vein with the songs of the Berlin schools. It resembles many numbers by Krause or Schulz. There is another snatch of birdsong in this work, the song of the quail at the close of "Summer". In "Autumn", after the brazen hunting chorus, described in another chapter, the countryfolk carouse and dance.

> Nun tonen die Pfeifen un wirbelt die Trommel,
> Hier kreischet die Fiedel, da schnarret die Leier,
> Und dudelt der Bock.

The pipes sound, the drums roll, the fiddles scrape, the hurdy-gurdy drones, the bagpipe skirls.

All these effects are faithfully shown in a brisk number in 6/8 time, with drones and fiddling tunes that suggest "Das ist ein Flöten und Geigen" from Schumann's *Dichterliebe*. This is followed by two character pieces in country style, a spinning song, "Knurre, schnurre, knurre", and a ballad, "Ein Mädchen, das auf Ehre hielt". In these songs, too, the closeness of these singspiel peasants to the Berlin repertoire is clearly shown.

There is an aesthetic change in the musical pastoral that crystallizes in these works of Haydn. Together with the cultural movement away from the classical Golden Age toward the philosophic elevation of nature and the idealization of contemporary peasants rather than Arcadian shepherds, derived from writers like Thomson and Sturm, they signal a personalization of the pastoral style, a movement toward songlike intimacy and individualized melody, often with lilting or rippling accompaniment figures. These musical features do not have a literary origin. Thomson's and Sturm's writings are thoughtful, abstract, generalizing, prosy. The charm, the inscape of Haydn's pastorals have a musical origin, connected with the evolution of the classical style.

(e) Beethoven's "Scene by the Brook"

In *The Sense of Music* I described an extraordinary example of cultural synchronicity. Just as the musical topic of the noble horse, signified by an imitation of the rhythm of the gallop, was establishing itself in the 1790s, so artists began to portray horses in the position of the *galop volant*. There was, apparently, no direct connection between the two developments; but nevertheless, they seem to signal a change in the mythology of the horse, connected with other changes like the use of the gallop in cavalry charges (older charges had proceeded at the trot), and the first compilation of the *General Stud Book* of the Jockey Club, basis of the line of racing thoroughbreds.

Beethoven's *Pastoral* Symphony, first performed in 1808, was part of the traditions of the *sinfonia caracteristica* and the *sinfonia pastorella*. There had been many such works, with evocative titles and sometimes with inner programs, during the previous couple of decades. Fétis compared Beethoven's symphony to the *Portrait Musical de la Nature* of Justin Henri Knecht (1784), and several other comparable works are cited by Jones (1995, 16–17). In common with some, but not all, of its predecessors, the Beethoven symphony gives titles to each of the movements: "Erwachen heiterer Empfindungen bei der Ankunft auf dem Lande" (Awakening of cheerful feelings on arrival in the country), "Szene am Bach" (Scene by the brook), "Lustiges Zusammensein der Landleute" (Merry gathering of country people), "Gewitter, Sturm—Hirtengesang: frohe, dankbare Gefühle nach dem Sturm" (Storm—song of shepherds: joyful, thankful feelings after the storm).

The composer wrote on the title page, and afterward insisted, that the symphony was "mehr Ausdruck der Empfindung als Malerei", more an expression of feeling than a picture. Apparently he wished to give allegiance to the current aesthetic of expressionism, and to dissociate the work from the trivial character-pieces that made up other "pastoral symphonies", and particularly from those grossly naïve "analyses pittoresques et poétiques" of music by Haydn and Mozart written by Jérôme-Joseph de Momigny (see Momigny 1806, vol. 1, 307–382; vol. 2, 387–403, 600–606). Nevertheless, the work contains obvious "pictures": the "storm", part of a tradition of musical storms extending at least from Vivaldi to Britten; the "brook", with its rippling accompaniment; and the celebrated bird imitations, nightingale, quail, and cuckoo. The sharpest distinction between this work and others of the same type is its consistent deploying of the signs of symphonism. It is dominated by a semiotic of structural logic, not one of representation; this was wittily asserted by Tovey in his *Essays in Musical Analysis:* "In the whole symphony there is not a note of which the musical value would be altered if cuckoos and nightingales, and country folk, and thunder and lightning, and the howling and whistling of the wind, were things that had never been named by man" (Tovey 1935, 45).

In spite of this, the work has been interpreted again and again by poetic commentators, by dance troupes, by moviemakers, and even by clever musicologists like Owen Jander, who found in it a narrative of the composer's spiritual development, culminating in his acceptance of his approaching deafness; it is "music's most amazing account of a human being's spiritual growth" (Jander 1993, 551).

Whatever the status of representation in this piece, it unquestionably embodies signs of pastoralism. Indeed, it may be called the central pastoral work of our whole tradition. And in spite of Tovey's wise strictures, it is semiotically different from the Fifth Symphony, its exact contemporary. The Fifth, also, carries signs that affiliate it to literary and cultural themes. But the *Pastoral* is embedded in a mythology that has formed a central pivot of our entire culture; and in any case, it declares its affiliation in a title, as the Fifth Symphony does not.

Undoubtedly, there are straightforward signs of pastoralism, in the sense that we have followed in older works. There are copious pedal points; a drone instantly places the work in pastoral country, at the very beginning of the first movement (and notice the passage in mm. 29–42, resolutely maintaining a pedal on F). There are several affectations of traditional dance tunes, especially in the first movement and in the scherzo ("Lustiges Zusammensein der Landleute"), where the second strain (m. 24) skirls over a tonic pedal point. The "Hirtengesang" begins with the pastoral *ranz des vaches*, as described above in chapter 7. The "storm", an entirely traditional feature, is not a pastoral signifier because it cannot be interpreted without a text or title; you cannot find storms in untitled works because there is no definable musical trait that means "storm", except for general storminess. The same limitation may be applied to the portrayals of birdsong; it seems unlikely that bird imitations can be found in the general repertoire, without titles or words, unless one considers Messiaen's ornithological excursions to function in this way.

The "Scene by the Brook", however, is indubitably a pastoral movement. The time signature, 12/8, is fairly rare at this stage of music history, at least with such a slow tempo marking—*andante molto mosso*—and the opening measures would almost be acceptable as a siciliana, the strings moving in eighth notes that define the meter. At m. 5 the instruments move into rippling sixteenth notes, imitating the purling of the brook. This seems a universal iconic motive that has manifested itself from Vivaldi to Debussy. The harmony is simple, no more than tonic and dominant, with a simple formula of cadence. There is even a trace of the pastoral horn (in mm. 19-20). But since the title implies no classical shepherds, no Golden Age, no *aulós*-players, satyrs, or fauns, we must firmly embrace the new conception of the pastoral, as a glorification of the landscape.

Like Haydn, Beethoven knew of the Enlightenment's theme of nature worship, in particular, through James Thomson (since he must have heard Haydn's *Seasons*) and Christian Sturm; the composer "owned a dog-eared copy" of Sturm's *Betrachtungen,* we learn from Anton Schindler (Jones 1995, 21), and often cites it in his breviary of favorite quotations.

At once, we may perceive an inconsistency between these literary works and Beethoven's symphonic movement. The older works were incoherent and formless. Samuel Johnson commented on Thomson: "The great defect of *The Seasons* is want of method. . . . Of many appearances subsisting all at once, no rule can be given why one should be mentioned before another" (Kroeber 1975, 97). Sturm's book is merely an assemblage of devotional fragments, switching from the heavens, winds, and tempests, to seeds, grass, and caterpillars with complete insouciance. But the "Scene by the Brook" is an extremely secure monothematic sonata movement, scrupulously crafted, modulating almost imperceptibly as far as B major (in a piece in B flat) and recapitulating with heightened firmness—even though the piece has to mold into extended unity a musical theme with the repeated emphatic closure of a folksong.

More remarkably, this long movement is a continuous cantilena, songlike, intimate and serene, the apotheosis of those "new siciliane" of Haydn in 6/8 time, like the siciliano of Symphony no. 27. Its closest companion is the duet "Von deiner Güt" from the *Creation,* another long movement based on an appealing cantilena with an undulating accompaniment. In the absence of voices, Beethoven's movement can engage with effects of pure originality, like the pauses on high trills (as at m. 40) that seem to move out of time into a pure moment of vision. But above all, its haunting melodic purity gives it an intimacy, an experiential reality, which is very close to the visionary embrace of Wordsworth. Of course, music cannot localize and familiarize, though the people of Heiligenstadt claim Beethoven's brook for their locale. But in any case, Wordsworth's purpose in focusing on the local and familiar was intended above all to stimulate a contact with the intimate spiritual center of the reader. This music achieves the same thing by its own means.

The whole movement demonstrates music's power to arrest time—the feature called "lyric temporality" (*Sense*, 81-114). In this respect, it is like a painting, but not a mere trivial illustration, the kind of "Malerei" that Beethoven rejected in composers like Knecht. It is more like the sort of visionary picture we associate with Samuel Palmer, or like the timelessness of lyric verse. Apparently, the mystic union of nature with the poet's experience, which we have observed in Wordsworth, accounts for the haunting purity of this work, which is so much more than a mere character piece or, *pace* its composer, a mere "expression of feeling". The mysticism of neoplatonic sentiment in the Renaissance pastoral has been replaced with a kind of secular hymnody. The *locus amoenus*, with its brook and its birdsong, has rediscovered its spiritual source.

Beethoven, presumably, had not read Wordsworth. Yet the poet seems to link hands with the composer in an experiential engagement with the landscape that was, perhaps, part of the changing collective unconscious. Like the galloping horses of Haydn and George Stubbs, the nature pieces of Wordsworth and Beethoven relate in the formation of a new consciousness, in this case that of Romanticism.

The most extensive study of the pastoral signifier in this period is that of Robert Hatten (Hatten 1994, 79–109). Examining the opening theme of Beethoven's Op. 109 piano sonata, he lists ten features that epitomize its pastoral qualities (97–99). It is, of course, an example of the "new siciliana" established by Haydn. In a slowish 6/8 time, with simple melody and harmony in a soft dynamic, it even has a trace of the bagpipe drone. Hatten draws attention also to a "water-like" rocking accompaniment and the movement in parallel thirds, which may, indeed, indicate a remote ancestry in the music of the *pifferari*. For our purposes, Hatten's chapter is chiefly remarkable in showing how a topical reference can form the basis of a whole movement, and indeed a whole work, in this period. This theorist also shows how the pastoral may be associated with the high, middle, and low styles; in this respect, the importance of the "rustic" pastoral in the nineteenth century, embodied in the associations of folksong, may be readily explained.

David Wyn Jones gives a comprehensive list of Beethoven's works with an overt pastoral reference (Jones 1995, 22–24). These include the "Pastorale" movement in the ballet *Die Geschöpfe des Prometheus,* and the "Pastoral" Sonata for piano, Op. 28. The latter was not so called by Beethoven, but the English publishers who invented the name were right in noticing pastoral pedal points in the first movement and the finale. They might also have sensed the pastoral spirit in the *Adagio* of the Sonata in E flat, Op. 27 no. 1; in the minor-key *Andante espressivo* of Op. 79 in G; in the slow movements of the String Quartets, Op. 74 and Op. 127; and in many other items of Beethoven's oeuvre.

(f) Berlioz's pastorals

As a descriptive composer, Berlioz made extensive use of expressive musical topics. He was much at home in the pastoral genre, though the "rustic pastoral" was rare in his works; his passionate and austere spirit led him to a new kind of Virgilian pastoral. Indeed, his very first published work was a simple pastoral song, "Le dépit de la bergère", a rudimentary new-siciliana published in 1819 (see Holoman 1989, 16, fig. 2.3). The early opera *Les Francs-juges,* part of which was later destroyed by the composer, is dominated by pastoral evocations, shepherds' pipes, the *ranz des vaches*, even a simple tune in 6/8 time called "mélodie pastorale".

A comparison of the "Scène aux Champs" from the *Symphonie Fantastique* with its possible model, Beethoven's "Scene by the Brook", reveals the great aesthetic distance between these two composers. They are, virtually, the two kinds of artist of Schiller's *Über naive und sentimentalische Dichtung*. The whole work is called an "episode in the life of an artist"; Berlioz is always concerned with expressing feelings, with portrayal, narrative, evocation. Musical topics are not especially good for the purpose of expressing personal feelings, in spite of Beethoven's declaration that this was his purpose. As Tovey noticed, the topical content of the "Scene by the Brook" is subordinate to the exquisite contrivance of the movement and the whole symphony; the 12/8 signature, the birdsong, the pedal points could not achieve the aim of reflecting a mystic vision, without the beauty of cantilena and the security of construction. Berlioz's movement cannot be said to display either of these features. On the contrary, the bony textures, the bleak unisons, the general bizarrerie reveal a composer wishing to surprise, to address, to persuade, to be original. Berlioz has feelings to embody, notably his despairing passion for Harriet Smithson. He wishes to be noticed as the subject of the discourse. He is a "sentimental artist". The topical material, then, is distorted and corrupted. The opening *ranz des vaches* is played, not on a horn (much less an alphorn) but on a cor anglais (first time in a symphony) and an offstage oboe. The new-siciliana theme in 6/8 time is presented by flute and violin, unaccompanied apart from laconic pizzicato interruptions. And when a shepherd's pipe (here a clarinet) is accompanied by a rippling figure in sixteenths, there is little harmony; the accompanying figure is played in octaves on violins and violas, snaking around the cantilena in the same register.

It is a paradox that program music and topical reference are poor bedfellows. The topic always refers to a convention, to a cultural world that is much broader than the work itself. But a program tries to tell a unique story, to individualize the expression to one place, one person, one subject. This is, of course, the reverse of Wordsworth's focusing devices, which place the description in a time and a place in order to reveal the infinite in the common. Berlioz wishes us to attend to his own voice, to hear his story, to sympathize with his overheated feelings. He composed the work "furiously", he tells us, his mind "boiling over"; we are meant to find "fire and tears within" (Holoman 1989, 99). Ideas have been found in this symphony from Chateaubriand, Shakespeare, Hugo. But none of these are musical ideas; they are not aspects of musical semantics, but intrusions of the artist's will. Even the implied respect for Beethoven—Berlioz, as a journalist, was after all responsible for establishing Beethoven at the center of our culture—is an intruding idea, something to place in a program note or on the page of a history book.

The much later *Enfance du Christ* occupies a different space. It is a neoclassical—or neo-baroque—piece, built around a choral item, the "Adieu des Bergers," that was originally offered, preposterously, as the work of a seventeenth-century composer. It is, moreover, a Nativity piece, its pastoralism linked to the ancient association of shepherds, heaven, the Golden Age, and the season of Christmas. This places its subjectivity on several layers; it is not a hand-on-heart expression like the symphony. Indeed, it is a religious work by one who possessed much religious sentiment, but no religious faith.

The famous "Adieu des Bergers" is, of course, a new-siciliana, though written in 3/8 time. The hypermeasure groups the measures consistently in twos; the piece is effectively in 6/8 time. Still, the departure from the 6/8 signature is somewhat significant, as we shall see. In addition, the voices are introduced in each strophe by an effect of skirling bagpipes, played on oboes and clarinets. There are two other new-siciliane, these having the expected 6/8 signature: the duet, "O mon cher fils", and the closing item of part 2, "Le Repos de la Sainte Famille". Like the "Adieu", both items are introduced by prominent passages for woodwind, a flute and an oboe in the second case. The duet in part 3, "Dans cette ville immense", may also be counted as a siciliana in 3/8 time; this number, too, has prominent wind parts, and begins over a pedal point. No composer since Scarlatti had ever written an extended work in which the siciliana meter played such a dominant part. One may suspect parody; there is an "exaggeration of stylistic norms", in the words of Esti Sheinberg in a different connection (2000, 25).

The Holy Family arrive at last at Sais, where they are entertained by the Ishmaelites. This is a chance for one of Berlioz's instrumental conjuring tricks. What instruments would biblical persons play? Certainly, they would play "pipes", and these, as we saw in the book of Isaiah, would be *auloi*. They might also play harps, since scripture is rich in harpers—one thinks of King David. We have, then, a trio for two flutes and harp, the standard mistranslation of *aulós* having been followed. The sentiment is entirely pastoral, with dotted triplet groups and the marking *andante espressivo*. But the signature (after a short introduction) is 9/8. Robert Hatten, in his summary of pastoral style, found that "pastoral movements are often in compound meters" (Hatten 1994, 97), implying that 9/8 might be found alongside 12/8 and 6/8. Even 3/8 may be admissible, if the hypermeasure is duple. There seems good reason to believe this, if we consider the Romantic repertoire.

(g) The new-siciliana, continued

The new-siciliana in 6/8 time has countless exemplars in the nineteenth century. Faced with a text descriptive of nature, Schubert sometimes produces a song in new-siciliana style. For example, the *Abendlied für die Entfernte*, a setting of August Schlegel, praises the spiritual refreshment to be gained from contemplation of the landscape.

> Hinaus, mein Blick! hinaus ins Thal!
> Da wohnt noch Lebensfülle,
> Da labe dich im Mondenstrahl
> Und an der heil'gen Stille.

> Go forth, my glance! forth into the valley! For in that place you will find fullness of life; there you will be refreshed by the light of the moon and the sacred peace.

Schubert's setting, in a moderate 6/8 time, combines a Haydnesque siciliana with the simplicity of a folksong. New-siciliane, in 6/8 time, appear frequently in the instrumental works; in the slow movements of the First and Fifth Symphonies, and of the String Quartet in E flat, D. 87, for example.

Mendelssohn, too, adopts this style, both in instrumental and vocal music. The chorus "How lovely are the messengers", from the oratorio *St. Paul,* presents an *andante con moto* in 6/8 time over a tonic pedal. The simple harmony, the key of G major, the gently moving accompaniment all guarantee the pastoral character of this piece, though the words do not specify it; it is a hymn of praise to those who spread the "gospel of peace". Perhaps the word "peace" brings a shadow of the Golden Age.

Brahms produces a very unusual and beautiful pastoral movement. In the normal way, his pastorals are not siciliane; the horn solo over a long pedal point at the start of the Serenade in D, Op. 11, is in *alla breve* time, and there is a similar simple melody over a pedal point at the start of the Quintet in F, Op. 88, in this case in quadruple meter. But, writing for the clarinet, one of the *aulós*'s successors, he is moved to write a sort of new-siciliana. The *Adagio* of the Clarinet quintet, Op. 115, is in 9/8 time and begins over a pedal point in B major, the key of this movement. There is a murmuring accompaniment in the strings. The harmony is less than simple; it has that touch of chromatic fragrance that Brahms came to affect often. But the feeling of elegy, of serenity touched with regret, seems authentically pastoral.

A suggestion of the siciliana spirit can materialize in the most unpromising places. Goldmark's *Rustic Wedding Symphony* of 1877 is an irredeemably pretty work, full of echoes of operetta and the salon. Its five movements have rather general titles, but there is no real program. The third piece, "Serenade", is a charming tune out of comic opera, over a long pedal on tonic and dominant in D. The next, "Im Garten", is a dreamy andante, initially over a throbbing pedal point, but the second strain, *poco più lento,* is given a string accompaniment in triplets, written in 12/8 time against the predominant 4/4. When this expands into a soft tutti, with undulating sixteenths accompanying and initially a suggestion of a pedal point (D flat in this passage in G flat major), there is a distinct suggestion of the Romantic kind of siciliana (fig. 14.13).

Tchaikovsky's *Manfred* Symphony (1885) illustrates Byron's poem, so has a more clearly discernible program. The third movement, "Pastorale", is marked "simple, free and peaceful life of the mountain people". It is an *andante con moto, molto cantabile e espressivo,* in 6/8 time, played by a solo oboe over string accompaniment. The melody somewhat resembles the style of Berlioz. In any case, this is a paradigm of the new-siciliana. The oboist is clearly Arcadian rather than *abruzzese.*

Perhaps the most extreme pastoral in the musical repertoire is the *Andante pastorale* from Nielsen's Third Symphony, the *Sinfonia Espansiva* (1911). In this piece the composer aimed for "a sort of phlegmatically paradisal mood" (Lawson 1997, 134); he spoke also of the "strong tension . . . of the first movement which is completely eradicated in the second movement by idyllic calm". The leaping energy of the first movement, which apparently signaled Nielsen's vigorous rejection of the Danish tradition for agreeable, anodyne music, had to be stilled; and this pastoral sequel is peaceful, tranquil, almost bovine in its rustic torpor. Most of the pastoral

Figure 14.13.

signifiers are there. The opening presents a long-breathed string melody on a horn pedal point, without further harmony (since the contrabasses take part, the melody is partly below its accompanying drone). As a siciliana, new or otherwise, it is surely the slowest ever known; written in 3/4 time, it proceeds at about quarter note = 72. If it were in 12/8 time, the measures would come at 18 to the minute! The melody, in almost uniformly equal values, affects a flattened seventh, a rustic rather than pastoral feature.

In the second section (m. 32), a high flute sings a wandering, meditative figure, afterward imitated by oboe, clarinet, and bassoon. There is a long held pedal on contrabass, with a soft timpani roll. The warmth of the scene suggests Theocritean shepherds or Ovidian fauns; this was, after all, the composer who wrote the overture *Helios* in praise of Athenian sunshine. The opening music is later recapitulated on the full orchestra over an enormously long pedal point on bassoons, trombone, tuba, and low strings, joined immediately by the meditative flute figure, now on violins. As the movement closes, two wordless voices are heard, a soprano and a baritone, concluding with the mysterious sound of the lowest three notes of the flutes.

Nielsen brings the pastoral into the twentieth century. A few years later, an Italian work encloses no fewer than two pastoral episodes. Respighi's symphonic poem *Fontane di Roma* was completed in 1916. Its four sections visualize different fountains at different moments of the day. The composer gives a short verbal commentary on the scene. The first part portrays the "fountain of the Valle Giulia at dawn". We see "un paesaggio pastorale: mandre di pecore passano e si dileguano nella bruma fresca e umida di un'alba romana", a pastoral landscape in which flocks of sheep are passing and vanishing in the chilly, damp mists of a Roman dawn. In a very slow tempo (written in 6/4), muted strings play an undulating figure—the water of the fountain—and a solo oboe, over low pedal points, intones a decorated

Figure 14.14.

cantilena, bringing into view an *aulós* player from ancient times (fig. 14.14). Later, oboes imitate birdsong. In spite of its slow tempo, this evocation is a highly traditional pastoral; its descent from the pastorals of Handel is perfectly clear. After the fountains of morning and midday, the fountain of the Villa Medici (a tiny jet in an exquisite garden overlooking the city) is sighted at sunset. It is pictured in a passage in 4/4, which dissolves into triplets in the flute and cor anglais, with a very soft pedal point on solo cello in the middle register. Again, clarinet and flute imitate birdsong. The spirit of a 12/8 siciliana is sufficiently suggested.

But there is an undeniable sense of the ancient in these symphonic poems of Respighi. Rome is the Eternal City, the seat of emperors and popes. *Fontane*'s companion piece, *Pini di Roma,* ends with a procession of praetorian troops marching up the Appian Way, in a dream of Rome's antique greatness. At this time in musical history, the conventions of pastoral signification have acquired a restrospective aura; *auloi,* syrinxes, shepherds, and shepherdesses suggest not only innocence and warm irresponsibility, but, almost as much, picturesque antiquity. New signifiers are needed for the authentic pastoral sentiments of modern times.

15 New Pastorals

(a) The "rustic" pastoral: Schubert and folksong

We have seen, in Haydn and Beethoven, the adapted folksong functioning as a pastoral signifier. There were, of course, folksongs in the music of older composers; Bach's *Peasant Cantata* (no. 212) is based on several of these. This signifier comes to dominate the pastoral topic in the nineteenth century, however. We may classify this as the "rustic" pastoral; it plays a major part in Romantic melos.

For example, the melodic style of Schubert's lieder seems rooted in the tradition of the salon folksong. It is lyric, engaging, metric, tonal, and simple. But Schubert writes songs of many kinds, dramatic and declamatory as well as merely lyric. When he chooses the simplicity of the volkslied, there is usually some prompting in the text. An example has been given above of a text descriptive of nature which produces a "new siciliana". Another such example—a very well known song—shows that the dominant spirit is less a memory of the siciliana than a reflection of the Berlin-school folksong. The first section of Wilhelm Müller's *Frühlingstraum* from *Winterreise* describes a dream of May flowers.

> Ich träumte von bunten Blumen
> So wie sie wohl blühen im Mai.
>
> I dreamed of colored flowers, as they bloom in May.

Although Schubert sets these words in 6/8 time, the simplicity, the balance of phrases and cadences, the exact matching of the musical structure to the poetic prosody clearly evoke a folksong (fig. 15.1).

Elsewhere, in some very celebrated songs, the composer has no need for the siciliana meter. Two water pieces materialize as light volkslieder in 2/4 time, with short regular phrases, rippling accompaniment, and simple construction, initially with the simplest harmony: *Wohin* from *Die schöne Müllerin* ("Ich hört' ein Bächlein rauschen . . ."), and *Die Forelle* ("In einem Bächlein helle . . .").

Trees, like brooks, may be rendered with the simplicity of folksong; Claudius's *Das Lied vom Reifen* portrays a row of trees, their twigs glistening with frost. It is rendered as a simple and symmetrical tune in 6/8 time, with accompaniment in sixteenths. This is a plain strophic song, its fifteen strophes sung to the same music, just like a folksong. Even among the radical through-composed masterpieces of *Winterreise*, the image of a lime tree (*Der Lindenbaum*) yields a song in moderate triple meter whose symmetry and simple structure are so like a volkslied that the first section, before Schubert begins to develop the music to follow the trajectory of the poem, has been taken into the folksong repertoire itself; it appears, slightly rearranged, in the collection *Deutsche Heimat* (Andersen ca. 1910, 8), as a simple

Etwas bewegt

Ich träum - te von bun - ten Blu - men, so wie sie wohl blü - hen im Mai; ich träum - te von grü - nen Wie - sen, von lus - ti - gem Vo - gel - ge - schrei, _____ von _____ lus - ti - gem Vo - gel - ge - schrei.

Figure 15.1.

sixteen-measure tune, sung three times to accommodate the poem that is treated so much more inventively in the original setting. Thus an advanced art song returns to its background in the "folk".

As well as nature descriptions, valleys, fields, brooks, and trees, there are songs about innocent children which take the form of volkslieder. Friedrich Schlegel's *Der Knabe* has a boy imagining himself to be a bird. Schubert's setting in 2/4 time, "heiter" (cheerful), is perhaps his most childlike melody. In another song, a setting of Heinrich Heine's *Das Fischermädchen,* the folksong spirit is suggested by the naïveté of the words.

> Du schönes Fischermädchen,
> Treibe den Kahn an's Land;
> Komm zu mir und setze dich nieder,
> Wir kosen Hand in Hand.

> You lovely fisher girl, push the boat off, come to me and sit down, we'll nestle hand in hand.

The music, symmetrical and charming, is in 6/8 time, though too fast ("etwas geschwind") to be a siciliana.

Innocent simplicity is an essential pastoral quality, of course, and nature description advanced to dominate pastoral expression during the eighteenth century. In Schubert's songs, then, both of these may prompt the ingratiating melodic ring of the folksong, which is to say the German traditional song as it was civilized and adapted for community singing and for the middle-class salon, with metrical regularity, tonal structure, short balanced phrases, and harmony of tonic and dominant.

(b) Brahms: the *Liedhaft*

Brahms believed that folksong lay at the root of all song composition. He wrote to Clara Schumann: "The song is at present sailing on a course so false, that one cannot fix firmly enough in one's mind its true ideal. And that, for me, is folk-song" (quoted by Rummenhöller 1992, 39). Peter Rummenhöller believes that the *Liedhaft*—the style of the volkslied—may be considered a *topic* in the music of Brahms. "The *Volksliedhaft* must be admitted to the ranks of musical topoi—and this is proved over and over again in the works of Brahms, even and especially in the instrumental music" (Rummenhöller 1992, 40). The composer was well acquainted with the kind of folksongs that people admired in the early nineteenth century. His settings of nursery songs, the *Volks-Kinderlieder,* came out in 1858. In the same year he wrote a collection of adult folksong arrangements, though this was not published until after his death. There are a number of settings of folksongs among the many song collections, and there are also arrangements for accompanied and unaccompanied chorus. At the end of his life he published the great seven-volume collection, *Deutsche Volkslieder.* The huge majority of these songs are taken from the collection of Kretzschmer and Zuccalmaglio, the *Deutsche Volks-lieder mit ihren Original-Weisen,* mentioned above.

Werner Morik argues convincingly that Brahms's whole melodic style is founded on his feeling for folksong (Morik 1953). But is this relevant to a study of the musical pastoral? In other words, is the *Liedhaft* a branch of the pastoral topic? The answer to this must focus on the writings of Herder, which Brahms had been reading in the years before his first major output of folksong arrangements (he speaks of Herder in a letter to Clara Schumann of June 1855; Morik 1953, 297n1). Herder believed that a good folksong had a "soul" of its own, independent of any possible composer or social origin; "the soul of the song," he wrote, "which alone affects the spirit and moves the feelings of the singers, this soul is immortal and goes on working for ever" (quoted by Morik 1953, 297). The folksong was for Herder "nature in the true sense, as one speaks of *Naturvolk* [aboriginal people]." Primitive peoples had no philosophy; for them, poetry was the only language. Their songs, therefore, embody all the wisdom of unlettered folk.

The pastoral essence of this view has been discussed in chapter 13. The "natural" properties of folksong were related to the naturalness of the Berlin community song tradition; but the early Romantics also imagined countryfolk to possess a naturalness, an uncorrupted simplicity, that the urban middle class had lost. We may recall Arnim's farm servants and villagers, singing together amid the trees, in the essay that concludes the first volume of *Des Knaben Wunderhorn.*

Brahms's Second Symphony, especially its first movement, is dominated by *liedhaft* melody. It has been called a "symphonic idyll". After the first performance in Leipzig, a reviewer wrote:

> In ideational content the first movement may be described as the most important: it strikes up such an endearing and cheerful pastoral tone, and although this is supplanted at times by the solemn sounds of trombones, like storms erupting over the calm, magnificent spring landscape, it always regains the upper hand, so that one imagines oneself transported back in time to the age of the idyll, which no savage passions were tearing apart. (*Neue Zeitschrift für Musik,* 25 January 1878, 47; quoted by Brinkmann 1995, 199)

This consciousness of the worship of landscape—this awareness of the pastoral myth at the heart of *liedhaft* melody—seems remarkable, but the reviewer was not the only one to see a romantic landscape in this pure lyric movement. Theodor Billroth, having received from Brahms the piano reduction of the symphony, had enthused, in a letter to the composer of 14 November 1877: "Why, it is all blue sky, babbling of streams, sunshine and cool green shade!" (Brinkmann 1995, 13).

Reinhold Brinkmann, who brings us these quotations, feels that Brahms's pastoralism is "skeptically broken"; "the idyllic nature-metaphor at the beginning of Brahms's Second Symphony is itself charged with history . . . [and with] that melancholy which is the product of 'mourning' for a 'lost possession'" (Brinkmann 1995, 200). "Mourning for a lost possession" is Schelling's definition of *melancholy*. "Thus etched on the Brahmsian idyll, with its reflective intensity, is the consciousness of a late period which is excluded from the pure representation of an Arcadian state. . . . This was called an idyll broken in melancholy fashion." Brinkmann considers that the symphony marks Brahms as a "sentimental" artist, in Schiller's terminology. He is undoubtedly right. But the elegiac longing for a lost period of happiness was always a pastoral theme, as we have found. It may be traced back at least to Virgil's Fourth Eclogue. Brahms's pastoral elegy is not sentimental because it is an elegy, but because it is self-conscious.

Morik finds that the composer's relation to folksong was variable. There may be a respect for the habitual strophic arrangement of folksong, but there is commonly also a modification of the strophes, tending eventually toward through-composition. Simple, monodic arrangement is observed alongside the sophisticated working out of folksong material, leading by a direct route into the art song, and finally the seamless instrumental melody.

We may observe a folksong formula evolving by stages. A traditional song called "Da unten im Tale", the version of Krezschmer and Zuccalmaglio, is arranged by Brahms as no. 6 of the *Deutsche Volkslieder* (fig. 15.2a). The poem is set by Brahms in folksong style as Op. 97 no. 6; the same formula is clearly present, though repetition of words leads to an extension of the musical unit from 8 to 12 measures (fig. 15.2b). Another folksong setting, *Spannung* (Op. 84 no. 5), shows a lengthening of phrases and some chromaticism in this minor-key melody; the unit has spread to 17 measures (fig. 15.2c). The words of *Spannung* remind us of the favorite *Wiegenlied*, Op. 49 no. 4, which is a simpler example of the same formula. The Waltz in E, Op. 39 no. 2, is an instrumental version of the formula.

The same kind of tonal simplicity, with short balanced phrases and regular cadences, is observed in the Intermezzo, Op. 117 no. 1, where the strumming of the high E flat, above the melody, suggests plucked strings (perhaps the separate topic of "serenade"). Brahms attaches the words of a lullaby from Herder's *Volksliedern:*

Schlaf sanft mein Kind,
Schlaf sanft und schön!
Mich dauert's sehr,
Dich weinen sehn.

(a) **Sanft bewegt**

Da ___ un - ten im Ta - le läufts Was - ser so trüb und i

kann dirs nit sa - gen i hab di so lieb.

(b) **Anmutig bewegt**

(Piano)

p

Da un - ten im

Ta - le läufts Was - ser so trüb, läufts Was - ser so trüb, und i kann dirs net

sa - gen, i hab di so lieb, i hab di so lieb.

(c) **Bewegt und heimlich**

Piano *p*

Gut'n A - bend, gut'n

A - bend, mein tau - si - ger Schatz, ich sag ___ dir gu - ten A -

bend; komm du ___ zu mir, ___ ich kom - me zu dir, du sollst ___ mir

Ant - wort ge - ben, mein En - - - gel!

Figure 15.2.

(a) **Langsam und leise**

Im - mer lei - ser wird mein Schlum - mer, nur wie Schlei - er liegt mein

Kum - mer zit - ternd ü - ber mir, __ ü - ber mir. __

(b) **Andante**

mp espr.

f

p

Figure 15.3.

Sleep softly, my child, sleep softly and well; it grieves me sore to see you weep.

Herder's words are, in fact, a translation of a Scottish poem, *Lady Anne Bothwell's Lament* from Percy's *Reliques*.

One step away from this ineffably pastoral piece is another intermezzo, Op. 119 no. 3, which copies the effect of the plucked stringed accompaniment, but re-arranges and develops the melody through repetitions and elisions, making it hard to subject to a simple analysis (Nattiez's complicated attempt is famous: Nattiez 1975, 300–319). The pastoral spirit, the spirit of nature, is still present, but overlaid with *Genie,* a quality which Goethe considered also to be natural (Morik 1953, 297).

A more extreme example of this process, the encounter of pastoralism and genius, is revealed by comparing the song "Immer leiser wird mein Schlummer", Op. 105 no. 2, with the cello solo in the third movement of the Second Piano Concerto, Op. 83 (fig. 15.3a,b). The poem is a lament, sophisticated and not pastoral in flavor, but the setting has the short phrases and balanced cadences of the volks-lied.

> Immer leiser wird mein Schlummer,
> Nur wie Schleier liegt mein Kummer
> Zitternd über mir. (Hermann Lingg)

My sleep gets ever more peaceful, yet my grief lies trembling over me, like a veil.

The instrumental melody is clearly derived from the same melodic idea (it antedates the song, of course). It is, however, one of those long-breathed, ceaselessly drawn-out lines that characterize Brahms, not composed of balanced short phrases or recurrent cadences. Its poignancy and beauty might be called "pastoral" by one using the term in the loose sense. We are now in a position to justify this by tracing its remote origin in the simple patterns of the folksong. We have here reached the boundary of the pastoral topic in Brahms, however. His music is rich in topical reference, not only pastoral, but venatory and military, as well as related to dance, to historic styles, and the many other associations of historic topics. The slow introduction to the last movement of the First Symphony is an extraordinary anthology of topics.

The instrumental works are, in fact, all full of topical figures, including quotations of actual folksongs. In the very first publication, the Piano Sonata Op. 1, the slow movement is based on what the score calls an "old German Minnelied", taken from Kretzschmer-Zuccalmaglio. Many of the tunes in the *Academic Festival Overture* are taken from collections of student songs. But at this point, we encounter an intrusion. The most memorable of these tunes is "Wir hatten gebauet ein stattliches Haus", these words coming from a poem by August Binzer (1819). As I have explained in *Sense* (129–130), there was another text to this tune, written almost contemporaneously with Binzer's:

> Ich hab mich ergeben
> Mit Herz und mit Hand
> Dir, Land voll Lieb und Leben
> Mein deutsches Vaterland. (Hans Ferdinand Massmann, 1820)

> I devote myself with heart and hand to thee, O land full of love and life, my German fatherland.

If Brahms meant to refer to this other text, which is likely—he was an ardent patriot—then the volkslied here is not a sign of pastoralism, but of *political nationalism*. There were, after all, whole categories of folksong connected with the national spirit: *Soldatenlieder, Heimatslieder, Heldenlieder*. This is the other side of the semantics of folksong. It will not be discussed here. Its origins lie in the same doctrine of the *Volksseele* that inspired the pastoral side of nineteenth-century topical signification, Herder's belief in the mysterious truths understood by the unlettered masses, and Arnim's applying of this to the spirit of the German nation. It powered the regional nationalisms of the century; it is hard to attribute purity and innocence to the folk spirit of Liszt, Smetana, Dvořák, Moniuszko, Balakirev, Mussorgsky, Bartók. Doubtless, pastoral references can be found in their operas and instrumental works, but these composers could not avoid political motivation, for in some cases the traditional material on which they based their styles was not generally familiar (the German and Scottish collections were widely known). It had to be brought to international attention, and at the same time the political enslavement of the eastern nations was trumpeted. Here lies an important study, on which I shall not embark.

(c) The *Liedhaft* in modern times

Mahler was not an arranger of folksongs, unless one counts the grotesque version of *Bruder Martin*, for contrabass solo, in the First Symphony. But he wrote many "new" folksongs to words from *Des Knaben Wunderhorn*, or to his own words. Some of these found their way into the symphonies. And like Brahms, Mahler developed the simple strophic form of some songs into complex through-composed structures, and finally into a vein of *liedhaft* melody in which the spirit of folksong is still apparent.

Undoubtedly he believed that the *Volk* embodied the spirit of anonymous nature. Although the "people" who spoke in Mahler's own folksongs were imaginary—since the melodies were composed by Mahler himself—they were nevertheless present in the inspiration of the composer. "One is just an instrument", he said, "on which the universe plays" (quoted in *Sense*, 175). Since I have spoken at some length on this aspect of Mahler's ideas, there is no need to recapitulate here (see *Sense*, 172–176). In summary, one can say that no musician so comprehensively adopted the Herderian view of folksong as nature.

If we take a single example from the manifold quotations in the symphonies, we shall engage with several other issues: first, the question of subjectivity (see also *Sense*, 147–195) and "autobiography", whatever this might mean in music; and second—and more important—the indwelling of the erotic in the heart of the nature-pastoral. The embedding of the song "Ging heut' morgens übers Feld", in the first movement of the First Symphony, may be shown at once to refer to nature-mysticism. The work begins with an evocation of landscape, an introduction full of icons and topics, picturing the sunlit scene through which the hero strolls. All stringed instruments, including the contrabasses, play a high A in harmonics. "With the first note," Mahler said to Natalie Bauer-Lechner, "the long-held A in harmonics, we are in the midst of nature: in the woods, where the sunlight of a summer day trembles and flickers through the branches" (quoted by Danuser 1991, 75). This strange noise—like an old-fashioned steam engine, according to Adorno—is marked "wie ein Naturlaut", like a natural sound. Distant horn calls are heard; we hear the cry of a cuckoo (a descending perfect fourth on the clarinet, marked "der Ruf eines Kukkuks nachzuahmen"). Then, in a clever transition passage, the cuckoo's cry turns into the first two notes of the song, which is played by the cellos. Danuser describes aptly the conversion of a static mood into a dynamic process, as the nature picture turns into a scene of movement, the hero strolling across the field.

"Ging heut' morgens" is the second of the *Lieder eines fahrenden Gesellen*, Mahler's first published collection of synthetic folksongs. The words are his own, but the whole impression, poetic style, melos, periodicity, harmonic plainness, is authentic. In almost all his composed folksongs, the composer conjures up a *liedhaft* manner that is more real than any "real" folksong, the apotheosis of the Kretzschmer-Zuccalmaglio myth. These songs were composed just before and during the composition of the symphony. Like Schubert's *Winterreise*, they portray, through a series of vignettes, an unhappy love affair. In the first song, "Wenn mein Schatz

Hochzeit macht" (the only one with a background in the *Wunderhorn*), the poet imagines his beloved's wedding to somebody else. In "Ging heut' morgens übers Feld" he tries to enjoy the spring weather, but cannot forget his sadness. The rationale of the symphony is much more complex. Because of the cyclic routines of the sonata movement, the "self-pity" (Raymond Knapp's word: Knapp 2003, 177) of the protagonist has to be worked out in a more mature way. In the cycle, the singer finally gives way to despair and a desire for death (in the last song, "Die zwei blauen Augen", also quoted later in the symphony); in the symphony, the sentiments of the hero are recalled, assessed, in a narrative present. In his subtle account of this work, Knapp allows himself to find Mahler's own subjectivity, at last, in the finale—and thus implies an aspect of "autobiography". Here lies an interesting debate (Knapp 2003, 154–193).

Whatever the case, the motivation of the song cycle was a love affair of the young Mahler. While at Kassel, he became attached to a singer called Johanna Richter, but the affair ended unhappily. Michael Kennedy finds in both song cycle and symphony "a remarkable autobiographical commentary on Mahler's youth. . . . The symphony, then, is a love story" (Kennedy 1990 [1974], 115). Whether we side with Knapp's relegation of the symphony to a remembered and overcome past, or with Kennedy's portrayal of both cycle and symphony as testaments to a living experience, we must accept that the young man who strolls across the fields is, in Mahler's eyes, the composer himself. The lost love that is mourned in the song is Gustav's love for Johanna. Within the nature reference of the symphony, and the lyricism of the song, is the erotic spirit, the spirit of young love, the loves of Aminta and Silvia, of Corydon and Alexis, of Daphnis and Chloe. All idealisms, it seems, are ultimately erotic. And since Eros always leads to elegy, the song cycle ends sadly. The symphony, as Knapp so well shows, is a more complicated matter.

Of course, the meeting of nature worship and elegiac eroticism could have been illustrated throughout the story of the *Liedhaft*. But as culture began to move away from the worship of landscape, the focusing of the simple lyric on the topic of young love became more habitual. Older people can only approach Eros by imagining themselves young, like the Feldmarschallin in Strauss's opera *Der Rosenkavalier*, preferably by love affairs with impossibly young lovers like Octavian. Alongside this existentially impossible project, the consummate artist Hofmannsthal (Strauss's librettist) places a truly young love affair, mirroring the protagonists (though involving one of them) but not yet worked out—and therefore, apparently, happy. This is the relation of Octavian and Sophie. As though to indicate that the whole opera was an erotic dream, Strauss ends the score with a volkslied, "Ist ein Traum, kann nicht wirklich sein" (synthetic, of course; it is hard to imagine a folksong setting by this composer). The text of this lovely duet encapsulates the whole unreality, yet fundamental truth, of the pastoral spirit.

> Ist ein Traum, kann nicht wirklich sein,
> Dass wir zwei bei einander sein,
> Bei einand für alle Zeit
> Und Ewigkeit.

Figure 15.4.

> It's a dream, it cannot be real, that we two are together, together for all time and eternity. *Sophie's words; Octavian's are different.*

Apart from the ecstatic drawing out of the phrases, Strauss's tune is symmetrical, simple, with regular cadences and harmonies centered around tonic and dominant (fig. 15.4).

Before we commence weeping with Strauss, the old confectioner, let us turn, finally, to a composer whose deep seriousness forbids us to stand back in pensive appraisal of the erotic myth. Janáček's opera *Kát'a Kabanová* bespeaks his pan-Slavic political consciousness—being based on a Russian play—so we would expect any reference to folksong to have a nationalist edge. Again, there are two love affairs, one between a married woman and her bourgeois lover, the other between two young innocents. Kát'a is an unhappily married woman who has responded to Boris's rapturous approaches; Kudrjáš is a clerk, Varvara a young foster child. For the younger couple this humane artist succeeds, in fact, in manufacturing new folksongs that avoid political suggestion and perfectly evoke the spirit of pastoral love, of the thoughtless love of young country people, of "S'ei piace, ei lice," in contrast to the forbidden love of the protagonists. In act 2 both pairs meet: Kát'a and Boris, Kudrjáš and Varvara. As the adults are carried further into urgent passion, the two young people sing of their carefree feelings in the freshness of the night. Ostrovsky, the Russian playwright whose work forms the basis of the opera, gives the young ones three folksongs. Originally Janáček set all three of these in Czech translations, though he afterward replaced the first, the song Kudrjáš sings to his guitar while waiting for Varvara. In Ostrovsky this was a song of a Cossack who thinks of murdering his wife. Janáček set this to music, but afterward replaced the text with another, also Russian, "about a young man bringing gifts to an independent-minded young girl (who loves another)" (Tyrrell 1982, 58; the song is on p. 87 of the Universal Edition vocal score). Clearly the composer wanted to avoid the dark suggestions of Ostrovsky's song; the other songs are, respectively, about a boy who thinks his girl looks like a Tsarina (p. 94), and a girl who made love all night, till "dawn was in the sky" (p. 110). The words are, apparently, traditional (though translated), but Janáček's tunes are new, "adapted to the Russian vernacular", according to Hollander (1963, 141). The last song is the sunniest and most innocent, in the major key, metrically plain, in short, cadenced phrases, its shameless words enwreathed in ingenuous charm.

Figure 15.5.

> KUDRJAŠ: A girl once strolled out for a time
> for a time at evening
> aj, leli, leli, leli
> for a time at evening
> VARVARA: And I am a girl and young
> and I made love till the day
> aj, leli, leli, leli
> till the earliest light of day.
> (Translation by Michael Ewans)

This "folksong" epitomizes the very essence of the pastoral tradition, youth, innocence, the delightful air of the garden, the spirit of nature, touched by slight regret.
It is, perhaps, the most telling example of synthetic folksong used to conjure pastoral sentiments (fig. 15.5).

(d) The *fête galante*

Nevertheless, there were other pastoral traditions in the nineteenth and
twentieth centuries, not connected with folksong. During the 1860s there was a
remarkable cultural change in France, the beginning, perhaps, of the fin de siècle.
The pastoral painters of the Louis XIV period, Watteau, Lancret, Boucher, Fragonard, had been heartily rejected by the age of the Revolution. In 1791 nine Watteau
drawings fetched a miserable three francs in Paris (Bornecque 1969, 22). During
the 1830s interest began to grow again in these artists; Théophile Gautier was fas-
cinated with Watteau. His nostalgic poem named for the painter ("C'était un parc
dans le goût de Watteau") dates from 1838. Soon, mere nostalgia turned to a more
serious engagement with Watteau's greatness. The breakthrough came with Arsène
Houssaye's influential *Histoire de l'Art Francais au Dix-huitième Siècle* of 1860. "If
painting consists, not in translating tragedies on to canvas, but in poetic invention
and colorful impressionism, Watteau is the greatest of French painters; no one has
surpassed him in love of nature and the sentiment of the ideal; he creates an immense and infinite nature, which he envelops in a luminous atmosphere. . . . [He
was] above all the painter of spirit and love, the painter of *fêtes galantes*" (quoted
by Bornecque 1969, 29). These *fêtes galantes* (the genre of most of Watteau's can-

vases) were pastoral in spirit, but they seldom portrayed shepherds. The Abbé du Bos had suggested that the true pastoral should be a dialogue of people of tone in a lovely natural setting; Watteau, who died in 1721, usually showed aristocrats in old-world costume (that of the time of Louis XIII) mixing with characters from the *commedia dell'arte*, the whole in delightful parkland lit by refulgent sunlight. Nevertheless, there is always an atmosphere of irresponsible innocence; there is "a shift . . . from the evocation of a supposed past arcadian reality to the fabrication of an ideal, present bucolic existence" (Posner 1984, 179).

The classic example of this genre is the *Embarquement de Cythère*, painted as Watteau's reception piece to the Académie Royale. It was the only painting of Watteau displayed in the Louvre in the mid-nineteenth century, and was thus the work from which the poet Paul Verlaine derived his impression of the *fête galante* (the riches of the Lacaze collection reached the Louvre a little too late; Bornecque 1969, 15n1). It shows a group of young people in old-fashioned courtly dress, some engaged in love play, apparently descending a hill away from a marble figure of a Herm, to enter a boat and voyage to the happy isle of Cythera. There are no shepherds, but the spirit is erotic, melancholy, fragrant.

Occasionally Watteau portrays actual pastoral characters, as he does in *The Shepherds* in the gallery of Charlottenburg, Berlin (plate 2). Their peasant character is belied, however, by the pastel satins and lawns of their costumes. The painting is an essay on love; its exquisite curve begins at bottom left, in the dog with prominent genitalia, passes through a pair of rustic lovers, a player of the musette (an aristocratic instrument; two chanters and a bourdon cylinder can be observed), two dancers in the graceful pose of a minuet, and finally a church on the right of the frame: from physical to divine love. In the background can be seen a girl on a swing, symbol of love's fickleness. This piece of pure erotic pastoral may be contrasted with the "real" peasants of plate 7, whose music and dancing are patently rustic.

Watteau's invention of the *fête galante* led to a whole series of imitators, some of them great artists in their own right. His pupil Nicolas Lancret, the virtuosic Chardin, and the sentimental Fragonard all owed their style, in part, to Watteau. But it was François Boucher (1703–70) who came to epitomize the rococo pastoral. Where Watteau chose mainly people of high tone, Boucher portrayed real shepherds and peasants. They wear the clothing of country people: the girls have skirts, aprons, and short petticoats, the boys wear loose jackets and baggy trousers rolled up to the knee; all are barefoot. Yet the impression is utterly and entirely unreal. In fact, only the coloring is truly false; real peasants wore drab, but Boucher's young people wear a rainbow of pastel colors, rose, yellow, and sky blue. Yet their impersonal loveliness, the coyness of the girls, the refined gestures, and the vague love play estrange them radically from real countryfolk. This painter was renowned for his lascivious nudes, and he even undresses his shepherdesses at times—or at least disorders their dress to reveal interesting flesh.

Nevertheless, his best pastorals—the *Pastorale d'Automne* and *Pastorale d'Eté*, both in the Wallace Collection, London, are his masterpieces—have a naturalness of pose, an exquisite accomplishment, a gaiety and ease which defy criticism.

Diderot dismissed this art as mere decoration. But in many ways, it influenced the pastoral image of several centuries to an even greater degree than the work of Watteau. Today, when most of us love to scoff at the pastoral, it is probably the art of Boucher that we invoke chiefly for our ridicule.

These, then, were the pastoral painters who suddenly came to prominence in the mid-nineteenth century. The Goncourt brothers, Edmond and Jules, took up this theme. In a series of articles in their *Journal,* produced from 1851 to 1895 (though Jules died in 1870), and in their masterpiece *Eighteenth-Century Painters,* they praised the taste, the hedonism, the delicate feeling, the poetry, the sophistication of these artists, and above all their quality of grace. In spite of the symbolic content of paintings like *The Shepherds,* the Goncourts had very little understanding of the lofty neoplatonic allegory of the pastoral. These modern writers, in fact, reveled in irresponsibility; Watteau's setting is pure pleasure, with no claim to any kind of reality.

> Here is a region that conspires with his mood—amorous woods, meadows overflowing with music, echoing groves and overarching branches hung with baskets of flowers; solitary places, remote from the jealous world . . . , refreshed with springs and inhabited by marble statues, by naiads dappled with the trembling shadows of leaves. . . . It is an amiable and pleasant country, where there are suns setting in apotheosis, beautiful lights sleeping upon the lawns, a verdant foliage, pierced, translucent, shadowless, where the palette of Veronese—that flashing harmony as of golden locks wreathed with red violets—lies slumbering. (Goncourt 1981, 2)

There is music, but it is the music of the stage, "villages dazed by the sounds of flutes and violins proceeding towards some baroque temple for the nuptials of Nature with the Muse of the Opera" (3). The scenery is embellished by the brush of the theatrical designer; "the *comédie-française* has mounted the stage and the *commedia dell'arte* trips lightly across it."

Pastoralism and erotism came together in these lyric evocations, which conveyed

> a poetry as unique as it is delightful, the poetry of dandalled ease, of the colloquies and songs of youth, of pastoral recreations and leisurely pastimes, a poetry of peace and tranquillity . . . beneath that cottage roof on the horizon, Time lies sleeping. . . . A Lethean stream spreads silence through this land of forgetfulness. . . . It is Love; but it is poetic Love, the Love that contemplates and dreams, modern Love with its aspirations and its coronal of melancholy. (Goncourt 1981, 5–8)

Boucher's shepherds had no reality for the Goncourts; their peasant clothes were fancy dress. "He presents them in the most chivalrous disguise, in the vesture of the masked balls of the court. Rustic life at his touch became an ingenious romance of nature, an allegory of pleasures and loves, virtues subsisting, remote from city and society. . . . He evoked Sylvio, Phyllis, Lycidas, Alexis, Celadon, Sylvanus, in all those compositions arranged, so to speak, on the banks of the Lignon" (67). The "banks of the Lignon" are a reference to *Astrée*. Thus the Goncourts recognized the continuity of the French pastoral. These eighteenth-century court painters, they felt, thought of *Astrée* when they portrayed their shepherds, "all satin, paniers, beauty spots, necklets of ribbon". But not only of *Astrée*: "It is a society dropped upon the green turf of a pastoral by Guarini, a song upon its lips and pink rosettes upon its shoes. It is an eclogue of the kind of which Fontenelle spoke when he said, as if foreseeing the phantasy of Boucher: 'It appears to me that the eclogue is gradually becoming analogous with the peasant costumes in a ballet'" (67–68).

The extraordinary boldness of these sophisticated critics, in praising something that seemed inseparable from the vapidities of the *ancien régime,* awoke a final burst of pastoralism in the France of the fin de siècle. The estrangement, the world-weariness of the Decadence warmed, just a little, to an art that avoided grandeur, that laughed at realism, that went shamelessly for pleasure: "the new emotional humours of an ageing humanity" (Goncourt 1981, 7).

(e) Debussy's syrinx

Verlaine's little collection of poems, the *Fêtes Galantes,* came out in 1867. They reflect Watteau's world in many ways; we find therein the sad, languorous young people in their "long gowns and high heels", "playing the lute and dancing", wandering through a "half light shining through high branches" amidst marble fountains, dreaming of love and sadness; and we find Pierrot, Harlequin, Colombine, Scaramouche, Pulcinella, all the personnel of the Italian *commedia.* And many of Verlaine's poems were set to music, of course, by Fauré and Debussy. However, it is not possible to speak of a *fête galante* topic, because neither composer adopted any unique means to portray this Watteauesque world. The songs (especially Fauré's *Cinq Mélodies de Venise* of 1891, and Debussy's two sets of *Fêtes Galantes* of 1891 and 1904) are fine works of their composers' maturity which do not differ, in terms of technical means, from their other collections (Debussy's earlier set of *Fêtes Galantes,* dating from 1882, is less than mature). We may find shreds of common ground with the pastoral tradition; Debussy's first song, "En Sourdine", presents the song of a nightingale in the piano accompaniment.

Just as there had been a break in the tradition of the literary pastoral—the last gasps of the classical shepherd came with the pastoral verses of André Chenier and Salomon Gessner, and the pastoral took flight into the nature poetry of Wordsworth— so musicians had largely forgotten the traditions that associated pastoralism with the siciliana, with imitations of the *aulós* on flute and oboe, with the bass drones of the bagpipe. The Goncourts and Verlaine reinvented the pastoral for modern readers, and Debussy had to discover new ways of evoking erotic innocence. Curiously, although the siciliana was thought in the eighteenth century to be an old dance of Sicily, the new composers had to respond to a new nostalgia, the feeling that pastoralism was itself a sign of an old and lost world. Brinkmann considered that Brahms's nostalgia was something different from the longing that is at the heart of all pastoralism; and the new French poets also understood the pastoral world as a sign of ancient times, a fragrant past that embraced all the periods—the Renaissance, the time of Louis XIII and *Astrée,* the world of Metastasio and *opera seria*—that had themselves sighed for the loss of the Golden Age. Now, the siciliana had been largely forgotten as a sign of the antique, though Fauré put one into the incidental music he wrote for *Le Bourgeois Gentilhomme* (and afterward arranged it for violin and cello). Even Debussy may have his siciliana: the third piece of the *Six Epigraphes Antiques*, "Pour que la Nuit soit Propice" (So that the night may be propitious) is in a slow 12/8 time.

More commonly, other dances like the minuet and the sarabande evoked the *ancien régime* for these people. This was the era when French baroque music was being edited and revived; Debussy himself edited *Les Fêtes de Polymnie* for Saint-Saëns's complete edition of Rameau (1908). When the composer, in 1882, set a poem called *Fête Galante* by Théodore de Banville ("Voilà Sylvandre et Lycas et Myrtil"), he chose a *tempo di minuetto*, and this song eventually metamorphosed into the menuet from the *Petite Suite* for piano. There is a sarabande in the suite *Pour le Piano*. A minuet is again chosen for the "Placet Futile" from *Trois Poèmes de Stéphane Mallarmé*. This predilection for clavecin dances to evoke the spirit of Louis XV is typified by the genres chosen by Ravel in his *Tombeau de Couperin* suite: forlane, rigaudon, menuet.

The sort of stately dance that signifies "antique" for Debussy is typified by the first of the piano *Préludes, Danseuses de Delphes*. The tempo, the signature, and occasionally the rhythm suggest a sarabande. This topic may be found in many places; the mysterious prelude *Feuilles Mortes*, in the second book, begins with a snatch of sarabande-like rhythm (can there be a suggestion in the title of *feuille-morte*, the sepia color seen in old photographs?). Earlier, another prelude, *Les Sons et les Parfums Tournent dans l'Air du Soir*, extends the triple rhythm to five beats (the title comes from Baudelaire's poem *Harmonie du Soir*, which Debussy set as one of the *Cinq Poèmes de Baudelaire*, and which uses octatony as a signifier of mystery—see Monelle 1992a).

Curiously, an English work, Arthur Bliss's *Pastoral: Lie Strewn the White Flocks*, a cantata for chorus, flute, timpani, and strings of 1928, though there is very little pastoral about it (except for a general sentiment of peacefulness, and persistent bird imitations on the flute), contains an item called "Pan's Sarabande". The forest god, you may have thought, would have been happier with a siciliana, but the French had accustomed him to the world of the clavecin.

We must examine a pastoral signifier that appears to be Debussy's invention. It may be that the cor anglais figure in *Nuages*, the first of the orchestral *Nocturnes*, and the almost identical motive for cor anglais in the second movement of *La Mer* imitate the sound of the *aulós*, placing Debussy in the same tradition as Handel's "Love in her eyes sits playing", for example. But the French composer was a prolific inventor of his own topical signifiers. One of these was, it seems, an imitation of the syrinx. Few people can have heard the sound of this ancient instrument in 1890. Even today, we know it mainly from the Andean panpipes. But Debussy imagined that the lips were applied to the pipe of highest pitch, then slid across the instrument, producing a rapid downward scale or arpeggio (or perhaps the reverse). This is easily imitated on the modern flute. It is heard in the most famous three measures of his whole oeuvre, which Pierre Boulez called "the birth of modern music": the opening of the *Prélude à l'Après-midi d'un Faune*.

The question is: what instrument was played by the faun in Mallarmé's *églogue*, of which the *Prélude* is an illustration? The whole historical confusion about the nature of the *aulós* is epitomized in this example. In line 19 of the poem the faun refers to his instrument as a "flûte", and describes shortly afterward the action of cutting hollow reeds to make it ("je coupais ici les creux roseaux"). We are aware that classical *auloi* were made from hard materials, wood or metal; but a poet may perpetuate the myth of the *avena,* the oat-straw, from which the *aulós* was supposed to have originated. Then follows the most evocative passage.

> Mais, bast! arcane tel élut pour confident
> Le jonc vaste et jumeau dont sous l'azur on joue:
> Qui, détournant à soi le trouble de la joue,
> Rêve, dans un solo long, que nous amusions
> La beauté d'alentour par des confusions
> Fausses entre elle-même et notre chant crédule;
> Et de faire aussi haut que l'amour se module
> Évanouir du songe ordinaire de dos
> Ou de flanc pur suivis avec mes regards clos,
> Une sonore, vaine et monotone ligne.

> But enough! some secret chose as its confidante the vast twin reed, played beneath the blue sky: which, itself absorbing the cheek's trouble, dreams, in a long solo, that we amused the beauty of the landscape with the false confusions between itself and our credulous song; and, as high as love is modulated, to banish from the ordinary dream of back and pure side followed by my half-shut eyes, a sonorous, vain, and monotonous line.

It is clear from this passage that the instrument is a double *aulós* (a "jonc vaste et *jumeau*") and that the cheeks are blown out in playing it, suggesting the effort required for the double reeds of the mouthpieces. The acoustic effect, however, seems puzzling. Played by a single player, the performance would indeed be a "solo", yet the two reeds would sound different parts, like a duet. The "vain and monotonous line" sounds dreamy and vague, unlike the piercing sound of the *aulós,* and in any case there would be *two* lines, one for each pipe! We must conclude that the poet is getting confused about the nature of the instrument. And indeed, he refers to it immediately as "maligne Syrinx". The syrinx, for certain, was made from reeds, but it was not "twin" and did not cause the "cheek's trouble".

From this extraordinary mixture was born Debussy's beautiful evocation. The musician obviously imagined the faun as a player of the syrinx, not the *aulós.* The recurrence of the lazy opening scale, unaltered and usually at the same pitch, conveys the "monotony" of this "long solo", while the intervening music develops constantly. The flute is at once answered by two horns, each playing a fragment of two different pentatonic scales. Most of the remainder of the piece derives from pentatonic effects, except for the interventions of the chromatic "long solo". The piece, thus, is bi-isotopic; I have suggested elsewhere that another poetic text is reflected in this bi-isotopy, a passage from Verlaine's *Art Poétique* (see Monelle, 1997a).

> Oh! la nuance seule fiance
> Le rêve au rêve et la flûte au cor!

Figure 15.6.

Oh! only the nuance joins dream to dream and flute to horn!

What is above all revealed by this extraordinary encounter of two inventive artists is that neither found themselves enclosed within an existing tradition of pastoral signification. Mallarmé does not echo Guarini, and Debussy gives no hint of Handel. Instead, the music is an entirely new evocation, and indeed an idea that will recur often in the composer's output. The pastoral is being reborn.

The same topic appears in the first of the *Trois Chansons de Bilitis,* settings of poems by Pierre Louys which were said by the poet to be translations of a woman poet of antiquity (this was a fiction). "La Flûte de Pan" portrays, in the words of Pan's female lover, a scene in which the god presents a flute to her for the "day of Hycacinths"; they play together, their lips coming closer together until at last they kiss. The dynamics of the situation make only one instrument feasible: the syrinx, which could, rather inconveniently, be played simultaneously by two players. And indeed, "syrinx" is the word used by Louys ("une syrinx de roseaux bien taillés", a syrinx of well-cut reeds). In an admirable demonstration of topical signification, the piano introduction presents Debussy's effect of the lips sliding across the reeds, followed by one measure of a stately dance, the signifier of the "antique"; Bilitis, as well as Pan, was part of the ancient world (fig. 15.6).

A rather extreme form of the "syrinx" topic appears at the start of the song *Le Faune,* from the second set of *Fêtes Galantes.* The opening gesture is a very rapid arpeggio across two octaves; later, this mutates into something more sedate and more like the gesture of "La Flûte de Pan". If the faun is playing a syrinx, then it is an instrument of thirteen reeds, which happens to be the extreme limit of the classical syrinx. What is even more interesting is that the poem (apart from describing a faun made of terra-cotta, thus presumably silent) makes no mention of the faun's playing music; he is merely said to "laugh". His laughter is, perhaps, reflected in the exotic dance that forms the other topical reference of this song.

The *Six Epigraphes Antiques* are arrangements for piano duet (also for piano solo) of music written for two flutes, two harps, and celesta for a dramatic presentation of the *Chansons de Bilitis* in 1900–1901. They contain two versions of the syrinx topic: the first piece, "Pour Invoquer Pan, Dieu du Vent d'Eté" (To invoke Pan, god of the summer wind), has sweeping scales for two "flutes"; no. 4, "Pour la Danseuse aux Crotales", for the dancer with antique cymbals, extends this motive to its greatest extent, in a figure that encompasses two octaves and a fifth. Elsewhere it could, however, cover a much narrower space; the main thematic figure of *Voiles*, from the first book of *Préludes*, sounds like two syrinxes playing together, and spans an augmented fifth (two together? Has the confusion about the double *aulós* returned?). Even the cor anglais motives already mentioned have the character of the syrinx figure, especially the one in *Nuages*, which travels scalewise up an augmented fourth, then descends slowly.

Most of the works discussed here have no direct connection with Watteau, Verlaine, or the theme of the *fête galante*. However, the pastoral subjectivity in this period has, partly through Verlaine's little collection of poems, become impersonalized and alienated. There is the usual sense of elegy, but it is "much more cerebral, premeditated, willed, or at least complacent"; the poems have become "impersonal" in their sensuality (Bornecque 1969, 18). This impersonality spreads to the broader world of the fin de siècle pastoral, to Mallarmé, Louys, and the other poets of this circle. The atmosphere of slightly alienated fantasy influences Debussy's style, removing his pastoral works from the old tradition. An ancient world, pagan, mysterious, sunlit, is evoked. It may, indeed, be a pastoral world. But the image of innocence, of happy love, is rendered crystalline, is slightly colored with risk. It is the world in which every nymph is threatened by Pan and his satyrs. Its irresponsibility is no longer a means to freedom, but becomes an animal quality, beautiful but grotesque. This is the fin de siècle pastoral, sensuous, heavily fragrant, disingenuous. It should have presented a final coda to the whole pastoral story. But there was more to come.

(f) The English pastoral

"Ralph Vaughan Williams is often characterized by commentators as a master of the musical *pastoral*" (Clark 2003, 55). This seems an undeniable truism. Every measure of his music recalls the modal and gapped scales of English folksong, and he spoke continually of the beauty of the old English songs and the urgent need to collect and preserve them before they were lost forever. Also, he wrote a *Pastoral* Symphony. His works return again and again to pastoral themes: *Flos Campi, An Oxford Elegy, Shepherds of the Delectable Mountains*. When he was not invoking shepherds or biblical pastorals he was arranging real folksongs or setting verse by pastoral poets like Housman and Spenser, or writing orchestral pieces evocative of the countryside, such as *In the Fen Country, Norfolk Rhapsody*, and *The Lark Ascending*.

Vaughan Williams was, of course, one of the leading collectors of folksong. His collecting began in 1903; by 1913 he had collected over 800 songs. In speaking of the reasons for collecting this material, he revealed that his pastoralism was less than simple. In a series of lectures in Bournemouth in 1902, he summarized the importance of folksong.

1. Folk songs contained the nucleus of all further developments in music;
2. They invariably affected the style of great composers;

3. National music was a sure index to national temperament;
4. Folk songs were supremely beautiful. (quoted by Kennedy 1980 [1964], 34)

Of these criteria, only the first and last are truly pastoral. The composer clearly thought that country people possessed the originary music of the world; sophisticated musicians should return to the source of their whole tradition and technique. Reason no. 3, clearly a reflection of the Herderian *Volksseele,* is more worrying. This was the period of militarism, of the arms race, of aggressive nationalism across the world. The English, belatedly, were seeking to shed German influence over their music, and wanted to develop a tradition of their own as an expression of Englishness. This was a different nationalism from those older nationalisms of Bohemia and Hungary. Britain was not a subject state buried in a great empire, but a powerful and aggressive country that would dominate European politics if it could. Musicians must do their best to demonstrate a "national temperament". It was the bugbear of modern pastoralism, a cultivation of rural innocence as an element of sentimental political jingoism.

However, Vaughan Williams truly believed that the roots of all music lay in the songs of the countryside. In another lecture, he imagined a young student seeking the sources of everything he has to learn.

> Before I take up the study of music . . . I will try and find out the absolutely unsophisticated, though naturally musical, man—one who has no learning, and no contact with learning, one who cannot read or write, and thus repeat anything stereotyped by others, one whose utterance, therefore, is purely spontaneous and unself-conscious. Will such a man be able to invent any form of music? And, if he does, will it contain the germs of those principles and rules which my professors wish to teach me? (Vaughan Williams 1953, 206)

The student's search is rewarded, for of course this is exactly what he finds in folksong. The description of prelapsarian man is complete; here is the shepherd of the Golden Age, the unspoiled innocent untouched by society, by learning, or by tradition.

> We do really find in every country among those people whose utterances must of necessity be spontaneous and unsophisticated—namely, the unlettered and untravelled portion of the community—a form of musical art, unwritten, handed down by tradition, hardly self-conscious, which is their special property. . . . [It] has in it the germ of all those principles of beauty, of expression, of form, climax and proportion which we are accustomed to look for in the highly developed compositions of great masters. (206–207)

The English pastoral differed in certain ways from the older German interest in rustic song. In the same lecture, Vaughan Williams laments the lateness with which English musicians have come around to collecting folksong; songs are already beginning to disappear, and are often known only by the oldest people in rural communities. Another generation, he felt, and everything would be lost. But this also had its advantages.

> Most of the folk-music of foreign countries, and much of that of Scotland, Wales and Ireland, was collected and published about 120 years ago, a period when musicians

Figure 15.7.

had no respect for what they found, and had no scruple in altering and "improving" their folk-songs to make them fit the supposed "correct style" of the period: thus none of the tunes of these early collectors are above suspicion as faithful records.

But nowadays a new spirit animates the collector; he wishes to preserve and put before the public exactly what he has heard—neither more nor less—and we can be sure that whatever we find in the collections of modern investigators is an accurate transcript of the songs of traditional singers. (201–202)

Compared to Kretzschmer and Zuccalmaglio, the new English collectors, especially Vaughan Williams and Cecil Sharp, were indeed more accurate and scrupulous. The effect of this was to generate a body of folk material that was stylistically quite unfamiliar to the musical public, whereas the songs of the German collectors had been in a style that was intimately familiar to the bourgeois, and which was, indeed, judged to be "natural" only if it sounded easy and familiar. The aspects that the Germans had removed in order to make the material acceptable to the salon became the very features that guaranteed the authenticity of English songs: "irregular rhythm, strange modal cadences and lack of modulations, and unexpected intervals" (Kennedy 1980 [1964], 27). The English composers, as well as creating a style for themselves in reaction to the Germanism of Parry and Stanford, wanted to turn the attention of the bourgeois listener to the country people who had previously been ignored. Thus, the younger group of composers—Vaughan Williams, Holst, Butterworth—were modernists; their turning to folksong was revolutionary, homiletic, challenging. Their music presented an obstacle to their audiences' complacency. It was a statement of music-political conviction, a credo. This was an opposite position to that of Brahms in imitating the friendly caress of the volkslied.

These strange cadences and unexpected intervals permeate the whole of Vaughan Williams's oeuvre, from *The Wasps* to the Ninth Symphony. Even his more radical works, like *Flos Campi,* are built on the melos of English song and the type of parallel harmonies that he developed in order to harmonize it. And here we encounter a difficulty for our theory. If topics are "characteristic figures" that are "subjects for musical discourse", as Ratner originally specified (Ratner 1980, 9), then Vaughan Williams's pastoralism is not a topic, for he is never out of it. It is a *style,* not a topic. There are, indeed, melodic formulae which behave like topics; the little pentatonic motive that appears in the first movement of the Fifth Symphony, in the opening flute solo of *Flos Campi,* and at the beginning of the finale of the *Pastoral* Symphony is a certain fingerprint of the composer (fig. 15.7). But it has no special signification; it is just part of the whole folk-oriented ambience.

In the sense we have described, this artist is a pastoral composer, because his every gesture witnesses to a belief in the originary wisdom and purity of country-folk. Ratner also spoke of "styles which are topics", but he meant styles that could be cited or echoed, like the rhythm of the French overture. Vaughan Williams does not *cite* the pastoral style; it is his very soul. It is true that traces of the old pastoral topic appear from time to time in his output. *An Oxford Elegy* begins, apparently, with a new-siciliana in 6/8 time over a pedal point. But it is easy to find also the hunt and the military topics in this music. Such an inquisition is trivial; it may be undertaken for all music before the time of true modernism (and continued into other musics, popular music and movie scores). Vaughan Williams, like Theocritus, is a pastoral artist.

The English Georgians are clearly part of the story of the musical pastoral, even if they cannot quite be made relevant to a study of the pastoral *topic*. This topic, with its quite distinct signifiers, is closely bound into a complex cultural tradition, which begins with and always centers on the literary. A study of the musical pastoral, then, is bound to expand beyond the limits of topic theory.

(g) The meaning of pastoral

From the literary point of view, the pastoral world is complex and many-sided. Originally set in a sunlit meadow where shepherds engaged in singing contests, it took on a yearning for the Golden Age, which could be associated with the Christian heaven; it was associated with Christmas, because the Nativity was first revealed to shepherds. Always amoral, it became the scene of lovers' yearnings; sophisticated courtiers found in it the extolment of erotic love and an allegory of music. The beauty of the meadow expanded into a worship of the whole landscape, fields, rivers, and mountains, and eventually a vision of the divinity within ourselves. Yet the amorality of Eros persisted; young, irresponsible lovers continued to speak the words of pastoralism.

Some of these features could be reflected in music. Throughout our history, the shepherd's pipe has sounded to signify pastoralism, though a mistranslation led composers to think of it as a flute (as well as an oboe). The shepherds of the Abruzzi, with their noisy *zampogne* and *pifferi,* might replace the lost tones of Greek shepherds, and the meter of their music could be refined into a languorous dance. Since pastoral personnel were always country people (when they were not supernaturals, satyrs, and fauns), a fashion for a kind of salon-tamed folksong provided a new signifier. This was succeeded, at least in one country, by a much more radical use of folksong, returning to the real songs of the peasantry, in spite of their unfamiliarity to concert audiences.

But music is much nearer to its final significations than literature, because it does not have to stop at concepts. The pastoral is about finding perfection in innocence, heaven in the uncorrupted, true morality in the irresponsible, the mystic vision of maturity in an allegory of youth and simplicity. These are the meanings universally expressed by composers of all ages, from the pellucid Monteverdi to the overheated Strauss, from the clear-edged Vivaldi to the lyric Brahms, from the fragrant Scarlatti to the picture-postcard Respighi, from the pious Bach to the atheist Janáček, the sensualist Debussy and the agnostic Vaughan Williams.

16 Epilogue

There has been time to present no more than a few illustrations of the working of these three topical genres. Any musician or music lover could give many additional examples of all three. But this is a book of theory, not an encyclopedic survey. It has, at least, been possible to show that a topical view of musical expression can shed new lights on the processes of signification. The most remarkable outcome is the discovery that musical semantics offers a map of culture, a map that is more direct, less tendentious, than any essay or exemplary fiction of a writer in words. This map is reflected, naturally, in literary semantics and in the worlds of visual art and the theater. It is also related dialogically to social history; cultural themes may reflect social realities, but they are also remarkable in their obstinate defiance of social realities. Still, an observation of the themes of historical culture must be informed by a study of social history; without it, one cannot know whether the social world is being reflected or lied about. The vicious *chasse aux toiles* is nowhere shown in the musical topics of the eighteenth century, because musical semantics was busy hiding social reality, not manifesting it. Post-Renaissance Europe is full of happy, soigné, innocent shepherds and shepherdesses, but they are found in books, pictures, and musical scores, never in the countryside.

Of course, the profoundest enterprise of criticism, what is now called "comparative studies", has had the purpose of drawing this cultural map, but it was hitherto not thought possible to ground it in music. Yet music is, in some ways, the truest cartographer. When society fragments—when the educated bourgeois, for example, quits traditional heroics for the intimacy of the novel—music persists in witnessing to the things that thrill people, in showing that the brave soldier is still a myth that people believe in. The century that invented self-consciousness also invented the Victoria Cross.

There are no extended analyses of music in this work. Such analyses may be found in the work of Robert Hatten (notably in his brilliant essay on Beethoven's Sonata in A, Op. 101; Hatten 1994, 91–111), in Kofi Agawu's remarkable analyses of Haydn, Mozart, and Beethoven (Agawu 1991), and in Elaine Sisman's analytical chapter on Mozart's *Jupiter* Symphony (Sisman 1993, 46–79). Bill Caplin's reservations about analysis have been reported in chapter 1, above. Our enthusiasm for analysis should be tempered, perhaps, by a sensible reluctance to expend much effort for little reward. Claude Palisca remarks that "theory is now understood as principally the study of the structure of music" (Palisca 1980, 741), though the article prefaced by this comment proves that the study of structure—that is, analysis—entered the world of theory only with eighteenth-century writers like Scheibe, Riepel, and Sulzer, and cannot be said to dominate until the next century, in the work of Marx and Riemann. Most theorists of the past have been concerned with

Pythagorean views of interval and consonance, or with Boethian ideas of moral content. And much music is more amenable to narrative comprehension than analysis—not only operatic scenes, of course, like the opening scene of *Der Rosenkavalier*, which tells a musical story of noble hunting, melting chromatic passion, military spirit, elegant Viennese society, with the "Habt Acht!" echoed on horns and suggested by the trumpet, but also the long symphonic paragraphs of Mahler. One may follow music as one follows written prose or a long narrative poem—event by event, moment by moment, turn by turn, following not the structural layout but the semantic sense.

Finally, let us say again: the three great topical genres, hunting, military, and pastoral, represent only one kind of musical topic. The world of dance measures has quite a different rationale; iconic topics, like the *pianto* and the noble horse, function differently again. The three major genres are of special interest because of their links with literature and general culture. For this reason, their study may lead in many directions and may connect with discourses not primarily musical. They may help to reunite us with students of language, literature, and the other arts, with history and anthropology. This is an important undertaking of comparative studies, for musicians and other scholars have been apt to eye each other suspiciously, each suspecting that the others want to create distraction from the proper concerns of their science.

The nightmare of modernism made some of us think that musical meaning, in any ordinary sense, was finished. But all that is past. Postmodern composers again write meaningful narratives, even suggesting familiar topics: the rustic pastoral in James MacMillan's *Confession of Isobel Gowdie* and William Sweeney's Fantasias for wind, the hunting horn in Ligeti's Horn trio and Henze's *König Hirsch*, the military march in Gideon Lewensohn's *Serenade* for chamber orchestra, the military trumpet in André Hajdu's cantata *Dreams of Spain*. Perhaps a new topical map needs to be drawn, recalling that Debussy and Vaughan Williams found new topical worlds and that topics grow, prosper, and decline like everything in music. What topics may be found in the music of the twenty-first century? Perhaps the topics of democracy, internationalism, and global communication. But then again, perhaps not.

Appendix 1

French hunting horn calls of the Dampierre era

Calls are quoted from Jean Serré de Rieux, *Les Dons des Enfans de Latone: la Musique et la Chasse du Cerf,* 1734; Antoine Gaffet de la Briffardière, *Nouveau Traité de Vénerie,* 1742; Marc-Antoine, Marquis de Dampierre, *Recueil de Fanfares pour la Chasse,* 1776; and Le Verrier de la Conterie, *Venerie Normande, ou l'Ecole de la Chasse aux Chiens Courants,* 1778. Sometimes calls are given in two parts as *bicinia;* the "Dampierre" collection of 1776 is particularly rich in these arrangements. Thus, "La Royale" is given from Gaffet, with the two-part version from the 1776 "Dampierre" collection.

The 1734 and 1776 sources notate as sounding (i.e., in D) rather than as written (in C). In Appendix 1 all calls are notated in C as written. Some sources indicate ornaments with small crosses; the exact meaning is not clear.

The calls of Dampierre and his imitators are largely in the diatonic fourth register of the horn, but a few merely triadic calls survive into the latest period (notice, for example, Gaffet's "Requête," which is identical in the very late Le Verrier set), and some which remain triadic, even in the fourth register (see Gaffet's "L'apel"). One call takes in the thirteenth harmonic (the high A: Gaffet's "La Charoloise"). In addition, there are some that consist largely of repetitions of the same note, like some very ancient calls, and, of course, the calls of the natural oxhorn.

The selection has been made to illustrate the musical topic, not as a record of social history. The substantial family of calls named after individuals and places ("L'Anjou"; "La Petitbourg") is scantily represented, as less likely to be echoed in concert music. In most cases, calls are quoted from the collection of Serré de Rieux, the earliest source, though some standard calls are not recorded in that collection. Two calls are quoted in two parts, from the collection of 1776.

The collection published as *französische Parforcejagd-Signale* by G. F. D. aus dem Winckell (1807) is largely drawn from Gaffet. The calls in this collection are entirely in two parts.

Ton pour la quete (1734)

Ton pour chien (1734) (in the source: "Autre ton pour chien")

* A in source

La Sourcillade (1734)

Première vue (1742)

L'Apel (1742)

Pour le debuché (1734)

La retraite (1734)

La Royale (1742)

La Royalle (in two parts, 1776)

La Saint Hubert (1734)

La Dampierre (1734)

La Charoloise (1742)

Appendix 2

Military trumpet and bugle calls

Appendix 2 shows an anthology of military calls, mainly from the nineteenth century, some of them quoted incomplete. Calls are selected for their relevance to musical topic theory, not their importance in the history of military music. A few calls are given from the eighteenth century, but the steady adaptation and refinement of the signals makes the later examples more metric and melodic and thus more like manifestations of the topic in concert music.

French trumpet and bugle calls are from the Royal Ordinance of 1 June 1766; the list compiled by David Buhl and accepted by the Military Commission in 1825; and Melchior's list of bugle calls, 1831 (all in Kastner 1848). The old royal calls are extremely plain; the *retraite* (not shown) is almost identical to the *boute selle*, for example. Prussian trumpet calls are presented in two versions, the "new version" of 1846 and an "old version", presumably approximating to the Popitz series of 1751. The Prussian bugle calls were published for the *chasseurs* or light infantry in 1846 (Kastner 1848).

In both the French and the Prussian examples, bugle ("clairon") calls are evidently played on an instrument that sounds middle C as second harmonic, since the E above is missing: presumably a Flügelhorn or bugle. The higher tessitura of this instrument is apparent. The kinship of bugle calls to hunting calls is suggested by the French bugle *pas de charge* and *ralliement sur la réserve*, and the Prussian *retraite du soir*.

Austrian exercier reglements have been consulted from 1751, 1807, and 1901 (the first two from Lackner 1997; the most recent from the published exercier reglement itself, in the Austrian National Library, which is almost identical to the undated collection shown in Rameis 1976). Two specific comparisons are made: the similarity is striking between the 1751 *Marsch* and the 1901 *Generalmarsch*, and the 1751 *hocher Ruf* and the 1901 *ganzer Ruf*. Unlike the French tradition, Austrian trumpeters seem to have been highly conservative. Indeed, Rameis considers that some of these calls (for example, the *Retraite* and the *Kirchenruf*) are much older than their first appearance in notation.

The Austrian reglements do not specifically distinguish between trumpet and bugle calls. In some cases (for example, the *Fussmarsch*) one assumes that an infantry bugler would have adapted the call. This must have been so when the same call had a different function for cavalry and infantry; the infantry *Vergatterung* (changing of the guard), for example, is also the cavalry *Aufsitzen* (the command to mount).

Many calls are almost confined to a single note (like the French *la marche*). Few of these are given, but this should not indicate that they are rare; this effect is, of course, common in concert music. It is interesting to find similarities between calls of different nations, especially when these have a similar function: the Prussian *Appel* (first post) is virtually identical to the Austrian *Habt Acht!*, while the French *la marche* resembles the Prussian *marche pour la parade* and the Austrian *General-marsch*, and, incidentally, the British *parade march* in Hyde's *New and Compleat Preceptor* of 1800. Those who have served in the British forces may, indeed, find some of the calls familiar. Some sources give calls in two, three, or four parts. These somewhat rare arrangements are not included here.

There are plenty of sources for Italian, Russian, Hanoverian, Bavarian, Belgian, and other military signals. Indeed, British sources are plentiful also. The calls shown in Appendix 2 are thought to be more clearly relevant to the concert music and opera in the established repertoire.

(a) FRENCH TRUMPET CALLS

L'assemblée (1825)

Allegro

La marche (1825)

Allegro

twice

La charge

(a) 1766

très vivement   (1er. couplet)

2e.

(b) 1825

Presto

another 8 mm.

La retraite (1825)

Allegro non troppo   another 12 mm.

Le ralliement
(a) 1766
Très vivement

(b) 1825
Presto

(b) FRENCH BUGLE CALLS (1831)

L'assemblée
Andante $\mathrel{d}[\mathrel{d}.?] = 80$

1.

2.

Le rappel
Andante $\mathrel{d} = 80$

Au drapeau
Andante $\mathrel{d} = 80$

another 8 mm. and DC.

Le pas ordinaire
Maestoso $\mathrel{d} = 76$

another 6 mm., repeated

Le pas accéléré

Allegro ♩ = 100

another 8 mm., repeated

Le pas de charge

Allegro ♩ = 115

another 8 mm. and DC.

Le revéil

Allegro ♩ = 110

another 8 mm. and DC.

La retraite

Andante ♪ [♩. ?] = 115

Le rappel aux clairons

Presto ♩ = 160

(c) PRUSSIAN TRUMPET CALLS

Tirez le sabre (new)

Remettre le sabre (old)

Remettez le sabre (new)

Pansage (old)

Pour le pansage (new)

Marche pour la parade (new)

another 8 mm.

Retraite et réveil du matin (new: excerpts)

I

16 mm. II

5 mm.

III 10 mm.   evening: three times

morning: repeat three times

(d) PRUSSIAN BUGLE CALLS (1846)

Pas ordinaire

Pas redoublé

Réveil

Retraite du soir

Alarme ou rassemblement

(e) AUSTRIAN CALLS

Marche (3rd post, 1751)

Generalmarsch (1901)

Etwas langsamer als im Marschtempo

another 4 mm.

Der hoche Ruf (1751)

1st post   2nd post

about 2/3 of the whole

Ganzer Ruf (1901)

Etwas langsamer als im Marschtempo

Habt Acht! (1901)

Im Marschtempo

Abblasen (1901)

Im Marschtempo

Fußmarsch (1901)

♩ = 115   another 12 mm.

Beschleunigung (1901)

Galopp (1901)

Im Marschtempo

Attacke (1807)

Vergatterung [or] Aufsitzen (1901)

Im Marschtempo

Retraite (1901)

Etwas langsamer als im Marschtempo

Beginning of Kirchenruf

another 12 mm.

Bibliography

Abrams, M. H. 1971. *Glossary of literary terms*. New York: Holt, Rinehart and Winston.

Agawu, V. Kofi. 1991. *Playing with signs: A semiotic interpretation of classic music*. Princeton: Princeton University Press.

Allanbrook, Wye Jamison. 1983. *Rhythmic gesture in Mozart:* Le nozze di Figaro *and* Don Giovanni. Chicago: University of Chicago Press.

Altenberg, Johann Ernst. 1795. *Versuch einer Anleitung zur heroisch-musikalischen Trompeter- und Pauker-Kunst*. Halle: Hendel. Facsimile edition, New York, Broude, 1966.

Andersen, L., ed. ca. 1910. *Deutsche Heimat, die schönsten Volks-, Wander- und Studentenlieder*. Mainz: Schott.

Andrews, Richard. 1996. "Theatre". In *The Cambridge history of Italian literature*, edited by P. Brand and L. Pertile, 277–298. Cambridge: Cambridge University Press.

Aristotle. 1958. *Aristotelis topica et sophistici elenchi*. Oxford: Clarendon.

Arnim, Achim von, and Clemens Brentano. 1979 [1806–1809]. *Des Knaben Wunderhorn: alte deutsche Lieder*. Edited by Heinz Rölleke. 9 vols. Stuttgart: Kohlhammer.

Bachmann-Geiser, Brigitte. 1981. *Die Volksmusikinstrumente der Schweiz*. Zürich: Atlantis.

Baines, Anthony. 1976. *Brass instruments: Their history and development*. New York: Scribner.

——. 1983. "Aulos." In *The new Oxford companion to music*, edited by D. Arnold, 1:116. Oxford: Oxford University Press.

——. 1995 [1960]. *Bagpipes*. Oxford: Pitt Rivers Museum (Occasional papers on technology, 9).

Benveniste, Émile. 1971 [1939]. "The nature of the linguistic sign". Originally published in *Acta Linguistica*, I, Copenhagen. Reprinted in English in *Problems in general linguistics*, translated by Mary Elizabeth Meek. Coral Gables, Fla.: University of Miami Press, 43–48.

Binni, Walter. 1963. *L'Arcadia e il Metastasio*. Florence: La Nuova Italia.

Blaine, Delabere P. 1852. *An encyclopaedia of rural sports*. London: Longman.

Bornecque, Jacques-Henry. 1969. *Lumières sur les Fêtes galantes de Paul Verlaine*. Edn. augmentée. Paris: Nizet.

Bourgue, Daniel. 1982. "The French hunting horn: its history, its technique and its music". *Brass Bulletin* 39: 26–38.

Brand, Peter, and Lino Pertile, eds. 1999 [1996]. *The Cambridge history of Italian literature*. Cambridge: Cambridge University Press.

Bretonnière, V. 1860. *L'art du chasseur et du veneur*. Paris: Meissonnier.

Brinkmann, Reinhold. 1995. *Late idyll: The Second Symphony of Johannes Brahms*. Cambridge, Mass.: Harvard University Press.

Bröcker, Marianne. 1998. *Volksmusik*. In *Die Musik in Geschichte und Gegenwart*, 2nd ed. Sachteil 9: 1733–1737.

Broughton, Leslie Nathan. 1920. *The Theocritean element in the works of William Wordsworth*. Halle: Niemeyer.

Burnham, Scott. 1995. *Beethoven hero*. Princeton: Princeton University Press.

Caplin, William E. 2002. "On the relation of musical topoi to formal function." Paper delivered at the Conference of the International Musicological Society, Leuven, August 2002.

Carrara, Ernesto. 1909. *La poesia pastorale.* Milan: Vallardi.

Chambry, Pierre. 1994. *Fanfares de circonstance et d'animaux.* Brussels: Gerfaut.

Chegai, Andrea. 1998. *L'esilio di Metastasio: forme e riforme dello spettacolo d'opera fra Sette e Ottocento.* Florence: Casa Editrice Le Lettere.

Chew, Geoffrey. 1980. "Pastorale", sections 1, 2, 4–6. *The new Grove dictionary of music and musicians,* 14: 290–296. London: Macmillan.

Clark, Walter Aaron. 2003. "Vaughan Williams and the 'night side of nature': Octatonicism in *Riders to the sea*". In *Vaughan Williams essays,* edited by B. Adams and R. Wells, 55–71. Aldershot: Ashgate.

Clausewitz, Carl von. 1976 [1831]. *On war.* Translated by Michael Howard and Peter Paret. Princeton: Princeton University Press.

Cody, Richard. 1969. *The landscape of the mind: Pastoralism and Platonic theory in Tasso's Aminta and Shakespeare's early comedies.* Oxford: Clarendon.

Contamine, Philippe. 1984 [1980]. *War in the middle ages.* Translated by Michael Jones. Oxford: Blackwell.

Corvisier, André. 1979 [1976]. *Armies and societies in Europe, 1494–1789.* Translated by Abigail T. Siddall. Bloomington: Indiana University Press.

Crescimbeni, Giovanni Maria. 1731 [1698]. *L'istoria della volgar poesia.* Third impression. Venice.

Csiba, Gisela, and Jozsef Csiba. 1994. *Die Blechblasinstrumente in Johann Sebastian Bachs Werken.* Kassel: Merseburger.

Cummins, John. 1988. *The hound and the hawk: The art of medieval hunting.* London: Weidenfeld and Nicolson.

Curtius, Ernst Robert. 1990 [1948]. *European literature and the Latin middle ages.* Translated by Willard R. Trask. Princeton: Princeton University Press.

Dahlhaus, Carl. 1979 [1971]. *Richard Wagner's music dramas.* Translated by Mary Whittall. Cambridge: Cambridge University Press.

Dampierre, Marc-Antoine, Marquis de. 1776. *Recueil de fanfares pour la chasse.* Paris: Le Clerc.

Danuser, Hermann. 1991. *Gustav Mahler und seine Zeit.* Laaber: Laaber Verlag.

Dent, E. J. 1960 [1905]. *Alessandro Scarlatti, his life and works.* London: Arnold.

Dietrich, Albert, and J. V. Widmann. 1904. *Recollections of Johannes Brahms.* Translated by D. Hecht. London: Seeley.

Döbel, Heinrich Wilhelm. 1783 [1754]. *Neueröffnete Jäger-Practica.* Leipzig: Heinsius.

Duffy, Christopher. 1987. *The military experience in the age of reason.* London: Routledge.

Dufrane, Louis. 1927. *Gossec: sa vie, ses oeuvres.* Paris: Fischbacher.

Dunoyer de Noirmont. 1863. *Histoire de la chasse en France, depuis les temps les plus reculés jusqu'à la Révolution.* 3 vols. Paris: Bouchard-Huzard.

Eckardt, Hans Wilhelm. 1976. *Herrschaftliche Jagd, bäuerliche Not und bürgerliche Kritik.* Göttingen: Vandenhoek.

Eco, Umberto. 1979 [1976]. *A theory of semiotics.* Bloomington: Indiana University Press.

Esposito, Joseph L. 1999. "Peirce's theory of semiosis: Toward a logic of mutual affection." Lecture 6 of *Semiosis: The philosophic significance of signification.* Cyber Semiotic Institute <http://www.univie.ac.at/Wissenschaftstheorie/srb/cyber/espout.html>.

Ewans, Michael. 1977. *Janáček's tragic operas.* London: Faber.

Farmer, Henry George. 1912. *The rise and development of military music.* London: Reeve.

Fawkes, Francis, trans. 1767. *The idylliums of Theocritus.* London: Dryden Leach.

Fehr, Max. 1954. *Musikalische Jagd.* Zürich: HUG.

Fensterer, M. 1984. *Jagdhornschule: theoretische und praktische Anleitungen für Fürst-Pless-Horn und Parforcehorn.* Munich.

Fitzpatrick, Horace. 1970. *The horn and horn-playing, and the Austro-Bohemian tradition from 1680 to 1830.* London: Oxford University Press.

Flemming, H. F. von. 1724. *Der vollkommene teutsche Jäger.* 2 vols. Leipzig: Martini.

Fouilloux, Jacques du. 1606 [1561]. *La vénerie de Jacques du Fouilloux.* Paris: l'Augelier.

Friedlaender, Max. 1902. *Das deutsche Lied im 18. Jahrhundert: Quellen und Studien.* Stuttgart: Cotta.

Gaffet de la Briffardière, Antoine. 1742. *Nouveau traité de vénerie.* Paris: Mesnier.

Gaston III Phoebus, Conte de Foix. 1994 [1387]. *Das Jagdbuch des Mittelalters; Ms. fr. 616 der Bibliothèque nationale in Paris.* Edited by Wilhelm Schlag and Marcel Thomas. Graz: Akademische Druck u. Verlagsanstalt.

Gerber, Ernst Ludwig. 1792. *Historisch-biographisches Lexicon der Tonkünstler.* Leipzig: Breitkopf.

Gerhardt, Mia I. 1950. *La pastorale: essai d'analyse littéraire.* Assen: Van Gorcum.

Gilbert, James. 1804. *The bugle horn calls of riflemen and light infantry.* London.

Goechhausen, H. F. von. 1751 [1710]. *Notabilia venatoris, oder Jagd- und Weidwercks-Anmerckungen.* Weimar: Hoffmann.

Goldschmidt, Hugo. 1900–1901. Das Orchester der italienischen Oper im 17. Jahrhundert. *Sammelbände der internationalen Musikgesellschaft* 2: 16–75.

Goncourt, Edmond, and Jules de Goncourt. 1981. *French eighteenth-century painters.* Translated by Robin Ironside. Oxford: Phaidon.

Goodwin, Sarah Webster. 1988. *Kitsch and culture: The Dance of Death in nineteenth-century literature and graphic arts.* New York: Garland.

Goury de Champgrand. 1769. *Traité de venerie et de chasses.* Paris: Herissant.

Greenlee, Douglas. 1973. *Peirce's concept of sign.* The Hague: Mouton.

Grout, Donald J. 1979. *Alessandro Scarlatti: An introduction to his operas.* Berkeley: University of California Press.

Halfpenny, Eric. 1953–1954. "Tantivy: an exposition of the 'ancient hunting notes.'" *Proceedings of the Royal Musical Association* 80: 43–58

Hammerstein, Reinhold. 1980. *Tanz und Musik des Todes: die mittelalterlichen Totentänze und ihr Nachleben.* Bern/Munich: Francke.

Hatten, Robert S. 1994. *Musical meaning in Beethoven: Markedness, correlation, and interpretation.* Bloomington: Indiana University Press.

Head, Matthew. 2000. *Orientalism, masquerade and Mozart's Turkish music.* London: Royal Musical Association.

Heartz, Daniel. 1975–1976. "The hunting chorus in Haydn's *Jahreszeiten* and the 'airs de chasse' in the *Encyclopédie*". *Eighteenth-century Studies* 9: 523–539.

Heinitz, Wilhelm. 1928. *Instrumentenkunde. Handbuch der Musikwissenschaft.* Wildpark, Potsdam: Akademische Verlagsgesellschaft Athenaion.

Hibberd, John. 1976. *Salomon Gessner: His creative achievement and influence.* Cambridge: Cambridge University Press.

Hoboken, Anthony van. 1957. *Joseph Haydn, thematisch-bibliographisches Werkverzeichnis.* 2 vols. Mainz: Schott.

Hofer, Achim. 1988. *Studien zur Geschichte des Militärmarsches.* 2 vols. Tutzing: Schneider.

——. 1993. "Zur Erforschung und Spielpraxis von Märschen bis um 1750". In *Militär-*

musik und 'zivile' Musik: Beziehungen und Einflüsse. Bericht über ein Symposion beim Tag der Musik am 14. Mai 1993 in Uffenheim, edited by Armin Griebel and Horst Steinmetz, 41–54. Stadt Uffenheim.

Holden, Anthony, trans. 1974. *Greek pastoral poetry: Theocritus, Bion, Moschus, the pattern poems.* Harmondsworth: Penguin.

Hollander, Hans. 1963. *Leos Janáček: His life and work.* Translated by Paul Hamburger. London: Calder.

Holoman, D. Kern. 1989. *Berlioz.* London: Faber.

Howard, Albert A. 1893. The αυλοσ or tibia. *Harvard Studies in Classical Philology* 4: 1–60.

Howard, Michael. 1976. *War in European history.* London: Oxford University Press.

Howes, Frank. 1954. *The music of Ralph Vaughan Williams.* London: Oxford University Press.

Hughes, Rosemary. 1970 [1950]. *Haydn.* London: Dent.

Hyde, J. 1800. *A new and compleat preceptor for the trumpet and bugle horn.* London: published by the author.

Jäger, Ralf Martin. 1996. "Janitscharenmusik". In *Die Musik in Geschichte und Gegenwart,* 2nd ed. *Sachteil* 4: 1315–1330. Kassel: Bärenreiter.

Jander, Owen. 1993. "The prophetic conversation in Beethoven's 'Scene by the brook'". *Musical Quarterly* 77: 508–560.

Jarman, Douglas. 1989. "Alban Berg, Wilhelm Fliess, and the secret programme of the Violin Concerto." In *The Berg companion,* edited by D. Jarman, 181–194. London: Macmillan.

Jessulat, Ariane. 2000. *Die Frage als musikalischer Topos: Studien zur Motivbildung in der Musik des 19. Jahrhunderts.* Berlin: Studio Verlag.

Jullien, Ernest. 1868. *La chasse, son histoire et sa législation.* Paris: Didié.

Jones, David Wyn. 1995. *Beethoven: Pastoral Symphony.* Cambridge: Cambridge University Press.

Jung, Hermann. 1980. *Die Pastorale: Studien zur Geschichte eines musikalischen Topos.* Bern: Francke.

Kappey, J. A. 1894. *Military music: A history of wind-instrumental bands.* London: Boosey.

Kastner, Georges. 1848. *Manuel général de musique militaire à l'usage des armées françaises.* Paris: Didot.

Keegan, John. 1993. *A history of warfare.* London: Pimlico.

——. 1997 [1989]. *The Second World War.* London: Pimlico.

Kennedy, Michael. 1980 [1964]. *The works of Ralph Vaughan Williams.* London: Oxford University Press.

——. 1990 [1974]. *Mahler.* London: Dent.

Kermode, Frank. 1952. *English pastoral poetry, from the beginnings to Marvell.* London: Harrap.

Kidwell, Carol. 1993. *Sannazaro and Arcadia.* London: Duckworth.

Kirby, F. E. 1970. "Beethoven's Pastoral Symphony as a *Sinfonia caracteristica*". In *The creative world of Beethoven,* edited by P. H. Lang, 103–121. New York: Norton.

Knapp, Raymond. 2003. *Symphonic metamorphoses: Subjectivity and alienation in Mahler's re-cycled songs.* Middletown, Conn.: Wesleyan University Press.

Kobbé, Gustave. 1987. *Kobbé's complete opera book.* 10th ed. Edited and revised by the Earl of Harewood. London: Bodley Head.

Koch, Heinrich Christoph. 1964 [1802]. *Musikalisches Lexikon.* Hildesheim: Olms. Facsimile of 1802 ed., Frankfurt.

Kristeva, Julia. 1969. *Semeiotike: recherches pour une sémanalyse.* Paris: Le Seuil.

Kroeber, Karl. 1975. *Romantic landscape vision: Constable and Wordsworth.* Madison: University of Wisconsin Press.

Krohn, Ilmari. 1955. *Anton Bruckners Symphonien: Untersuchung über Formenbau und Stimmungsgehalt.* Helsinki: Suomalaisen Tiedeakatemien Toimituksia.

Lackner, Hannes. 1993. *Die Trompete als Signalinstrument in Geschichte und Gegenwart.* Master's dissertation, University of Vienna.

———. 1997. *Studien zu Signaltrompete und militärischer Signalmusik Österreich-Ungarns und Beispiele ihrer Übernahme in die Kunst- und Blasmusik von ca. 1750 bis 1918.* Ph.D. dissertation, University of Vienna.

Lawson, Jack. 1997. *Carl Nielsen.* London: Phaidon.

Le Verrier de la Conterie. 1778. *Venerie normande, ou l'école de la chasse aux chiens courants.* Rouen: Dumesnil.

Lenz, J. M. R. 1972. *The Soldiers.* Translated by William E. Yuill. Chicago: University of Chicago Press.

Léon, Pierre. 1970. *Economies et sociétés préindustrielles. Tome 2: 1650–1780: Les origines d'une accélération de l'histoire.* Paris: Armand Colin.

Leppert, Richard D. 1978. *Arcadia at Versailles: noble amateur musicians and their musettes and hurdy-gurdies at the French court. c. 1660–1789.* Amsterdam: Swets and Zeitlinger.

Little, Meredith Ellis. 1995 [1980]. "Siciliana". In *The new Grove dictionary of music and musicians* 17: 291–293.

Loughrey, Bryan, ed. 1984. *The pastoral mode: A casebook.* London: Macmillan.

LSM. See Monelle 1992b.

McCarthy, Julian. 1997. *The Ottoman Turks: An introductory history to 1923.* London: Longman.

Marinelli, Peter V. 1971. *Pastoral.* London: Methuen.

Marks, Paul F. 1971. "The rhetorical element in musical *Sturm und Drang:* Christian Gottfried Krause's *Von der musikalischen Poesie*". *International Review of the Aesthetics and Sociology of Music* 2, no. 1: 49–64.

Marolles, Gaston de. 1979. *La trompe de chasse et Gaston de Marolles.* Edited by Joël Bouëssée. Paris: Fédération Internationale des Trompes de France et Société de Vénerie.

Martinez, José Luiz. 1998. "A semiotic theory of music, according to a Peircean rationale". Paper delivered to the Sixth International Conference on Musical Signification, Aix-en-Provence.

Mercier, Louis-Sébastien. 1974 [1770]. *Le déserteur.* Edited by Simon Davies. Exeter: University of Exeter.

Mitchell, Jerome. 1977. *The Walter Scott operas: An analysis of operas based on the works of Sir Walter Scott.* Tuscaloosa: University of Alabama Press.

Mollo, John. 1972. *Military fashion.* London: Barrie & Jenkins.

Momigny, Jérôme-Joseph de. 1806. *Cours complet d'harmonie et de composition.* Paris.

Monelle, Raymond. 1992a. "A semantic approach to Debussy's songs". *The Music Review* 51, 3: 193–207.

———. 1992b. *Linguistics and semiotics in music.* Chur: Harwood.

———. 1997a. "Binary semantic opposition in Debussy". In *Semiotics around the world: Synthesis in diversity,* edited by I. Rauch and G. F. Carr, 647–650. Berlin: Mouton de Gruyter.

———. 1997b. "Scottish music, real and spurious". In *Music and nationalism in 20th-century Great Britain and Finland,* edited by T. Mäkelä, 87–110. Hamburg: von Bockel.

———. 2000. *The sense of music: Semiotic essays*. Princeton: Princeton University Press.

———. 2001. "Horn and trumpet as topical signifiers". *Historic Brass Society Journal* 13: 102–117.

Morik, Werner. 1953. *Johannes Brahms und sein Verhältnis zum deutschen Volkslied*. Dissertation, University of Göttingen.

Murray, David. 1994. *Music of the Scottish regiments*. Edinburgh: Pentland Press.

Nattiez, Jean-Jacques. 1975. *Fondements d'une sémiologie de la musique*. Paris: Union Générale d'Editions.

Nef, John U. 1950. *War and human progress: An essay on the rise of industrial civilization*. London: Routledge.

Nowak, Leopold. 1955. "Beethovens *Fidelio* und die Österreichischen Militärsignale". *Österreichische Musikzeitschrift*, Jg 10, Heft 1: 373–375.

———. 1985. *Uber Anton Bruckner: gesammelte Aufsätze*. Vienna: Musikwissenschaftlicher Verlag.

Ogden, C. K., and I. A. Richards. 1923. *The meaning of meaning: A study of the influence of language upon thought and of the science of symbolism*. London: Paul, Trench, Trubner.

Olleson, Edward. 1968. "The origin and libretto of Haydn's *Creation*". *Haydn Yearbook* 4: 148–168.

Palisca, Claude V. 1980. "Theory, theorists". *The new Grove dictionary of music and musicians*, 18: 741–762. London: Macmillan.

Panoff, Peter. 1938. *Militärmusik in Geschichte und Gegenwart*. Berlin: Siegismund.

Panofsky, Erwin. 1957. *Meaning in the visual arts*. New York: Doubleday.

Pärson, Johann Wilhelm von. 1734. *Der edle Hirsch-gerechte Jäger*. Leipzig: Weidmannische Buch-Laden.

Peirce, Charles Sanders. 1940. *The philosophy of Peirce, selected writings*. Edited by Justus Buchler. London: Kegan Paul.

Pilka, Jiři. 1972. *Hunting music of old Czech masters*. Sleeve note to Supraphon 1111156.

Pirrotta, Nino, and Elena Povoledo. 1982 [1969]. *Music and theatre from Poliziano to Monteverdi*. Translated by Karen Eales. Cambridge: Cambridge University Press.

Poggioli, Renato. 1975. *The oaten flute: Essays on pastoral poetry and the pastoral ideal*. Cambridge, Mass.: Harvard University Press.

Pöschl, Josef. 1996. "Jagdmusik". In *Die Musik in Geschichte und Gegenwart*, 2nd ed. *Sachteil* 4: 1309–1315. Kassel: Bärenreiter.

———. 1997. *Jagdmusik: Kontinuität und Entwicklung in der europäischen Geschichte*. Tutzing: Schneider.

Posner, Donald. 1984. *Antoine Watteau*. London: Weidenfeld and Nicolson.

Pulikowski, Julian von. 1933. *Geschichte des Begriffes Volkslied im musikalischen Schrifttum: ein Stück deutscher Geistesgeschichte*. Heidelberg: Winter.

Quadrio, Francesco Saverio. 1739. *Della storia e della ragione d'ogni poesia*. Milan: Agnelli.

Ramann, L. 1887. *Franz Liszt als Künstler und Mensch*, vol. 2, section 1. Leipzig: Breitkopf & Härtel.

Rameis, Emil. 1976. *Die österreichische Militärmusik—von ihren Anfängen bis zum Jahre 1918*. Edited by E. Brixel. Tutzing: Schneider.

Ratner, Leonard G. 1980. *Classic music: Expression, form, and style*. New York: Schirmer.

———. 1992. *Romantic music: Sound and syntax*. New York: Schirmer.

Ravenscroft, Thomas. 1971 [1614]. *A briefe discourse of the true use of charact'ring the degrees*. Amsterdam: Da Capo.

Redman, Harry Jr. 1991. *The Roland legend in nineteenth-century French literature.* Lexington: University Press of Kentucky.

Reed, William H. 1939. *Elgar.* London: Dent.

Richards, I. A. 1967 [1925]. *Principles of literary criticism.* London: Routledge.

Ringer, Alexander L. 1953. "The *chasse* as a musical topic of the 18th century". *Journal of the American Musicological Society* 6: 148–159.

Robinson, Harlow. 1987. *Sergei Prokofiev, a biography.* London: Hale.

Rooney, Anne. 1993. *Hunting in middle English literature.* Woodbridge: Boydell.

Rosenmeyer, Thomas G. 1969. *The green cabinet: Theocritus and the European pastoral lyric.* Berkeley: University of California Press.

Rougemont, Denis de. 1962 [1940]. *Passion and society.* Rev. ed. Translated by Montgomery Belgion. London: Faber.

Rummenhöller, Peter. 1992. "'Liedhaftes' im Werk von Johannes Brahms". In *Brahms als Liedkomponist,* edited by Peter Jost, 38–46. Stuttgart: Steiner.

Rutherford, Andrew. 1978. *The literature of war: Five studies in heroic virtue.* London: Macmillan.

Sachs, Curt. 1940. *The history of musical instruments.* London: Dent.

Samuels, Robert. 1995. *Mahler's Sixth Symphony: A study in musical semiotics.* Cambridge: Cambridge University Press.

Saussure, Ferdinand de. 1974 [1916]. *Course in general linguistics.* Edited by Charles Bally and Albert Sechehaye. Translated by Wade Baskin. Glasgow: Fontana/Collins.

Schick, I. T., ed. 1978. *Battledress: The uniforms of the world's great armies, 1700 to the present.* London: Weidenfeld.

Schlesinger, Kathleen. 1939. *The Greek aulos.* London: Methuen.

Schneider, David M. 1968. *American kinship: A cultural account.* New York: Prentice-Hall.

Schneider, Helmut, ed. 1988. *Deutsche Idyllentheorie im 18. Jahrhundert: mit einer Einführung und Erläuterungen.* Tübingen: Narr.

Schweitzer, Albert. 1911 [1905]. *J. S. Bach.* 2 vols. Translated by E. Newman. London: Black.

Sée, Henri. 1921. *Esquisse d'une histoire du régime agraire en Europe aux XVIIIe et XIXe siècles.* Paris: Giard.

Selincourt, M. de. 1683. *Le parfait chasseur.* Paris: Quinet.

Sense. See Monelle 2000.

Serré de Rieux, Jean. 1734. *Les dons des enfans de Latone: la musique et la chasse du cerf.* Paris: Prault.

Shaw, Stanford. 1976. *History of the Ottoman empire and modern Turkey.* Vol. 1: *Empire of the Gazis: The rise and decline of the Ottoman empire, 1280–1808.* Cambridge: Cambridge University Press.

Sheinberg, Esti. 2000. *Irony, satire, parody and the grotesque in the music of Shostakovich.* Aldershot: Ashgate.

Signell, Karl. 1967. Mozart and the mehter. *The Consort* 24: 321–333.

Sisman, Elaine R. 1993. *Mozart: The "Jupiter" Symphony, no. 41 in C major, K. 551.* Cambridge: Cambridge University Press.

———. 1997. Genre, gesture and meaning in Mozart's "Prague" Symphony. *Mozart Studies 2,* edited by Cliff Eisen, 27–84. Oxford: Clarendon.

Smernoff, Richard A. 1977. *André Chénier.* Boston: Twayne.

Stewart, Pamela D. 1999 [1996]. "Boccaccio". In *The Cambridge history of Italian literature,* edited by P. Brand and L. Pertile, 70–88. Cambridge: Cambridge University Press.

Sturm, Christoph Christian. 1819 [1772]. *Reflections on the works of God and of his providence throughout all nature.* Anonymous translation. London: Bumpus.

Tagg, Philip. 1979. *Kojak, 50 seconds of television music: Toward the analysis of affect in popular music.* Studies from the Department of Musicology, Göteborg, no. 2.

Tarasti, Eero. 2000. *Existential semiotics.* Bloomington: Indiana University Press.

Tarr, Edward H. 1970. "Monteverdi, Bach und die Trompetenmusik ihrer Zeit". Gesellschaft für Musikforschung, Kongressbericht, 592–596. Bonn.

Taut, Kurt. 1927. *Die Anfänge der Jagdmusik.* Leipzig: n.p.

Thackray, R. M. 1963. *Playing for dance.* London: Novello.

Thorburn, W. A. 1969. *French army regiments and uniforms, from the Revolution to 1870.* London: Arms and Armour Press.

Tiby, O. 1954. "Il problema della 'siciliana' dal Trecento al Settecento". *Bolletino del Centro di studi filologici e linguistici siciliani* 2: 245.

Tieghem, Paul Van. 1930. *Le préromantisme: études d'histoire littéraire européenne.* Vol. 2: *La poésie de la nuit et des tombeaux; les idylles de Gessner et le rêve pastoral.* Paris: Alcan.

Toliver, Harold E. 1971. *Pastoral forms and attitudes.* Berkeley: University of California Press.

Tovey, Donald Francis. 1935. "Beethoven: Sixth Symphony in F major. Sinfonia pastorale, Op. 68". In *Essays in musical analysis, volume 1; symphonies,* 44–56.

Trumpet and bugle sounds for the army. 1909. London: His Majesty's Stationery Office.

Tyrrell, John, ed. 1982. *Leoš Janáček: Kat'a Kabanová.* Cambridge: Cambridge University Press.

Vaughan Williams, Ralph. 1953. "English folk-songs". Appendix 1 in Percy M. Young, *Vaughan Williams.* London: Dobson, 200–217.

Verrier de la Conterie, Le. 1778. *Venerie normande, ou l'ecole de la chasse aux chiens courants.* Rouen: Dumesnil.

Wendt, Ulrich. 1908. *Kultur und Jagd: ein Birschgang durch die Geschichte.* Vol. 2. *die neuere Zeit.* Berlin: Reimer.

Will, Richard. 1997. "Time, morality and humanity in Beethoven's Pastoral Symphony". *Journal of the American Musicological Society* 50: 269–329.

Winckell, Georg Franz Dietrich aus dem. 1898 [1805]. *Handbuch für Jäger, Jagdberechtigte und Jagdliebhaber.* 3 vols. Neudamm: Neumann.

Wind, Edgar. 1967 [1958]. *Pagan mysteries in the Renaissance.* Harmondsworth: Penguin.

Winternitz, Emanuel. 1967. *Musical instruments and their symbolism in western art.* London: Faber.

Wiora, Walter. 1971. *Das deutsche Lied: zur Geschichte und Ästhetik einer musikalischen Gattung.* Wolfenbüttel: Möseler.

Wörner, Karl H. 1910. "Die Darstellung von Tod und Ewigkeit in der Musik". In *Die Musik in der Geistesgeschichte: Studien zur Situation der Jahre um 1910. Abhandlungen zu Kunst-, Musik- und Literaturwissenschaft,* 92.

Zuckerová, Olga. 1983. *Staré lovecké Fanfary* (Old hunting fanfares.) Prague: Supraphon.

Index

Kirnberger, Johann Philipp, 86, 226
Knaben Wunderhorn, Des, 105–106, 178, 222, 223, 253, 258; afterword, "Von Volksliedern," 222
Kojak television theme, 84, 99
Komzák, Karl, 130; *Erzherzog Albrecht*, 124, 130, 131
Krause, Christian Gottfried, 221, 222, 241

Leclair, Jean-Marie, 85
Lenz, J. M. R.: *Die Soldaten*, 149–150, 175
Lévi-Strauss, Claude, 32
Lewensohn, Gideon, 273
liedhaft, the, 252–261
Ligeti, György, 97, 273
Liszt, Franz, 32, 87, 257; *Festival March*, 131; *Grand Solo de Concert*, 178; *Hungaria*, 165; symphonic poems, 170–171
locus amoenus, 12, 13–16, 185, 204, 206, 235, 245
Lord of the Rings, The, soundtrack, 181
Lortzing, Albert: *Der Wildschütz*, 79–80
Lully, Jean-Baptiste, 40, 74, 115, 229

MacMillan, James, 273
Mahler, Gustav, 8, 9, 17, 18, 27–28, 273; *Der Tamboursg'sell*, 178; *Lieder eines fahrenden Gesellen*, 258–259; *Rewelge*, 165, 178; Symphony no. 1, 98, 258–259; Symphony no. 3, 130, 164–165, 166; Symphony no. 6, 179, 258; *Wo die schönen Trompeten blasen*, 178–179; associated with trumpet, 99
Mallarmé, Stéphane, 208, 265–267
Manet, Edouard, 27
march, 113–133, 160; types of march, 125; harpsichord marches, 126–127; processional marches, 127; wedding marches, 127; funeral march, 127–130. *See also* concert marches
marching in step, 113–115, 116, 120, 122, 127, 133
Marenzio, Luca, 215
Marolles, Gaston de, 44, 50–51
Marschner, Heinrich: *Hans Heiling*, 79
mehter. See "Turkish music"
Méhul, Etienne-Nicolas: *Le Jeune Henri*, 76
Mendelssohn, Felix: *A Midsummer Night's Dream*, incidental music, 104–105, 127, 167; *Athalie*, 181; *Jagdlied*, Op. 84 no. 3, 92; *Jagdlied*, Op. 120 no. 1, 92–93; Octet, 180; Overture, *The Hebrides*, 174–175; Piano Concerto in G minor, 181; *St. Paul*, 248; *Sommerlied*, 93; *Song Without Words*, Op. 19 no. 3 ("Hunting Song"), 82
Mercier, Louis-Sébastien: *Le Déserteur*, 148–149, 175

Mersenne, Marin, 37, 137
Metastasio, Pietro, 160, 188, 191–194, 264; *Angelica*, 192–193; opera libretti, 193
Meyerbeer, Giacomo, 127, 167, 181
military academies, 147–148
military bands, modern, 119, 122–123
military topic, 5–6, 9, 113–181
military trumpet. *See* trumpet, military
military uniforms, 144, 151, 157–159, *Plate 1*; dress and undress uniforms, 158
Milton, John, 15
Mondonville, Jean-Joseph Cassanéa de, 85
Monteverdi, Claudio, 135, 271; *Orfeo*, 189, 216, 220–221
Morin, Jean-Baptiste, 46, 51, 74
Mouret, Jean-Joseph, 87
Mozart, Leopold, 53, 194; *Die Jagd*, 68, 86; *Sinfonia di Caccia*, 75, 87–88
Mozart, Wolfgang Amadeus, 8, 130, 243, 272; *Eine kleine Nachtmusik*, 122, 173; *Haffner* Serenade, 161; *Haffner* Symphony, 172, 173; Piano Concerto in B flat, K. 595, 173; Piano Concerto in C, K. 415, 173; Piano Concerto in E flat, K. 271, 172; Quartet, K. 593, 83, 98; Quintet, K. 614, 98; Serenade, K. 320, 84; Sonata in A, K. 331, 6, 238; Symphony no. 41, "Jupiter," 178, 272
STAGE WORKS: *Così Fan Tutte*, 161; *Die Entführung aus dem Serail*, 6, 119; *Die Zauberflöte*, 127, 176; *Don Giovanni*, 4; *Il Re Pastore*, 193; *Il Sogno di Scipione*, 193; *La Clemenza di Tito*, 193; *Le Nozze di Figaro*, 150, 175–176
musette, 210, 212–214, *212*, 262, *Plate 2*

new-siciliana. *See* siciliana
Nibelungenlied, 11
Nielsen, Carl: Overture, *Helios*, 249; Symphony no. 3, *Espansiva*, 248–249

Ogden, C. K., and I. A. Richards: *The Meaning of Meaning*, 20–21
oxhorn. *See cor de chasse*

pace of marching, 119–122
Paganini, Niccolò, 85–86
parforce hunt, 49, 54–55, 59, 60, 107
part-songs describing the hunt, 73. *See also* Gherardello da Firenze, "Tosto che l'Alba"
pastoral horn, 100–107, 160, 244
pastoral topic, 5, 13
pastoralism: prejudice against, 185; classical pastoral, 185–187; Renaissance pastorals, 187–189; French pastorals, 189–191; allegory of

the imagination, 189, 196, 206; meaning of, 195–198, 271; religious, 198–200; high and low pastoral, 227–228; pastoral genres, 229; in music, 229–250; and death, 232, 233; "rustic" pastoral, 251–252; fin de siècle, 268; English pastoral, 268–271

peasantry, European, poverty of, 200–202

Peirce, Charles Sanders, 22, 24, 26–27, 29, 31

Peri, Jacopo: *Euridice*, 215–216, 240

Philidor, André Danican, l'aîné, 44, 46, 49, 51, 99, 115, 137

Philidor, François-André (the younger): *Tom Jones*, 76; *Ernelinde*, 161

Phoebus, Gaston. *See* Gaston Phoebus

pifferari, *Plate 3*; visitors to Rome, 198–199; instruments of, 210; relation to siciliana, 217, 219, 220; echoed in concert music, 229–230, 234, 236; in Beethoven, 245; replacing Greek shepherds, 271

pitch of brass instruments, 50

Pless, Fürst (Hans Heinrich, Count of Hochberg), 53–54, 71; Fürst-Pless Horn, 63, 71

Poliziano, Angelo, 187, 197, 198

Polybius, 186, 189, 232, 233

Pope, Alexander, 13, 185, 200

posthorn, 84

Praetorius, Michael, 37, 39, 209–210

Prokofiev, Sergey: *Lieutenant Kizhe*, 176–177, 178; *The Love for Three Oranges*, 176, 177

Purcell, Henry, 36, 72, 127

Ratner, Leonard G., xii, 6, 7, 8, 35, 82, 270

Ravenscroft, Thomas: *Briefe Discourse*, 72

referentialism, 20–22

Respighi, Ottorino, 109, 271; *Fontane di Roma*, 91, 249–250; *Pini di Roma*, 79, 250

Ricoeur, Paul, xi

Riffaterre, Michael, 18

rifle, introduction of the, 145

Ringer, Alexander, 76, 85, 86, 89

Roland, story of, 152–154

Rosen, Charles, 7

Rossini, Gioachino: *Armida*, 15; *Guillaume Tell*, 42, 79, 102, 163, 167; *La Gazza Ladra*, 162, 163

Samuels, Robert, 16, 18

Sannazaro, Jacopo: *Arcadia*, 187, 191, 200; *De Partu Virginis*, 200

Saussure, Ferdinand de, 21, 22, 82

Scarlatti, Alessandro, 217–219, 271

Scheibe, Johann Adolf, 221, 272

Schubert, Franz, 27, 258; *Alfons und Estrella*, 79, 91–92; "Great C major" Symphony, 113, 181;

Marche Militaire, Op. 51 no. 1, 122, 162; Quartet in E flat, D. 87, 248; Quartet in A minor, D. 804, 8; *Trois Marches Héroiques*, 162 SONGS: *Abendlied für die Entfernte*, 247–248; *Das Fischermädchen*, 252; *Das Lied vom Reifen*, 251; *Der Alpenjäger*, 91; *Der Jäger*, 92; *Der Knabe*, 252; *Der Lindenbaum*, 251; *Der Tod und das Mädchen*, 16; *Die böse Farbe*, 92; *Die Forelle*, 251; *Ellens Gesang* I and II, 84, 92, 169–170; *Erlkönig*, 24, 26, 30; *Frühlingstraum*, 251; *Jägers Liebeslied*, 91; *Lied des gefangenen Jägers*, 92; *Romanze des Richard Löwenherz*, 162; *Trost*, 91–92; *Wohin*, 251

Schulz, Johann Abraham Peter, 223, 225, 241

Schumann, Robert, 242; *Der wilde Reiter*, 5; "Er, der herrlichste von allen," 180; *Jagdlieder*, 93; *Konzertstück*, 93

Scott, Sir Walter, 84, 92, 154, 162, 169

Scottish songs, 222, 223–224

Serré de Rieux. *See Dons des Enfans de Latone, Les*

Shakespeare, William, 11, 104, 105, 197, 246

Sheinberg, Esti, 176, 178, 247

Shelley, Percy Bysshe, 15

Shostakovich, Dmitri: Symphony no. 7, 177–178

Sibelius, Jean, 107

siciliana (siciliano), 229, 237, 241, 264, 271; origins of, 215–220; as pastoral signifier, 227, 230; in concert music, 231, 232, 233, 235; new-siciliana, 238, 239, 241, 244, 245, 246, 247–250, 251; in Haydn, 239; in Beethoven, 244

Sisman, Elaine, 4, 272

snare drum effects, 80

Sousa, John Philip, 122, 130; *Hail to the Spirit of Liberty*, 124; *The Stars and Stripes for Ever*, 124; *Washington Post*, 123

Sporck, Count von, 41–42, 88

Star-Spangled Banner, The, 7

Strauss, Johann, I: *Radetsky March*, 124

Strauss, Richard, 31, 271; *Daphne*, 185; *Der Rosenkavalier*, 6, 259–260, 273; *Don Juan*, 84, 99; *Don Quixote*, 100, 107; *Ein Heldenleben*, 83, 169; *Pilgers Morgenlied*, 93; *Till Eulenspiegel*, 97; enamored of the horn, 99

Stravinsky, Igor, 17, 37

Stubbs, George, 24, 245

Sturm, Christoph Christian: *Betrachtungen über die Werke Gottes in der Natur*, 70–71, 203–204, 206, 242, 244

Suppé, Franz von, 165

Sweeney, William, 273

syrinx, 30, 208, 230, 250, 264; imitation of, 265–268